Pokémon® Diamond Version Pearl Version

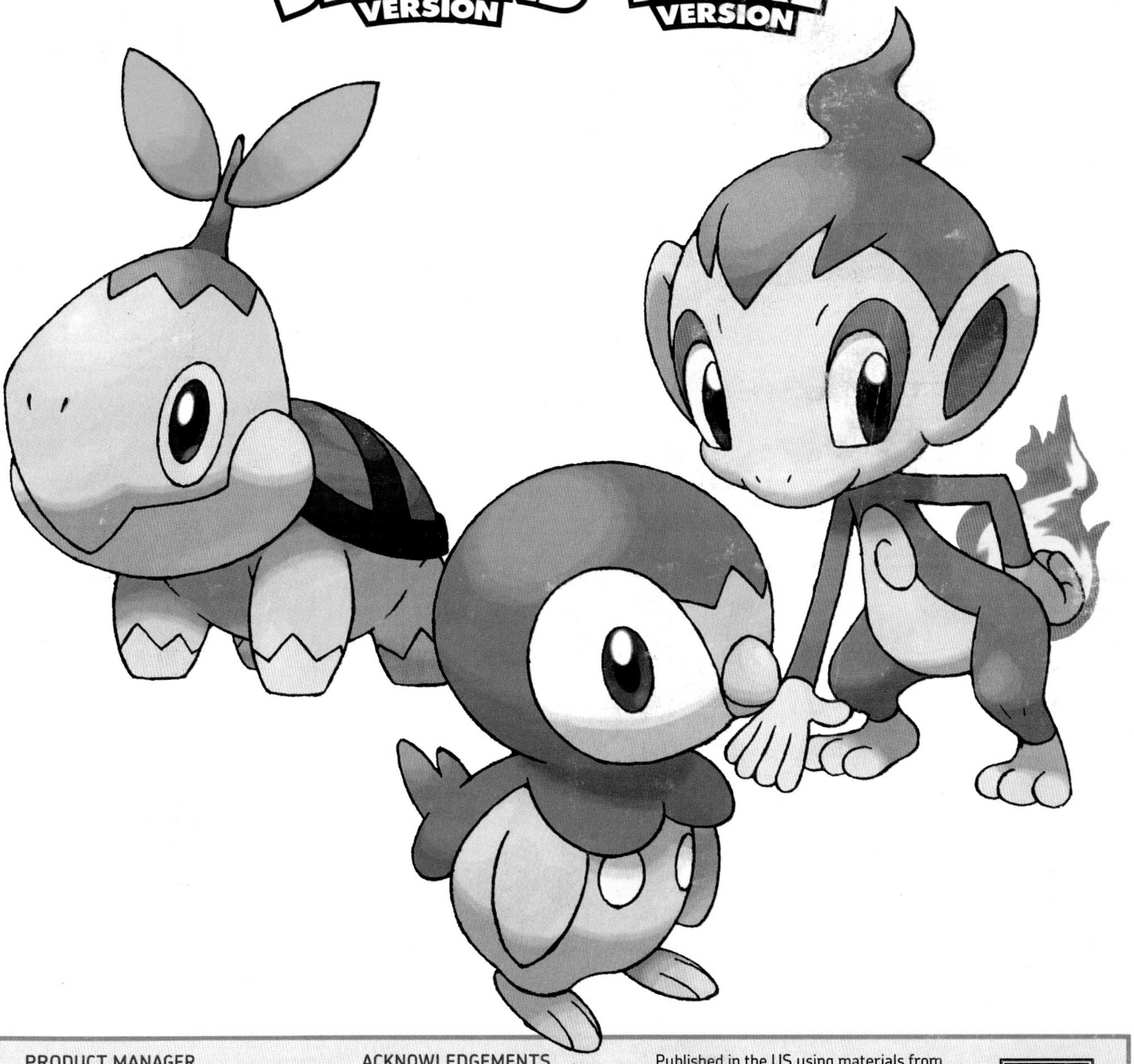

PRODUCT MANAGER
Mario De Govia

CONTRIBUTING EDITORS
Lawrence Neves
Katherine Fang
Kristina Naudus
Cris Silvestri

PRODUCTION MANAGER
Stephanie Sanchez

ACKNOWLEDGEMENTS
Simon Schatzmann
Koji Kondo
Maya Nakamura
Chris Brixey
John Hershberger

DESIGN & PRODUCTION
Big Yellow Taxi, Inc.
www.BigYellowTaxi.com

Published in the US using materials from Pokémon Diamond/Pearl Official Adventure Clear Guide. Published in Japan October 2006 by Media Factory, Inc.

SPECIAL THANKS TO:
Editor:
Shyunsuke Motomiya and ONEUP, inc.
Design & Layout:
RAGTIME CO., LTD. and SUZUKIKOUBOU, INC.

YOU ARE A POKÉMON TRAINER...

... and about to embark on an adventurous journey with your Pokémon.

CHOOSE YOUR MAIN character (boy or girl) in this magnificent story and get ready to explore the awesome, adventure-packed world of Pokémon!

TURTWIG CHIMCHAR PIPLUP

START WITH THE STARTERS...

TO BEGIN, PICK OUT ONE POKÉMON as your partner (Turtwig, Chimchar, Piplup). One of these three Pokémon above will be your first partner. Which one will you choose?

GOAL 1: WIN THE POKÉMON LEAGUE CHAMPIONSHIP IN THE SINNOH REGION

YOUR PRIMARY GOAL in this adventure is to become the champion of the Pokémon League by defeating other Pokémon Trainers. Together with your partner Pokémon, you should be able to beat all your rivals!

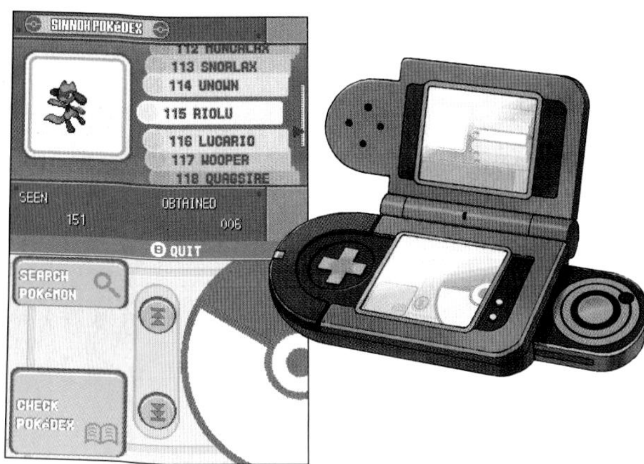

GOAL 2: FIND ALL THE POKÉMON AND COMPLETE YOUR POKÉDEX

THE NEXT GOAL is to find all the Pokémon you can and add them to your Pokédex. This may seem like a long and difficult process, but it isn't. It is, however, one of the greatest achievements a Pokémon Trainer can attain!

ENCOUNTERS WITH VARIOUS POKÉMON

AS YOU MOVE FORWARD, you will see many different types of Pokémon. Learning about them and getting to know their strengths and weaknesses will always bring you great joy and satisfaction as a Trainer. They are the most amazing creatures you'll ever meet!

CONTENTS

INTRODUCTION 12

SINNOH ADVENTURE 38

POKÉDEX 210

CONTESTS 224

WIRELESS FUNCTION 238

CHARTS AND INFO 256

COLUMNS

SINNOH REGION WORLD MAP

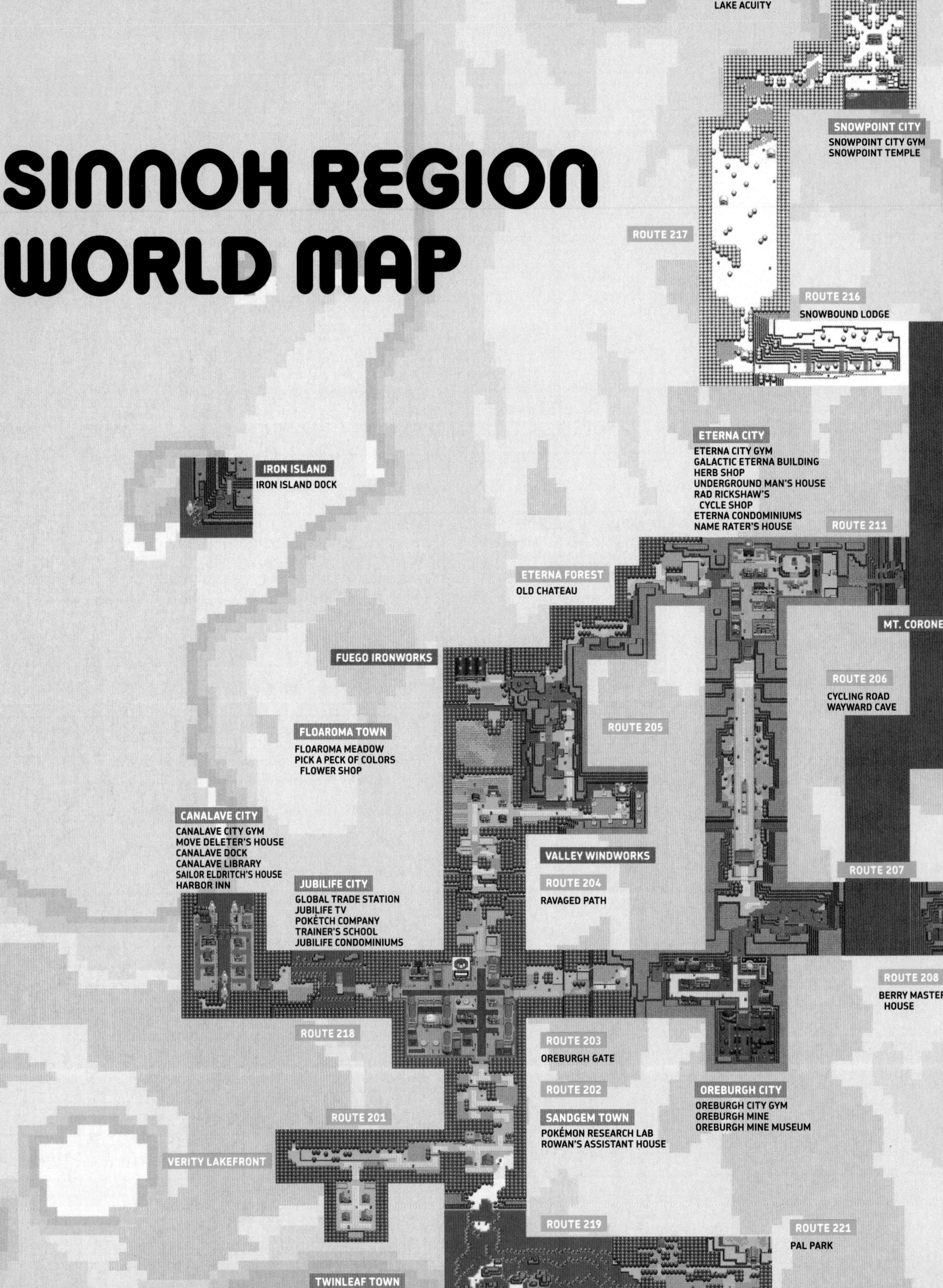
ACUITY LAKEFRONT
LAKE ACUITY
SNOWPOINT CITY
SNOWPOINT CITY GYM
SNOWPOINT TEMPLE
ROUTE 217
ROUTE 216
SNOWBOUND LODGE
ETERNA CITY
ETERNA CITY GYM
GALACTIC ETERNA BUILDING
HERB SHOP
UNDERGROUND MAN'S HOUSE
RAD RICKSHAW'S CYCLE SHOP
ETERNA CONDOMINIUMS
NAME RATER'S HOUSE
ROUTE 211
IRON ISLAND
IRON ISLAND DOCK
ETERNA FOREST
OLD CHATEAU
MT. CORONET
FUEGO IRONWORKS
ROUTE 206
CYCLING ROAD
WAYWARD CAVE
ROUTE 205
FLOAROMA TOWN
FLOAROMA MEADOW
PICK A PECK OF COLORS FLOWER SHOP
CANALAVE CITY
CANALAVE CITY GYM
MOVE DELETER'S HOUSE
CANALAVE DOCK
CANALAVE LIBRARY
SAILOR ELDRITCH'S HOUSE
HARBOR INN
VALLEY WINDWORKS
ROUTE 207
JUBILIFE CITY
GLOBAL TRADE STATION
JUBILIFE TV
POKÉTCH COMPANY
TRAINER'S SCHOOL
JUBILIFE CONDOMINIUMS
ROUTE 204
RAVAGED PATH
ROUTE 208
BERRY MASTER'S HOUSE
ROUTE 218
ROUTE 203
OREBURGH GATE
ROUTE 202
OREBURGH CITY
OREBURGH CITY GYM
OREBURGH MINE
OREBURGH MINE MUSEUM
ROUTE 201
SANDGEM TOWN
POKÉMON RESEARCH LAB
ROWAN'S ASSISTANT HOUSE
VERITY LAKEFRONT
ROUTE 219
ROUTE 221
PAL PARK
TWINLEAF TOWN
MAIN CHARACTER'S HOUSE
RIVAL'S HOUSE
ROUTE 220

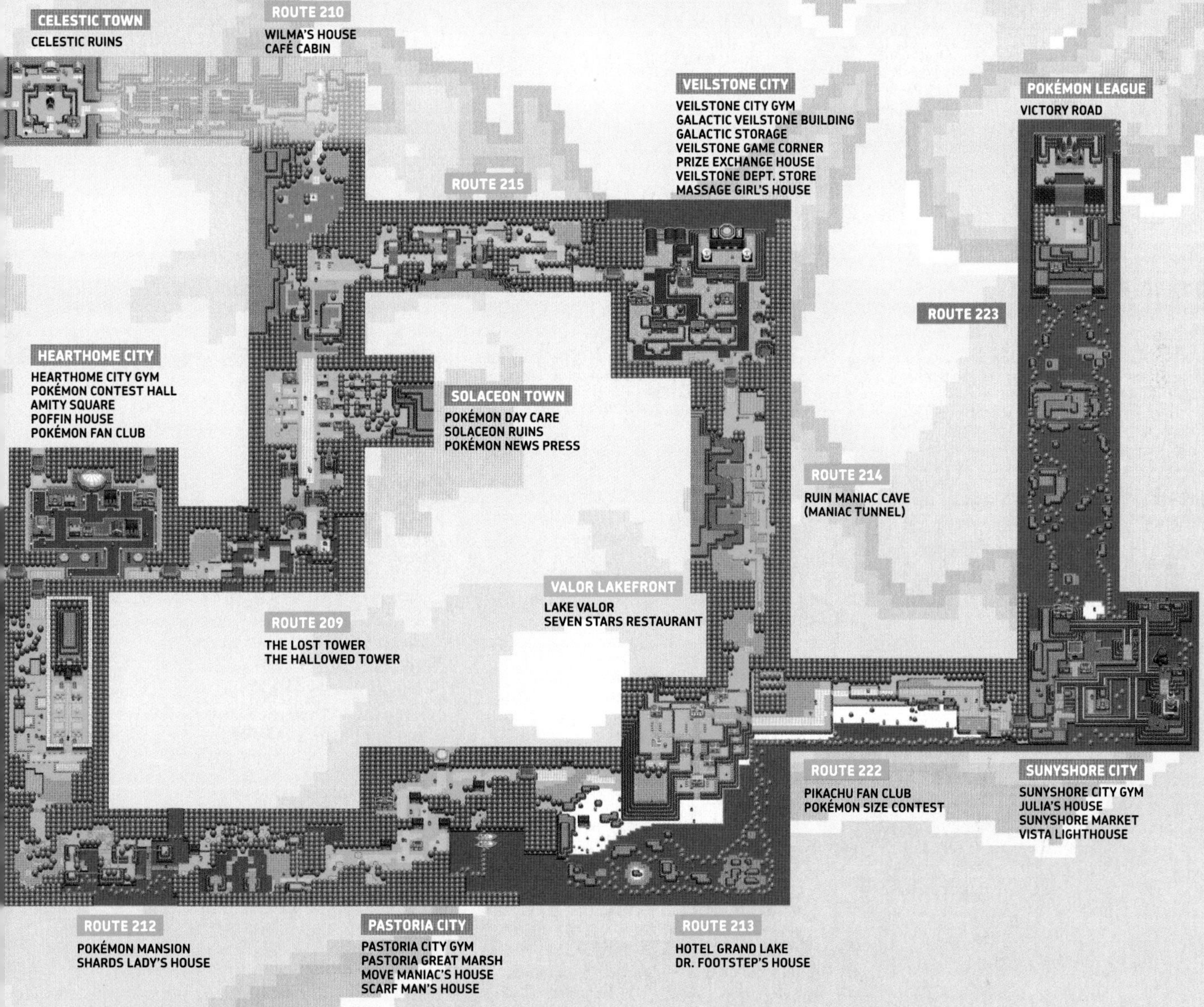

CELESTIC TOWN
CELESTIC RUINS

ROUTE 210
WILMA'S HOUSE
CAFÉ CABIN

VEILSTONE CITY
VEILSTONE CITY GYM
GALACTIC VEILSTONE BUILDING
GALACTIC STORAGE
VEILSTONE GAME CORNER
PRIZE EXCHANGE HOUSE
VEILSTONE DEPT. STORE
MASSAGE GIRL'S HOUSE

POKÉMON LEAGUE
VICTORY ROAD

ROUTE 215

ROUTE 223

HEARTHOME CITY
HEARTHOME CITY GYM
POKÉMON CONTEST HALL
AMITY SQUARE
POFFIN HOUSE
POKÉMON FAN CLUB

SOLACEON TOWN
POKÉMON DAY CARE
SOLACEON RUINS
POKÉMON NEWS PRESS

ROUTE 214
RUIN MANIAC CAVE
(MANIAC TUNNEL)

VALOR LAKEFRONT
LAKE VALOR
SEVEN STARS RESTAURANT

ROUTE 209
THE LOST TOWER
THE HALLOWED TOWER

ROUTE 222
PIKACHU FAN CLUB
POKÉMON SIZE CONTEST

SUNYSHORE CITY
SUNYSHORE CITY GYM
JULIA'S HOUSE
SUNYSHORE MARKET
VISTA LIGHTHOUSE

ROUTE 212
POKÉMON MANSION
SHARDS LADY'S HOUSE

PASTORIA CITY
PASTORIA CITY GYM
PASTORIA GREAT MARSH
MOVE MANIAC'S HOUSE
SCARF MAN'S HOUSE

ROUTE 213
HOTEL GRAND LAKE
DR. FOOTSTEP'S HOUSE

QUICK WALK THROUGH

Here is a quick walk through to blaze you through this adventure in the Sinnoh region. Check back here whenever you want to know where you are, where to go next, or what's coming your way in Pokémon Diamond and Pokémon Pearl.

1 TWINLEAF TOWN PG 40

- Meet your rival in front of his house.
- Go to the 2 FL of his house.

2 ROUTE 201 PG 44

- Head out to Lake Verity with your rival.

3 LAKE VERITY (FIRST VISIT) PG 47

- Meet Prof. Rowan and Rowan's assistant.
- Find a bag that Prof. Rowan left.
- Choose one out of Turtwig, Chimchar, Piplup.

4 ROUTE 201 PG 44

- Reunite with Prof. Rowan and Rowan's assistant.

5 TWINLEAF TOWN PG 41

- Get Running Shoes from your mom.

6 SANDGEM TOWN PG 49

- Rowan's assistant takes you to visit Pokémon Laboratory.
- Get Pokédex from Prof. Rowan.
- Rowan's assistant shows you around town.

7 TWINLEAF TOWN PG 42

- Get the Journal from your mom.
- Keep Parcel for your rival's mom.

8 ROUTE 202 PG 55

- Get five Poké Balls from Prof. Rowan's assistant.

9 JUBILIFE CITY PG 57

- Deliver Parcel to your rival at Trainers' School.
- Get Town Map from your rival.
- Obtain three coupons by correctly answering the quizzes given by three clowns.
- Trade the coupons for a Pokétch.
- Get Old Fishing Rod from a fisherman.

10 ROUTE 203 PG 60

- The first battle against your rival.

11 OREBURGH GATE PG 63

- Get HM06 Rock Smash from a man.

12 OREBURGH CITY PG 65

- Pokémon Wi-Fi Club opens in the basement of the Pokémon Center.
- Get Pal Pad from Teala.

13 OREBURGH MINE PG 66

- Go talk to Roark, a Gym Leader from Oreburgh City.

14 OREBURGH CITY PG 67

- Gym Battle #1 - Battle Gym Leader Roark.

15 JUBILIFE CITY PG 59

- Reunite with Prof. Rowan and Rowan's assistant.
- Help Rowan's assistant fight a tag battle against Team Galactic.
- Get the Fashion Case after beating the Galactic Grunts at the Jubilife TV Station.
- Now you can take photos of Pokémon at Jubilife TV.
- Get the Pokétch app Memo Pad from the president of the Pokétch Company.

16 ROUTE 204 PG 74

17 RAVAGED PATH PG 74

18 ROUTE 204 PG 75

- The first Double Battle against a Pokémon Trainer.

19 FLOAROMA TOWN PG 76

- Get Sprayduck Watering Can from an employee of Pick a Peck of Colors Flower Shop.

20 ROUTE 205 PG 82

- A girl asks you to help her dad.

21 VALLEY WINDWORKS PG 85

- Team Galactic battle—lock them in!

22 FLOAROMA MEADOW PG 76

- Get Works Key from Team Galactic.

23 VALLEY WINDWORKS PG 85

- Enter the Windworks using Works Key.
- Battle Team Galactic Commander, Mars.
- Rescue the girl's dad.

24 ROUTE 205 PG 80

25 ETERNA FOREST PG 86

- Travel through the forest with Cheryl.

26 ROUTE 205 PG 80

27 ETERNA CITY PG 91

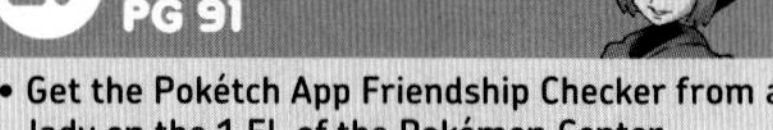

- Get the Pokétch App Friendship Checker from a lady on the 1 FL of the Pokémon Center.
- Get Explorer Kit from the Underground Man.
- Now you can access the Underground.
- Get HM01 Cut from Cynthia.
- Gym Battle #2 - Battle Gym Leader Gardenia.

28 ETERNA FOREST PG 86

- Go to Old Chateau using Cut.

29 OLD CHATEAU PG 87

30 ROUTE 211 PG 96

31 MT. CORONET (#1)
PG 98

32 GALACTIC ETERNA BUILDING
PG 103

- Battle Team Galactic Commander, Jupiter.

33 ETERNA CITY
PG 90

- Get Bicycle from a shop manager of a bike shop.
- Get Exp. Share from Prof. Rowan's assistant.

34 ROUTE 206
PG 104

35 WAYWARD CAVE
PG 105

- Pass through the cave with Mira.

36 ROUTE 207
PG 71

- Get Pokétch app Vs. Seeker and Dowsing Machine from Rowan's assistant.

37 MT. CORONET
PG 100

- Meet a mystery man.

38 ROUTE 208
PG 109

- Get the Pokétch app Berry Searcher from a girl at the Berry Master's house.
- Get Odd Keystone from a man on the street.

39 HEARTHOME CITY
PG 111

- Get a Pokémon Egg from a hiker.
- Get Poffin Case from the president of Pokémon Fan Club.
- Meet the Gym Leader Fantina.
- Get Tuxedo or Dress from your mom.
- Now you can compete in the Super Contest.
- Battle again with your rival.

40 ROUTE 209
PG 117

- Get Good Rod from a fisherman.
- Use Odd Keystone on The Hallowed Tower.

41 THE LOST TOWER
PG 118

- Get HM04 Strength from an old lady on the 5 FL.

42 SOLACEON TOWN
PG 122

- Get the Pokétch app Pokémon History from a man in town.
- Get Seal Case.
- After leaving your Pokémon at the Pokémon Day Care, get the Pokétch app Day Care Checker from a man in the Pokémon Day Care.

43 SOLACEON RUINS
PG 121

44 ROUTE 210
PG 128

- In the back of Café Cabin, a group of Psyduck is blocking the way.

45 ROUTE 215
PG 127

46 VEILSTONE CITY
PG 132

- Get the Pokétch app Counter at reception on the 2FL of the Veilstone Dept. Store.
- Get Coin Case from a clown in a house.
- Gym Battle #3 - Battle Gym Leader Maylene.
- Tag battle Team Galactic with Rowan's assistant.

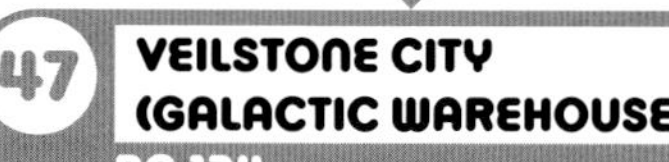

47 VEILSTONE CITY (GALACTIC WAREHOUSE)
PG 134

- Get HM02 Fly.

48 JUBILIFE CITY
PG 59

- Get a Pokétch app Marking Map from the president of Pokétch Company.

49 ROUTE 214
PG 139

50 RUIN MANIAC CAVE / MANIAC TUNNEL
PG 144

51 VALOR LAKEFRONT
PG 139

52 ROUTE 213
PG 139

53 PASTORIA CITY
PG 147

- Gym Battle #4 - Battle Gym Leader Wake.
- Chase Team Galactic grunts and talk to them twice.
- The third battle with your rival.

54 PASTORIA GREAT MARSH
PG 147

- Get HM05 Defog from a man near the entrance.

55 ROUTE 213
PG 141

- Chase Team Galactic grunts.

56 VALOR LAKEFRONT
PG 141

- Chase Team Galactic grunts some more and then battle them.
- Get Secret Potion from Cynthia.

57 ROUTE 212
PG 152

58 POKÉMON MANSION
PG 153

59 ROUTE 210
PG 128

- Use SecretPotion on a group of Psyduck.
- Keep Old Charm for Cynthia.

60 CELESTIC TOWN
PG 157

- Get the Pokétch app Analog Watch from a man in the house.
- Defeat Team Galactic at the entrance of a cave.
- Give the Old Charm to Cynthia's grandmother.
- Examine a fresco in the back of the ruin.
- Get HM03 Surf.
- Meet Cyrus.

61 HEARTHOME CITY
PG 114

- Gym Battle #5 - Battle Gym Leader Fantina.

62 JUBILIFE CITY
PG 59

- Get the Pokétch app Link Searcher from the president of the Pokétch company.

63 ROUTE 219-221
PG 53

- You can go to Pal Park but it's under preparation and they won't let you enter.

64 ROUTE 218
PG 73

- Prof. Rowan's assistant adds to your Pokédex a function to show you Pokémon in both gender forms.

65 CANALAVE CITY
PG 161

- The fourth battle with your rival.
- Gym Battle #6 - Battle Gym Leader Byron.

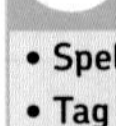
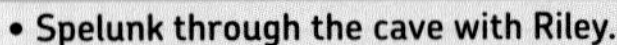

66 IRON ISLAND
PG 166

- Spelunk through the cave with Riley.
- Tag battle Team Galactic with Riley.
- Get a Pokémon Egg from Riley.

67 CANALAVE CITY
PG 163

- Go to Canalave Library.
- Dr. Rowan asks you to go find a Legendary Pokémon.
- A big earthquake takes place.

68 LAKE VALOR
PG 169

- Battle Team Galactic Commander Saturn in Valor Cavern.

69 LAKE VERITY (SECOND VISIT)
PG 171

- Battle Team Galactic Commander Mars.

70 ROUTE 211
PG 97

71 MT. CORONET
PG 98

72 ROUTE 216
PG 172

73 ROUTE 217
PG 173

- Get HM08 Rock Climb.

74 ACUITY LAKEFRONT
PG 172

75 SNOWPOINT CITY
PG 177

- Gym Battle #7 - Battle Gym Leader Candice.

76 JUBILIFE CITY
PG 59

- Get the Pokétch app Move Tester from the president of the Pokétch company.

77 ROUTE 213
PG 143

- Go to a cottage using HM08 Rock Climb and get a Pokétch app Coin Toss from a man there.

78 LAKE ACUITY
PG 179

- Meet your rival and Team Galactic Commander, Jupiter.
- Chase Jupiter, who's on the way to headquarters.

79 VEILSTONE CITY
PG 134

- Get Storage Key from Team Galactic grunts at the entrance of Galactic HQ.

80 GALACTIC STORAGE
PG 182

- Enter the Galactic Warehouse using Storage Key.
- Get Galactic Key on the passage to the building.

81 GALACTIC VEILSTONE BUILDING
PG 183

- Battle Team Galactic Boss, Cyrus.
- Get a Master Ball from Cyrus.
- Underground, discover the Legendary Pokémon, Mesprit, Azelf, and Uxie in captivity.
- Battle Team Galactic Commander, Saturn.
- Free the three imprisoned Pokémon.

82 MT. CORONET (#2)
PG 184

83 SPEAR PILLAR
PG 186

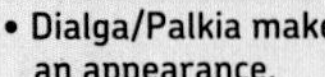

- Dialga/Palkia makes an appearance.
- Tag battle Team Galactic Commanders Mars and Jupiter with your rival.
- The second battle against Team Galactic Boss, Cyrus.
- Capture Dialga/Palkia.

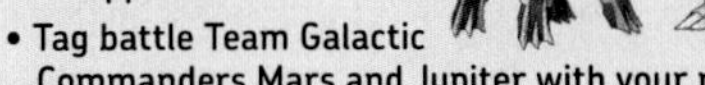

84 LAKE ACUITY
PG 189

- Capture Uxie in Acuity Cavern.

85 LAKE VALOR
PG 190

- Capture Azelf in Valor Cavern.

86 LAKE VERITY
PG 191

- Find Mesprit in Verity Cavern. Talking to it will record it in the Sinnoh Pokédex. It starts traveling.
- Capture Mesprit.

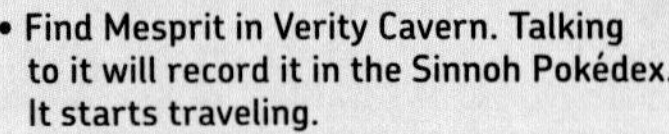

87 ROUTE 222
PG 192

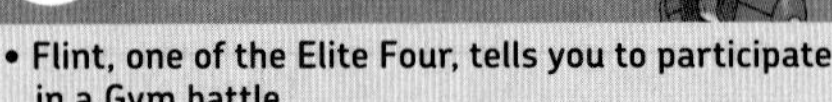

88 SUNYSHORE TOWN
PG 195

- Flint, one of the Elite Four, tells you to participate in a Gym battle.
- Talk to Gym Leader Volkner at Vista Lighthouse.
- Get a Pokétch app Calendar from a man in a house by showing him a Pokémon that has a Serious Character.
- Get the Pokétch app Dot Artist from a man in the house that has an Innocent Character.
- Get a Pokétch app Roulette from a man in a house by showing him a Pokémon that has Capricious Character.
- Gym Battle #8 - Battle Gym Leader Volkner.
- Get HM07 Waterfall from Jasmine.

89 ROUTE 223
PG 198

90 VICTORY ROAD
PG 200

91 POKÉMON LEAGUE
PG 203

- Battle the Elite Four, and the champion, Cynthia.

92 TWINLEAF TOWN
PG 208

93 SANDGEM TOWN
PG 208

- Rowan's assistant tells you to go to Celestic Town.

94 CELESTIC TOWN
PG 209

- The elder shows you an old book.
- Dialga/Palkia will be recorded in Sinnoh Pokédex.

95 SANDGEM TOWN
PG 209

- Prof. Oak comes to Pokémon Laboratory.
- Have Prof. Oak upgrade your Sinnoh Pokédex to the National Pokédex.

POKÉMON DIAMOND/ POKÉMON PEARL

How to use this guide.

THIS IS THE OFFICIAL STRATEGY GUIDE for Pokémon Diamond and Pokémon Pearl. The story navigates you through your adventure to conquer the Pokémon League Championship, and the Pokédex instructs you on how to complete your records in the Sinnoh Pokédex. Start with a chapter of your choice. Post-ending strategies and the guide on "how-to-complete" the National Pokédex will be introduced in the Official Pokémon Diamond and Pearl National Pokédex on sale in May of 2007.

KNOW MORE ABOUT POKÉMON!
INTRODUCTION

TO PG 012

THIS CHAPTER provides you with all the basic information needed to prepare yourself for your adventure. If you're a first-timer, it is recommended that you start with this chapter.

BEGIN YOUR JOURNEY
SINNOH ADVENTURE

TO PG 038

FULL OF THE IN-DEPTH instructions and helpful navigations from the beginning to the end!! Make your way to the top of the league smoothly.

COMPLETE YOUR RECORDS WITH THE
SINNOH POKÉDEX

TO PG 210

GO HERE TO DISCOVER how to find all 150 Pokémon in the Sinnoh region, and complete your records for the Sinnoh Pokédex.

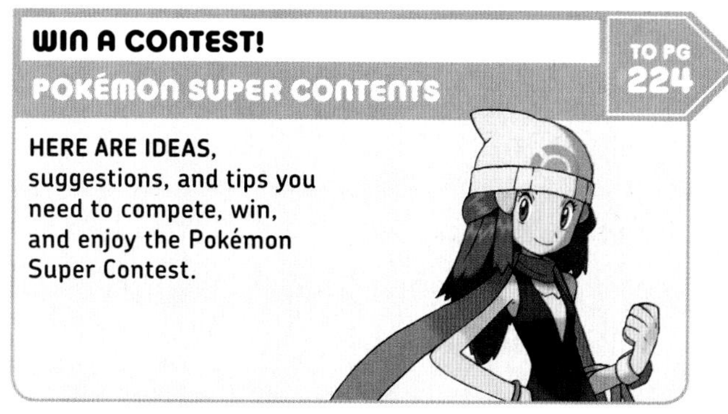

WIN A CONTEST!
POKÉMON SUPER CONTENTS

TO PG 224

HERE ARE IDEAS, suggestions, and tips you need to compete, win, and enjoy the Pokémon Super Contest.

FIND OUT WHAT FUN THINGS YOU CAN DO
WIRELESS FUNCTION

TO PG 238

INTRODUCES and familiarizes you with various connected playing modes such as Nintendo DS Wireless Connection and Nintendo Wi-Fi Connection.

LEARN ABOUT POKÉMON MOVES
CHARTS

TO PG 256

VERY USEFUL LISTS that contain important information about Pokémon moves, effectiveness of items and how and where to obtain them.

SECTION 1

INTRODUCTION

RAISE YOUR POKÉMON WITH CARE!

There are many types of Pokémon.

POKÉMON ARE VERY MYSTERIOUS creatures - there is so much more to them than meets the eye!! Some live in the wild and some live in cities and towns with humans. More and more new species are being discovered every day!

GOTTA CATCH 'EM ALL!

OWN AS MANY POKÉMON AS YOU CAN!! You will need their help and cooperation in order to achieve your goal ...and to advance through the Pokémon League Championship! Here are some ways to capture them successfully.

PRIMARY METHODS TO CATCH POKÉMON

CATCH WILD POKÉMON

Many Pokémon live in bushes, caves, and oceans. The most basic method of collecting Pokémon is to find them in their wild habitats and catch them.

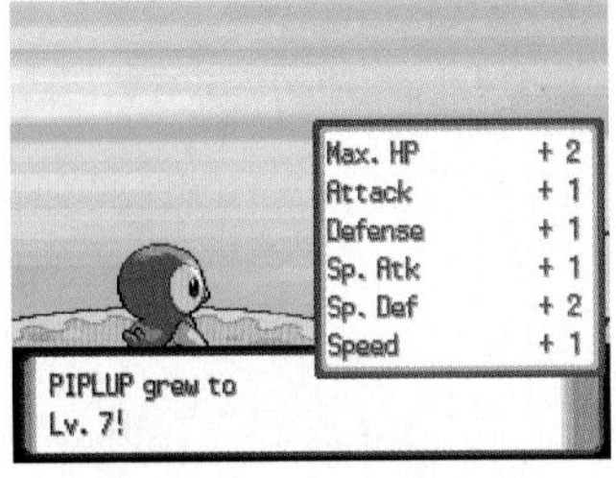

LET THEM EVOLVE THROUGH BATTLES

Train your Pokémon and let them battle other Pokémon. They will grow and eventually evolve. When evolved, they assume different names and appearances and even learn new moves and Abilities!

EARN AN EGG FROM A STRANGER

Help people out, do them favors and you may earn a Pokémon Egg. Look around and see if somebody needs your help.

TRADE POKÉMON WITH FRIENDS

When it comes to types that are rare and very hard to catch, try trading Pokémon with your friends. It's another efficient way to increase the number of Pokémon in your Pokédex!

BATTLES MAKE THEM STRONGER!

POKÉMON GROW UP and get stronger as they battle. Each time they win, their experience points accumulate – when enough points have built up, they level up, which makes their Attack and Defense power also rise. Raise and train your Pokémon well!

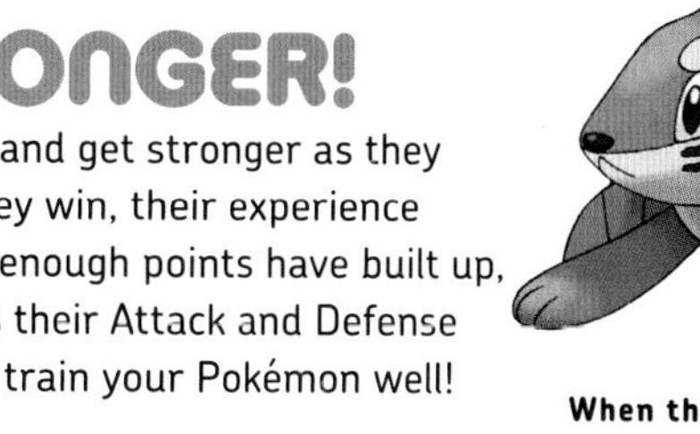

When their experience points hit certain levels, Pokémon level up.

LEVELING LEADS TO EVOLUTION

SOME POKÉMON EVOLVE into different creatures when they level up. Although there are several ways to make your Pokémon evolve, the most basic method is to make them battle and earn experience points for them to level up.

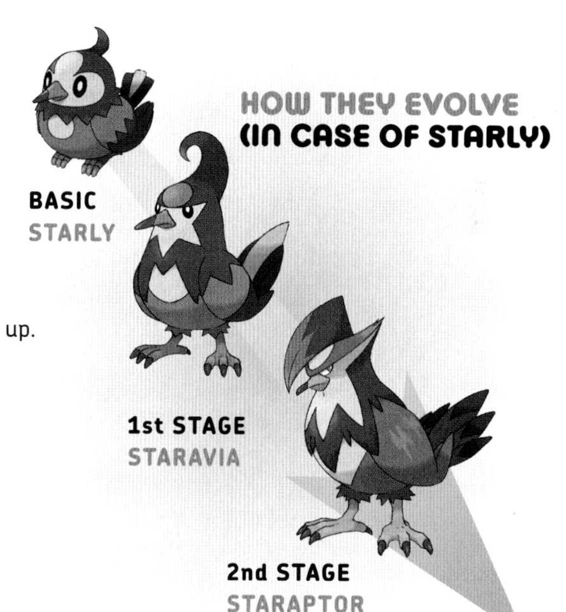

OTHER METHODS FOR EVOLVING

GIVE THEM A SPECIAL STONE

Using stones that have special power like the Shiny Stone, Dusk Stone, or Thunderstone, is also another way to level up certain Pokémon.

Welcome to the Pokémon Fan Club!
Oh, your PIPLUP...

BOND WITH YOUR POKÉMON

Breed them with tender loving care and they will become happily attached to you. In some special cases, this is the only way certain Pokémon can evolve.

MAKE THEM LEARN MORE MOVES

For some Pokémon, leaning moves are the key to an Evolution. Make them level up after they have learned or mastered a specific move.

CONNECTION TRADE

Use the buddy system! Some Pokémon can only evolve when traded!

BE AN EXPERT AT CATCHING WILD POKÉMON

YOU NEED TO USE a Poké Ball to catch wild Pokémon, but often times, that's not enough. Some will escape the Poké Ball, and others won't surrender easily. Here are three basic techniques to help you successfully capture them.

BASIC METHODS TO CATCH WILD POKÉMON

1 BRING DOWN THEIR HP AS LOW AS POSSIBLE

Every wild Pokémon has HP (Hit Points) which shows how strong they are. High HP means Pokémon are very energetic, while zero HP means a Pokémon has fainted and can no longer be used in battle. To capture them, it is very important to first decrease their HP by attacking them. When their HP bar goes into the red, you will be able to capture them without difficulty.

2 ATTACK THEM WITH STATUS CONDITIONS

In battles, Pokémon sometimes fall under certain status conditions - like Poison and Paralyze (see p.25) - because of the effects of their opponent's moves. This is another situation that makes Pokémon easier to catch. Sleep and Freeze are two conditions that make Pokémon extremely vulnerable. When placed in these conditions, combined with low HP, there won't be much a Pokémon can do to avoid capture.

3 USE DIFFERENT KINDS OF POKÉ BALLS

As you can tell from the list on the next page, there are many different kinds of Poké Balls. They have their own unique strengths and weaknesses, and work differently depending on what type of Pokémon you use them on. For instance, a Net Ball works best on Water- and Bug-type Pokémon. Make sure you use the right Poké Ball for the right situation.

WHICH POKÉ BALL SHOULD YOU USE?

YOU WILL BE USING 15 DIFFERENT POKÉ BALLS through the course of your adventure in Pokémon Diamond/Pearl. As explained previously, every Poké Ball has a different effectiveness. Familiarize yourself with them all and master how to use them to catch the Pokémon of your choice!!

POKÉ BALL

The most basic Poké Ball. The Professor's assistant will give you five near the start of your adventure, but after that, you have to buy them.

HOW TO OBTAIN: Purchase it.

HEAL BALL

Restores HP of the Pokémon you caught and helps them recover from Special Conditions.

WHERE TO BUY: Jubilife City, Oreburgh City etc.

TIMER BALL

The more turns the battle last, the better this Poké Ball works.

WHERE TO BUY: Celestic Town, Snowpoint City etc.

GREAT BALL

Slightly more effective than a Poké Ball.

HOW TO OBTAIN: Collect 3 Gym badges (win Veilstone City Gym battle).

NET BALL

For the capture of Bug-type and Water-type Pokémon.

WHERE TO BUY: Oreburgh City, Floaroma Town etc.

REPEAT BALL

High effectiveness against Pokémon you have previously captured.

WHERE TO BUY: Canalave City, Pokémon League

ULTRA BALL

Slightly more effective than Great Ball.

HOW TO OBTAIN: Collect 5 Gym badges (win Hearthome City Gym battle).

DUSK BALL

Works well at night or in a dark place like a cave.

WHERE TO BUY: Solaceon Town, Pastoria City etc.

DIVE BALL

High effectiveness against Pokémon living in water.

HOW TO OBTAIN: Work part-time at Pokémon News Press.

MASTER BALL

An ultimate ball that enables you to capture just about any Pokémon!!

HOW TO OBTAIN: Gain it from Team Galactic boss, Cyrus in Galactic Veilstone Building.

NEST BALL

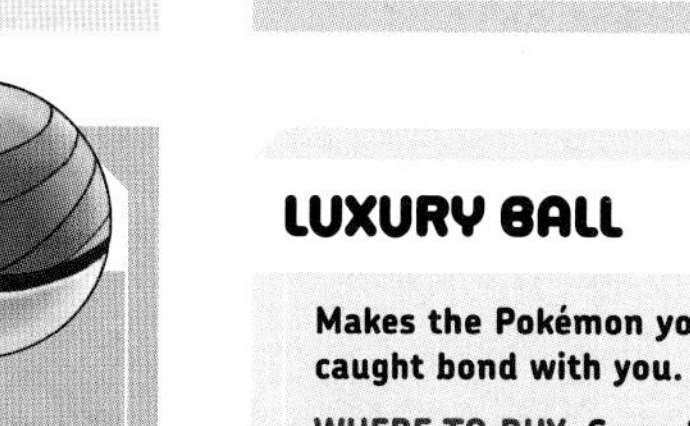

The weaker the Pokémon, the better it catches them.

WHERE TO BUY: Eterna City, Hearthome City

LUXURY BALL

Makes the Pokémon you've caught bond with you.

WHERE TO BUY: Sunyshore City, Pokémon League

PREMIER BALL

Has the same efficiency as Poké Ball. It's free!

HOW TO OBTAIN: Buy 10 Poké Balls in one purchase.

QUICK BALL

Use it as soon as a battle begins for better effectiveness.

WHERE TO BUY: Pastoria City, Celestic Town etc.

SAFARI BALL

For the use in Pastoria Great Marsh only!

HOW TO OBTAIN: Pastoria Great Marsh

POKÉMON MOVES MAKE THE DIFFERENCE

POKÉMON LEARN VARIOUS MOVES that are very useful in battles and adventures. There are more than 380 moves and each one of them has a specific effect of its own. Special moves make each Pokémon unique.

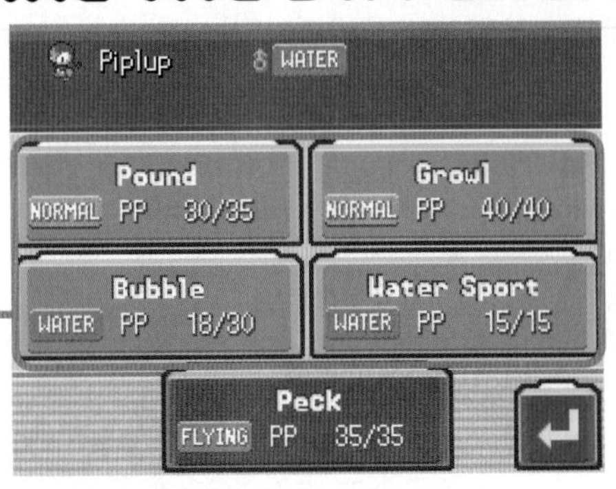

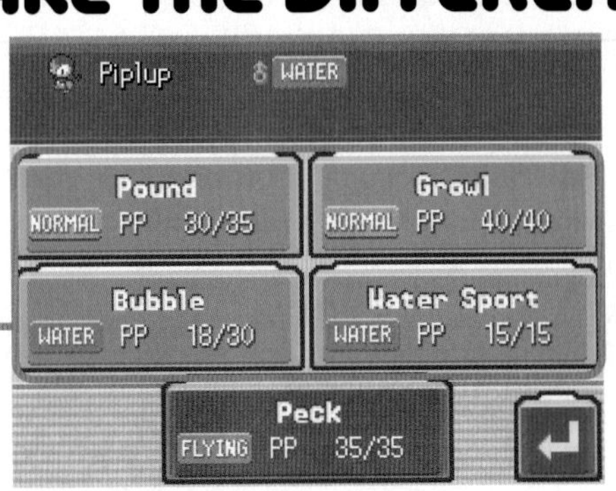

They can learn up to 4 moves at a time.

MOVES COME IN THREE TYPES

ATTACK MOVES

Used to attack their enemies and do damage to them. In addition to simply injuring the opponents, they can also do various more damaging things like casting Special Conditions over them such as poison, burn or paralyze. There are also moves that let you strike first.

DEFENSE MOVES

Used to defend against opponents' attacks. These moves restore your HP and cure your Pokémon's Special Conditions. You can also increase your HP while (by) doing damage to your opponent, and gradually restore your HP every turn.

SPECIAL MOVES

Lets you strengthen yourself or give your enemy disadvantages. You can intensify your Pokémon's Stats or take away your enemy Pokémon's HP by affecting them with Special Conditions such as Poison and Burn.

HOW TO MAKE YOUR POKÉMON LEARN MOVES

LEVEL UP

They learn new moves at certain levels. When they level up and are ready and able, they learn new moves.

USE TMS

TMs are the items you use to make your Pokémon learn their moves. Remember, though, that it is good for only one use. So be very careful and use it wisely!!

USE HMS

HMs are the items that have special moves (see p.21) registered in them. Unlike TMs you can use them repeatedly on more than one Pokémon.

TEACH THEM WELL

During your adventure you'll meet people who are great Trainers. Take advantage of these opportunities and let your Pokémon get schooled!

POKéMON AND THEIR ABILITIES

POKÉMON HAVE DIFFERENT ABILITIES depending on their types. For instance, Pikachu has an Ability called Static, which can inflict the Paralyze condition, and attracts Electric-type Pokémon (when Pikachu is the lead in your group). Some are useful in battle, and some are helpful in capturing wild Pokémon.

Some Pokémon may have two Abilities. In such cases, they usually can only possess one of the two.

EXAMPLES OF ABILITIES AND THEIR EFFECTS

PICKUP

When in battle, they pick up items. The items they can pick up vary depending on their level. (see p.290)

POKÉMON: Pachirisu, Munchlax

ANTICIPATION

If an opponent has moves that are very effective on them, they detect them right at the very beginning of the battle.

POKÉMON: Wormadam, Croagunk

RUN AWAY

No matter whom it is that you're in a battle with, you can run from them. It bears no effect in battles between Pokémon Trainers.

POKÉMON: Buneary, Ponyta

BOND WITH YOUR POKÉMON

ESTABLISH A GOOD RELATIONSHIP with your Pokémon. If you make them happy by doing things they like, naturally they will become more bonded to you. If you annoy them, don't expect them to play nice.

HOW TO BOND WITH YOUR POKÉMON

ALWAYS KEEP THEM IN YOUR PARTY

Keep them in your Party and travel with them. The more time you spend with them, the better they bond with you.

CAPTURE THEM WITH THE LUXURY BALL

Using a Luxury Ball in capturing them definitely makes this bonding business easier.

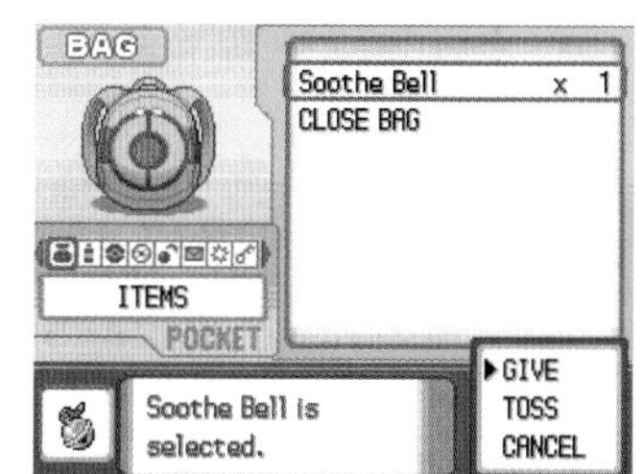

GIVE THEM THE SOOTHE BELL

Give them an item to hold called the Soothe Bell and they bond with you better than they do without it.

GIVE THEM AN ABILITY ITEM

Bringing up their basic points by giving them items like Protein, Zinc or Iron is another solution for happier Pokémon.

YOU MAKE ME FEEL LIKE A NATURAL POKÉMON

EACH AND EVERY POKÉMON has its own nature. There are 25 of them in total including brave, serious, quirky. Depending on Pokémon's Nature, their stats change upon leveling up.

Look here for their Nature.

THE DIFFERENCE IN NATURE AFFECTS...

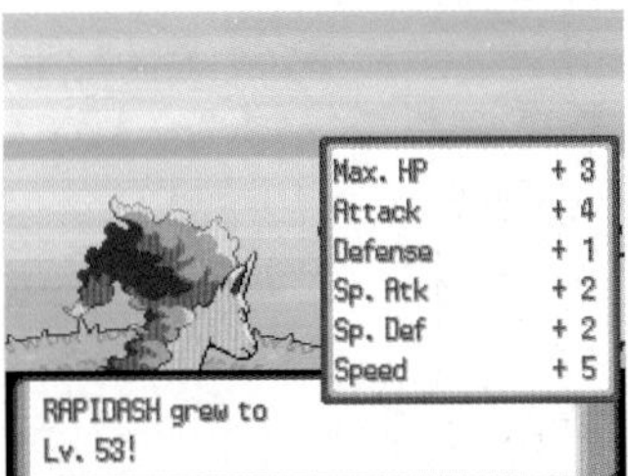

HOW THEY ADVANCE IN THEIR ABILITIES

1 When they level up, their stats advance, too. Pokémon with different Nature differ in the way their stats grow.

EFFECTIVENESS OF BERRIES

2 Some berries can restore Pokémon's HP when given to them. But if Pokémon dislike the flavor of it, it can often make them Confused.

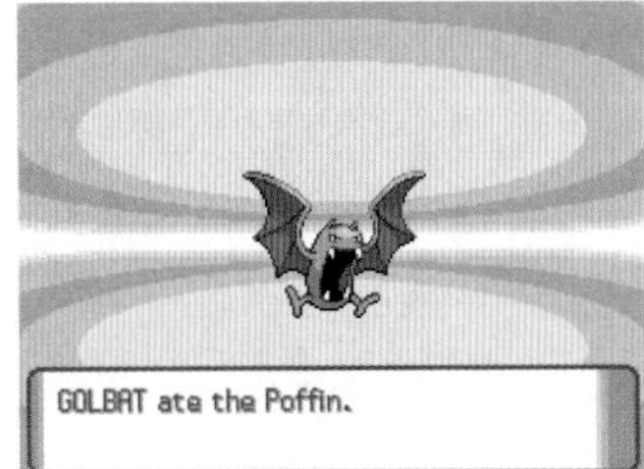

TASTE FOR POFFIN

3 They have different tastes for Pokémon food. Feed them Poffin they like, and their condition gets better.

NATURE ATTRACTS

4 Give your Pokémon Everstone and leave it with a Pokémon breeder. Chances are better than a Pokémon with the same Nature will be born.

SEE P.272 FOR A LIST OF THE POKÉMON'S CHARACTERISTICS

WHAT ABOUT CHARACTERISTICS?

A POKÉMON'S CHARACTERISTICS INDICATE which stats will develop the best. For instance, if your Pokémon is sensitive to sound, its Speed stat will increase. Try and improve the stats that will grow the fastest.

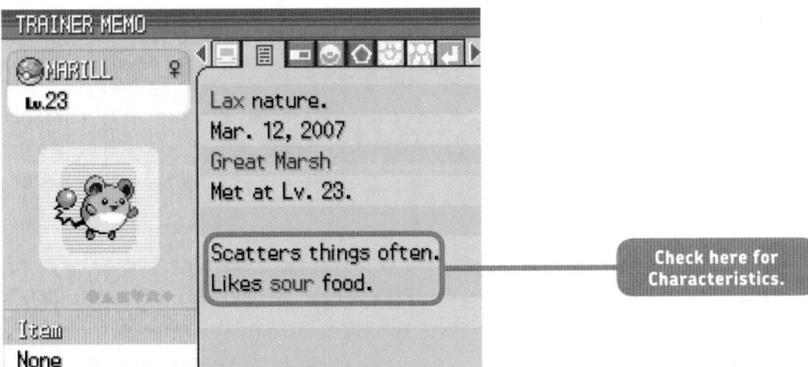

SEE P.272 FOR A LIST OF THE POKÉMON'S CHARACTERISTICS

AIN'T NO MOUNTAIN HIGH ENOUGH

AMONGST THE MANY MOVES POKÉMON USE, there are some granted through items known as Hidden Machines (HMs). When taught to a Pokémon and used on the field, there won't be a single place you can't go. They simply get rid of all the obstacles you will come across on the way. Each move requires a specific Gym badge in order to activate the move in the field.

FIELD MOVES THAT ARE EFFECTIVE FOR TRAVELING

HM 1: CUT

Chops down small trees so you can move forward.

WHERE TO GET IT:
Get it from Cynthia in Eterna City.

HM 2: FLY

Flies you to towns you've visited before. You will land in front of the town's Pokémon Center.

WHERE TO GET IT: Obtain it in Galactic Storage.

HM3: SURF

You can surf freely on the waters of rivers and oceans.

WHERE TO GET IT:
Get it from an elder in Celestic Town.

HM4: STRENGTH

Use this power to move heavy rocks with ease.

WHERE TO GET IT:
The old lady on the fifth floor of the the Lost Tower.

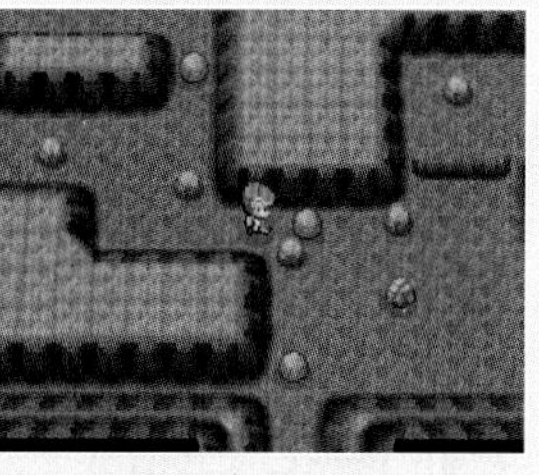

HM5: DEFOG

Dissipate the thick fog and you can see clearly now.

WHERE TO GET IT:
Get it from a man in Pastoria Great Marsh.

HM6: ROCK SMASH

Crush these huge obstacles into pieces and keep on going.

WHERE TO GET IT:
Get it from a man at Oreburgh Gate.

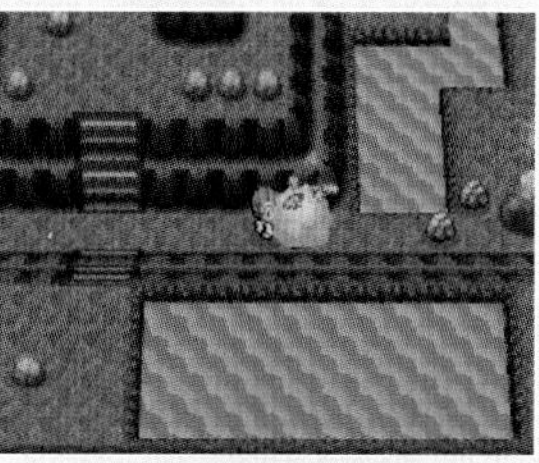

HM7: WATERFALL

Climb up vast waterfalls with ease.

WHERE TO GET IT:
Get it from Jasmine in Sunyshore City.

HM8: ROCK CLIMB

You can climb up and down on rough, craggy surfaces of mountains.

WHERE TO GET IT:
Get it on Route 217.

REGULAR MOVES THAT CAN BE USED ON THE FIELD

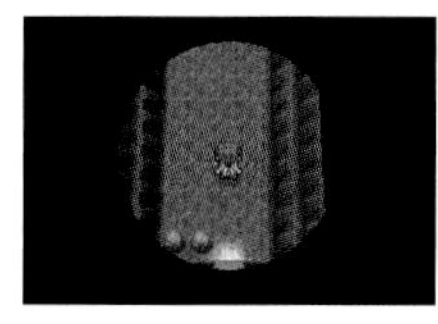

FIELD MOVES ARE VERY USEFUL MOVES that make it easier to travel on roads and caves, but there are regular moves that also can do similar tasks. For instance, Flash comes in very handy when you need something to light your way through the pitch black darkness in Wayward Cave right under the Cycling Road.

TECHNIQUES TO WIN

Type Casting.

YOU SHOULD KNOW by now that all Pokémon have different types like Normal, Fire, Water, Grass, etc. There are 17 types in total and every Pokémon belongs to one of those groups. Type is a very important factor that impacts the results of battles. Make sure you know them well so you have a head start for wins in your future battles!

17 TYPES OF POKéMON IN ALL!

Normal

Glameow

Fire

Chimchar

Water

Piplup

Grass

Turtwig

Electric

Pachirisu

Ice

Snover

Fighting

Lucario

Poison

Skorupi

Ground

Hippopotas

Flying

Starly

Psychic

Chingling

Bug

Kricketot

Rock

Cranidos

Ghost

Drifloon

Dragon

Gible

Dark

Stunky

Steel

Bronzor

HAVE TYPES, WILL TRAVEL

JUST BECAUSE a Pokémon is a certain type doesn't mean that it is limited to learning moves of that type. Take Piplup, for example. Although it is a Water-type, they can learn moves of different types.

PIPLUP'S CASE

Piplup
Water
Uses Move Peck:
• Flying-type

MOVE TYPE AFFECTS THEIR ATTACKS

Attacks the opponent, Bidoof, with a Flying-type move

Attacks with the move Peck

POKéMON TYPE AFFECTS THEIR DEFENSES

Receives Bidoof's attack against its Water-type defense

Receives the attack Headbutt

PIN-POINT THEIR WEAKNESS! TURN THE BATTLE UPSIDE-DOWN!

HERE IS THE POKÉMON GOLDEN RULE. Water-types dominate Fire-types, but is vulnerable against Grass-types. Kind of reminds you of rock, paper, scissors, right? This is where type effectiveness comes in to play. For example, if the attacker's move type is effective on the defender's Pokémon type, the damage done here will be double that than under normal circumstances.

COMPATIBILITY

IF IT'S EFFECTIVE (FIRE VS. GRASS) THE DAMAGE IS 2X!

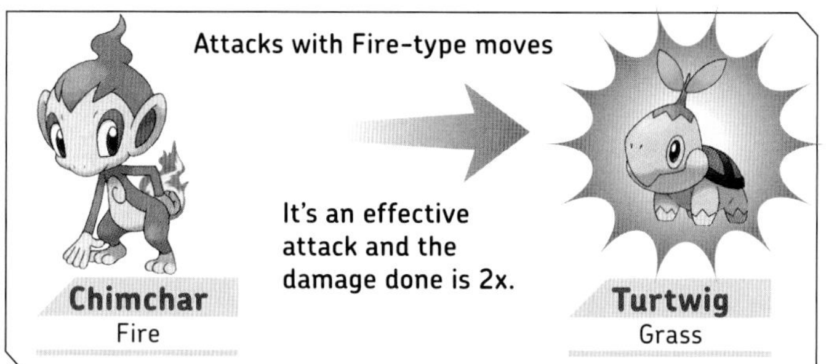

IF NOT EFFECTIVE, THE DAMAGE IS ONLY 1/2

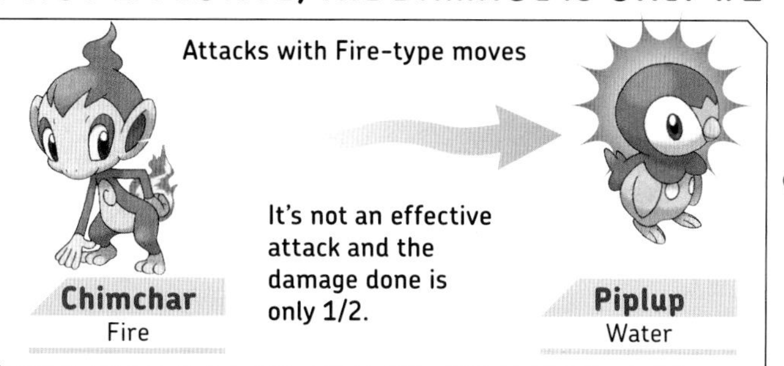

MULTIPLY THE DAMAGE OF YOUR ATTACKS!

YOU CAN INCREASE the damage to your opponents by more than 1.5x by meeting certain requirements. And since the more damage you do to your opponent, the closer you get to your victory, why not give it a try? Here are three basic conditions that will make victory possible.

1: USE THE SAME MOVE TYPE AS YOUR POKÉMON'S:

If the type of the move is the same as the type of your Pokémon, the power of the move is 1.5x. Damage: 1.5x

2: ATTACK YOUR OPPONENT'S WEAKNESS

Use the type of move that your opponent is vulnerable against, and the damage increases to 2x. Damage: 2x

3: HITTING YOUR OPPONENT WITH A CRITICAL HIT

If you land a critical hit, the damage increases another 2x. Damage: 2x

REFER TO THE IN-BATTLE MESSAGES FOR THE AMOUNT OF DAMAGE YOU ARE CREATING

MESSAGE	EFFECTIVENESS	DAMAGE
Super Effective!	Effective	2 to 4x
Not very effective	Not Effective	1/2 or less
(No message)	Normal	Normal
Not effective at all	No Effect	No damage
It is a critical hit	-	2x

INTRODUCTION

THE NUMBERS GAME: POKÉMON'S STATS

EACH POKÉMON has 6 main statistics: HP, Speed, Attack, Defense, Special Attack, and Special Defense. The higher each statistic, the stronger it is!

HP
Pokémon's physical strength. When attacked the points decreases. If it goes all the way down to zero, your Pokémon faints.

SPEED
Quick attacks, quick moves! Pokémon who have high speed points are faster than others in making initial moves.

RELATED TO PHYSICAL MOVES
Attack
Higher points mean more damage they do with physical moves.

DEFENSE
Higher points mean less damage they receive from physical moves.

RELATED TO SPECIAL MOVES
Special Attack
Higher points mean more damage they do with special moves.

SPECIAL DEFENSE
Higher points mean less damage they receive from special moves.

STATS AFFECT EFFECTIVENESS OF MOVES

ALL THE MOVES can be divided into three categories: Physical, Special, and Status - all of which are closely related to their stats. An example: Let a Pokémon that is strong in Attack learn physical moves that will cause a great deal of damage to your opponents.

EFFECTIVENESS OF MOVES CAN BE DIVIDED IN THREE DIFFERENT CATEGORIES

PHYSICAL MOVES

Includes all the contact moves such as Bite, Thunderpunch and Hi Jump Kick.

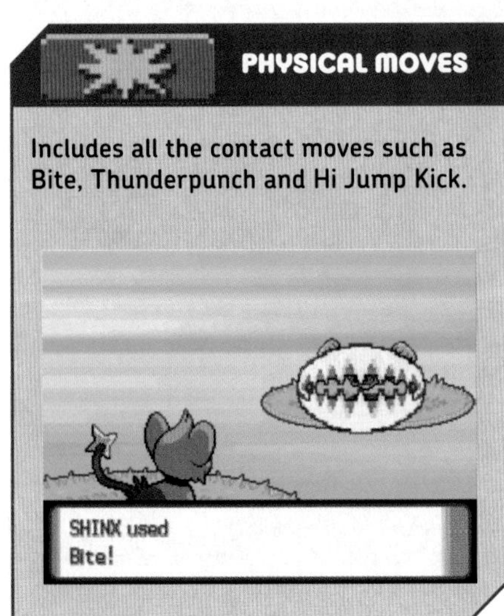
SHINX used
Bite!

SPECIAL MOVES

Includes all non-contact moves such as Shock Wave, Ember and Bubblebeam.

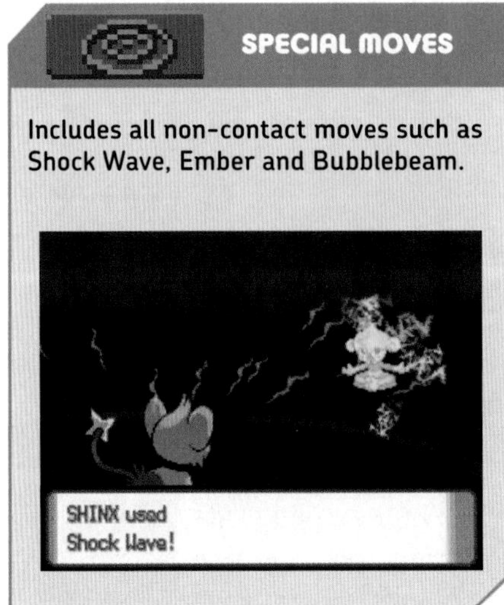
SHINX used
Shock Wave!

STATUS MOVES

All the moves that change both your stats and your opponent's stats or conditions during battle, like Swagger.

GRAVELER Lv27
SHINX Lv29
72/72
SHINX used
Swagger!

STATUS CONDITIONS

STATUS CONDITIONS affect an opponent's ability to battle. While they don't always do damage, they can definitely make a difference! In addition to the 6 main status conditions, there are some possible semi-special conditions. A Pokémon can be affected by both a status condition and a special condition at the same time, but you can't affect a Pokémon with two status conditions (with the exception of Confusion) or two special conditions.

The effects of special conditions are absolutely powerful! Execute them as often as you can and see the results for yourself!

THE SIX SPECIAL CONDITIONS

POISON

Reduces your HP every turn. Doesn't heal automatically during battle.

1 Effect: Reduces your opponent's HP.

PARALYSIS

Decreases your speed and deprives you of one attack out of every four. Doesn't heal automatically during battle.

2 Effect: Lessens your opponent's turns to attack. You get to attack first.

BURN

Lowers your attack and reduces your HP with every turn. Doesn't heal automatically during battle.

3 Effect: Reduces your opponent's HP. Makes your opponent's attacks less powerful.

SLEEP

Makes you unable to attack. Allows you to heal yourself after several turns.

4 Effect: Prevents your opponent from attacking you. Provides you with a safe environment.

FREEZE

Makes you unable to attack. Allows you to heal yourself after several turns.

5 Effect: Prevents your opponent from attacking you. Provides you with a safe environment.

CONFUSE

Target may be confused enough to attack itself. Wears off after several turns.

6 Effect: Lessens your opponent's turns to attack. Reduces your opponent's HP.

ADDITIONAL EFFECTS FROM CONDITIONS

SOME MOVES PERFORM just like special conditions. In fact, you can use them in conjunction with special conditions to bring about more effects. For example: You can make already poisoned Pokémon even weaker by using Attract.

CURSE

Reduces your HP by 1/4 of your max HPs each turn.

ATTRACT

Makes it difficult for you to attack your opponents of opposite gender.

FLINCH

Makes you Flinch and unable to attack during that turn.

LEECH SEED

Reduces your HP each turn and lets your opponent absorb it.

THE RULES IN EXECUTING THESE MOVES

 You can't combine special conditions (except for Confuse)

 You can combine semi-special conditions

MAKE THE MOST OF POKéMON ABILITIES

EACH TYPE OF POKéMON has its own special Abilities. Utilizing them in battles will expand your advantage for successful wins. Master them and use them together with your various moves.

Abilities control battles.

ABILITIES THAT THE FIRST THREE POKéMON POSSESS

OVERGROW
TURTWIG
When HP decreases to less than 1/3, the power of Grass-type moves will be strengthened by 1.5x.

BLAZE
CHIMCHAR
When HP decreases to less than 1/3, the power of Fire-type moves will be strengthened by 1.5x.

TORRENT
PIPLUP
When HP decreases to less than 1/3, the power of Water-type moves will be strengthened by 1.5x.

ABILITIES USEFUL IN BATTLE

INTIMIDATE
Upon entering into a battle, lowers opponent's Attack by one level.

POKéMON THAT HAVE IT:
Shinx, Staravia

LEVITATE
Immune to any Ground-type moves.

POKéMON THAT HAVE IT:
Misdreavus, Gastly

STATIC
Paralyzes opponents that come in contact with a 30% probability.

POKéMON THAT HAVE IT:
Pikachu, Raichu

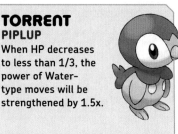

EQUIP ITEMS ONTO YOUR POKéMON

POKéMON CAN HOLD one item. Some battles can turn depending on the use of these helpful items. Use them wisely.

EXAMPLES OF USEFUL TOOLS AND ITEMS

SHELL BELL
Restores your HP by 1/8 of damage done to your opponent.

WIDE LENS
Raises the accuracy of your moves.

QUICK CLAW
Lets you attack first.

SILK SCARF
Makes Normal-type moves more powerful.

LUM BERRY
Cures special conditions.

CITRUS BERRY
Restores your HP by 1/4 of your max HPs.

USE YOUR TOOLS AND ITEMS

BAGS

BAGS CONTAIN TOOLS AND ITEMS you collect during the course of your adventure. They have eight pockets (Items, Medicine, Poké Balls, TMs and HMs, Berries, Mail, Battle Items, and Key Items) and will automatically categorize your tools and items and keep them separately in those pockets.

FOR BOYS

FOR GIRLS

REGISTER ITEMS OF FREQUENT USE

IT IS WISE TO REGISTER THE TOOLS like the Bicycle or the Fishing Rod that you repeatedly use. Once registered, you can access those items right away by pressing the Y-button. This will save a significant amount of the time you would waste rooting through your bag.

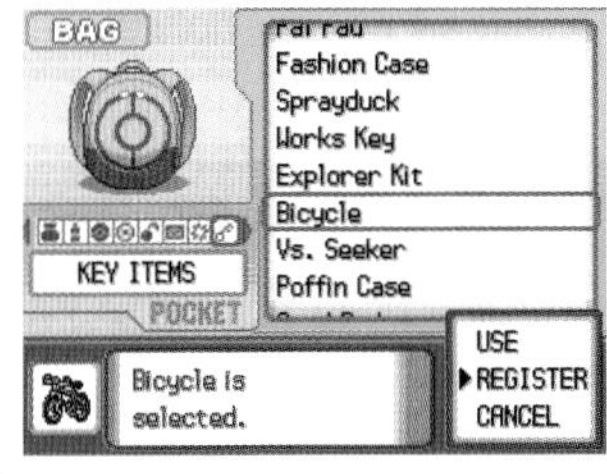

HOW TO REGISTER YOUR ITEMS?

Move the cursor to the item you want to use. Press a button and select Register.

ORGANIZE YOUR ITEMS

YOU WOULD WANT TO COLLECT as many useful items and tools as possible but after a while it becomes a time consuming task to go though your bag and find what you need if they are not sorted out and neatly in place. So start organizing your items early. Example: line up your Potions and Hyper Potions in order. You can pick up exactly what you want in the blink of an eye.

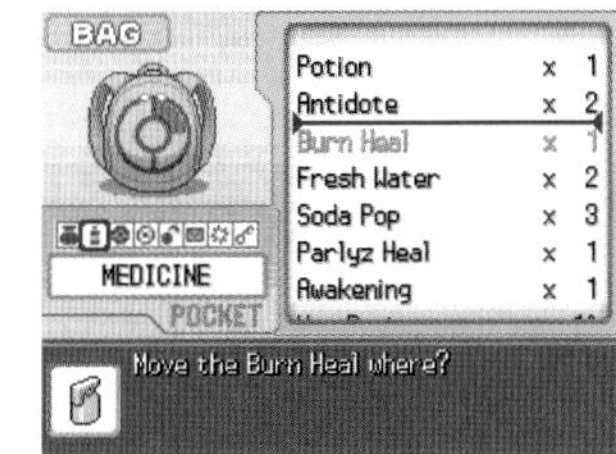

WHERE WILL YOU KEEP HYPER POTION?

How to organize your items:

- **Move the cursor to the items**
- **Rearrange them by pressing Select button.**

EXAMPLES: ITEMS YOU WANT TO TAKE WITH YOU

POKÉ BALL

An item with which you catch Pokémon. Collect as many kinds as you can so that you can use the right Poké Ball on the right Pokémon.

POTION

An item that heals your Pokémon. Collect as many kinds as you can so that you can choose the right one for the right situation.

REMEDY FOR SPECIAL CONDITIONS

An item that cures special conditions. Collect and carry all of them and you will be able to deal with all kinds of special conditions when they occur.

AN ITEM TO RESTORE THE PP

PP is an indicator of the number of moves Pokémon can use. PP restoration items are very valuable so use them carefully.

REPEL

Allows you to avoid encounters with Pokémon that are lower-level than yours. It's a time-saver when you're in a hurry to get somewhere.

ESCAPE ROPE

A tool that brings you back out to the entrance of a cave in an instant. It's a helpful tool you can use when you're stuck deep inside of a cave.

THE POKÉDEX

THE POKÉDEX IS A HIGH-TECH DEVICE that automatically registers information on Pokémon. When you come across Pokémon while traveling or see them in battles against other Trainers, The Pokédex records their names, appearances and habitats as the number you've found. When you capture them, it indicates their detailed biological information as the number you've captured.

THE PROCEDURE OF REGISTRATION

1 WHEN THERE IS NOTHING REGISTERED

Until you start seeing Pokémon, it just shows you pages with index numbers on them.

2 POKÉMON'S APPEARANCE AND HABITAT

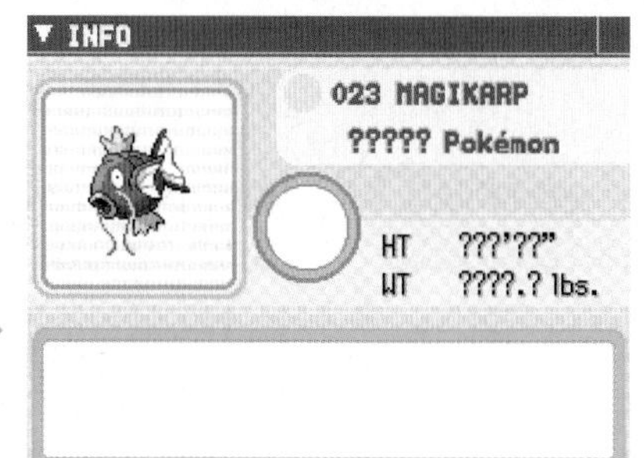

Once you find the Pokémon, the Pokédex shows their names and images. If they are wild Pokémon, the Pokédex indicates their habitats, too.

3 POKÉMON'S BIOLOGICAL DATA

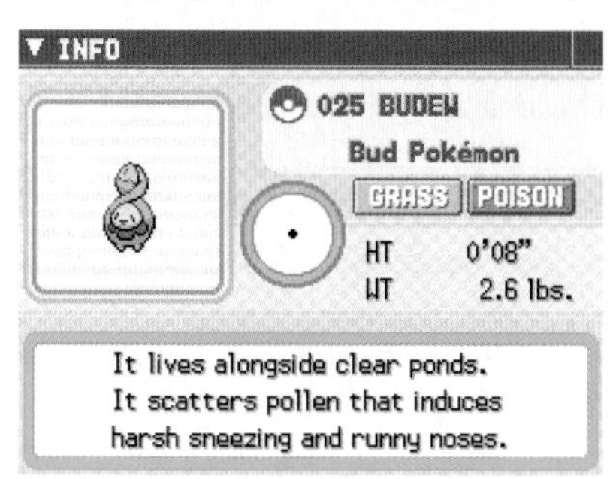

When you finally capture them, the Pokédex indicates Pokémon types, height and weight, and other detailed biological information. This completes the Pokémon registration procedure.

OTHER BASIC FUNCTIONS

AREA

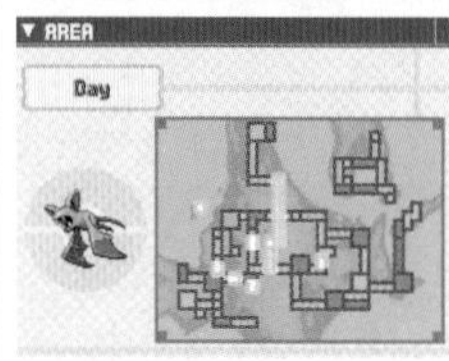

You'll see the area where caught Pokémon have appeared. Moving the sun on the bottom screen shows the areas during the morning, day, and night.

CRY

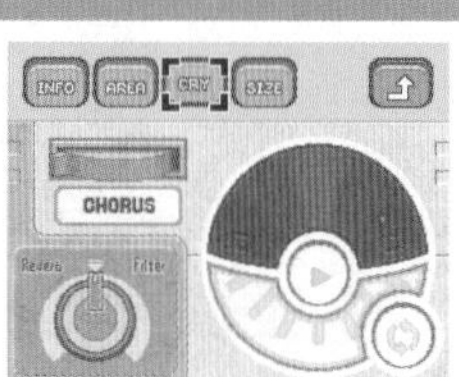

You can hear Pokémon's cries. You can also play sound effects such as Chorus and Pan.

SIZE

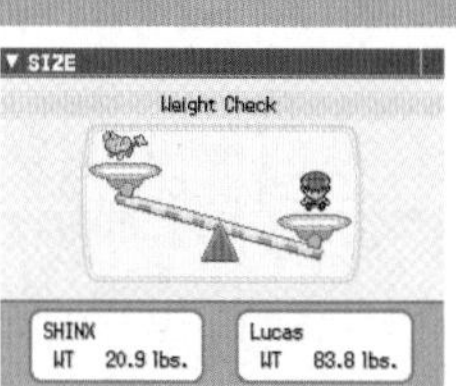

It shows Pokémon's size (height and weight) in comparison with yours.

FORMS

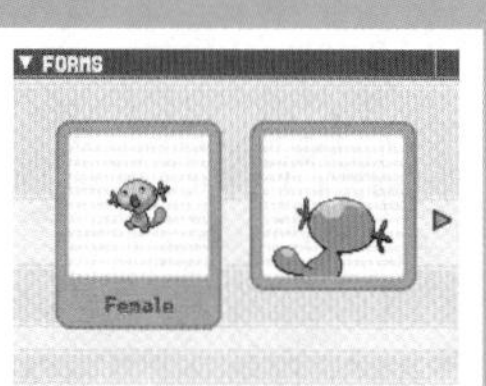

You can examine physical difference between males and females.

SORT FUNCTION

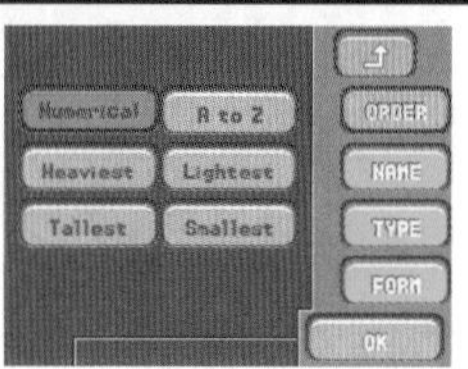

Sorts out data by Sinnoh Pokédex number, alphabetical order, weight etc.

VS. SEEKER

ARE THERE TRAINERS YOU'VE FACED before who want a rematch with you? Are you willing to fight them again? Who knows, they may have gotten better and now want to take a second shot at victory. This tool lets you find those foes by indicating "!!" above their heads.

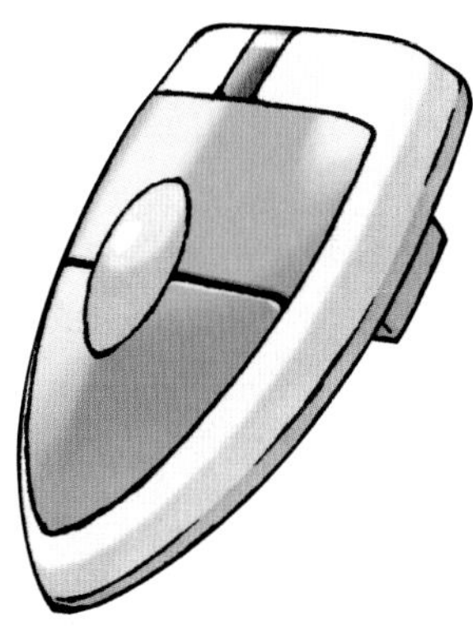

TAKE 100 STEPS TO RECHARGE

You have to recharge your Vs. Seeker after every use. How? Easy! Just take 100 steps and your Seeker is ready for use again. When the battery is dead, take a quick run to recharge it.

Number of steps required to fully charge the battery: 72

HOW MANY MORE STEPS?
No need to keep counting. This tool tells you the number of steps needed to complete charging.

THEY GET BETTER AND STRONGER, TOO!

Your old opponents get better and come at you with new moves and techniques. So do your homework on their Pokémon, and their Pokémon. Make these rematches as beneficial to you as possible.

I'm still on my journey...
Let's have a battle!

ENJOY YOUR BATTLES
Rematch Trainers even act and talk differently which makes rematch battles more fun.

THE BICYCLE

A VERY CONVENIENT TOOL that lets you travel much faster than just using your Running Shoes. It's a new model with automatic gear changes. Press the B Button and the gear goes from 3RD gear, which lets you make easy turns, to 4TH gear, which helps you travel on loose surfaces like sandy slopes.

SANDY SLOPES

Loose, shifty sand is difficult enough to walk on, and worse when going uphill. Put the gear in 4TH and give your Bike a running start. This should get you up there.

JUMP STAND

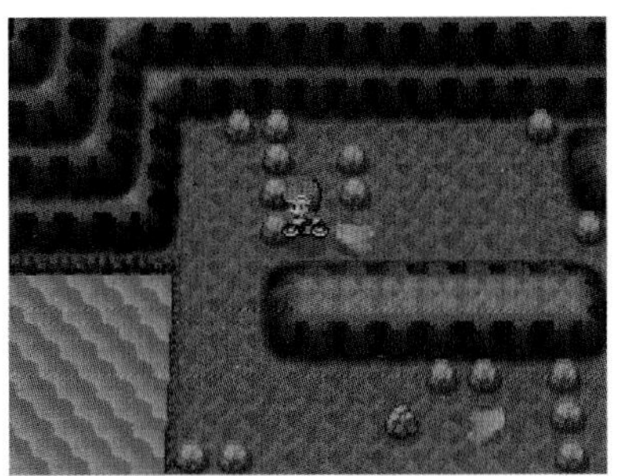

If you stumble across annoying boulders sticking out of the ground in caves, shift the gear to 4TH gear and give your Bike a running start to jump over them. One jump is equivalent to two walking steps.

NARROW BRIDGE

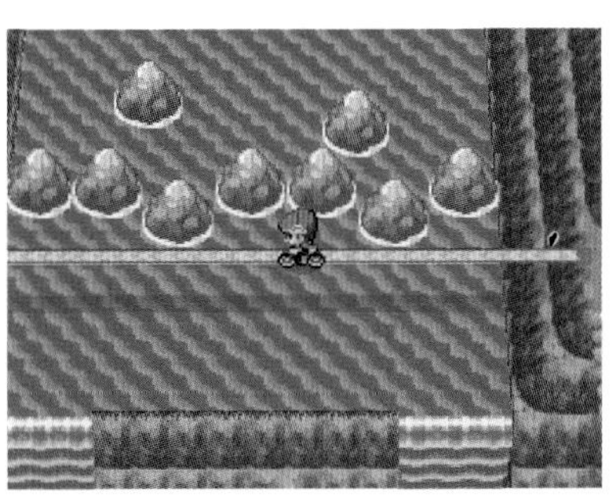

Wow, these are just barely wide enough for your wheels. Have the gear in either 3RD or 4TH and leave the rest to your Bicycle.

POKÉMON WATCH – THE POKÉTCH

THE POKÉMON WATCH, aka Pokétch, is a high-performance, small-sized computer you can wear on your wrist. You can add various features to this efficient device by getting the applications from the The Pokétch Company and other sources.

BOY'S MODEL

GIRL'S MODEL

FEATURES & FUNCTIONS

DIGITAL WATCH

Comes in digital format. If you press on it with your finger, the whole screen flashes.

HOW TO OBTAIN:
Comes with the watch.

PEDOMETER

Tells you the number of steps you have taken. Press C to reset.

HOW TO OBTAIN:
Comes with the watch.

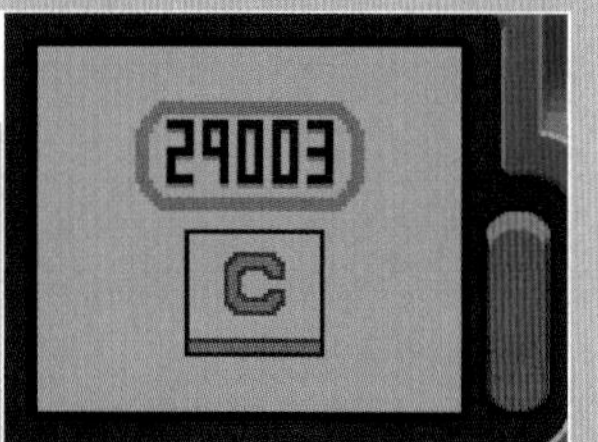

MEMO PAD

With a pencil and eraser, you can jot down anything you want.

HOW TO OBTAIN:
Get it from the president of The Pokétch Company in Jubilife City after winning the Gym battle in Oreburgh City.

DOWSING MACHINE

If you touch the monitor, and there's a tool to be found, it responds.

HOW TO OBTAIN:
Get it from Rowan's assistant on Route 207.

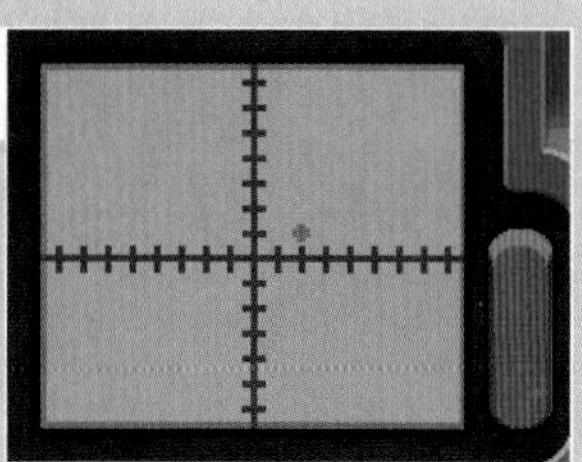

CALCULATOR

When you press on selected number keys and then on = , the cry of a matching Pokémon is heard.

HOW TO OBTAIN:
Comes with the watch.

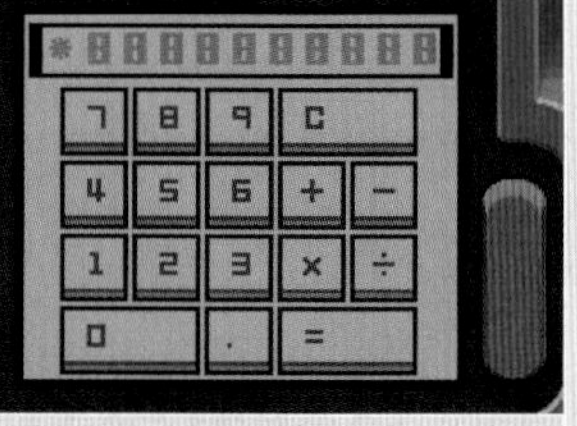

POKÉMON LIST

Indicates Pokémon in your collection. Touch these Pokémon and you hear their cries.

HOW TO OBTAIN:
Comes with the watch.

FRIENDSHIP CHECKER

Tells you how happy your Pokémon is. If it's happy, it will come to where you touch on the screen, or responds with ♥ on the screen.

HOW TO OBTAIN:
Woman on the 1 FL of the Pokémon Center in Eterna City.

BERRY SEARCHER

Tells you where they are buried. It updates itself when you touch the monitor.

HOW TO OBTAIN:
Get it from a girl on Route 208.

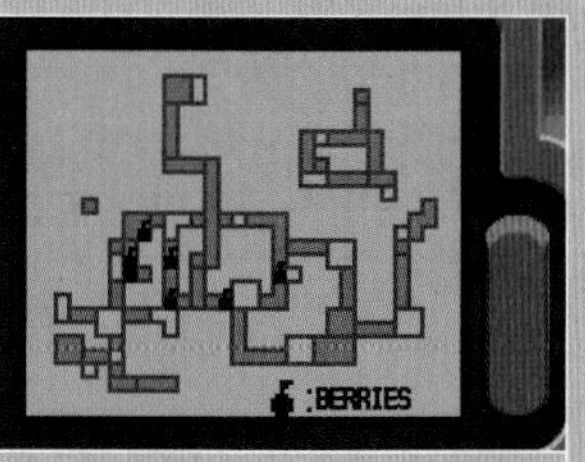

DAY CARE CHECKER

Shows you how your Pokémon is doing at the Day Care.

HOW TO OBTAIN:
Get it from a man at a Day Care in Solaceon Town.

COUNTER

It starts counting by pressing +. Can be used for various purposes.

HOW TO OBTAIN:
Get it at reception on the second floor of Veilstone Dept. Store.

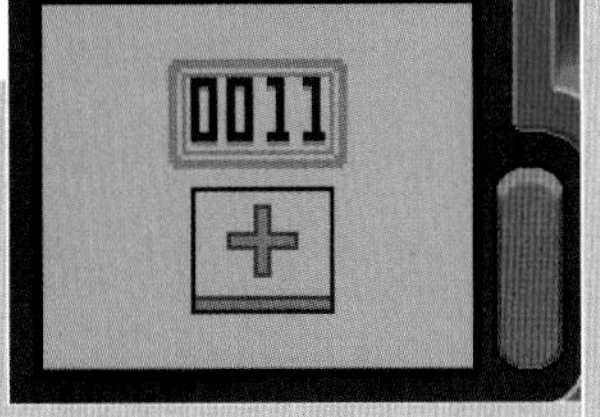

MARKING MAP

Move around ● or ◆ with your touch pen to put marks on your map.

HOW TO OBTAIN:
Get it from the president of the The Pokétch Company after winning the Gym battle in Veilstone City.

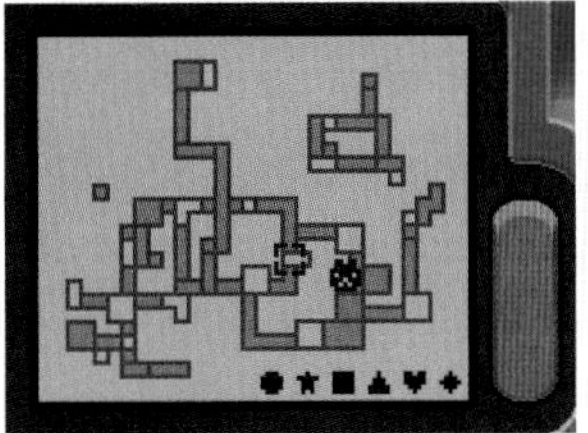

COIN TOSS

Tosses Magikarp's coin and see if it's head or tail. Can be used for various purposes.

HOW TO OBTAIN:
Get it from a couple staying at the Hotel Grand Lake on Valor Lakefront.

CALENDAR

You can mark the dates by touching on them.

HOW TO OBTAIN:
Get it from a man in a house by showing him a Pokémon that is Serious.

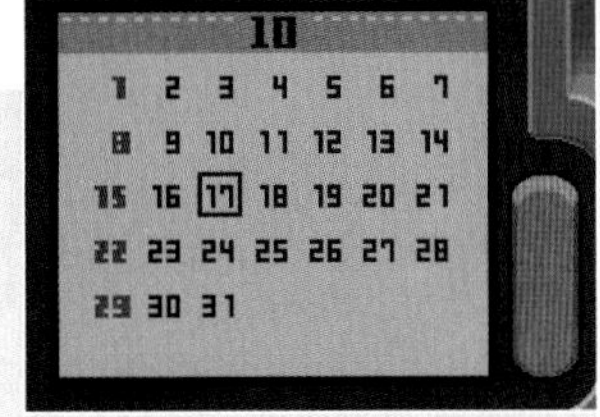

ROULETTE

Customize it as you like it by writing letters and drawing pictures.

HOW TO OBTAIN:
Get it from a man in a house by showing him Pokémon that is Quirky in Nature.

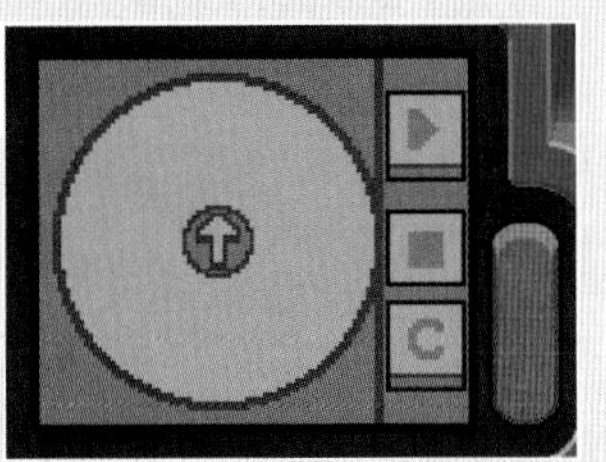

POKÉMON HISTORY

Shows your last twelve captured Pokémon.

HOW TO OBTAIN:
Get it from a man in Solaceon Town.

ANALOG WATCH

Comes in an analog format. The whole monitor flashes just by touching it.

HOW TO OBTAIN:
Get it from the president of the The Pokétch Company after winning the Gym Battle in Veilstone City.

LINK SEARCHER

Looks for other players who are on Nintendo DS Wireless Connection.

HOW TO OBTAIN:
Get it from the president of the Pokétch Company in Jubilife City after winning the Gym battle in Hearthome City.

MOVE TESTER

Compares the move types of your Pokémon and that of your opponent's Pokémon.

HOW TO OBTAIN:
Get it from the president of the Pokétch Company after winning the Gym battle in Snowpoint City.

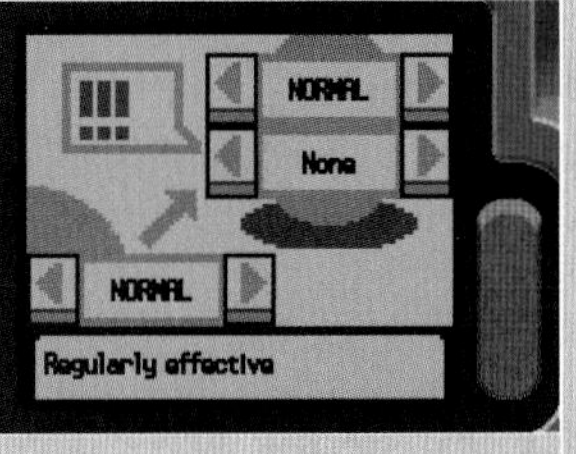

DOT ARTIST

Make your own dot art – the pressure you apply determines the line thickness.

HOW TO OBTAIN:
Show a man in a house a Pokémon that is Naive in Nature. Who's down with LCD? Yeah you know me!

UTILIZE TOWN FACILITIES

POKÉMART

THE POKÉMART SELLS useful items and tools that will help you progress in the game. The items in the Pokémart will change as you win more battles, adding even more helpful items to their inventory. There are two salespeople - the one on the right sells common items, while the one on the left specializes in town specialties. If you talk to people in the shop, you may end up with great advice, a chuckle or two, or even some useful information.

ITEMS YOU CAN BUY AT POKÉMART AND HOW TO OBTAIN THEM

ITEM	PRICE	CONDITIONS	DESCRIPTION
Poké Ball	200	○	Use to catch wild Pokémon.
Great Ball	600	▲	Use to catch wild Pokémon. More effective than the Poké Ball.
Ultra Ball	1200	■	Use to catch wild Pokémon. More effective than the Super Ball.
Potion	300	○	Restores 20 HP.
Super Potion	700	●	Restores 50 HP.
Hyper Potion	1200	■	Restores 200 HP.
Max Potion	2500	◆	Restores HP to full.
Full Restore	3000	★	Restores HP to full and heals any status conditions.
Revive	1500	▲	Revives a fainted Pokémon with half its HP.
Antidote	100	○	Heals a poisoned Pokémon.
Parlyz Heal	200	○	Heals a paralyzed Pokémon.
Awakening	250	●	Awakens a sleeping Pokémon.
Burn Heal	250	●	Heals a burned Pokémon.
Ice Heal	250	●	Thaws a frozen Pokémon.
Full Heal	600	■	Heals all status conditions.
Escape Rope	550	●	Lets you instantly escape caves and similar areas.
Repel	350	●	Repels weak wild Pokémon for 100 steps.
Super Repel	500	▲	Repeals weak wild Pokémon for 200 steps.
Max Repel	700	■	Repels weak wild Pokémon for 250 steps.

○ They are sold at Pokémart from the beginning
● After winning Oreburgh City Gym battle (After obtaining 1 Gym badge)
▲ After winning Veilstone City Gym battle (After obtaining 3 Gym badges)
■ After winning Hearthome City Gym battle (After obtaining 5 Gym badges)
◆ After winning Snowpoint City Gym battle (After obtaining 7 Gym badges)
★ After winning Sunyshore City Gym battle (After obtaining 8 Gym badges)

POKÉMON CENTER

THE POKÉMON CENTER IS A THREE-STORY BUILDING that provides Pokémon Trainers with various valuable services, as well as some fun activities. Let's visit each floor and see what's shakin' at the Center.

SECOND FLOOR: POKÉMON WIRELESS CLUB

HERE YOU CAN TRADE Pokémon and battle with your friends through Nintendo DS Wireless Connection. Pokémon Communication Club Colosseum is a section where you can challenge other Trainers in more serious battles. In Union Room, you get together with your friends and do things like trade Pokémon or mix records. At the reception area on the far left you can sign the back of your Trainer card.

FIRST FLOOR: POKÉMON CENTER

POKÉMON CENTER takes in Pokémon and heal them on the spot. Use the PC next to the reception for deposit and withdrawal activities. Since there are always people coming in and out of this place, sometimes you gain some helpful information or even a new Pokétch function by simply having conversations with them.

BASEMENT: POKÉMON WI-FI CLUB

HERE AT POKÉMON WI-FI CLUB, you can play, battle, or trade Pokémon with friends around the world using the Nintendo Wi-Fi Connection. In order for you to take advantage of this fabulous feature, go to the club and get the Pal Pad from Teala on your first visit. Exchange Friend Codes in advance and have them registered in each other's Pal Pad.

RAISE THEM WELL – THE FIRST 3 POKéMON

 BASIC 1 LEVEL THEM UP

AT THE BEGINNING of the story you'll find three Pokémon inside a briefcase Prof. Rowan forgot to take with him. From there you pick your partner Pokémon. All three of them have profound and specific capabilities, so it is crucial that you let them battle a lot to grow stronger.

MAKE THEM LEVEL UP
When they level up their Stats go up.

 BASIC 2 TEACH THEM MANY TYPES OF MOVES

IT BENEFITS YOU to teach Pokémon types of moves that are different from their own type. For instance, Piplup is a Water-type Pokémon and usually doesn't respond well to Grass-type moves. But with a Flying-type move like Peck, it can do 2x the damage on Grass-type opponents and should hold out well. Be selective with the moves you teach them.

Congratulations! Your Piplup
evolved into PRINPLUP!

MAKE UP FOR WEAKNESSES
Be careful, 2x damage will be dealt to you if your opponent attacks you on your weak point. Teach your Pokémon moves that protect or reduce these powerful moves.

SOMETIMES, IT IS IMPORTANT TO CANCEL AN EVOLUTION

YOU CAN CANCEL AN EVOLUTION by pressing the B button during the process. But why do this? Well, evolving slows down a Pokémon's ability to learn moves. In the basic form, Turtwig learns the move Mega Drain at Lv.25, but after having evolved into Grotle, it can only learn Mega Drain at Lv.27, which will obviously take much more time. So in some scenarios, it's better not to rush Evolution and instead focus on teaching them necessary moves first.

TURTWIG is evolving!

IF YOU CHOSE TURTWIG AS YOUR FIRST POKéMON

Lv	MOVES	TYPE	CLASSIFICATION	STRENGTH	ACCURACY	PP	RANGE	DIRECT ATTACK
Basic	Tackle	Normal	Physical	35	95	35	Normal	○
5	Withdraw	Water	Status			40	Self	
9	Absorb	Grass	Special	20	100	25	Normal	
13	Razor Leaf	Grass	Physical	55	95	25	Enemy 2	
17	Curse	?	Status			10	Normal/Self	
21	Bite	Dark	Physical	60	100	25	Normal	○
25	Mega Drain	Grass	Special	40	100	15	Normal	
29	Leech Seed	Grass	Status		90	10	Normal	
33	Synthesis	Grass	Status			5	Self	
37	Crunch	Dark	Physical	80	100	15	Normal	○
41	Giga Drain	Grass	Special	60	100	10	Normal	
45	Leaf Storm	Grass	Special	140	90	5	Normal	

TURTWIG EVOLVES INTO GROTLE AT LV.18.

Lv	MOVES	TYPE	CLASSIFICATION	STRENGTH	ACCURACY	PP	RANGE	DIRECT ATTACK
Basic	Tackle	Normal	Physical	35	95	35	Normal	○
Basic	Withdraw	Water	Status			40	Self	
5	Withdraw	Water	Status			40	Self	
9	Absorb	Grass	Special	20	100	25	Normal	
13	Razor Leaf	Grass	Physical	55	95	25	Enemy 2	
17	Curse	?	Status			10	Normal/Self	
22	Bite	Dark	Physical	60	100	25	Normal	○
27	Mega Drain	Grass	Special	40	100	15	Normal	
32	Leech Seed	Grass	Status		90	10	Normal	
37	Synthesis	Grass	Status			5	Self	
42	Crunch	Dark	Physical	80	100	15	Normal	○
47	Giga Drain	Grass	Special	60	100	10	Normal	
52	Leaf Storm	Grass	Special	140	90	5	Normal	

GROTLE EVOLVES INTO TORTERRA AT LV.32.

Lv	MOVES	TYPE	CLASSIFICATION	STRENGTH	ACCURACY	PP	RANGE	DIRECT ATTACK
Basic	Wood Hammer	Grass	Physical	120	100	15	Normal	○
Basic	Tackle	Normal	Physical	35	95	35	Normal	○
Basic	Withdraw	Water	Status			40	Self	
Basic	Absorb	Grass	Special	20	100	25	Normal	
Basic	Razor Leaf	Grass	Physical	55	95	25	Enemy 2	
5	Withdraw	Water	Status			40	Self	
9	Absorb	Grass	Special	20	100	25	Normal	
13	Razor Leaf	Grass	Physical	55	95	25	Enemy 2	
17	Curse	?	Status			10	Normal/Self	
22	Bite	Dark	Physical	60	100	25	Normal	○
27	Mega Drain	Grass	Special	40	100	15	Normal	
32	Earthquake	Ground	Physical	10	100	10	Enemy 2/Ally 1	
33	Leech Seed	Grass	Status		90	10	Normal	
39	Synthesis	Grass	Status			5	Self	
45	Crunch	Dark	Physical	80	100	15	Normal	○
51	Giga Drain	Grass	Special	60	100	10	Normal	
57	Leaf Storm	Grass	Special	140	90	5	Normal	

TIPS

FIRE-TYPE MOVES are Turtwig's weak point. But it can't learn Earthquake, the Ground-type move that is effective against Fire-type Pokémon until it evolves into Torterra. Your best bet is to raise a Water-type Pokémon that is strong against Fire-type Pokémon as back-up.

IF YOU CHOSE CHIMCHAR AS YOUR FIRST POKéMON

Lv	MOVES	TYPE	CLASSIFICATION	STRENGTH	ACCURACY	PP	RANGE	DIRECT ATTACK
Basic	Scratch	Normal	Physical	40	100	35	Normal	○
Basic	Leer	Normal	Status		100	30	Enemy 2	
7	Ember	Fire	Special	40	100	25	Normal	
9	Taunt	Dark	Status		100	20	Normal	
15	Fury Swipes	Normal	Physical	18	80	15	Normal	○
17	Flame Wheel	Fire	Physical	60	100	25	Normal	○
23	Nasty Plot	Dark	Status			20	Self	
25	Torment	Dark	Status		100	15	Normal	
31	Facade	Normal	Physical	70	100	20	Normal	○
33	Flame Spin	Fire	Special	15	70	15	Normal	
39	Slack Off	Normal	Status			10	Self	
41	Flamethrower	Fire	Special	95	100	15	Normal	

CHIMCHAR EVOLVES INTO MONFERNO AT LV.14.

Lv	MOVES	TYPE	CLASSIFICATION	STRENGTH	ACCURACY	PP	RANGE	DIRECT ATTACK
Basic	Scratch	Normal	Physical	40	100	35	Normal	○
Basic	Leer	Normal	Status		100	30	Enemy 2	
Basic	Ember	Fire	Special	40	100	25	Normal	
7	Ember	Fire	Special	40	100	25	Normal	
9	Taunt	Dark	Status		100	20	Normal	
14	Mach Punch	Fighting	Physical	40	100	30	Normal	○
16	Fury Swipes	Normal	Physical	18	80	15	Normal	○
19	Flame Wheel	Fire	Physical	60	100	25	Normal	○
26	Feint	Normal	Physical	50	100	10	Normal	
29	Torment	Dark	Status		100	15	Normal	
36	Close Combat	Fighting	Physical	120	100	5	Normal	○
39	Fire Spin	Fire	Special	15	70	15	Normal	
46	Slack Off	Normal	Status			10	Self	
49	Flare Blitz	Fire	Physical	120	100	15	Normal	○

MONFERNO EVOLVES INTO INFERNAPE AT LV.36.

Lv	MOVES	TYPE	CLASSIFICATION	STRENGTH	ACCURACY	PP	RANGE	DIRECT ATTACK
Basic	Scratch	Normal	Physical	40	100	35	Normal	○
Basic	Leer	Normal	Status		100	30	Enemy 2	
Basic	Ember	Fire	Special	40	100	25	Normal	
Basic	Taunt	Dark	Status		100	20	Normal	
7	Ember	Fire	Special	40	100	25	Normal	
9	Taunt	Dark	Status		100	20	Normal	
14	Mach Punch	Fighting	Physical	40	100	30	Normal	○
17	Fury Swipes	Normal	Physical	18	80	15	Normal	○
21	Flame Wheel	Fire	Physical	60	100	25	Normal	○
29	Feint	Normal	Physical	50	100	10	Normal	
33	Punishment	Dark	Physical		100	5	Normal	○
41	Close Combat	Fighting	Physical	120	100	5	Normal	○
45	Fire Spin	Fire	Special	15	70	15	Normal	
53	Calm Mind	Psychic	Status			20	Self	
57	Flare Blitz	Fire	Physical	120	100	15	Normal	○

TIPS

CHIMCHAR IS A FIRE-TYPE POKéMON and vulnerable to Rock-type moves. As a counter-measure, you might want to teach it Mach Punch, a Fighting-type move which is effective against Rock-types. Once evolved into Monferno, it acquires an additional type, Fighting.

IF YOU CHOSE PIPLUP AS YOUR FIRST POKÉMON

Lv	MOVES	TYPE	CLASSIFICATION	STRENGTH	ACCURACY	PP	RANGE	DIRECT ATTACK
Basic	Pound	Normal	Physical	40	100	35	Normal	○
4	Growl	Normal	Status		100	40	Enemy 2	
8	Bubble	Water	Special	20	100	30	Enemy 2	
11	Water Sport	Water	Status			15	All	
15	Peck	Flying	Physical	35	100	35	Normal	○
18	Bide	Normal	Physical			10	Self	○
22	BubbleBeam	Water	Special	65	100	20	Normal	
25	Fury Attack	Normal	Physical	15	85	20	Normal	○
29	Brine	Water	Special	65	100	10	Normal	
32	Whirlpool	Water	Special	15	70	15	Normal	
36	Mist	Ice	Status			30	Ally 2	
39	Drill Peck	Flying	Physical	80	100	20	Normal	○
43	Hydro Pump	Water	Special	120	80	5	Normal	

PIPLUP EVOLVES INTO PRINPLUP AT LV.16.

Lv	MOVES	TYPE	CLASSIFICATION	STRENGTH	ACCURACY	PP	RANGE	DIRECT ATTACK
Basic	Tackle	Normal	Physical	35	95	35	Normal	○
Basic	Growl	Normal	Status		100	40	Enemy 2	
4	Growl	Normal	Status		100	40	Enemy 2	
8	Bubble	Water	Special	20	100	30	Enemy 2	
11	Water Sport	Water	Status			15	All	
15	Peck	Flying	Physical	35	100	35	Normal	○
16	Metal Claw	Steel	Physical	50	95	35	Normal	○
19	Bide	Normal	Physical			10	Self	○
24	BubbleBeam	Water	Special	65	100	20	Normal	
28	Fury Attack	Normal	Physical	15	85	20	Normal	○
33	Brine	Water	Special	65	100	10	Normal	
37	Whirlpool	Water	Special	15	70	15	Normal	
42	Mist	Ice	Status			30	Ally 2	
46	Drill Peck	Flying	Physical	80	100	20	Normal	○
51	Hydro Pump	Water	Special	120	80	5	Normal	

PRINPLUP EVOLVES INTO EMPOLEON AT LV.36.

Lv	MOVES	TYPE	CLASSIFICATION	STRENGTH	ACCURACY	PP	RANGE	DIRECT ATTACK
Basic	Tackle	Normal	Physical	35	95	35	Normal	○
Basic	Growl	Normal	Status		100	40	Enemy 2	
Basic	Bubble	Water	Special	20	100	30	Enemy 2	
4	Growl	Normal	Status		100	40	Enemy 2	
8	Bubble	Water	Special	20	100	30	Enemy 2	
11	Swords Dance	Normal	Status			30	Self	
15	Peck	Flying	Physical	35	100	35	Normal	○
16	Metal Claw	Steel	Physical	50	95	35	Normal	○
19	Swagger	Normal	Status		90	15	Normal	
24	BubbleBeam	Water	Special	65	100	20	Normal	
28	Fury Attack	Normal	Physical	15	85	20	Normal	○
33	Brine	Water	Special	65	100	10	Normal	
36	Aqua Jet	Water	Physical	40	100	20	Normal	○
39	Whirlpool	Water	Special	15	70	15	Normal	
46	Mist	Ice	Status			30	Ally 2	
52	Drill Peck	Flying	Physical	80	100	20	Normal	○
59	Hydro Pump	Water	Special	120	80	5	Normal	

TIPS

PIPLUP IS VULNERABLE to Grass-type moves. So teach it Peck, a Flying-type move which is effective against Grass-types. Once evolved into Empoleon, it becomes a Steel-type Pokémon as well. We suggest you teach it a Steel-type move like Metal Claw.

SINNOH ADVENTURE STRATEGY GUIDE

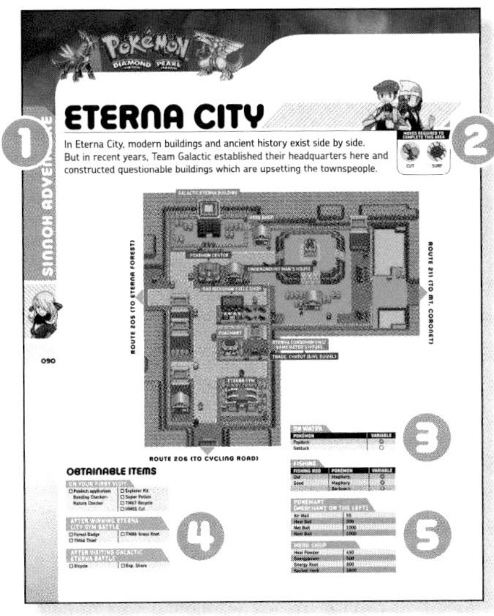

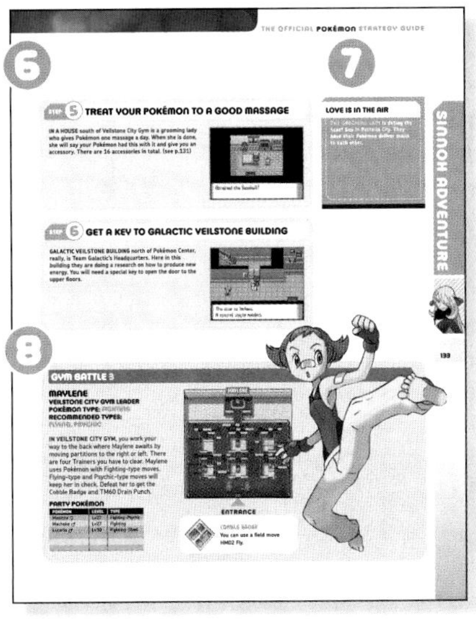

STORY

This gives you a brief introduction on the town's infrastructures, and the geographical characteristics.

HMS THAT ARE NECESSARY TO EXPLORE THE WHOLE AREA

Marked are the HMs you need to use in order to explore the whole area and collect all the items available.

Rock Smash

Cut

Defog

Surf

Strength

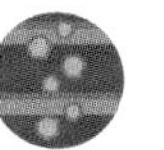
Rock Climb

Waterfall

3 WILD POKéMON YOU WILL ENCOUNTER IN THE AREA

It shows the types, time of appearance, etc, of wild Pokémon in the area.

APPEARANCE PROBABILITY			
◎	Very often	○	Normally
△	Rarely	▲	Hardly

TIME	
Morning	4:00am - 10:00am
Day	10:00am - 8:00pm
Night	8:00pm - 4:00am

DIFFERENT VERSION	
♦	Appears only in Diamond
●	Appears only in Pearl

TYPE OF FISHING ROD			
Old	An old fishing rod	Good	A good fishing rod

4 OBTAINABLE ITEMS

Shows you the items and tools that are obtainable in the area. If there are conditions, they are shown here as well.

5 POKéMART

A sales person on the left side of the shop will show you the goods that are sold there.

6 IN-DEPTH WALK-THROUGH TO THE END OF THE GAME

Goes over events, incidents and everything else you should experience in the area. You will find detailed instructions, such as order of activities and how to fulfill conditions, very helpful. Together with the quick walk through in the beginning of this book (see p.8) this will guide your way to the best ending!

7 MORE DETAILED INFORMATION

This will take a closer look at the details of the town's facilities, on-field events and incidents, what to know and who to go see etc. - useful knowledge that will help you out immensely.

GYM BATTLES

Gives you insights on things like the functions and features of the town's Pokémon Gym, the type of Pokémon the Gym Leader will use on you, and tips and hints to defeat them. Full of important information you should know before you actually enter a battle.

SECTION 2

SINNOH ADVENTURE

TWINLEAF TOWN

MOVES REQUIRED TO COMPLETE THIS AREA

SURF

After checking out a new special TV show called *The Search For Red Gyarados* in your room, you head downstairs to talk to your mom. She lets you know that your rival stopped by. What did he want? Go to his house to find out!

OBTAINABLE ITEMS

AFTER VISITING LAKE VERITY

☐ Running Shoes

AFTER OBTAINING POKÉDEX

☐ Journal | ☐ Package

ON WATER

POKÉMON	VARIABLE
Psyduck	◎
Golduck	○

FISHING

FISHING ROD	POKÉMON	VARIABLE
Old	Magikarp	◎
Good	Magikarp	◎
	Goldeen	○

LET'S GO TO YOUR RIVAL'S HOUSE

WHEN YOU GO DOWNSTAIRS in your house, your mom tells you that your rival came looking for you, and he looked flustered. After wondering what his deal-eo is, you leave and search him out (he's in the same town as you, Twinleaf Town).

MEET YOUR SCATTERBRAINED RIVAL

JUST AS YOU GET TO your rival's house, he comes running out. He's all worked up about the two of you going to the lake. As you go upstairs, he runs up, grabs something, and takes off. So much for being a BFF.

THE ROUTE, THE ROUTE, THE ROUTE IS ON FIRE

GO DOWNSTAIRS and talk to your rival's mom. She'll let you know that your rival is probably already on his way to Route 201, which is to the north of Twinleaf Town. Don't wait for an invitation, go!

LAKE VERITY (1ST VISIT)
GET THE RUNNING SHOES FROM YOUR MOM

AFTER CERTAIN EVENTS have transpired, go back and tell your mom what happened on Route 201. She tells you to go see Professor Rowan and explain to him why you used his Pokémon without his permission. She then gives up the Running Shoes – you remember these from past games – simply press the B Button while moving and you'll zip along!

POSTER PROPS

TAKE A LOOK at the posters in your house and in other people's houses. They contain basic information about the operation of the game – don't forget to check them out!

DO I SEE A WII?

IN YOUR RIVAL'S room you spot a brand new Nintendo Wii game system. Wonder what he's been playing?

AFTER OBTAINING THE POKÉDEX
GET THE JOURNAL FROM YOUR MOM

AFTER OBTAINING the Pokédex from Professor Rowan in Sandgem Town, go back and tell your mom. She gets all up in your fa-shizzle, then gives you a Journal which automatically records all the happenings of your adventure.

Lucas obtained
the Journal!

AFTER OBTAINING THE POKÉDEX
HOLD A PARCEL FOR YOUR RIVAL

AFTER YOU GET the Journal, your rival's mom comes by and asks you to deliver a package to him – but he's already left for Jubilife City. Head out to Jubilife City to deliver the package.

Lucas obtained
the Parcel!

AFTER OBTAINING THE POKÉDEX
FOLLOW YOUR RIVAL TO JUBILIFE CITY

JUBILIFE CITY is located further north of Sandgem Town. On your way there you will encounter plenty of wild Pokémon and Pokémon Trainers. Make the most of the experience you'll gain, but make sure to talk to your mom first – she'll restore your Pokémon's HP and PP.

CHECK OUT THE PCS

CHECK OUT the PC on your desk and you'll be treated to a primer on Pokémon. Remember to check out all PCs you find, as well as the posters.

PAY ATTENTION TO TV

THE TVS IN THE GAME are just as full of information as the PCs and wall posters. Make a habit of checking out every flashing TV set you see.

ROUTE 201, VERITY LAKEFRONT

Route 201 and Verity Lakefront are located along a pleasant woody path in the forest. You can go west on Route 201 to Lake Verity, or you can head east to Sandgem Town. Let's go west and check out the action at Verity Lake.

OBTAINABLE ITEMS

AFTER OBTAINING RUNNING SHOES

- ☐ Potion

LAKE VERITY ■ VERITY LAKEFRONT ■ ROUTE 201

IN GRASS

POKéMON	M	D	N
Starly	◎	◎	◎
Bidoof	◎	◎	◎

Starly
Normal-Flying
Abilities:
• Keen Eye

Bidoof
Normal
Abilities:
• Simple
• Unaware

HEAD OUT TO VERITY LAKE WITH YOUR RIVAL

YOUR RIVAL is well on his way to capturing his own red Gyarados. Proceed west on Route 201 towards Lake Verity.

AVOID GRASSY BRUSH

FORGET ABOUT GOING east for now – although you may be tempted, you don't have any Pokémon to battle with. Keep west and stop being so curious!

MOTHER KNOWS BEST

IF YOU DO venture east, you mother will sound a stern warning. Your mom knows what she's talking about – stay away from the bush until you have your own Pokémon!

AFTER VISITING VERITY LAKE
REUNITE WITH PROFESSOR ROWAN AND HIS ASSISTANT

AFTER DEFEATING STARLY at Lake Verity, come back to Route 201. You'll find Professor Rowan and his assistant there waiting for you. The Professor seems a little put-off, and eventually leaves. The assistant suggests you come by the lab later.

AFTER OBTAINING THE RUNNING SHOES
RAISE AND TRAIN YOUR POKÉMON

ONCE YOU HAVE your own Pokémon, then you should aggressively seek out wild Pokémon. Step into any grassy brush and start leveling up your Pokémon as much as you can.

HEAL. NOW SIT.

AT THIS POINT, every time your Pokémon gets wounded in battle and is close to fainting, head home and heal up. If all of the Pokémon in your party faint, you lose some of your acquired Poké Dollars.

AFTER OBTAINING THE RUNNING SHOES
TALK TO A SALES PERSON IN THE POKÉMART

IN THE GRASSY BRUSH, you'll come across a sales person from the local Pokémart. When you talk to her, she'll hand over a Potion. The Potion will heal up to 20 HP (hit points) of damage. If you need it now, use it!

Here, let me give you a Potion as
a free sample. First one's free!

ALWAYS CARRY HEALING POTIONS

THERE WILL BE TIMES when Pokémon Centers and Pokémarts are few and far between. Always carry a supply of healing Potions, including those that cure status ailments, like Sleep and Freeze.

AFTER OBTAINING THE RUNNING SHOES
CHECK OUT THE BULLETIN BOARD

THE BULLETIN BOARDS that you sometimes see on the road are another great source of information. Check them out whenever you find them.

Trainer Tips!

AFTER OBTAINING THE RUNNING SHOES
HEAD TO JUBILIFE CITY

REMEMBER EARLIER that your rival's mom said he was headed to Jubilife City? Jubilife City is located north of Sandgem Town. Make sure to deliver that Parcel you're holding for your Rival. Head east, and when you get to Sandgem Town, head north.

LAKE VERITY

You've made it to Lake Verity, hoping to find some rare Pokémon with your rival. Instead, you come across Professor Rowan and his assistant — but when you approach Professor Rowan's briefcase, a wild Starly attacks!

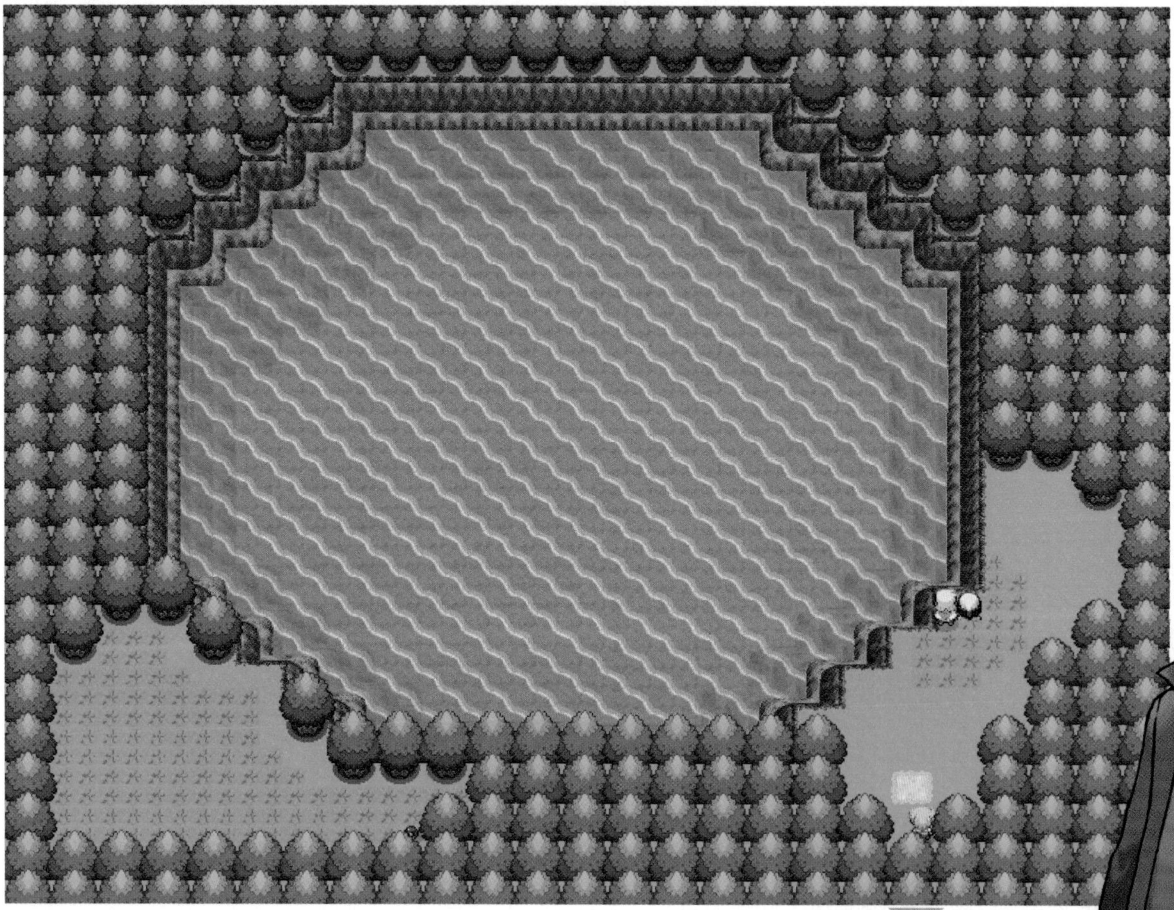

VERITY LAKEFRONT (TO TWINLEAF TOWN)

IN GRASS

POKÉMON	M	D	N
Starly	◎	◎	◎
Bidoof	◎	◎	◎

STEP 1 MEET PROFESSOR ROWAN AND HIS ASSISTANT

NEAR VERITY LAKE you'll meet Professor Rowan, an authority on Pokémon, and his assistant. Professor Rowan seems a bit disturbed by some environmental changes that have been taking place around the lake over the years. After some conversation, they take off for Route 201.

Professor: Excuse me.
Let us pass, please.

YOU'VE GOT (FE)MALE

IF THE MAIN character is a girl, Rowan's assistant is a boy. Choose a girl as the main character and she gets a male friend as a supportive companion who will lead your way through your journey.

STEP 2 CHOOSE A POKéMON

PROFESSOR ROWAN left his briefcase in the bush. When you approach it, you get ambushed by a wild Starly. Counterattack it using one Pokémon in the briefcase. Be careful in making this choice since this Pokémon will be given to you by the professor later and will be your very first partner Pokémon.

Look! These are Poké Balls!
Let's battle using these!

PICK YOUR POKéMON

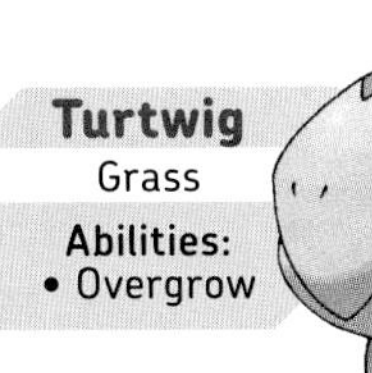

Turtwig
Grass
Abilities:
• Overgrow

Chimchar
Fire
Abilities:
• Blaze

Piplup
Water
Abilities:
• Torrent

STEP 3 GET BACK TO TWINLEAF TOWN

AFTER BATTLING STARLY and defeating it, the assistant reappears to get the Professor's briefcase. She looks concerned about the fact that you used Rowan's Pokémon without his permission. Let's get back to Twinleaf Town for now.

I don't know what's going on.
Lucas, let's get out of here.

SANDGEM TOWN

You come to apologize to Professor Rowan for having used his Pokémon without asking him. But surprisingly, the Professor isn't angry at all and will even assign you the task of completing a Pokédex.

Route 202 (To Jubilife City)

Pokémon Lab

Pokémon Center

PokéMart

Route 201 (To Twinleaf Town)

Rival's House

Route 219 (To Pal Park)

OBTAINABLE ITEMS

☐ Pokédex

VISIT POKéMON LAB

WHEN YOU REACH Sandgem Town, the Professor's assistant is there waiting for you. She (he) takes you to see Professor Rowan, when suddenly you bump into your rival who has already been there. He tells you the Professor is one crazy geezer, then leaves.

WHAT'S IN THE FRIDGE, MIDGE?

IN THE BACK of the Pokémon Lab is a refrigerator. Inside are lots of sweets. Does Rowan have a sweet tooth? I hope he brushes daily.

GET A POKéMON FROM PROFESSOR ROWAN

YOU'RE KIND OF SURPRISED that the Professor is not upset with you about having used his Pokémon earlier. You're even more shocked when he gives you the Pokémon you used at Verity Lake. He says that you've already established a bond with it.

GIVE YOUR POKéMON A NICKNAME

YOU CAN create nicknames for your Pokémon using up to 5 letters for each. Come up with unique ones that will help you and your Pokémon bond better!

SET OUT TO UPGRADE YOUR POKéDEX

PROFESSOR ROWAN has assigned you a very important mission. He gives you a Pokédex and says he wants you to go find all Pokémon living in the Sinnoh region, and record them into the Pokédex. So let's get started!!!

POKéDEX

STOP BY AT A POKéMON CENTER

MOST TOWNS HAVE A POKéMON CENTER, a facility where they heal Pokémon. When you visit a new town, go there first and have your wounded Pokémon healed. You may even gain some useful information from people on the premises.

THE WI-FI CLUB WILL OPEN SOON

THE WI-FI CLUB area in the basement of the Pokémon Center is still under construction – you won't be able to enter it yet. As a matter of fact, you won't be able to enter it until you visit Oreburgh City.

STEP 5 SIGN YOUR TRAINER CARD

ON THE UPPER floor of Pokémon Center is a Pokémon Wireless Club where you can battle and trade via the Wi-Fi Connection. When you talk to a lady on the far left at the reception, she will let you sign the back of a Trainer Card. Sign using your stylus.

STEP 6 STOP AND SHOP BEFORE YOU HEAD OUT

AT THE POKÉMART you can purchase lots of items and tools. The numbers of items sold by the merchant on the right will increase as you obtain more Gym badges. The sales person on the left sells the special products that are only available in a particular town.

VISIT ROWAN'S ASSISTANT'S HOUSE

THE ASSISTANT'S house is in Sandgem Town, too. His/her sister and grandfather are there. It probably is a good idea to pay them a courtesy visit.

STEP 7 GET BACK TO TWINLEAF TOWN

AFTER RECEIVING a Pokédex from Professor Rowan, the assistant suggests that you go home to tell your family about the adventure you're about to embark on. Let's take Route 201 back to Twinleaf Town to talk to your mom.

WHAT ARE THE DIFFERENCES BETWEEN DIAMOND AND PEARL?

Pokémon Diamond and Pokémon Pearl have, for the most part, the same plotline as each other, except for some minor variations such as different species of Pokémon appearing in certain parts of the game. Let's compare these two different versions and see what those differences are.

DIFFERENCE 1 OPENING GRAPHICS

JUST LIKE THE GAME box cover, the first images that come up on the loading screen are not the same. Pokémon Diamond has a silhouette of Dialga, and Pokémon Pearl has that of Palkia. They both gleam and glow beautifully. Get together with your friends and compare these two nice pieces of art.

DIAMOND

© 2007 GAME FREAK inc.

PEARL

© 2007 GAME FREAK inc.

DIFFERENCE 2 SPECIES OF WILD POKÉMON

THERE ARE SOME parts in the game in which different wild Pokémon species appear in each version. Let's look at a grassy bush on Route 209. In Pokémon Diamond you encounter Mime Jr., as opposed to Bonsly in Pokémon Pearl version. There are some species that appear only in one version of the two.

DIAMOND

MIME JR.
A wild MIME JR. appeared!

PEARL

BONSLY
A wild BONSLY appeared!

DIFFERENCE 3 LETTERS ON THE POKÉMON STATUE IN ETERNA CITY

IN ETERNA CITY, you marvel at the gigantic statue of a Legendary Pokémon that it is said to have created the world in ancient times. The letters engraved on the pedestal on the statue are different between the two versions. In Pokémon Diamond, they are about Dialga -who ruled time - and in Pokémon Pearl, they are about Palkia – who ruled space.

DIAMOND

The same time flows...
...the blessing of Dia...

PEARL

To arrive in the same univer...
...the blessing of Pal...

DIFFERENCE 4 POKÉMON THAT APPEAR AT SPEAR PILLAR

AT THE CLIMAX of the story, Cyrus, the boss of Team Galactic, resurrects a Pokémon from the ancient myth in order to accomplish his evil ambition. In Pokémon Diamond, he resurrects Dialga, as opposed to Palkia, that is brought back to life in Pokémon Pearl.

DIAMOND

DIALGA: Guguugubah!

PEARL

PALKIA: Gagyagyaah!

ROUTE 219, 220, AND 221

Just below Sandgem Town there is a white sand beach that leads to a beautiful ocean. Beyond the ocean there is Pal Park where you will be meeting new Pokémon. You will need HM03 Surf in order to reach it.

MOVES REQUIRED TO COMPLETE THIS AREA

SURF

OBTAINABLE ITEMS

ON YOUR FIRST VISIT

- ☐ Antidote

AFTER WINNING HEARTHOME CITY GYM BATTLE

- ☐ Ether
- ☐ Carbos
- ☐ Honey
- ☐ Pecha Berry
- ☐ Pure Incense (when you show an old man the Pokémon of his wish)
- ☐ Splash Plate
- ☐ Protein
- ☐ Leppa Berry
- ☐ Mago Berry
- ☐ TM81 X-Scissor
- ☐ Black Belt
- ☐ Expert Belt
- ☐ Focus Sash

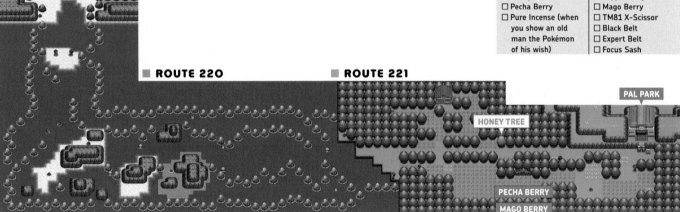

SANDGEM TOWN

ROUTE 219

ROUTE 220

ROUTE 221

HONEY TREE

PAL PARK

PECHA BERRY

MAGO BERRY

HONDEW BERRY

LEPPA BERRY

ROUTE 221

IN GRASS

POKÉMON	M	D	N
Stunky ♦	○	○	○
Gastrodon ♦	○	○	○
Gastrodon ●	◎	◎	◎
Skuntank ♦	○	○	○
Sudowoodo ●	○	○	○
Floatzel	○	○	○
Roselia	○	○	○
Shellos	○	○	○
Wingull	○	○	○

ROUTE 219, ROUTE 220

ON WATER

POKÉMON	Variable
Tentacool	◎
Wingull	◎
Tentacruel	△
Pelipper	△

FISHING

FISHING ROD	POKÉMON	Variable
Old	Magikarp	◎
Good	Magikarp	◎
	Finneon	○

Skuntank
Poison-Dark

Abilities:
- Stench
- Aftermath

 STEP 1 YOU NEED TO SURF TO GO ACROSS THE OCEAN

GO SOUTH of Sandgem Town and you'll eventually come to a beach - but you'll need HM03 Surf to proceed on water. You will gain it after a Gym battle in Hearthome City. Battle first and come back here after.

YOU WILL GET SURF IN CELESTIC TOWN

HM03 SURF is necessary for you to travel on water and will be given to you by the elder of Celestic Town that you will visit much later.

 AFTER WINNING HEARTHOME CITY GYM BATTLE
SURF'S UP, DUDE!

ONCE YOU'VE obtained HM03 Surf by winning the Gym battle in Hearthome City, visit Sandgem Town and go east on the ocean. You'll encounter a lot of Pokémon Trainers on the way, so be prepared - stock up on items and make sure you have leveled up your Pokémon.

 AFTER WINNING HEARTHOME CITY GYM BATTLE
COLLECT ITEMS BY SHOWING POKéMON TO DIFFERENT PEOPLE

WHEN YOU TALK to the old man in the house on Route 221, he'll give you a number. Put a Pokémon whose level matches this number in the front of your party and show it to him. He'll give you a Black Belt item. Do it twice more and receive the Expert Belt and Focus Sash as your rewards.

Show me a Pokémon that's Lv. 33.
If you can, I'll reward you.

 AFTER WINNING HEARTHOME CITY GYM BATTLE
PAL PARK IS IN PREPARATION

WHEN YOU REACH Pal Park, you see two working men. When you talk to them, they'll tell you that Pal Park is still under construction. Come back here after conquering the Pokémon League and you'll earn the National Pokédex.

Pal Park isn't open yet.
We're still setting up.

USE FLY TO RETURN

AFTER ONLY ONE visit to Pal Park, you'll be able to go back there after earning the National Pokédex by using HM02 Fly. This makes it much easier and more convenient because you no longer have to sail across the ocean.

ROUTE 202

You should be on your way to Jubilife City to deliver the Parcel to your rival. On your way there, you'll see Rowan's assistant, who's been waiting to show you how to catch Pokémon.

OBTAINABLE ITEMS	
☐ Poké Ball x5	☐ Potion

JUBILIFE CITY

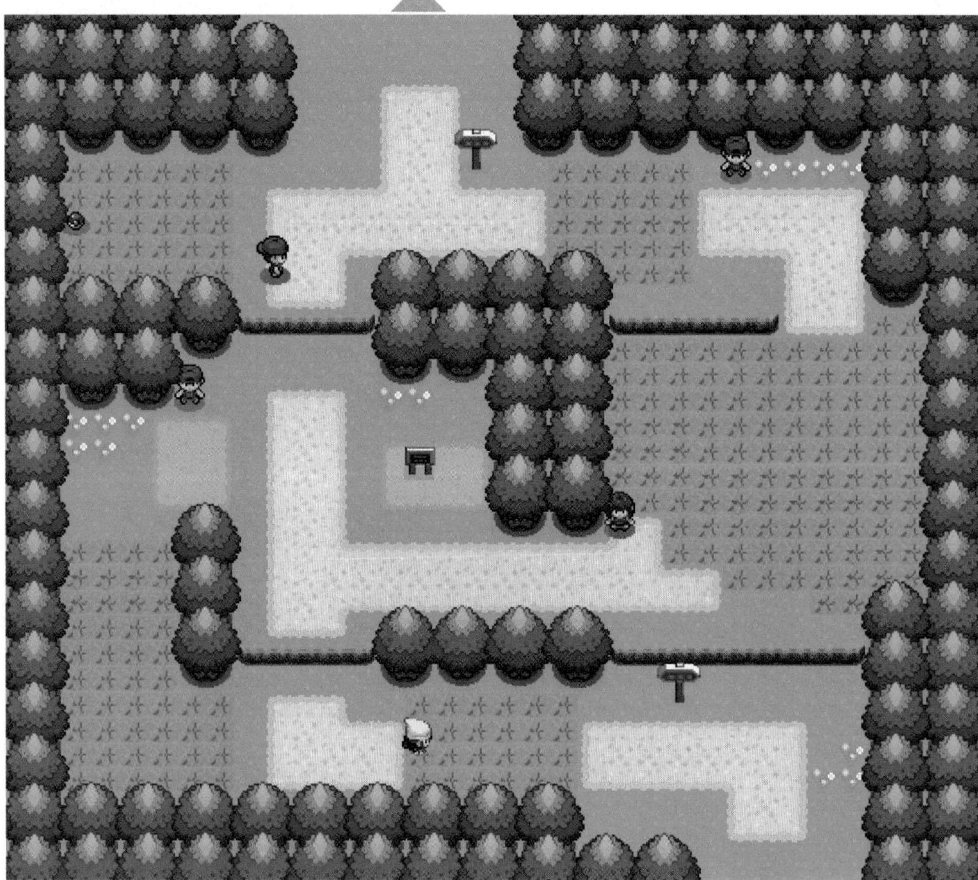

SANDGEM TOWN

IN GRASS			
POKÉMON	M	D	N
Shinx	◎	◎	◎
Bidoof	◎	◎	◎
Starly	◎	◎	○
Kricketot	○	✕	○

Shinx
Electric
Abilities:
- Rivalry
- Intimidate

Kricketot
Bug
Abilities:
- Shed Skin

LEARN HOW TO CATCH POKÉMON

ENTER A GRASSY field on Route 202 and you'll find Rowan's assistant waiting for you. He/she says they will teach you how to catch Pokémon. Watch the assistant closely and learn how to reduce a Pokémon's HP and capture it.

LET'S CAPTURE WILD POKÉMON

THE ASSISTANT GIVES you 5 Poké Balls. Use them to capture Pokémon living in the grassy bush along this route, and increase your travel companions. On Route 202 you will encounter four kinds of Pokémon in total, including Shinx and Bidoof.

USE DIFFERENT POKÉ BALLS

AS THE GAME progresses, you will obtain various kinds of Poké Balls. Different Poké Balls work on different Pokémon (see page 276 for descriptions and effectiveness). Use them properly.

BATTLE OTHER POKÉMON TRAINERS

YOU'LL COME ACROSS other Pokémon Trainers on the road. The minute they make eye contact with you, they'll come after you. These battles are good opportunities to level up your Pokémon, so try not to flee. Also, winning Trainer battles will reward you with money to purchase items.

HEAD TO JUBILIFE CITY

YOUR DESTINATION, Jubilife City, is north of Route 202. If your Pokémon are hurt, have a condition status, or are low on HP, go back to Sandgem Town and cure them at a Pokémon Center, or give them Potion from your supplies.

JUBILIFE CITY

Jubilife City is a big city that includes buildings like Jubilife TV and the Global Trade Station. Deliver the Parcel to your rival before you start sight-seeing!

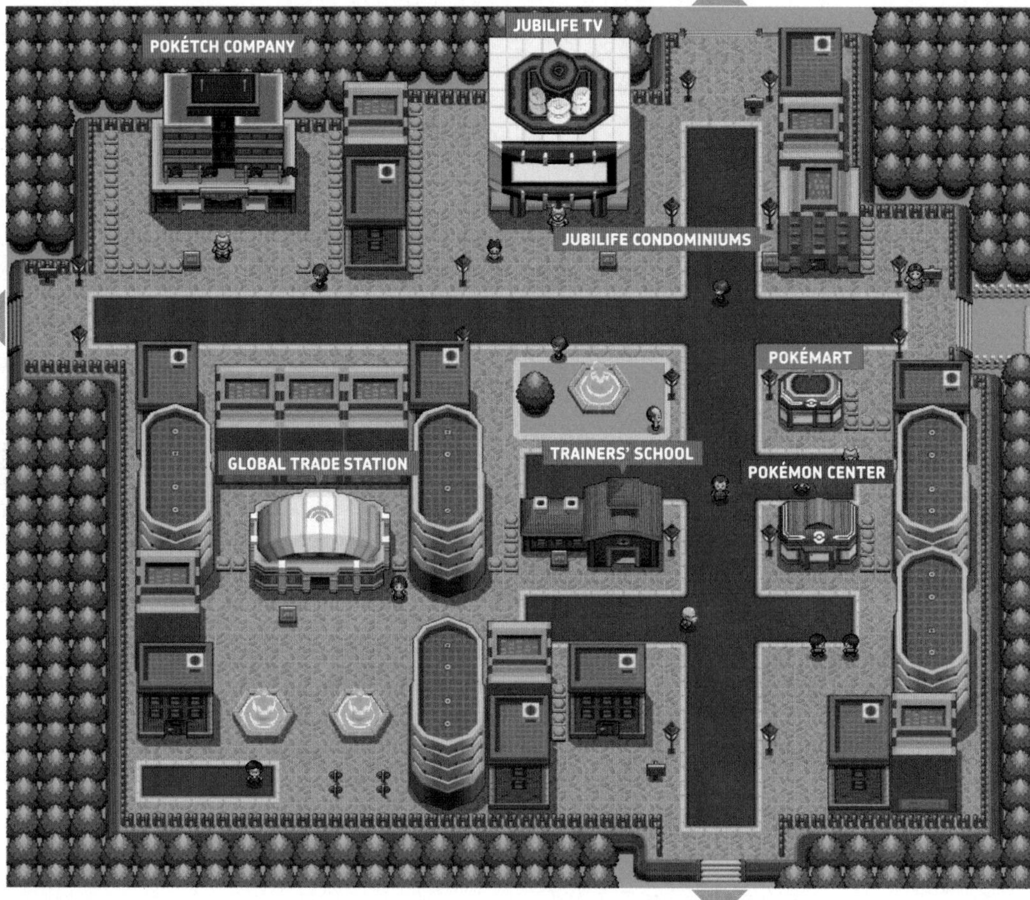

OBTAINABLE ITEMS

ON YOUR FIRST VISIT

- ☐ Town Map
- ☐ Coupon 1
- ☐ Coupon 3
- ☐ Quick Claw
- ☐ TM10 Hidden Power
- ☐ Coupon 2
- ☐ Pokétch
- ☐ Old Rod

AFTER WINNING OREBURGH CITY GYM BATTLE

- ☐ Fashion Case
- ☐ Pokétch application Memo Paper
- ☐ One of the following: Turtwig Mask Chimchar Mask or Piplup Mask

AFTER WINNING VEILSTONE CITY GYM BATTLE

- ☐ Pokétch application Memo paper

AFTER WINNING HEARTHOME CITY GYM BATTLE

- ☐ Pokétch application Connection Searcher

AFTER WINNING SNOWPOINT CITY GYM BATTLE

- ☐ Pokétch application Move Effectiveness Checker

POKÉMART (MERCHANT ON THE LEFT)

Air Mail	50
Heal Ball	300

POKÉMON LOTTERY AT JUBILIFE TV

Prizes	Matching numbers	Accesories
Grand Prize	5	Master Ball
1st Prize	4	Max Revive
2nd Prize	3	Exp. Share
3rd Prize	2	PP Up
4th Prize	1	Accessory Backgound

GET THE TOWN MAP FROM YOUR RIVAL

YOUR RIVAL WAS STUDYING about Pokémon at the Trainers' School. You give him the Parcel - which turned out to be Town Maps. There were two of them so he let you keep one.

REGISTER ITEMS YOU USE MOST

IT IS RECOMMENDED that you register the frequently used items like Town Maps (also good for items Fishing Rods, Potions, etc). Doing so allows you to access them easily just by pressing the Y-Button.

USE TMS ON YOUR POKÉMON

AFTER WINNING BATTLES at the Trainer's School you'll earn TM10 Hidden Power. TMs are valuable tools teach moves to your Pokémon. Get as many as you can and teach them new moves - you never know when they will come in handy!

READ THE BLACKBOARD

A BLACKBOARD at the Trainers' School provides you with detailed knowledge about special conditions such as Poison and Burn. You know that special conditions can be a big factor in determining a victory or defeat, so study hard and master them.

STEP 3 CAN'T ENTER GTS UNTIL YOU EARN A GYM BADGE

THE GLOBAL TRADE STATION (GTS) is located west of the Trainers' School. On your first visit to Jubilife City, though, you can't enter - you need to go to Oreburgh City first and earn a Gym badge.

STEP 4 CLOWN AROUND FOR A POKÉTCH

YOU SEE A MAN near the Trainers' School that is advertising a Pokétch. He tells you to find three clowns in town, answer their quizzes, and come back with three coupons - after which he'll give you a Pokétch. Where are the clowns? Send in the clowns. They're already here.

POKÉTCH (BOY)

POKÉTCH (GIRL)

STEP 5 GET THE OLD ROD FROM A FISHERMAN

WHEN YOU ENTER a gate that leads to Route 218, you'll meet a fisherman. Speak to him and he'll give you the Old Rod. This comes handy when you want to capture sea-faring Pokémon living in oceans, streams, and lakes.

KEEPING IT REEL!

AFTER CASTING your line, you may see a "!" pop up above your head which indicates that you've snagged a Pokémon. Respond quickly by pressing the A button to reel it in.

STEP 6 GET IN THE MIX

BY SPEAKING to a person near a fountain you can form a group or join other groups to mix records. This creates lots of zany situations - like broadcasting your friend's records on TV in the game! (see p. 244)

Yay, cool! What do you want to name
your group?

STEP 7 EQUIP YOUR POKÉMON WITH NEW ITEMS

SPEAK TO A WOMAN on 1 FL of the Jubilife Condominiums and she'll give you the Quick Claw - a useful item that lets your Pokémon attack first in battle. Equip this item on the Pokémon you use most frequently in battles.

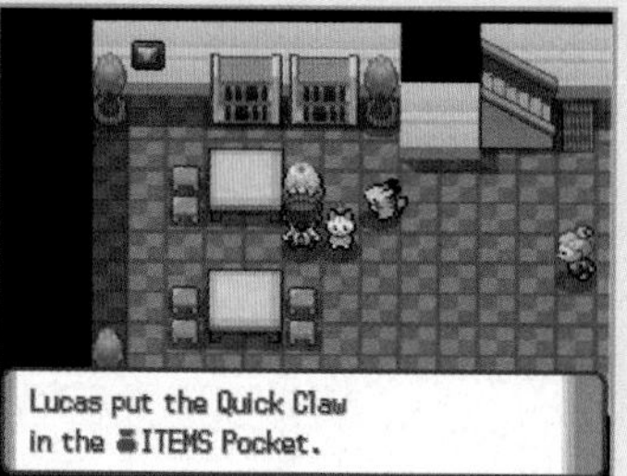

Lucas put the Quick Claw
in the ITEMS Pocket.

ITEMS TO EQUIP

BESIDES QUICK CLAW, there are many other items you can benefit greatly from. For instance, Luck Incense doubles your prize money when you win a battle.

STEP 8 HEAD TO A POKÉMON GYM IN OREBURGH CITY

ONCE YOU'VE GONE through town, head over to Oreburgh City where they have a Pokémon Gym. It's located in the east, right past Route 203. Stop by the Pokémart before you leave and stock up on items to prepare yourself for upcoming battles.

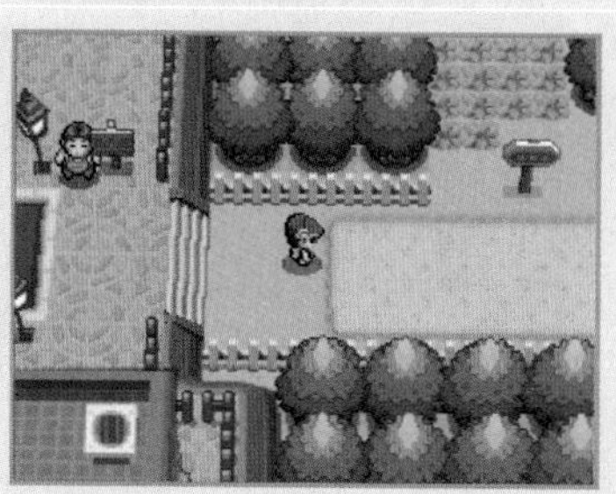

AFTER WINNING OREBURGH CITY GYM BATTLE
TRADE YOUR POKéMON

UPON YOUR VICTORY at Oreburgh City Gym, you've earned one Gym badge and also access to GTS (Global Trading Station). GTS is a facility where you can trade with people across the country using Nintendo's Wi-Fi Connection. (see p.240)

Welcome! This is the Global Trade Station, or GTS for short.

LET YOUR POKéMON DELIVER MESSAGES

BUY MAIL at a Pokémart and attach them to your Pokémon (as Hold Items). You can write a message on the mail and when you trade with your friends they can read your messages!

AFTER WINNING OREBURGH CITY GYM BATTLE
COLLECT AS MANY POKéTCH APPLICATIONS AS YOU CAN!

AT POKéTCH COMPANY, a company that manufactures Pokétch, they're constantly developing new devices that add more features to your Pokétch. Come back to the Pokétch Company after obtaining one, three, five, and seven Gym badges. They'll have new functions ready for your Pokétch.

READ THE MANUAL

ON 3 FL of the Pokétch building, they have a PC that provides you with an instruction manual for your Pokétch. More instructions are added as they introduce new Pokétch applications. If you come across functions you don't know how to use, this PC will help you.

AFTER WINNING OREBURGH CITY GYM BATTLE
BATTLE AGAINST TEAM GALACTIC

NEAR THE JUBILIFE Condominiums, you'll see Team Galactic grunts muscling Professor Rowan for his cooperation. Punish them! This is going to be a double battle in which you and Rowan's assistant fight as a team. Two heads are definitely better than one - work together and defeat Team Galactic!

These miscreants are babbling utter nonsense that I just can't stomach.

NUMB3RS

YOU GET TO play the Pokémon Lottery at a reception on the first floor of the Jubilife Television building. If the daily drawn number matches your Pokémon ID number (on your Trainer's Card), you get a prize. Check out your chances every day.

AFTER WINNING OREBURGH CITY GYM BATTLE
TAKE A PHOTO OF YOUR POKéMON AT JUBILIFE TV

WHEN YOU DEFEAT the Team Galactic grunts, an employee of Jubilife TV comes by and gives you a Fashion Case. Now you can take a photo of your primped and preened Pokémon on the 2 FL of the Jubilife TV building. They'll even frame the picture and put it up on the wall for you.

YES
NO
I will snap a photo when you're done. You will do this, won't you?

PICTURE PERFECT

WHEN YOU MIX records, pictures of your friends' Pokémon will also be exhibited on the second floor of the Jubilife TV building. They display up to 10 pictures at a time.

ROUTE 203

Route 203 is a passage way to your next destination, Oreburgh City. On your way there, your rival will challenge you. His Pokémon have grown exponentially – don't underestimate him.

OBTAINABLE ITEMS

ITEMS TO OBTAIN

☐ Poké Ball	☐ Repel

IN GRASS

POKÉMON	M	D	N
Starly	◎	◎	○
Shinx	○	○	○
Bidoof	○	○	○
Abra	○	○	○
Kricketot	○	✕	○
Zubat	✕	✕	○

ON WATER

POKÉMON	VARIABLE
Psyduck	◎
Golduck	○

FISHING

FISHING ROD	POKÉMON	VARIABLE
Old	Magikarp	◎
Good	Magikarp	◎
	Goldeen	○

BATTLE YOUR RIVAL 1

RIVAL

When you enter Route 203, your rival will find you – and then it's on!

IF YOUR STARTER WAS TURTWIG: YOUR RIVAL WILL CHOOSE:

POKÉMON	LEVEL	TYPE
Starly ♂	Lv7	Normal-Flying
Chimchar ♂	Lv9	Fire

IF YOUR STARTER WAS CHIMCHAR: YOUR RIVAL WILL CHOOSE:

POKÉMON	LEVEL	TYPE
Starly ♂	Lv7	Normal-Flying
Piplup ♂	Lv9	Water

IF YOUR STARTER WAS PIPLUP: YOUR RIVAL WILL CHOOSE:

POKÉMON	LEVEL	TYPE
Starly ♂	Lv7	Normal-Flying
Turtwig ♂	Lv9	Grass

TRADE YOUR POKÉMON WITH TOWNSPEOPLE

So, you now know you can trade Pokémon with your friends, family, co-workers, and other Pokémon fans from across the country using Nintendo's DS Wireless Connection or Nintendo Wi-Fi Connection. But did you know you can also trade with other characters in the game as well?

RARE POKÉMON

YES
NO
Wanna trade it for my CHATOT?

IN THE COURSE of your journey you'll meet people who'll want to trade Pokémon with you. When they offer you a trade, do what you can to complete the trade – not only is it beneficial to you, but it helps you practice for trading with other Pokémon players. You may be able to obtain rare Pokémon like Abra or Haunter – and trading will also bring you closer to completing the Pokédex.

TRADES YOU CAN COMPLETE BEFORE THE HALL OF FAME

TRADE 1 A WOMAN IN OREBURGH CITY

ABRA APPEARS on Route 203 or 215, but they are very elusive. If you find it difficult to capture, you can resort to trading with the woman in Oreburgh City. She'll want Machop in return, which you can find abundantly on Route 207. It also appears on Route 208.

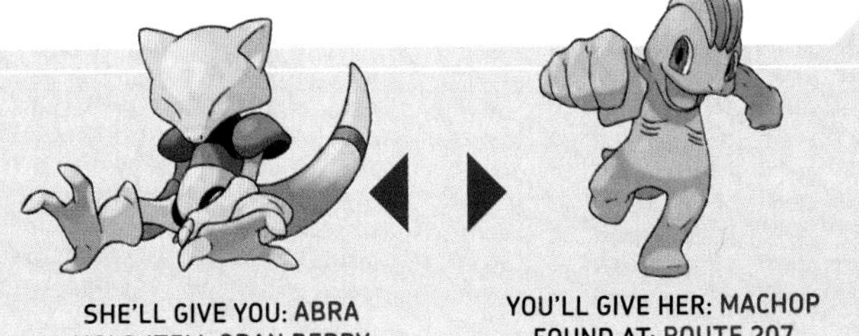

SHE'LL GIVE YOU: ABRA
HOLD ITEM: ORAN BERRY

YOU'LL GIVE HER: MACHOP
FOUND AT: ROUTE 207

TRADE 2 A BOY IN ETERNA CITY

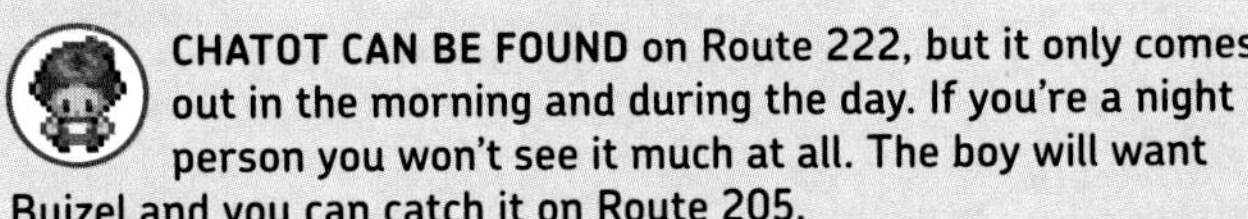

CHATOT CAN BE FOUND on Route 222, but it only comes out in the morning and during the day. If you're a night person you won't see it much at all. The boy will want Buizel and you can catch it on Route 205.

HE'LL GIVE YOU: CHATOT
HOLD ITEM: LEPPA BERRY

YOU'LL GIVE HIM: BUIZEL
FOUND AT: ROUTE 205

TRADE 3 A WOMAN IN SNOWPOINT CITY

A WILD HAUNTER won't come into the picture until you obtain a National Pokédex. You can also raise your Gastly to Lv25 but it is time-consuming. It's easier to get it from the woman in Snowpoint City. She'll want Medicham, which you can find on Route 217 or Victory Road.

SHE'LL GIVE YOU: HAUNTER
HOLD ITEM: EVERSTONE

YOU'LL GIVE HER: MEDICHAM
FOUND AT: ROUTE 217, VICTORY ROAD

OREBURGH GATE

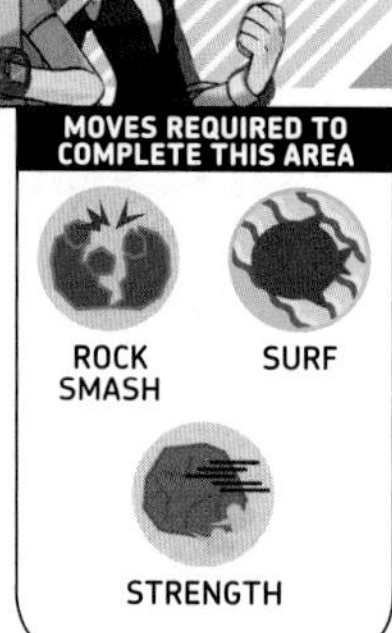

Oreburgh Gate is a cave inside a mountain located on the west side of Oreburgh City. You can only pass through it on your first visit, but you'll be able to proceed to the back of the lower level once you learn some new moves.

MOVES REQUIRED TO COMPLETE THIS AREA

ROCK SMASH
SURF
STRENGTH

OBTAINABLE ITEMS

ON YOUR FIRST VISIT

- ☐ HM06 Rock Smash

AFTER WINNING OREBURGH CITY GYM BATTLE

- ☐ TM70 Flash
- ☐ Stardust

AFTER OBTAINING BICYCLE

- ☐ TM31 Brick Break

AFTER WINNING CANALAVE CITY GYM BATTLE

- ☐ Earth Plate
- ☐ TM01 Focus Punch

■ 1 FL

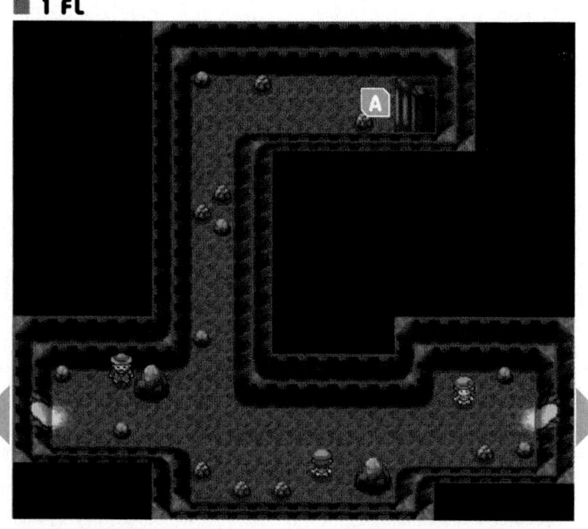

■ B1F

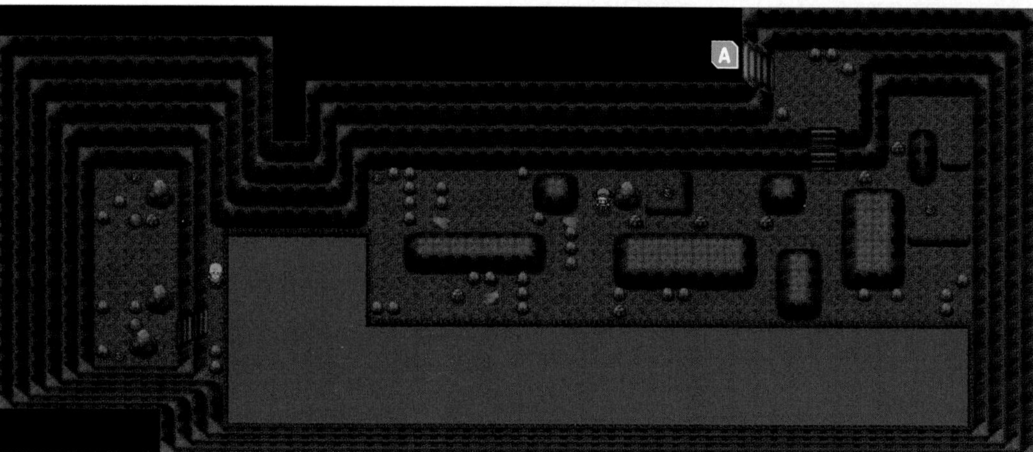

■ 1 FL

IN CAVE

POKÉMON	M	D	N
Geodude	◎	◎	◎
Zubat	○	○	○

■ B1F

IN CAVE

POKÉMON	M	D	N
Zubat	◎	◎	◎
Psyduck	◎	◎	◎
Geodude	○	○	○

ON WATER

POKÉMON	VARIABLE
Zubat	◎
Psyduck	◎
Golbat	△
Golduck	△

FISHING

FISHING ROD	POKÉMON	VARIABLE
Old	Magikarp	◎
Good	Magikarp	◎
	Barboach	○

STEP 1 ROCK ON!

UPON ENTERING a cave you'll find a hiker – when he sees your Pokétch, he'll give you HM06 Rock Smash. In order for you to use Rock Smash, you'll need to win a Gym battle in Oreburgh City and earn the Coal Badge.

Oh, lookie there!
You've got a Pokétch!

FIRST, GO TO OREBURGH CITY!

OREBURGH GATE has a lake in the basement, but since you're not able to use HM06 Rock Smash yet, you can only pass through the ground level. Head east to Oreburgh City, and win that Gym badge!

AFTER WINNING OREBURGH CITY GYM BATTLE
USE ROCK SMASH AT BACK OF CAVE

AFTER YOU WIN at Oreburgh City Gym, you'll be able to use HM06 Rock Smash. Use it to bust up the rocks to the lower level of the cave, and search out TM70 Flash. Flash is an invaluable move that will give you light in very dark places.

▶YES
NO
This rock appears to be breakable.
Would you like to use Rock Smash?

AFTER WINNING OREBURGH CITY GYM BATTLE
JUMP OVER A JUMP STAND ON BICYCLE

COME BACK to the cave again after obtaining the Bicycle in Eterna City – you'll be able to jump over a bike ramp and go further towards the back of the Basement Level. When you jump over the stand, you find TM31 Brick Break.

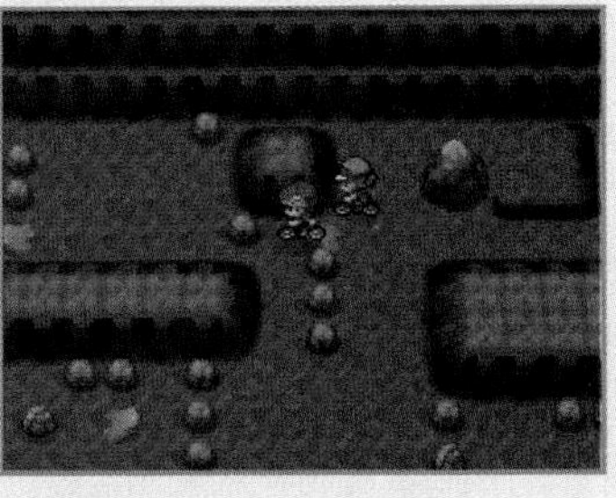

AFTER WINNING OREBURGH CITY GYM BATTLE
GO DEEPER INTO THE BACK OF THE CAVE USING STRENGTH

AFTER YOU WIN at Canalave City Gym, you'll be able to use the HM04 Strength. Using Strength, you can go even farther in this cave and obtain the Earth Plate and TM01 Focus Punch.

WHAT DO YOU USE THE EARTH PLATE FOR?

CERTAIN PLATES, equipped on Pokémon, can improve the power of certain types of moves. For instance, the Earth Plate effectively increases the power of Ground-type moves.

OREBURGH CITY

Oreburgh City is a vigorous coal-mine town that is blessed with beautiful nature. There is a museum that exhibits materials related to coal mining. You came here to challenge the Gym Leader, Roark, but he is nowhere to be found...

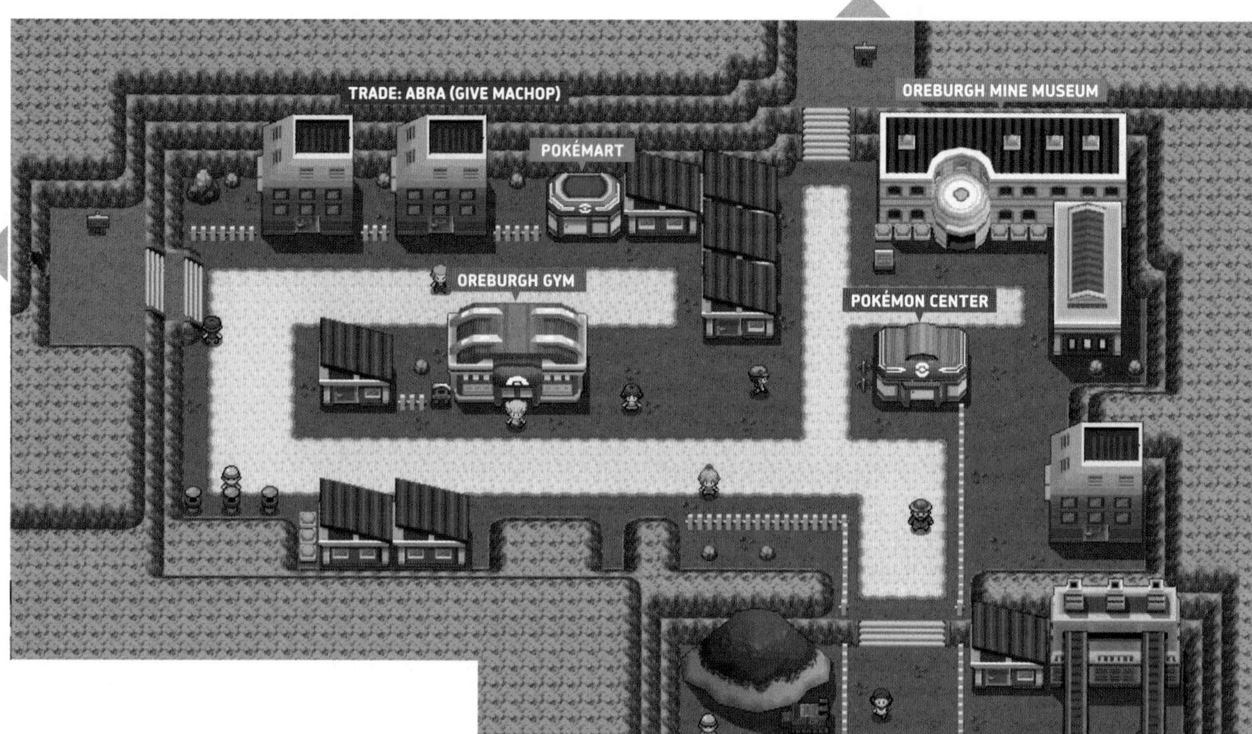

OBTAINABLE ITEMS

ON YOUR FIRST VISIT	
☐ Pal Pad	☐ Dusk Ball
☐ Great Ball	☐ Super Potion

WHEN YOU SHOW ZUBAT TO A MAN IN THE CONDOMINIUMS
☐ Heal Ball

AFTER WINNING OREBURGH CITY GYM BATTLE	
☐ Coal Badge	☐ TM76 Stealth Rock

POKÉMART (MERCHANT ON THE LEFT)	
Tunnel Mail	50
Heal Ball	300
Net Ball	1000

STEP 1 WHERE IS THE GYM LEADER, ROARK?

YOU SEE YOUR RIVAL in front of the Oreburgh Gym. He says that he's already won his battle and gained a badge. He also says that the Gym Leader, Roark, is currently at Oreburgh Mine, and not at the Gym. After you acquaint yourself with the town, go to the mine.

Oh, it's you, Lucas!
You finally got here?

STEP 2 WI-FI CLUB IN THE POKéMON CENTER OPENS

YOU VISIT a Pokémon Center to find that Pokémon Wi-Fi Club in the basement has been opened. Enter the club and a guide named Teala will give you the Pal Pad. With this, you'll be able to enjoy trading or battling with friends from all over (see p. 240).

My name is Teala, and I'm your guide

FUHGEDDABOUTIT! YA GOTTA BE CONNECTED

IN ORDER FOR YOU to truly enjoy the Nintendo Wi-Fi connection, you need a PC with a wireless router, or the Nintendo Wi-Fi USB Connector (sold separately - see p. 240 for details).

STEP 3 PICK YOUR APPEARANCE FOR CONNECTION

TALK TO THE BOY on 1 FL of the Pokémon Center, and he'll ask you who your favorite Trainer is. You'll be represented by the look of the Trainer you choose when in the Union Room. Choose wisely!

Which kind of Trainer would you like

STEP 4 ABRA TRADE-DABRA

WHEN YOU TALK to a woman in the condominium, she'll offer you a Pokémon trade. She says she'll give you Abra if you give her a Machop in exchange. Abra are hard to catch - you my want to take her up on this trade.

Would you be willing to trade your
MACHOP for my ABRA?

FREE TRADE AGREEMENT

IN THE SINNOH REGION, you'll have three opportunities to trade for rare Pokémon. Not only is it fun, but it will also help you attain your goal of an upgraded Pokédex!

STEP 1 ZUBAT-TER UP!

SPEAK TO A MAN on 2 FL of the condominium, and he'll ask you to show him a Zubat. When you get a Zubat, put it in front of your party and talk to him again. He'll thank you and give you a Heal Ball.

If you don't mind, how about showing me a Pokémon called ZUBAT?

STEP 2 GO VISIT THE MUSEUM

AT THE OREBURGH MINING MUSEUM, there is an exhibition of various items concerning the Oreburgh Mine. Admission is free so visit and see as much as you can. Also, if you dig out a Pokémon fossil in an Underground Pass, they'll restore it here for you.

Badly scarred wooden tools are displayed.

STEP 3 GO TO OREBURGH MINE TO SEE ROARK

ACCORDING TO YOUR RIVAL, the Gym Leader, Roark, is at Oreburgh Mine, south of Oreburgh City. You want to challenge him. Let's go to Oreburgh Mine to find him.

AFTER VISITING OREBURGH MINE PREPARE FOR A BATTLE

WHEN YOU SEE ROARK in Oreburgh Mine, you can finally participate in the Oreburgh City Gym battle. There are some tough customers in the Gym - make sure you stop by at the Pokémart to get supplies.

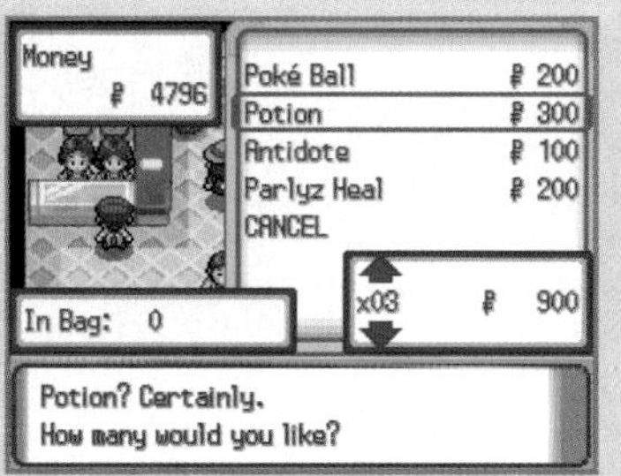

Potion? Certainly.
How many would you like?

ZUBAT A-PLENTY!

ZUBAT LIVE in and around Oreburgh City. You'll come across them at the coal mine as you look for Roark.

GYM BATTLE 1

ROARK

OREBURGH GYM LEADER
POKÉMON TYPE: ROCK
RECOMMENDED TYPES: WATER, GRASS

COAL BADGE:
Allows you to use HM06 Rock Smash in the field.

WELCOME TO OREBURGH CITY GYM – where you'll experience your first Gym battle! Inside the Gym, go up the stairs and face off against Roark who's waiting for you in the back. There are two other Pokémon Trainers in your way. Roark uses Rock-type Pokémon - you can make it an easy victory if you use either Water-, Grass-, Fighting-, or Ground-type moves. When you win, the Coal Badge and TM76 Stealth Rock are yours.

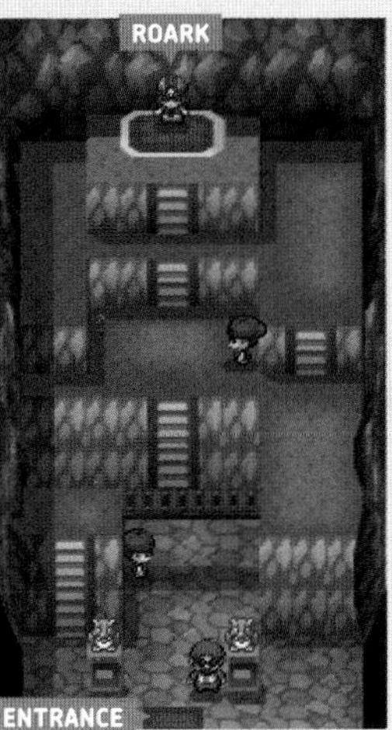

PARTY POKÉMON

POKÉMON	LEVEL	TYPE
Geodude ♂	Lv12	Rock-Ground
Onix ♂	Lv12	Rock-Ground
Cranidos ♂	Lv14	Rock

AFTER WINNING OREBURGH CITY GYM BATTLE
GO BACK TO JUBILIFE CITY

YOUR NEXT GYM BADGE BATTLE is in Eterna City, but you can't pass through Route 207 without the Bicycle. Do as your rival suggests and go back to Jubilife City and head back out to Eterna City via Floaroma Town.

So, I'm going back to Jubilife City.
Next stop, the Eterna Gym Badge!

AFTER OBTAINING THE EXPLORER KIT
HAVE YOUR FOSSIL RESTORED

WHEN YOU TALK TO UNDERGROUND MAN in Eterna City, he'll give you an Explorer Kit (see p.91). With the Explorer Kit, you can go underground in the Sinnoh region and dig for fossils of Pokémon in the walls. If you do find a fossil or two, go to the museum and have them restored.

I study Pokémon Fossils!
Me! Right here and now!

USE FLY TO RETURN

AFTER ONLY ONE visit to Pal Park, you'll be able to go back there after earning the National Pokédex by using HM02 Fly. This makes it much easier and more convenient because you no longer have to sail across the ocean.

OREBURGH MINE

Oreburgh Mine is a cave in which lies a vast coal reserve. Coal miners are hard at work here, and are even enlisting the help of Machop. Go inside and proceed towards the back of the cave to find the Gym Leader of Oreburgh City Gym.

MOVES REQUIRED TO COMPLETE THIS AREA

ROCK SMASH

■ B1F

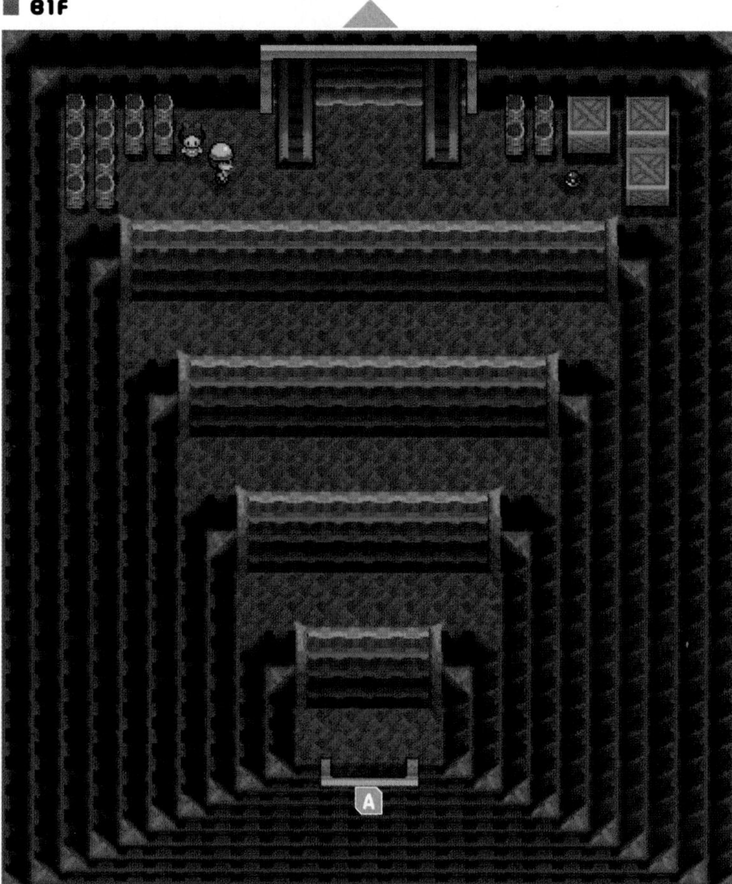

OBTAINABLE ITEMS

ON YOUR FIRST VISIT

☐ X Defend	☐ Potion
☐ Escape Rope	

■ B1F • B2F

IN CAVE

POKÉMON	M	D	N
Geodude	◎	◎	◎
Zubat	○	○	○
Onix	○	○	○

STEP 1 FIND THE GYM LEADER, ROARK

THE GYM LEADER, Roark is in front of a huge coal rock in the second sub-level of Oreburgh Mine. Speak to him and he'll tell you how to use HM06 Rock Smash – after which, he promptly will head back to his Gym. Go to Oreburgh City Gym and face him!!

Fallen boulders need to be smashed so they're out of the way.

THE ZURI IS DIG-LOCKED

IF YOU SPEAK to the miners, they will tell you that the sand pile they dig out is called Zuri Mountain. They also tell you it's called Bota Mountain in the Hoenn region.

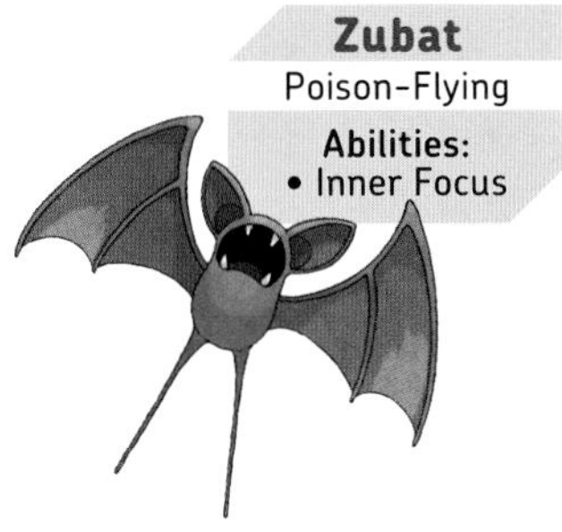

Zubat
Poison-Flying
Abilities:
• Inner Focus

Onix
Rock-Ground
Abilities:
• Rock Head
• Sturdy

B2F

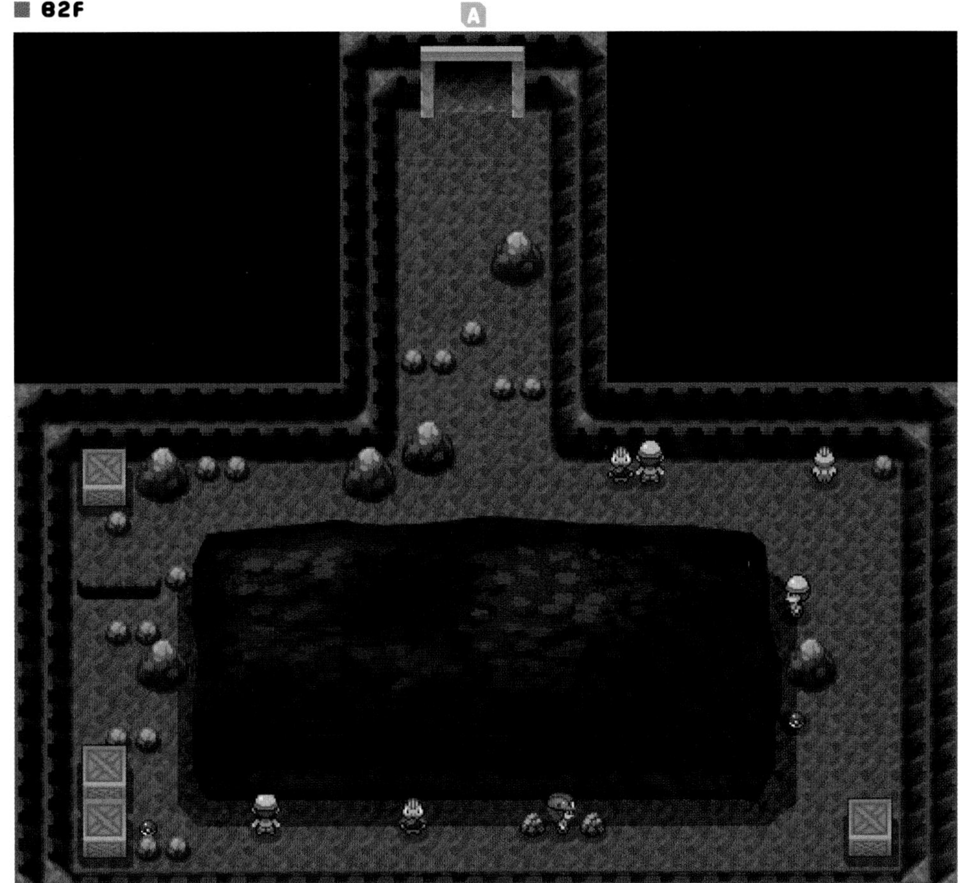

STEP 2 CAPTURE ZUBAT IN THE COAL MINE

OREBURGH MINE is inhabited by wild Zubat. These are the same Zubat that the man in Oreburgh City was asking about. Capture at least one and take it back to him – that Heal Ball he has as a reward is pretty sweet!

ROUTE 207

MOVES REQUIRED TO COMPLETE THIS AREA

ROCK CLIMB

Route 207 is a road that leads to a rocky mountain called Mt. Coronet. You'll need to have a Bicycle to climb up sandy slopes in this area. First, head to Eterna City to get the Bicycle.

OBTAINABLE ITEMS

AFTER OBTAINING A BICYCLE

- ☐ Battle Searcher
- ☐ Oran Berry x2
- ☐ Bluk Berry
- ☐ Dire Hit
- ☐ Super Potion
- ☐ A Pokétch application Itemfinder
- ☐ Cheri Berry
- ☐ Poké Ball

AFTER WINNING SNOWPOINT CITY GYM BATTLE

- ☐ Iron

IN GRASS

POKÉMON	M	D	N
Geodude	◎	◎	◎
Machop	◎	◎	○
Kricketot	○	✕	○
Zubat	✕	✕	○

Machop
Fighting

Abilities:
- Guts
- No Guard

CATCH NOW – TRADE LATER

ON YOUR FIRST VISIT through Route 207, you won't be able to proceed without the Bicycle. But you may want to hang around the grassy brush for a while and capture a wild Machop. There's a woman in Oreburgh City who will trade you an Abra for your Machop.

AFTER OBTAINING THE BICYCLE
ROWAN'S ASSISTANT GIVES UP THE GOODS

COMING FROM ROUTE 206, you'll bump into Rowan's assistant. The assistant will give you an item called a Vs. Seeker and a Pokétch application called an Dowsing Machine. The assistant will first tease you by asking which one you'll choose, but don't get your Poké Balls in a bunch – you'll get both!

YOU CAN FIND ITEMS WITH DOWSING MACHINE

DOWSING MACHINE, a Pokétch application you get from the Professor's assistant, is a very convenient tool that detects hidden or invisible items. If you come to a place that possibly have those items, touch on the bottom screen.

AFTER OBTAINING THE BICYCLE
PRACTICE SLOPE SLAMMING

WITH THE BICYCLE, you'll be able to climb hills of shifting sand. In order to run on the loose, sandy surfaces of certain slopes (say that five times really fast), you need to shift your bike to fourth gear and give it a running start. Get in lots of practice here.

AFTER OBTAINING THE BICYCLE
PROCEED TOWARDS MT. CORONET

HEAD EAST ON ROUTE 207 and you'll eventually reach Mt. Coronet. You haven't had a break since you left Eterna City so rest up at a Pokémon Center before you enter Mt. Coronet.

ROUTE 218

Route 218 is a short passage, but a good fishing spot that is very popular among fishermen. If you've obtained a Fishing Rod, you'll have a "reel" good time here. Once you've learned HM03 Surf, you can head to Canalave City.

MOVES REQUIRED TO COMPLETE THIS AREA

SURF

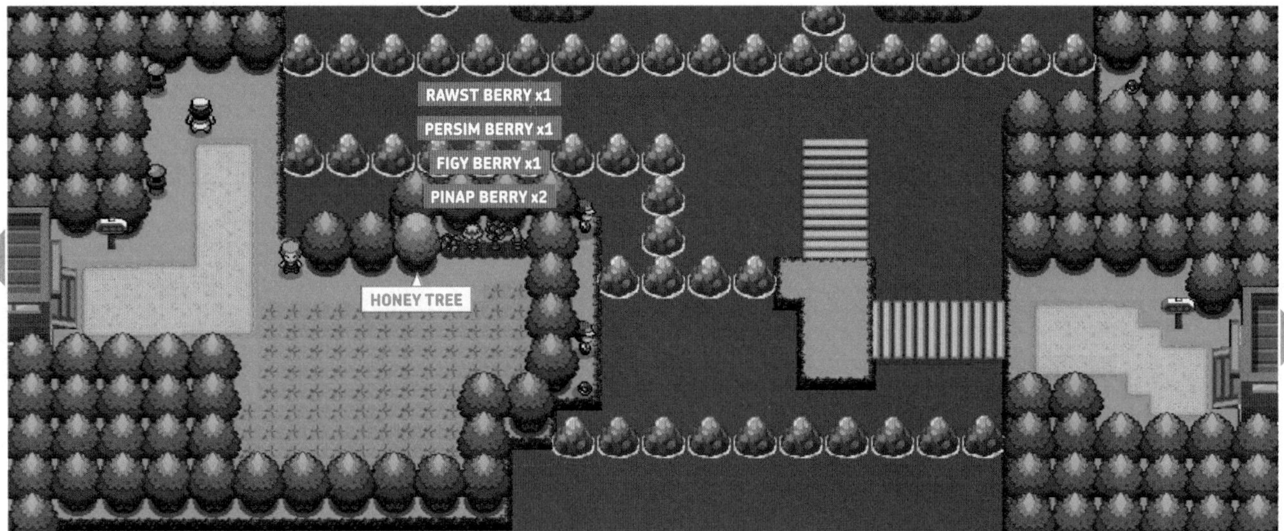

OBTAINABLE ITEMS

AFTER WINNING HEARTHOME CITY GYM BATTLE

☐ Rare Candy	☐ Honey
☐ Rawst Berry	☐ Persim Berry
☐ Figy Berry	☐ Pinap Berry x 2

IN GRASS

POKÉMON	M	D	N
Floatzel	◎	◎	◎
Shellos	○	○	○
Gastrodon	○	○	○
Mr. Mime ♦	○	○	○
Glameow ●	○	○	○
Wingull	○	○	○

ON WATER

POKÉMON	VARIABLE
Tentacool	◎
Wingull	◎
Tentacruel	△
Pelipper	△

FISHING

FISHING ROD	POKÉMON	VARIABLE
Old	Magikarp	◎
Good	Magikarp	◎
	Finneon	○

Mr. Mime
Psychic
Abilities:
• Sound Proof
• Filter

Glameow
Normal
Abilities:
• Limber
• Own Tempo

STEP 1 FISHING FOR DUMMIES

TRY AND ENJOY fishing here using the Old Rod that you've received at the gate outside of Jubilife City. You can only catch Magikarp with this ragged rod, but it's good enough for practicing.

IN ROD WE TRUST

WHICH POKÉMON you catch depends on which Fishing Rod you use. With the Old Rod you can only catch Magikarp, but with a Good Rod, you can catch Pokémon like Finneon.

STEP 2 NEXT STOP–FLOAROMA TOWN

YOUR RIVAL is already on his way to the next Gym, so hurry! First head to Floaroma Town, north of Jubilife City. If you have the Coal Badge (which you won by defeating Roark at the Oreburgh City Gym) you can use HM06 Rock Smash and pass through the Ravaged Path.

AFTER WINNING HEARTHOME CITY GYM BATTLE
HEAD TO CANALAVE CITY USING HM03 SURF

PROCEED WEST on the ocean using HM03 Surf until the gate that leads to Canalave City comes into view. Canalave City is a port town that houses the Canalave Library and a harbor. Go to the Library and read a book concerning Cynthia's recommendations.

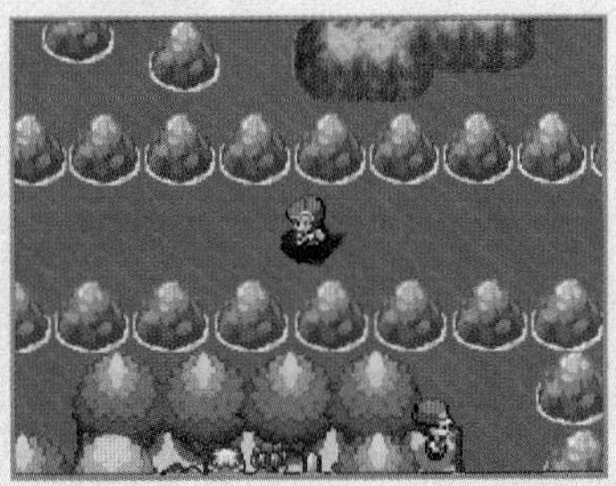

AFTER WINNING HEARTHOME CITY GYM BATTLE
HAVE YOUR POKÉDEX UPGRADED WITH NEW FUNCTIONS

WHEN YOU ENTER a gate that connects to Canalave City, Professor Rowan's assistant approaches you. Looks like the assistant was waiting to upgrade your Pokédex. After the upgrade, you'll be able to switch back and forth to see both genders for your Pokémon.

THE BIRDS AND THE BEEDRILLS

IN YOUR UPGRADED Pokédex, you can switch between male and female forms by choosing "Appearance" on the bottom screen. For example, in the case of Finneon, their lower fins are different in size.

ROUTE 204, RAVAGED PATH

Route 204 is a road of natural beauty that is lined with ponds and trees. In the middle of this unsurpassed vista is the Ravaged Path, a cave thruway that has been hollowed out over the years. You'll need a HM06 Rock Smash to pass through it.

MOVES REQUIRED TO COMPLETE THIS AREA

ROCK SMASH
CUT
SURF

OBTAINABLE ITEMS

ON YOUR FIRST VISIT	
☐ Parlyz Heal	☐ Antidote
☐ TM39 Rock Tomb	☐ Awakening
☐ TM09 Bullet Seed	

AFTER WINNING ETERNA CITY GYM BATTLE
☐ TM78 Captivate

AFTER WINNING HEARTHOME CITY GYM BATTLE	
☐ HP Up	☐ Sea Incense
☐ Luck Incense	☐ TM03 Water Pulse

ROUTE 204

FLOAROMA TOWN

JUBILIFE CITY

IN GRASS

POKÉMON	M	D	N
Starly	○	◎	○
Bidoof	○	○	○
Budew	○	○	○
Shinx	○	○	○
Kricketot	○	✕	○
Zubat	✕	✕	○

ON WATER

POKÉMON	VARIABLE
Psyduck	◎
Golduck	○

FISHING

FISHING ROD	POKÉMON	VARIABLE
Old	Magikarp	◎
Good	Magikarp	◎
	Goldeen	○

RAVAGED PATH

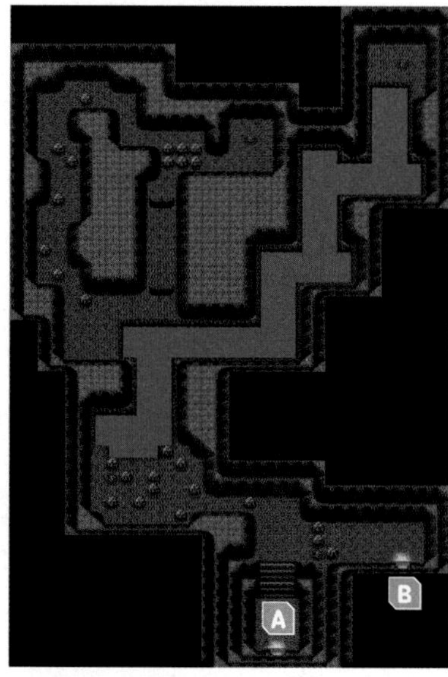

RAVAGED PATH

IN CAVE

POKÉMON	M	D	N
Zubat	◎	◎	◎
Geodude	○	○	○
Psyduck	△	△	△

ON WATER

POKÉMON	VARIABLE
Zubat	◎
Psyduck	◎
Golbat	△
Golduck	△

FISHING

FISHING ROD	POKÉMON	VARIABLE
Old	Magikarp	◎
Good	Magikarp	◎
	Barboach	○

STEP 1 ENTER THE RAVAGED PATH THROUGH THE CAVE

IN ORDER TO REACH Floaroma Town, you'll have to pass through the Ravaged Path that's smack dab in the middle of Route 204. You can enter it through a cave in the mountainside. Since you'll need HM06 Rock Smash to proceed, make sure one of your Pokémon has learned it.

STEP 2 PROCEED USING ROCK SMASH

ENTER RAVAGED PATH and head east then you will come out on the top of the eminence. However, there are many boulders blocking your way. Get rid of those obstacles using HM06 Rock Smash and keep going.

TO SURF, MAN

YOU'LL NEED HM03 Surf (and the ability to use it) to fully explore the whole cave. Win the Hearthome City Gym battle, then get the Relic Badge and come back.

STEP 3 CHALLENGE TWO TRAINERS IN A DOUBLE BATTLE

WHEN YOU COME OUT of Ravaged Path you'll face twin Pokémon Trainers who were there waiting for you. This is your very first Double Battle in which you use two Pokémon at the same time. Remember that in a Double Battle, the first two Pokémon in your party will enter.

AFTER WINNING ETERNA CITY GYM BATTLE COLLECT ITEMS USING CUT

WHEN YOU WIN the Eterna City Gym Battle and get the Forest Badge, you'll be able to use HM01 Cut to chop trees. Cut down trees on Route 204 and collect items that were previously unavailable to you.

DOUBLE YOUR EARNINGS WITH LUCK INCENSE!

THIS ITEM doubles your prize money when equipped on a Pokémon that fought in the battle. Use it to really rack up the cash!

FLOAROMA TOWN

Floaroma Town is filled with the sweet scent of beautiful blossoming flowers. Here you'll find Floaroma Meadow, and a flower shop operated by huge fans of the flora. The entrance of the meadow north of town is blocked by Team Galactic.

OBTAINABLE ITEMS

ON YOUR FIRST VISIT	
☐ Cheri Berry	☐ Oran Berry
☐ Sprayduck	☐ TM88 Pluck

AFTER VISITING VALLEY WINDWORKS	
☐ Works Key	☐ Honey

AFTER WINNING HEARTHOME CITY GYM BATTLE	
☐ Miracle Seed	☐ Leaf Stone

MERCHANT ON THE LEFT	
Bloom Mail	50
Heal Ball	300
Net Ball	1000

HONEY MAN	
Honey	100

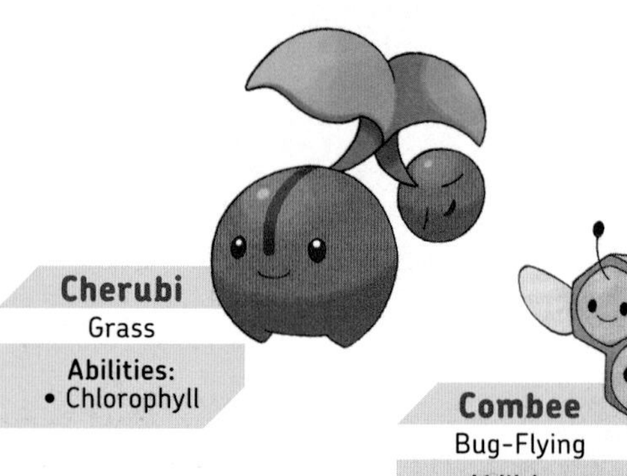

Cherubi
Grass
Abilities:
• Chlorophyll

Combee
Bug-Flying
Abilities:
• Honey Gather

FLOAROMA MEADOW

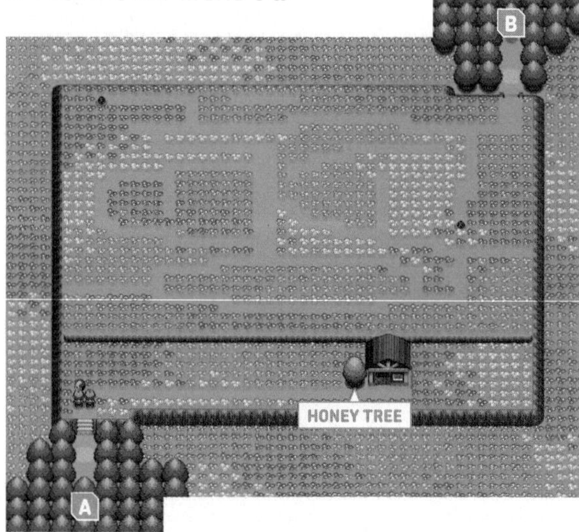

FLOAROMA TOWN

FUEGO IRONWORKS

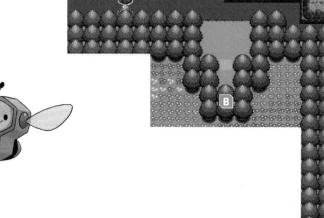

ROUTE 204 (TO JUBILIFE CITY)

ROUTE 205 (TO VALLEY WINDWORKS)

DO YOUR BERRY BEST

AT THE FLOWER SHOP, you can get berries that will grow in soft soil. Berries are useful items you can use or equip on Pokémon. Also, you can use them to make a new Pokémon food called Poffin.

PLANT AHEAD

YOU CAN BURY your berries in a soft soil and grow them. That increases the number of your berries. If you have only one of them, don't use it until you reproduce it.

TRADE FOR BERRY NICE ACCESSORIES

AT THE FLOWER SHOP, you can trade your berries for accessories which you can use to decorate your Pokémon for the photo shoot at the Jubilife TV station in Jubilife City (see p.59), or at the Pokémon Super Contest in Hearthome City (see p.113).

GET ALL DOLLED UP

IN THE POKÉMON Super Contest in Hearthome City, accessories can be a big factor in the judging. Collect as many accessories as possible and go for the grand prize.

ACCESSORIES YOU CAN TRADE FOR AT PICK A PECK OF COLORS FLOWER SHOP

ACCESORIES	REQUIRED BERRIES AND THE AMOUNT
Red Flower	Razz Berry x10
Pink Flower	Bluk Berry x10
White Flower	Nanab Berry x10
Blue Flower	Cornn Berry x30
Orange Flower	Magost Berry x15
Yellow Flower	Rabuta Berry x15
Googly Specs	Nomel Berry x20
Black Specs	Wepear Berry x20
Gorgeous Specs	Pinap Berry x40
Sweet Candy	Nanab Berry x30
Confetti	Razz Berry x30

ACCESSORIES YOU CAN TRADE FOR AT PICK A PECK OF COLORS FLOWER SHOP

ACCESORIES	REQUIRED BERRIES AND THE AMOUNT
Colored Parasol	Magost Berry x30
Old Umbrella	Pamtre Berry x50
Spotlight	Nomel Berry x80
Cape	Cornn Berry x250
Standing Mike	Bluk Berry x80
Surfboard	Wepear Berry x180
Carpet	Spelon Berry x100
Retro Pipe	Pamtre Berry x120
Fluffy Bed	Watmel Berry x150
Mirror Ball	Durin Berry x250
Photo Board	Belue Berry x200

STEP 4 WATER, WATER EVERYWHERE

SPEAK TO A WOMAN in the flower shop and she will give you a Sprayduck, which is a bottle to water berries you've planted. Always try to plant berries so you'll have a good supply when needed.

ONCE A DAY

THE WOMAN at the flower shop will give you one of these berries everyday: Cheri Berry, Chesto Berry, Pecha Berry, Rawst Berry, and Aspear Berry.

STEP 5 TEAM GALACTIC FOR THE BLOCK, TOM

THERE IS AN ENTRANCE to Floaroma Meadow in the north of town but grunts from Team Galactic are blocking the way and you can't enter the meadow. What are they doing in a flower meadow, anyway?

STEP 6 GET BACK TO TWINLEAF TOWN

YOUR RIVAL IS HEADED to Eterna City, off of Route 205 and the Eterna Forest. Proceed to Route 205 from the east end of town and go on to Eterna City.

AFTER VISITING VALLEY WINDWORKS OBTAIN A WORKS KEY

WHEN YOU ENTER Floaroma Meadow, you'll see Team Galactic threatening an old man, and attempting to steal Honey from him. Take care of Team Galactic and help the old man. As they take off, they drop the Works Key.

AFTER WINNING VALLEY WINDWORKS
BUY HONEY FROM THE OLD MAN

AFTER YOU CHASED Team Galactic away, you can buy Honey from the old man in the meadow. Honey is a very important item that lures Pokémon. This will contribute greatly to a more completed Pokédex. Spend lots of money on Honey – it will pay for itself.

WHAT'S SO SWEET ABOUT HONEY?

SPREADING HONEY around in the grassy brush will attract a lot of Pokémon. It's as effective as the move Sweet Scent (which also attracts Pokémon).

AFTER WINNING VALLEY WINDWORKS
LURE POKéMON WITH HONEY

YOU CAN LURE various Pokémon by putting Honey on Honey Trees. Once you put it on the tree, come back to check on it in half a day.

THE EFFECT ONLY LAST A DAY

THE EFFECT of the Honey on a Honey Tree lasts for only a day. Remember well on which tree you have put the Honey so that you can use the Honey efficiently.

AFTER WINNING HEARTHOME CITY GYM BATTLE
WALK AROUND THE MEADOW AND COLLECT ITEMS

ONCE YOU'VE LEARNED SURF, head west of Fuego Ironworks and enter Floaroma Town. You will now be able to cover every single part of Floaroma Meadow. Pick up all the items you can find and keep them for later use.

Burmy (Sandy Cloak)	Burmy (Plant Cloak)	Burmy (Trash Cloak)
Bug	Bug	Bug
Abilities: • Shed Skin	Abilities: • Shed Skin	Abilities: • Shed Skin

ROUTE 205, FUEGO IRONWORKS

MOVES REQUIRED TO COMPLETE THIS AREA

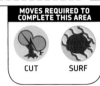

CUT SURF

Route 205 is on an winding piece of land that has a river running through it. In the east is the Valley Windworks, in the west Fuego Ironworks, and up north lies the Eterna Forest.

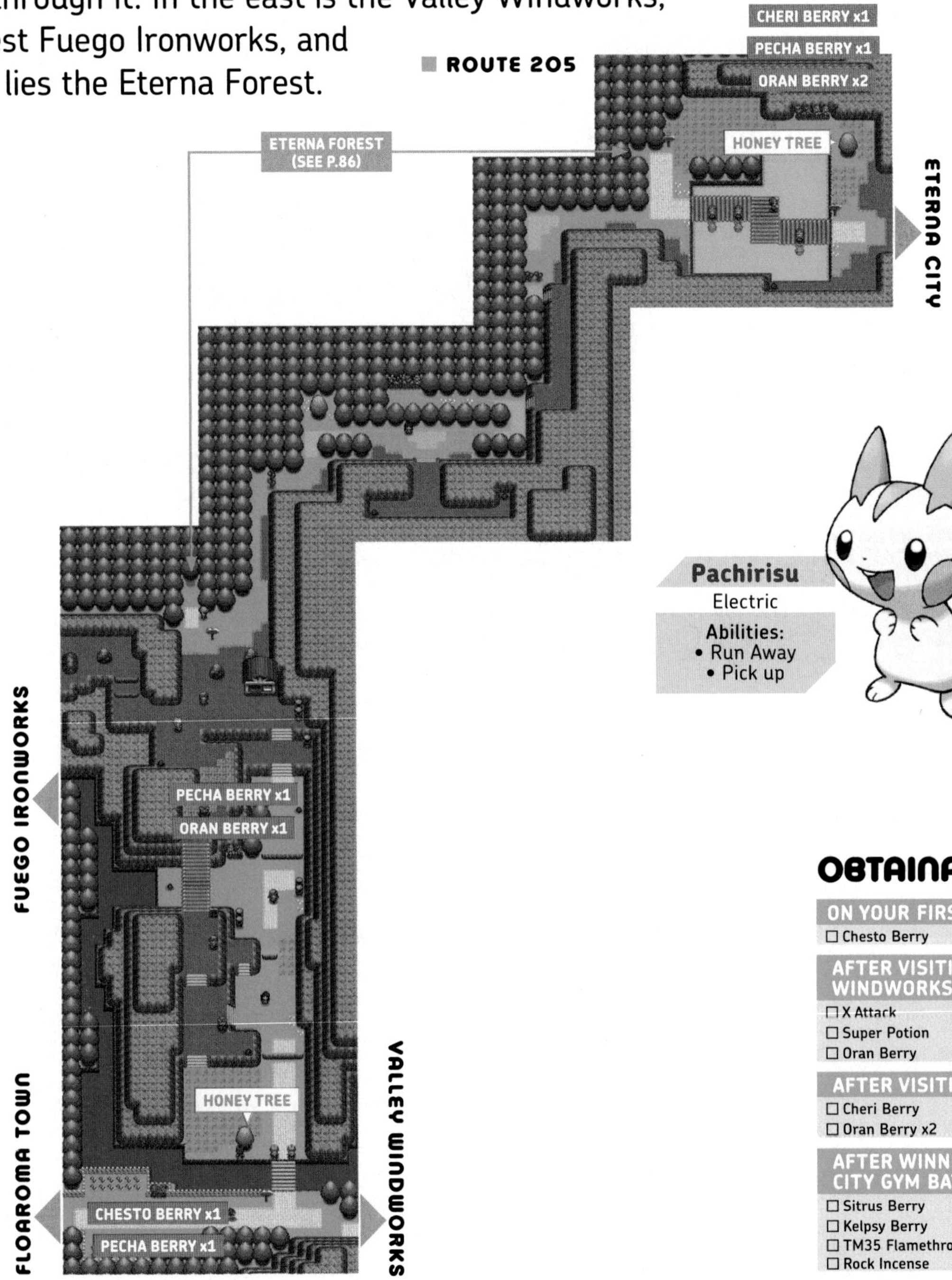

ROUTE 205

CHERI BERRY x1
PECHA BERRY x1
ORAN BERRY x2
HONEY TREE
ETERNA FOREST (SEE P.86)
ETERNA CITY
FUEGO IRONWORKS
PECHA BERRY x1
ORAN BERRY x1
HONEY TREE
FLOAROMA TOWN
VALLEY WINDWORKS
CHESTO BERRY x1
PECHA BERRY x1

Pachirisu
Electric
Abilities:
- Run Away
- Pick up

OBTAINABLE ITEMS

ON YOUR FIRST VISIT	
☐ Chesto Berry	☐ Pecha Berry

AFTER VISITING VALLEY WINDWORKS	
☐ X Attack	☐ Repel
☐ Super Potion	☐ Pecha Berry
☐ Oran Berry	☐ Poké Ball

AFTER VISITING ETERNA FOREST	
☐ Cheri Berry	☐ Pecha Berry
☐ Oran Berry x2	☐ Potion

AFTER WINNING HEARTHOME CITY GYM BATTLE	
☐ Sitrus Berry	☐ Wepear Berry x4
☐ Kelpsy Berry	☐ Burn Heal
☐ TM35 Flamethrower	☐ Fire Stone x2
☐ Rock Incense	

FUEGO IRONWORKS (OUTSIDE)

FUEGO IRONWORKS (OUTSIDE)

IN GRASS

POKÉMON	M	D	N
Floatzel	○	○	○
Shellos	○	○	○
Shinx	○	○	○
Luxio	○	○	○
Wingull	○	○	○
Gastrodon	○	○	○
Pachirisu	○	○	○

ON WATER

POKÉMON	VARIABLE
Tentacool	◎
Wingull	◎
Tentacruel	△
Pelipper	△

FISHING

FISHING ROD	POKÉMON	VARIABLE
Old	Magikarp	◎
Good	Magikarp	◎
	Finneon	○

FUEGO IRONWORKS

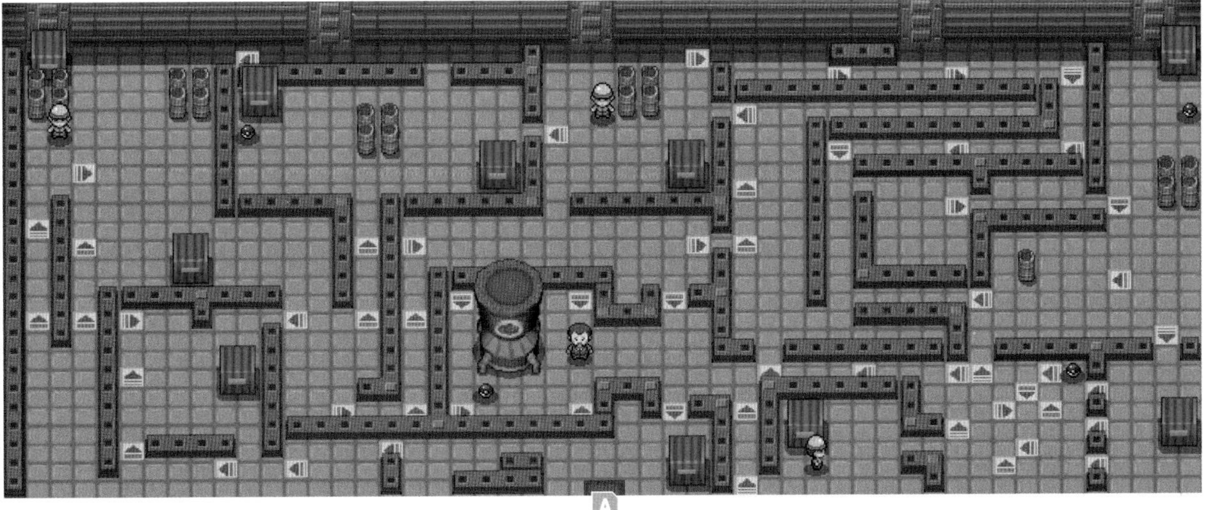

ROUTE 205 (ETERNA CITY SIDE)

IN GRASS

POKÉMON	M	D	N
Buizel	◎	◎	◎
Bidoof	◎	◎	◎
Shellos	○	○	○
Pachirisu	○	○	○

ON WATER

POKÉMON	VARIABLE
Psyduck	◎
Golduck	○

FISHING

FISHING ROD	POKÉMON	VARIABLE
Old	Magikarp	◎
Good	Magikarp	◎
	Barboach	○

ROUTE 205 (FLOAROMA SIDE)

IN GRASS

POKÉMON	M	D	N
Buizel	◎	◎	◎
Bidoof	◎	◎	◎
Shellos	○	○	○
Pachirisu	○	○	○

ON WATER

POKÉMON	VARIABLE
Tentacool	◎
Wingull	◎
Tentacruel	△
Pelipper	△

FISHING

FISHING ROD	POKÉMON	VARIABLE
Old	Magikarp	◎
Good	Magikarp	◎
	Finneon	○

Buizel
Water
Abilities:
• Swift Swim

Floatzel
Water
Abilities:
• Swift Swim

HELP A FATHER OUT

PROCEED TO ROUTE 205 from Floaroma Town. A girl will ask you to find her father - sounds like he works at Valley Windworks just ahead of here. Head over there.

COLLECT ITEMS WITH PICKUP

THERE ARE POKÉMON called Pachirisu that live in bushes and shrubs, and sometimes have an Ability called Pickup. If you add Pachirisu to your party, it picks up items while traveling - pretty soon you'll find your pack is packed with items!

FIND ANOTHER WAY

THE BRIDGE YOU'LL HAVE TO CROSS to proceed to Eterna Forest is closed by Team Galactic grunts. It seems like something is up in the forest. Take an alternate route to the east and hurry over to Valley Windworks.

AFTER RESCUING THE GIRL'S DAD
MOVE FORWARD IN THE ETERNA FOREST

AFTER YOU RESCUE the girl's dad, Team Galactic grunts leave the area and the bridge is open for traffic again. To get to Eterna City, cross the bridge and step into the Eterna Forest.

HEAL YOUR POKÉMON

THERE IS A HOUSE near the entrance of the forest where you can restore both your Pokémon's PP and HP. Stop by and rest before you go into the Eterna Forest.

AFTER VISITING ETERNA FOREST
ENTER ETERNA CITY

WHEN YOU COME OUT of Eterna Forest, you'll be back on Route 205. Proceed to the big bridge where fishermen gather and your next destination is right in front of you. Keep on going to Eterna City to challenge the next Gym.

SHORTCUT WITH CUT

USING HM01 CUT, chop down a tree on the right side of the entrance to Eterna Forest and proceed. You can't get to Eterna City without passing through the forest - as soon as you are able to use HM01 Cut, take this shortcut.

AFTER WINNING HEARTHOME CITY GYM BATTLE
HEAD TO FUEGO IRONWORKS USING SURF

USING HM03 SURF, proceed on a waterway right off of Route 205 coming from Floaroma Town, head to Fuego Ironworks. When you reach the dead-end of the waterway, you can go north to Fuego Ironworks, south to Floaroma Meadow.

AFTER WINNING HEARTHOME CITY GYM BATTLE
COLLECT ITEMS IN FUEGO IRONWORKS

IN FUEGO IRONWORKS, There are lots of directional floor tiles – step on one, and you'll be whisked away in the direction of the arrow imprinted on them. Plot out which direction you travel so that you can collect items scattered around the Ironworks. Near a smelting furnace is Fuego, the person in charge of this Ironworks.

EVOLVE YOUR POKéMON WITH FIRE STONE

AT FUEGO IRONWORKS, you will find an item called the Fire Stone which evolves a particular type of Pokémon. You will be using this item after you obtain the National Pokédex. Keep it in a safe place.

AFTER WINNING HEARTHOME CITY GYM BATTLE
GO TO A HIDDEN PLACE IN THE FLOWER GARDEN

HEAD SOUTH OF FUEGO IRONWORKS and you can get to the north side of the Floaroma Meadow, which was inaccessible from Floarama Town before. Walk around everywhere and collect all the items you can find. On your way back, just step down on to the lower part of ground which makes a shortcut to Floaroma Town.

Shellos

Water

Abilities:
- Sticky Hold
- Storm Drain

VALLEY WINDWORKS

At Valley Windworks, energy is generated through wind power, and a vast array of windmills. Team Galactic is after the energy the Windworks produces and they have occupied the plant.

MOVES REQUIRED TO COMPLETE THIS AREA

SURF

OBTAINABLE ITEMS

ON YOUR FIRST VISIT
- ☐ Potion

AFTER WINNING HEARTHOME CITY GYM BATTLE
- ☐ TM24 Thunderbolt

OUTSIDE

ROUTE 205 (TO FLOAROMA TOWN)

INSIDE

IN GRASS

POKÉMON	M	D	N
Buizel	◎	◎	◎
Shellos	◎	◎	◎
Pachirisu	○	○	○
Bidoof	○	○	○

FISHING

FISHING ROD	POKÉMON	VARIABLE
Old	Magikarp	◎
Good	Magikarp	◎
	Finneon	○

ON WATER

POKÉMON	VARIABLE
Tentacool	◎
Wingull	◎
Tentacruel	△
Pelipper	△

Drifloon
Ghost-Flying

Abilities:
- Aftermath
- Unburden

TEAM GALACTIC ARE IN LOCK DOWN MODE

THE FIRST TIME you visit this plant, a Team Galactic grunt is standing guard at the entrance. When you defeat him, he goes inside the plant and locks you out. Go to Floaroma Meadow to get the Works Key that'll open the entrance.

It's locked from inside!

AFTER OBTAINING WORKS KEY
PROCEED TO THE BACK OF THE PLANT

AFTER YOU OBTAIN the Works Key in Floaroma Meadow, open the entrance and go inside. Battle your way through the occupied plant and finally face off against the Team Galactic Commander, Mars, who is in the back. Beat her and you can rescue the girl's dad who was captured by the group.

You don't have an inkling of what
Team Galactic is trying to achieve!

GALACTIC BATTLE 1

MARS
GALACTIC TEAM COMMANDER

MARS, A TEAM GALACTIC COMMANDER, will send out two different types of Pokémon. Counterattack Zubat with Electric-, Ice-, Psychic-, or Rock-type moves, and go after Purugly with Fighting-type moves.

PARTY POKéMON

POKéMON	LEVEL	TYPE
Zubat ♀	Lv 14	Poison-Flying
Purugly ♀	Lv 18	Normal

AFTER OBTAINING WORKS KEY
HEAR ABOUT DRIFLOON FROM THE GIRL

AFTER YOU DEFEAT Team Galactic, the girl will tell you about a balloon-like Pokémon that comes to the plant often. It's called Drifloon. It appears in front of the plant every Friday. Capture it to help complete your Sinnoh Pokédex.

Flooooooon!

ETERNA FOREST AND THE CHATEAU

In Eterna Forest, a cluster of trees creates a natural maze. Deep in the forest an old deserted Chateau. Head east past the Chateau and you'll reach Eterna City in no time!

MOVES REQUIRED TO COMPLETE THIS AREA

CUT

INSIDE OF ETERNA FOREST

Beautifly
Bug-Flying
Abilities:
• Swarm

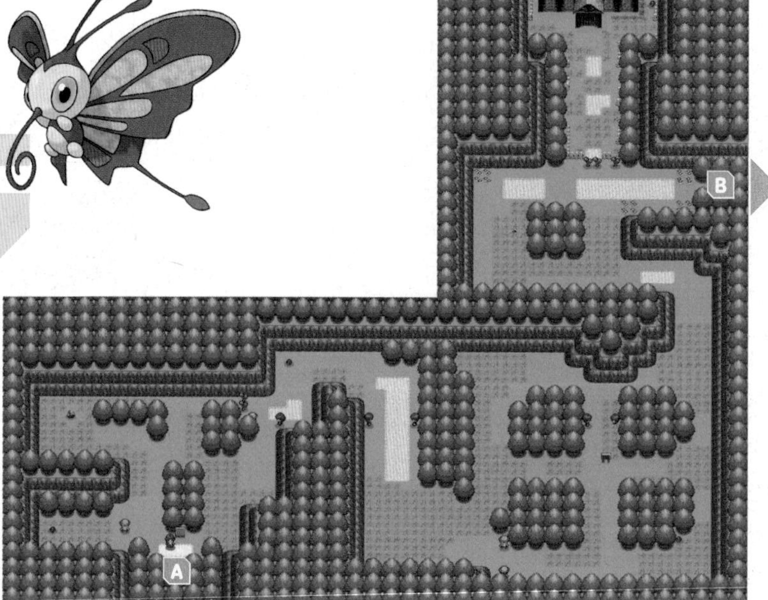

ROUTE 205 (TO ETERNA CITY)

ROUTE 205 (TO FLOAROMA TOWN)

OBTAINABLE ITEMS

ON YOUR FIRST VISIT

☐ Antidote	☐ Potion
☐ Parlyz Heal	☐ Honey
☐ Great Ball	

AFTER WINNING ETERNA CITY GYM BATTLE

☐ Elixer	☐ Cheri Berry
☐ Old Gateau	☐ Oran Berry x2
☐ TM90 Substitute	☐ Big Tree
☐ Dread Plate	☐ Silverpowder
☐ Razz Berry x2	☐ TM82 Sleep Talk
☐ Bluk Berry x2	

OUTSIDE OF ETERNA FOREST

Dustox
Bug-Poison
Abilities:
• Shield Dust

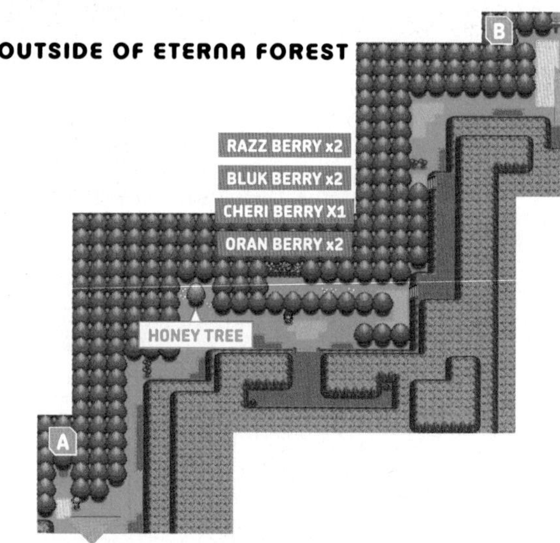

ROUTE 205 (TO ETERNA CITY)

ROUTE 205 (TO FLOAROMA TOWN)

IN GRASS

POKÉMON	M	D	N
Wurmple	◎	◎	○
Silcoon ♦	○	○	○
Cascoon ●	○	○	○
Murkrow ♦	✕	✕	○
Misdreavus ●	✕	✕	○
Budew	○	○	○
Buneary	○	○	○
Beautifly ♦	△	△	△
Dustox ●	△	△	△

OLD CHATEAU 2 FL

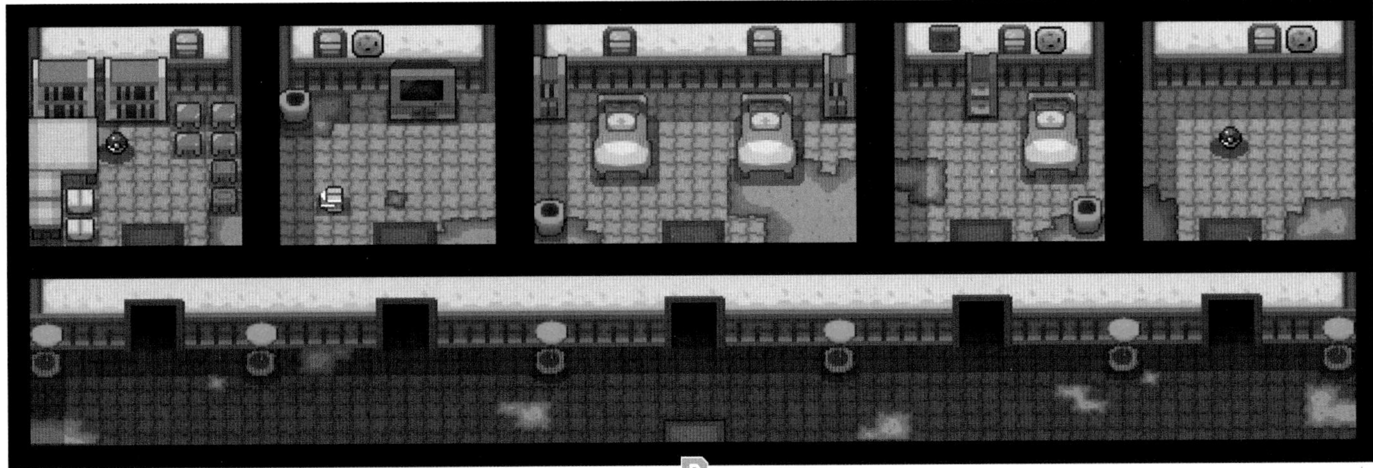

OLD CHATEAU 1 FL / DINING ROOM

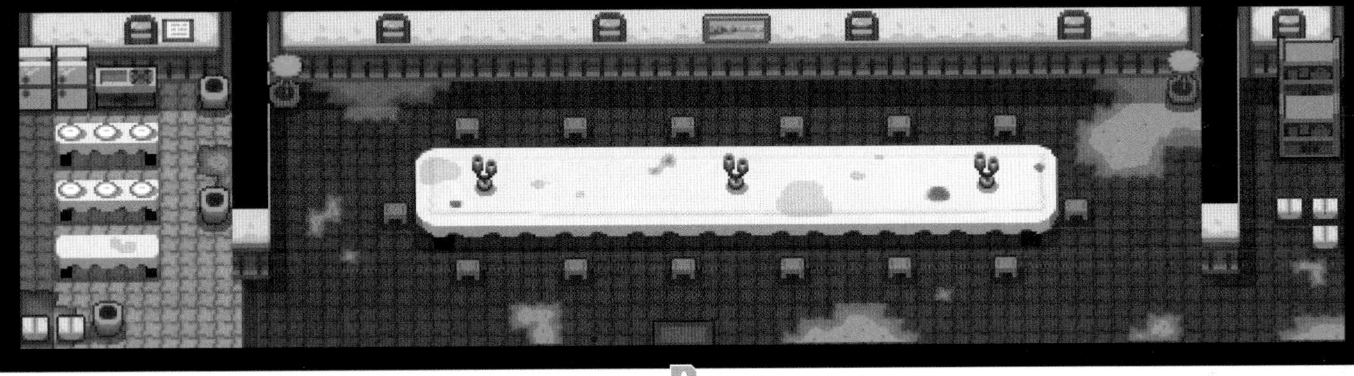

OLD CHATEAU

INSIDE CHATEAU

POKÉMON	M	D	N
Gastly	◎	◎	◎

Gastly
Ghost-Poison
Abilities:
- Levitate

CHERYL

STEP 1 PASS THROUGH THE FOREST WITH CHERYL

AS YOU ENTER THE FOREST, a woman named Cheryl speaks to you. She heard about Team Galactic roaming around the forest and got spooked. Do her (and yourself) a favor and accompany her to the exit of the forest.

Lucas decided to go with

CHERYL IS A GIVER

WHILE TRAVELING together in the forest, Cheryl will heal your Pokémon thoroughly after every battle. Not only can she restore their HP and PP, she can also cure special conditions like Sleep and Poison as well. It may be a good idea to take this opportunity to trick out your low-level Pokémon and earn them some experience points.

STEP 2 WILD POKÉMON DOUBLE UP

DURING THE TIME you're in the forest with Cheryl, you'll encounter two wild Pokémon at a time. Since every battle in the forest is a Double Battle, cooperate with Cheryl's Chansey and try to win every fight!

A wild BUDEW and
WURMPLE appeared!

BE PREPARED! THE PAIRED MUST BE UNPAIRED

THOSE PAIRED wild Pokémon you fight here can only be caught when they are unpaired. When you battle a Pokémon and see one you want, defeat its partner first and then throw a Poké Ball at your target.

STEP 3 SAY GOODBYE TO CHERYL

WHEN YOU REACH the exit of the forest, Cheryl thanks you and takes off. Keep going east and exit the forest. Eterna City is right around the corner! Pass through Route 205 and head to Eterna City.

Cheryl: Oh! There's the exit!
I'm so relieved... We finally got here.

MYSTERY MOSS

AT THE WEST exit of Eterna Forest, there is a strange rock covered with moss. This rock is needed for an Evolution of a Pokémon that you'll meet after you obtain the National Pokédex. When you have that Pokémon, come back again.

AFTER WINNING ETERNA CITY GYM BATTLE
GET TO THE MANSION IN THE FOREST USING CUT

USING HM01 CUT, chop down a tree and enter the Old Chateau. In the Chateau, you'll encounter Gastly, a Ghost-type Pokémon. It's totally immune to any Normal- or Fighting-type moves so don't use them.

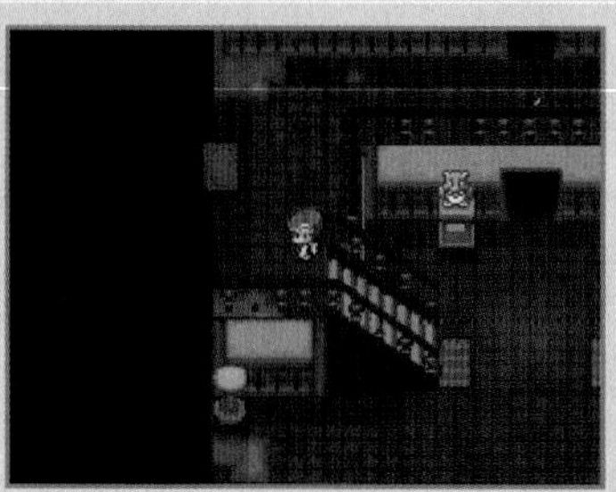

TREE'S A CROWD

You'll find certain trees in the Sinnoh region that give off a sweet fragrance. You can make them even more tempting to Pokémon by smearing Honey on them – you might even catch a rare Pokémon like Munchlax. It's certainly worth a try.

HOW TO HONEY UP YOUR POKÉMON

FIRST, SMEAR SOME HONEY on a honey tree and wait. After a while, a Pokémon will appear – some of the better trees can attract rare Pokémon. Try different trees until you find one that does the job well. But be aware – the effects from Honey last for only a day.

GET HONEY

You can buy it for 100 Poké Dollars from an Old Man in Floaroma Meadow.

GIVE IT SOME TIME

You can't catch them right away. Be patient. Give it about half a day.

POKÉMON THAT COME OUT FOR HONEY TREES

PROBABILITY	VERY OFTEN	SOMETIMES	RARELY	D/P VERSIONS
High	Wurmple	Combee	Munchlax	
	Silcoon	Burmy		Diamond Only
	Cascoon	Burmy		Pearl Only
	Combee	Cherubi		
	Burmy	Aipom		
	Cherubi	Heracross		
Low	Aipom	Wurmple		

HONEY UP AS MANY TREES AS YOU CAN!

THERE ARE APPROXIMATELY 20 honey trees in the Sinnoh region. Start with ones that are the easiest to spot. When a Pokémon appears sometimes the tree will shake. The bigger the shake is the more probable that a very rare Pokémon will appear.

LOCATIONS OF HONEY TREES

LOCATIONS	PAGE #
Route 205 x2	80
Route 206	104
Route 207	70
Route 208	108
Route 209	116
Route 210 x2	126
Route 211	96
Route 212 x2	152
Route 213	139
Route 214	139
Route 215	127
Route 218	72
Route 221	52
Route 222	192
Floaroma Meadow	76
Fuego Ironworks	81
Valley Windworks	84
Eterna Forest	86

ETERNA CITY

In Eterna City, modern buildings and ancient history exist side by side. But in recent years, Team Galactic established their headquarters here and constructed questionable buildings which are upsetting the townspeople.

ROUTE 205 (TO ETERNA FOREST)

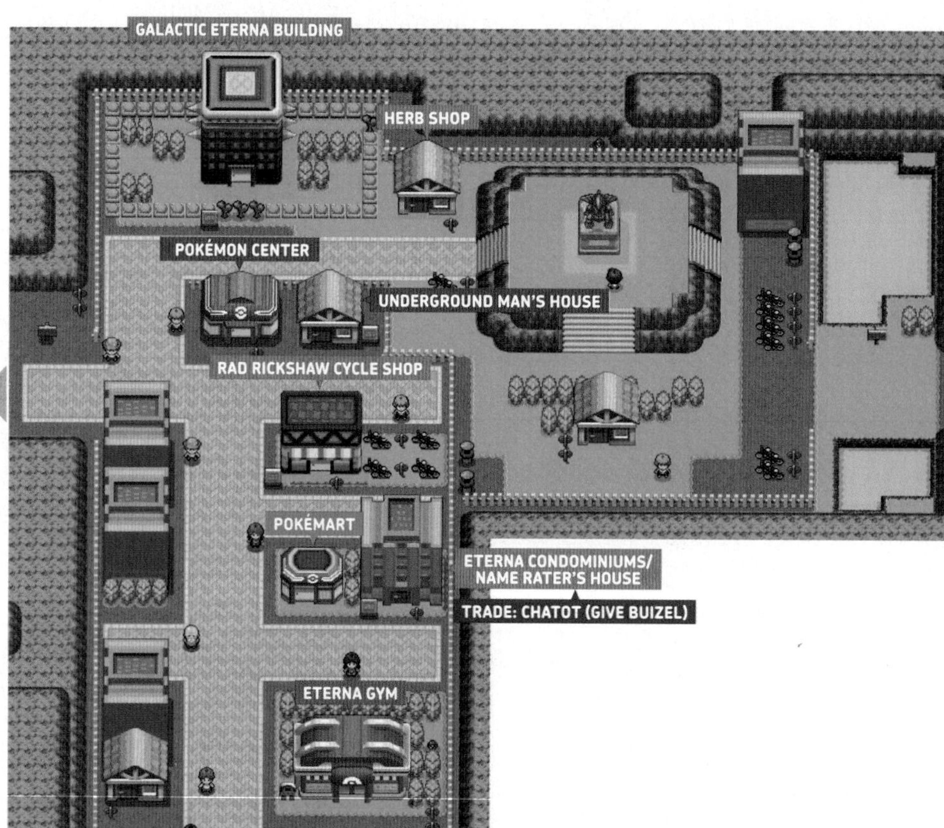

ROUTE 211 (TO MT. CORONET)

ROUTE 206 (TO CYCLING ROAD)

OBTAINABLE ITEMS

ON YOUR FIRST VISIT	
☐ Pokétch application Bonding Checker-Nature Checker	☐ Explorer Kit
	☐ Super Potion
	☐ TM67 Recycle
	☐ HM01 Cut

AFTER WINNING ETERNA CITY GYM BATTLE	
☐ Forest Badge	☐ TM86 Grass Knot
☐ TM46 Thief	

AFTER VISITING GALACTIC ETERNA BATTLE	
☐ Bicycle	☐ Exp. Share

ON WATER

POKÉMON	VARIABLE
Psyduck	◎
Golduck	○

FISHING

FISHING ROD	POKÉMON	VARIABLE
Old	Magikarp	◎
Good	Magikarp	◎
	Barboach	○

POKÉMART (MERCHANT ON THE LEFT)

Item	Price
Air Mail	50
Heal Ball	300
Net Ball	1000
Nest Ball	1000

HERB SHOP

Item	Price
Heal Powder	450
Energypowder	500
Energy Root	800
Revival Herb	2800

STEP 1 GET A POKÉTCH APP: FRIENDSHIP CHECKER

TALK TO THE WOMAN in Pokémon Center and she'll give you a Pokétch application called Friendship Checker. When you use the Checker and tap on the bottom screen, your Pokémon approach and let you know how happy they are.

STEP 2 THE NAME GAME

A MAN ON THE 1 FL of the Eterna Condominiums is a name rater - you can consult him about Pokémon names. You can change their nicknames as many times as you want.

Hello, hello!
I am the official Name Rater!

HE'S SUPER SLEEPY

THE SUPERINTENDENT of the building is on the 1 FL. If you speak to him between 12 am and 4 am, he is sleepy and unresponsive. During the day, though, he's much more alert and energetic.

STEP 3 GET THE EXPLORER KIT FROM UNDERGROUND MAN

UNDERGROUND MAN is the first person in the Sinnoh region who's tunneled underground, and he presents you with an Explorer Kit. Use it for the tasks he gives you - complete them and you'll become an excellent underground explorer. (see p. 246)

EXPLORER KIT

STEP 4 GET HM CUT

GO TO the Galactic Eterna Building and a woman will come to talk to you. She'll give you HM01 Cut and commend the mission you're on. But you won't be able to use HM01 Cut until after you defeat the Eterna City Gym battle.

Obtained the HM01!

WHO IS CYNTHIA?

CYNTHIA SAYS she's only a curious Pokémon Trainer who is studying ancient Pokémon. She also guesses that you're assisting Professor Rowan. Who is Cynthia, and where is she getting her information?

STEP 5 CHECK ON ROUTE 211

HEAD EAST of Eterna City and you will come to Route 211 which bisects Mt. Coronet. You can take Route 211 to try to enter Mt. Coronet, but you'll only get about halfway across because of a huge rock. Turn around and go back to Eterna City.

STEP 6 LOOK FOR THE BIKE SHOP MANAGER

RAD RICKSHAW'S CYCLE SHOP is the only bike shop available in the Sinnoh region. But they say that the shop manager has gone to the Galactic Eterna Building and hasn't returned. You'll need to use HM01 Cut to enter the Galactic Eterna Building so make sure to challenge and win the Eterna City Gym battle.

The manager's gone off to the Team Galactic building and hasn't returned.

GYM BATTLE 2

GARDENIA

ETERNA CITY GYM LEADER
POKÉMON TYPE: GRASS
RECOMMENDED TYPES: FIRE, FLYING

IN ETERNA GYM, there are 4 Trainers to deal with. Find three Trainers in hiding and fight them before you finally reach Gardenia. Her Pokémon are all Grass-type. Attack them with Fire-, Ice- and Flying-type moves. When you win, you'll get Forest Badge and TM86 Grass Knot.

FOREST BADGE

You can use HM01 Cut on the field. In case of a Pokémon raised by other Trainers, it will obey if it's under Lv30.

PARTY POKÉMON

POKÉMON	LEVEL	TYPE
Cherubi ♀	Lv19	Grass
Turtwig ♂	Lv19	Grass
Roserade ♀	Lv22	Grass-Poison

AFTER WINNING ETERNA CITY GYM BATTLE
SNEAK INTO THE GALACTIC ETERNA BUILDING

AFTER YOU BEAT Gardenia and obtain the Forest Badge, you will be able to use HM01 Cut and cut small trees. Sneak into the Galactic Eterna Building where the missing bike shop manager is, and see what is going on.

GO TO OLD CHATEAU BEFORE YOU GET THE BIKE

IF YOU TRY to go back to Route 205 after you've obtained the Bike, a boy will stop you. You no longer will be able to go back there at this point, so visit the Old Chateau before you get the Bike.

AFTER WINNING ETERNA CITY GYM BATTLE
GET THE BICYCLE FROM THE MANAGER OF THE BIKE SHOP

GO TO THE Bike Shop to see the manager, who is happy about getting back his Clefairy. He'll give you a Bicycle as a token of his gratitude. The Bike has a new gear-change mechanism.

RIDE EVERYWHERE

AT POKÉMON CENTERS or city entrances, they are bicycle lots, where you can easily hop on and off your Bike. Just press the A Button when you're near one of these lots.

AFTER OBTAINING THE BICYCLE
GET EXP. ALL FROM PROFESSOR ROWAN'S ASSISTANT

ENTER THE GATE that leads to Route 206 and you'll see Professor Rowan's lab assistant waiting for you. If you've seen more than 35 Pokémon, the assistant will give you Exp. Share. This number includes SEEN Pokémon, not the number caught so far.

EQUIP EXP. SHARE AND LEVEL UP FASTER

EXP. SHARE gives experience points to Pokémon that are not participating in battles. Equip this on weaker Pokémon that you don't bring out to battle so often.

AFTER OBTAINING THE BICYCLE
GO TO CYCLING ROAD

NEAR ROUTE 206 just north of Eterna City is a cycling road. Hop on the Bicycle that you got from the Bike Shop manager and go cycling.

CLEAR SIX TASKS AND GET FAMILIAR WITH THE UNDERGROUND

Underground Man is the first person in the Sinnoh region that started exploring Underground. He assigns you six tasks to see if you can become an excellent underground explorer. You will be rewarded with various items upon completion of each task. Go clear all of them.

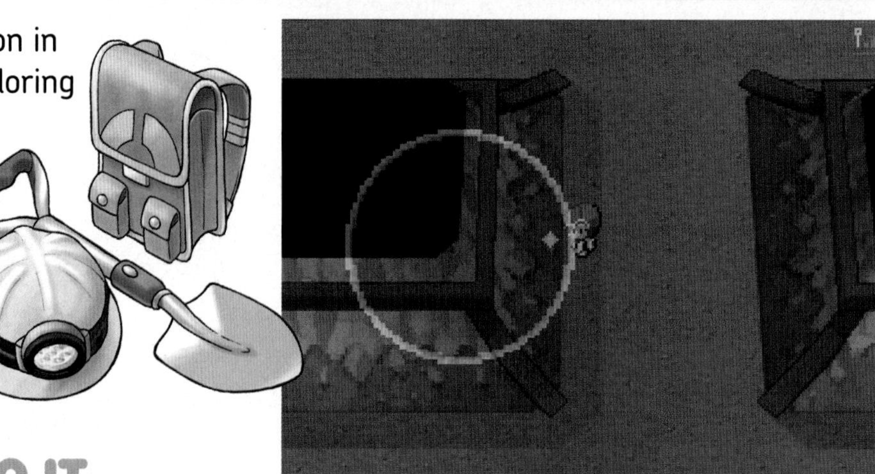

LET'S GET RIGHT ON IT

TASK 1 GET TO THE UNDERGROUND

Welcome to Sinnoh's Underground!

First things first - get to the Underground using the Explorer Kit. After checking things out, go back up to the 1 FL.

PRIZES Move Trap, Bubble Trap, Leaf Trap

TASK 2 DIG OUT A FOSSIL

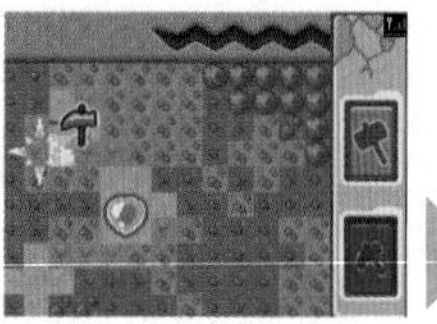

Check your underground radar and go to the spot shown in yellow. Tap the bottom screen and you'll locate where fossils are buried. Check on the wall that flashes and dig out the fossil using a hammer and pick.

PRIZES Prism Sphere, Red Sphere, Blue Sphere

TASK 3 BURY A SPHERE

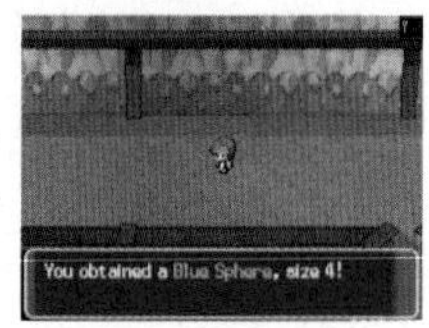

You obtained a Blue Sphere, size 4!

When you get down to the Underground, bury a sphere in the ground. The ball will grow while buried and will be much bigger when you dig it out later. Touch on the bottom screen to confirm where you buried it.

PRIZES Digger Drill

TASK 4 BUILD A SECRET BASE

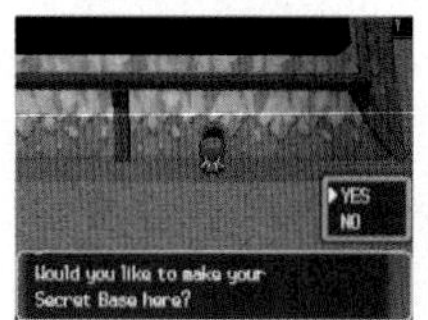

YES
NO
Would you like to make your Secret Base here?

In the Underground, you can build a secret base of your own. Pick a spot you like and build your secret base using the Digger Drill. At your secret base, you can have your own PC and a flag.

PRIZES Plain Table, Wooden Chair, Buneary Doll

TASK 5 DECORATE YOUR BASE

MOVE GOODS

Pick decoration goods stored on the PC and display them.

You can furnish your secret base and rearrange items to your liking. Put your reward goods from Task 4 (Plain Table, Wooden Chair, and Buneary Doll) where you want them.

PRIZES Chimchar Doll, Turtwig Doll, or Piplup Doll

TASK 6 SEIZE YOUR FRIEND'S FLAG

You've obtained the Flag from Lucas's Base!

Go Underground with your friend using the Nintendo DS Wireless Connection. Go to your friend's secret base, and seize their flag. Bring it to your secret base and complete your mission!

PRIZES Pretty Gem

POKÉMON THAT CHANGE UNDER CERTAIN CONDITIONS

Among the many different kinds of Pokémon living in the Sinnoh region are ones that are similar species, but have different appearances or features in accordance with their habitats and battle locations. Here, we take a look at Shellos and Burmy.

SHELLOS — THEY HAVE DIFFERENT APPEARANCES DEPENDING ON THEIR GEOGRAPHIC LOCATION

MT. CORONET, which stands in the center of the Sinnoh region, divides Shellos' habitats in two - the ones that live on the west side of the region are pink, as opposed to their eastern counterparts which are blue. In addition, they differ in the shape of their head and back as well. The same goes for their evolved version, Gastrodon - west side inhabitants look different from their eastern cousins.

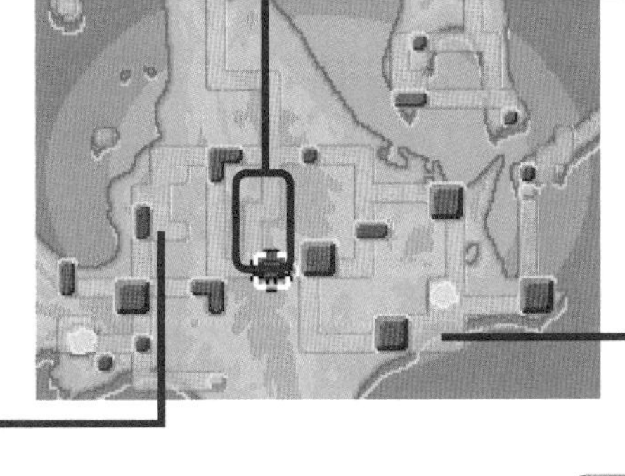

Shellos Pink
In West Sea
Main Location:
- Route 205

Shellos Blue
In East Sea
Main Location:
- Route 213

BURMY — BURMY TRANSFORM THEIR CLOAKS IN VARIOUS BATTLE LOCATIONS

BURMY CHANGE THE DESIGNS and effectiveness of their casing based on the topographic details of the battle site. They wear a Plant Cloak when fighting in grassy bush, a Sandy Cloak in a cave or on a craggy cliff, and a Trash Cloak on a hard, paved surface like in a building.

Go! BURMY!

Their cloaks change after the battle's over. Check their cloaks after the battle.

Burmy (Sandy Cloak)
Battle Locations:
- Caves
- Rocky Surface

Burmy (Plant Cloak)
Battle Locations:
- Grass
- Bushes

Burmy (Trash Cloak)
Battle Locations:
- In buildings

ROUTE 211

Route 211 is a mountain path that runs from east to west through Mt. Coronet, the biggest mountain in the Sinnoh region. You'll need HM06 Rock Smash and HM04 Strength to get to Celestic Town from Eterna City.

MOVES REQUIRED TO COMPLETE THIS AREA

CUT
ROCK SMASH
ROCK CLIMB
STRENGTH

OBTAINABLE ITEMS

ON YOUR FIRST VISIT

- ☐ TM12 Taunt

AFTER VISITING LAKE VERITY (SECOND TIME)

- ☐ Pecha Berry
- ☐ Iapapa Berry
- ☐ TM77 Psych Up
- ☐ Aspear Berry
- ☐ Grepa Berry

AFTER WINNING SNOWPOINT CITY GYM BATTLE

- ☐ TM29 Psychic

ROUTE 211 (ETERNA CITY SIDE)

MT. CORONET (SEE P.98)

ROUTE 211 (CELESTIC TOWN SIDE)

ROUTE 211 (ETERNA CITY SIDE)

IN GRASS

POKÉMON	M	D	N
Meditite	◎	◎	○
Bidoof	◎	◎	○
Geodude	○	○	○
Ponyta	○	○	○
Chingling	○	○	○
Zubat	☒	☒	○
Hoothoot	☒	☒	○

ROUTE 211 (CELESTIC TOWN SODE)

IN GRASS

POKÉMON	M	D	N
Meditite	◎	◎	◎
Graveler	○	○	○
Machoke	○	○	○
Chingling	○	○	○
Ponyta	○	○	△
Zubat	☒	☒	○
Noctowl	☒	☒	○

STEP 1 GO TO MT. CORONET

HEAD EAST from Eterna City and you'll come across Route 211. You will see an entrance to Mt. Coronet. It's a huge mountain that divides the Sinnoh region into east and west.

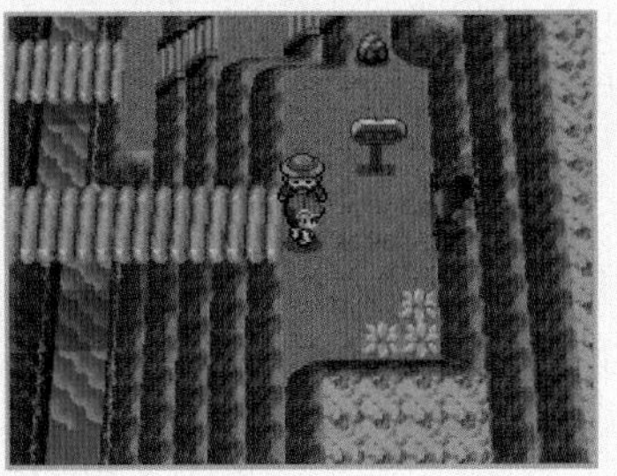

NINJA. BUSH. DUCK.

AS YOU ENTER Route 211 from Eterna City, you'll find a bush where a Ninja Boy is hiding. Find him.

STEP 2 GO BACK AND CHALLENGE GARDENIA

YOU'LL NEED TO be able to use HM04 Strength to pass through Mt. Coronet, but that won't happen for a while. Go back to Eterna City Gym to battle Gardenia, the Grass-type Gym Leader.

AFTER VISITING LAKE VERITY (SECOND VISIT) HEAD TO LAKE ACUITY THROUGH CELESTIC TOWN

GO AFTER Team Galactic, who by now have completed their nefarious plans in both Lake Valor and Lake Verity. Hurry to the third lake, Lake Acuity. Head to Celestic Town using HM02 Fly, then proceed west on Route 211 to Mt. Coronet. Enter the mountain.

Hoothoot
Normal-Flying
Abilities:
- Insomnia
- Keen Eye

Meditite
Fighting-Psychic
Abilities:
- Pure Power

MT. CORONET (1ST VISIT)

Mt. Coronet is the biggest mountain in the Sinnoh region. Inside the mountain are vast caves that connect Eterna City, Celestic Town, Oreburgh City, Hearthome City and Snowpoint City.

OBTAINABLE ITEMS

AFTER YOUR FIRST VISIT TO LAKE VERITY	
☐ Escape Rope	☐ Rare Candy
☐ TM69 Rock Polish	☐ Stardust
☐ Light Clay	☐ Soft Sand
☐ Revive	☐ Max Elixir
☐ Full Restore	

1 FL ❷

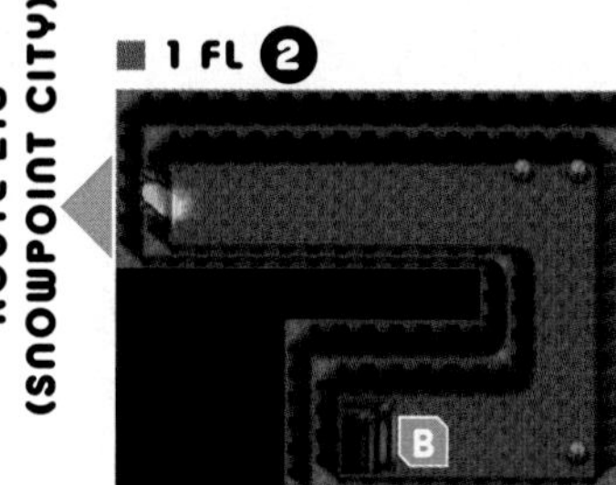

B1F

1 FL ❶ (ETERNA CITY CELESTIC TOWN)

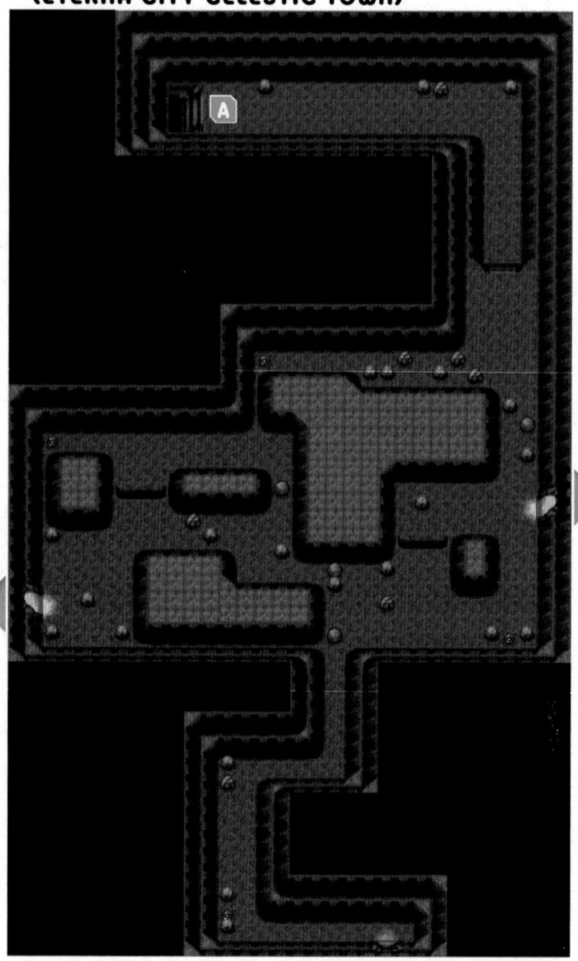

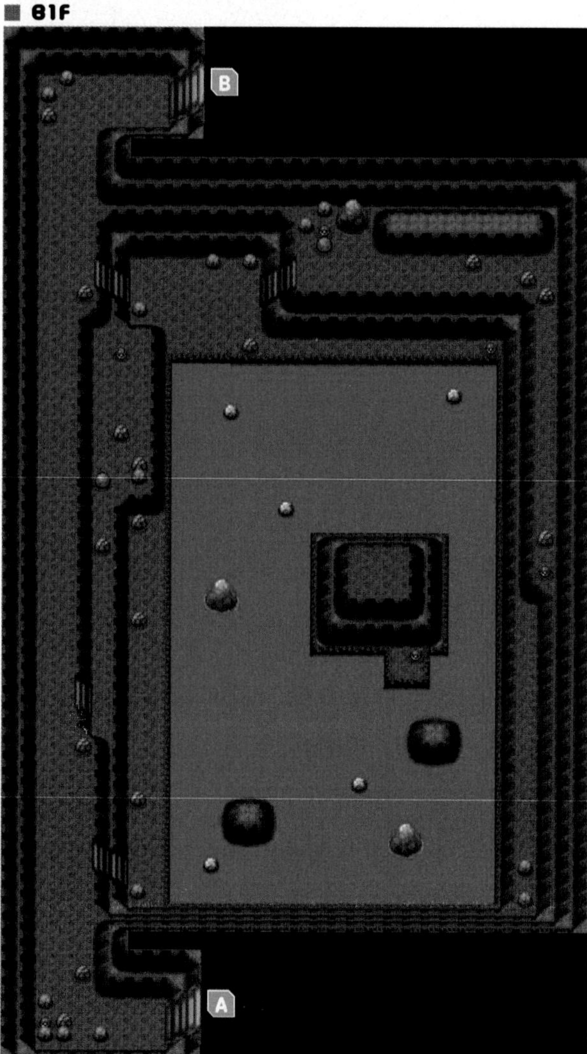

1 FL (OREBURGH CITY-HEARTHOME CITY)

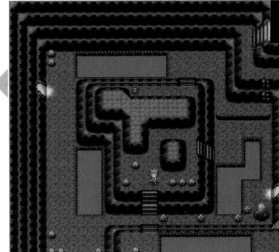

ROUTE 207 (TO OREBURGH CITY)

ROUTE 208 (TO HEARTHOME CITY)

B1F

IN CAVE

POKÉMON	M	D	N
Meditite	○	○	○
Graveler	○	○	○
Clefairy	○	○	○
Golbat	○	○	○
Machoke	○	○	○
Chingling	○	○	○

ON WATER

POKÉMON	VARIABLE
Zubat	◎
Golbat	○

FISHING

FISHING ROD	POKÉMON	VARIABLE
Old	Magikarp	◎
Good	Magikarp	◎
	Barboach	○

1 FL ❶

IN CAVE

POKÉMON	M	D	N
Geodude	○	◎	◎
Meditite	○	○	○
Machop	○	○	○
Zubat	○	○	○
Chingling	○	○	○
Cleffa	○	△	△

1 FL ❷

IN CAVE

POKÉMON	M	D	N
Meditite	○	○	○
Graveler	○	○	○
Clefairy	○	○	○
Golbat	○	○	○
Machoke	○	○	○
Chingling	○	○	○

1 FL ❸

IN CAVE

POKÉMON	M	D	N
Geodude	○	◎	◎
Meditite	○	○	○
Machop	○	○	○
Zubat	○	○	○
Chingling	○	○	○
Cleffa	○	△	△

ON WATER

POKÉMON	VARIABLE
Zubat	◎
Golbat	○

FISHING

FISHING ROD	POKÉMON	VARIABLE
Old	Magikarp	◎
Good	Magikarp	◎
	Barboach	○

Clefairy
Normal
Abilities:
- Cute Charm
- Magic Guard

Cleffa
Normal
Abilities:
- Cute Charm
- Magic Guard

STEP 1 ROUTE 211 WILL TAKE YOU TO THE MOUNTAIN

YOU'LL GET the first opportunity to enter the mountain when you come out of Route 211 on the Eterna City side. You'll need HM04 Strength to pass through, but you can't use it yet. Go back to Eterna City.

AFTER OBTAINING THE BICYCLE MEET THE MYSTERY MAN

WHEN YOU TAKE Route 207 (the closest route to Oreburgh City) into the mountain, a blue-haired man approaches you. He tells you there's a theory that the entire Sinnoh region started here at Mt. Coronet, and then he leaves. Who is he?

According to one theory, Mt. Coronet is where the Sinnoh region began.

WHO IS THE MYSTERIOUS MAN WHO SPEAKS TO YOU?

THIS BLUE-HAIRED strange man sounds as if he knows you. Have you met him before? Or is he related to somebody you know?

AFTER OBTAINING THE BICYCLE PROCEED TO THE EXIT THAT LEADS TO ROUTE 208

AFTER THE MYSTERIOUS man leaves, keep heading towards the exit on Route 208. Use the stairs so that you'll be able to get out of the cave without having to use HMs. When you come out to Route 208, head east to Hearthome City.

AFTER OBTAINING THE BICYCLE YOU WILL NEED HM SURF TO GO FURTHER INTO THE CAVE

YOU CAN PROCEED even deeper on the passageway in Mt. Coronet that connects Route 207 with Route 208, but only if you have HM03 Surf and HM08 Rock Climb. But if you don't, don't fret, just keep going east past the mountain.

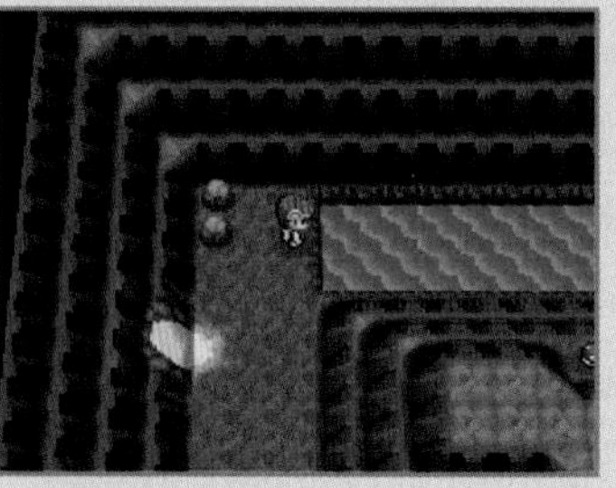

YOU'LL BE BACK, CHASING SOMEONE

AFTER VISITING all three lakes, Lake Valor, Lake Verity and Lake Acuity, you will come back to Mt. Coronet hot on the heels of the Team Galactic boss. This time, use HM03 Surf and HM08 Rock Climb and proceed to the back.

AFTER VISITING LAKE VERITY
PROCEED TO THE BACK OF THE CAVE USING HM STRENGTH

ENTER MT. CORONET from Celestic Town side. Go north using HM04 Strength and you will find a way to the B1F that is covered with a thick fog. Clear the fog using HM05 Defog and proceed further into the back.

▶YES
NO
Would you like to use Strength?

USE STRANGE CANDY EFFECTIVELY

RARE CANDY is an item that elevates Pokémon's level by 1 and can be found here in Mt. Coronet or Wayward Cave. This is a very rare item so you don't want to just toss it into their mouth easily unless you are in an absolutely critical situation.

AFTER VISITING LAKE VERITY
BLOCKED BY A ROCK

TAKE ROUTE 211 into Mt. Coronet. On the ground floor, there is a path that is blocked by a rock which you could move to the south side if you had the move HM04 Strength. This path leads to the innermost area of the cave called the Spear Pillar. You can't go there from this side anyway so don't bother. Keep moving.

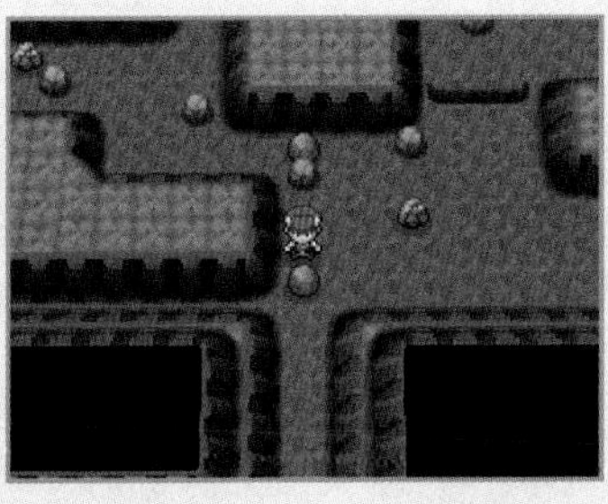

AFTER VISITING LAKE VERITY
PASS THROUGH TO SNOW-COVERED ROUTE 216

PROCEED TO THE BACK on a foggy B1F then take a stairway up to the 1 FL where you'll find an exit to outside. You will come to Route 216 which is covered with white snow all over. Keep going on the snow-falling Route 216 towards Lake Acuity.

GALACTIC ETERNA BUILDING

Galactic Eterna Building is a suspicious, questionable building that has been the talk of the town since Team Galactic moved into the area. As a matter of fact, the store manager of a bicycle shop has mysteriously disappeared lately. Sneak into the building to find him.

■ 4 FL

■ 3 FL

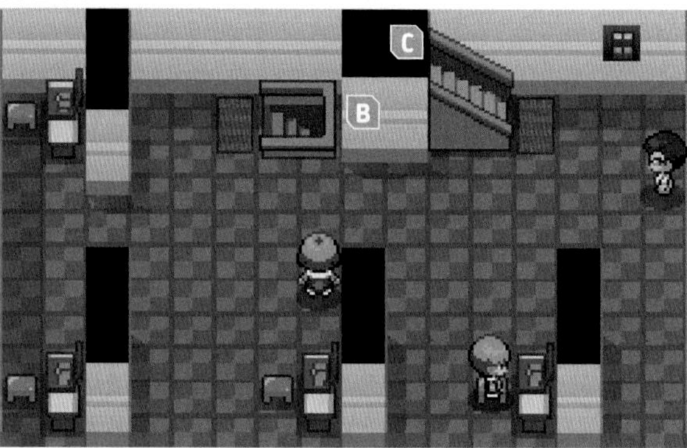

■ 2 FL

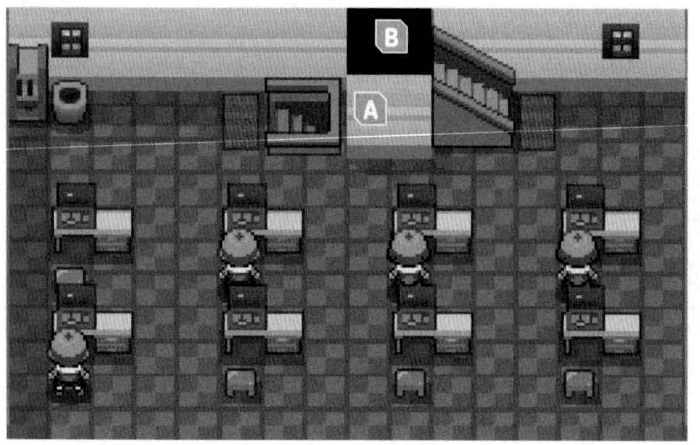

■ 1 FL

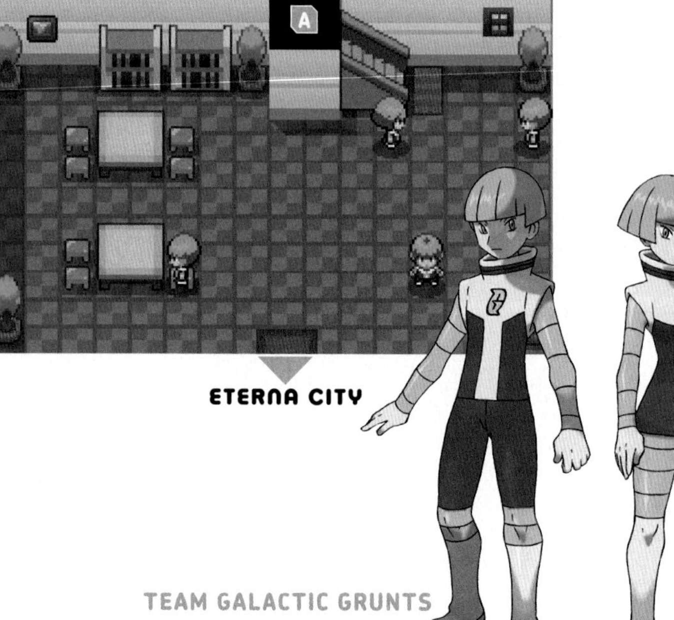

TEAM GALACTIC GRUNTS

FIGHT YOUR WAY UP TO THE 4 FL

THE GALACTIC ETERNA BUILDING is a four-story building. Each floor contains a Team Galactic grunt that's itchin' to fight, so be prepared, When you reach the 4 FL, you'll find the Team Galactic Commander, Jupiter, holding the Bike Shop manager hostage.

Your meddling won't be tolerated!

THAT GIRL IS POISON

THE POKÉMON that Team Galactic will employ are mostly Poison- and Bug-types. Chances are they'll come at you with moves that will give you the Poison condition, so be prepared and carry extra Antidote with you.

GALACTIC COMMANDER #1

JUPITER
TEAM GALACTIC COMMANDER

JUPITER, a Team Galactic Commander, will use Zubat and Skuntank. Either Electric-, Ice-, Psychic-, or Rock-type moves will be very effective on Zubat. On Skuntank, Ground-type moves are going to be most effective.

PARTY POKÉMON

POKÉMON	LEVEL	TYPE
Zubat ♀	Lv 18	Poison-Flying
Skuntank ♀	Lv 20	Poison-Dark

RESCUE THE BIKE SHOP MANAGER

WHEN YOU DEFEAT Jupiter, she leaves the building with a parting shot hinting about Legendary Pokémon and her boss. Rescue the Bike Shop manager and leave the building.

I got my CLEFAIRY back, and it's all thanks to you!

THE MANAGER IS LOOKING FOR HIS CLEFAIRY

IT TURNED OUT to be that the Bike Shop manager had come to the building to take back his Clefairy, which had been absconded by Team Galactic. Remember the kid at the Pokémon Center that told you about his Buneary being stolen? That Pokémon is here also.

ROUTE 206, WAYWARD CAVE

Route 206 is also known as the Cycling Road. Take a vigorous run on a paved street on your Bicycle. Under the Cycling Road is an entrance to the Wayward Cave.

OBTAINABLE ITEMS

ON YOUR FIRST VISIT	
☐ Flag	☐ Razz Berry x 2
☐ Full Heal	☐ Burn Heal
☐ Super Repel	☐ Rawst Berry x 2
☐ Poison Barb	☐ Escape Rope
☐ Rare Candy	☐ TM32 Double Team

AFTER WINNING CANALAVE CITY GYM BATTLE	
☐ Max Ether	☐ Grip Claw
☐ Revive	☐ TM26 Earthquake

ROUTE 206

IN GRASS

POKÉMON	M	D	N
Stunky ◆	◎	◎	◎
Geodude ◆	○	○	○
Geodude ●	◎	◎	◎
Ponyta	◎	◎	○
Bronzor	○	○	○
Kricketot	○	✕	✕
Kricketune	○	○	○
Zubat	✕	✕	○

ROUTE 206

ETERNA CITY

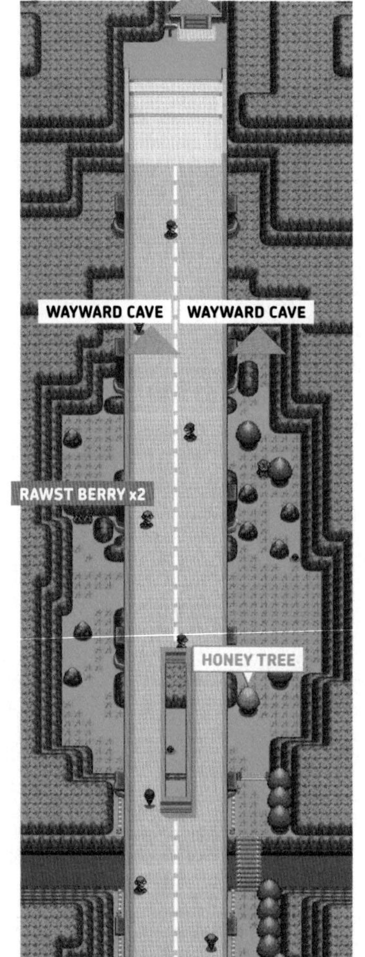

ROUTE 207
(TO OREBURGH CITY)

Kricketune
Bug
Abilities:
• Swarm

■ WAYWARD CAVE, 1 FL

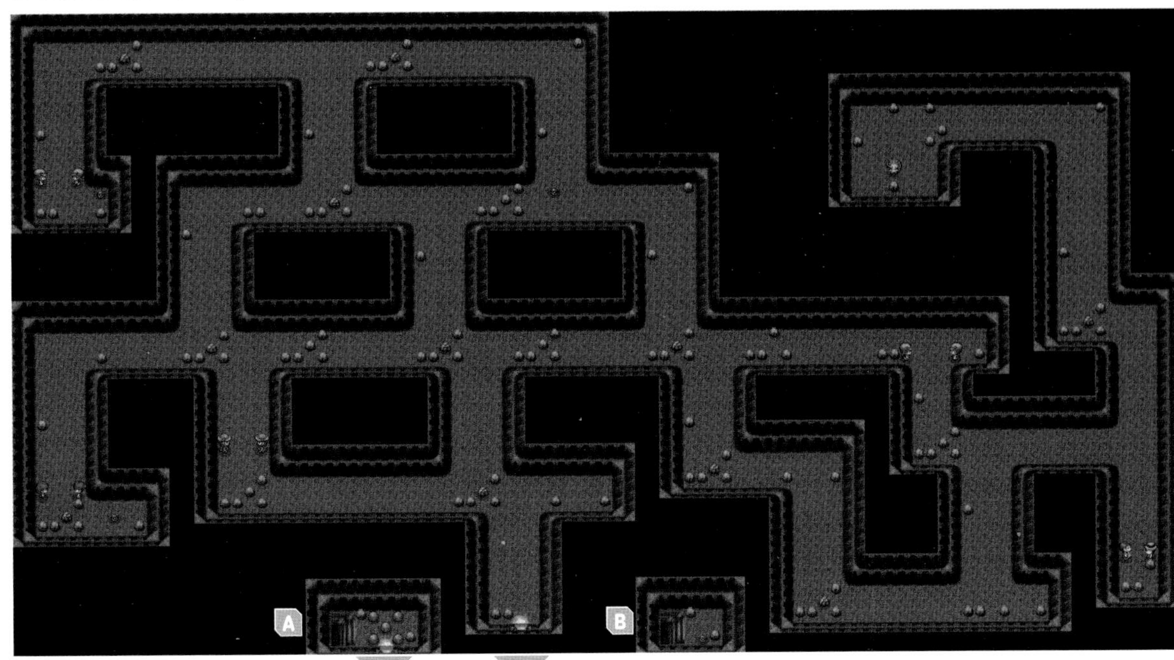

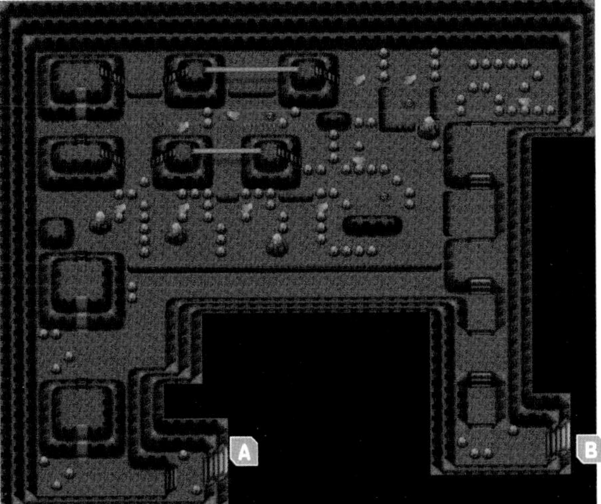

Bronzor
Steel-Psychic

Abilities:
- Levitate
- Heatproof

■ WAYWARD CAVE

B1F

POKÉMON	M	D	N
Bronzor	◎	◎	◎
Zubat	◎	◎	◎
Geodude	○	○	○
Gible	○	○	○

1 FL

POKÉMON	M	D	N
Bronzor	◎	◎	◎
Zubat	◎	◎	◎
Geodude	○	○	○

Gible
Dragon-Ground

Abilities:
- Sand Veil

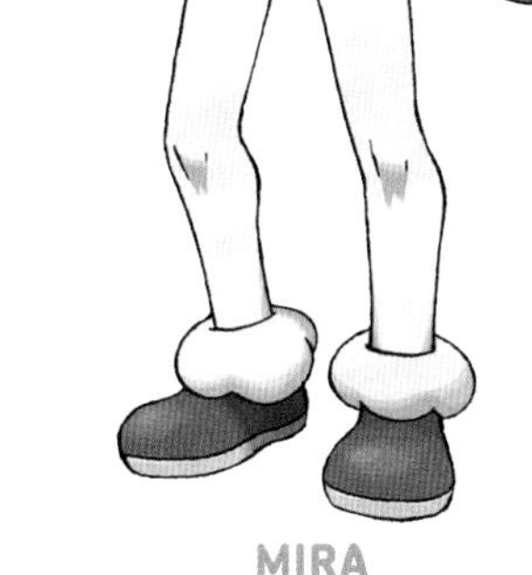

MIRA

STEP 1 RUN THROUGH ON CYCLING ROAD

WHEN YOU GET TO ROUTE 206 from Eterna City, you automatically mount your Bicycle. Cycling Road is all downhill, so you can take make the journey in one swift ride from Eterna City all the way to the south gate. Battle other Pokémon Trainers on the way.

GET YOUR FLAG ON

AS YOU RIDE your Bike south on Cycling Road, a woman at the gate will give you an accessory - a Flag. Use it in the Super Contest or to accesorize your Pokémon for the photo shoot at the Jubilife TV station.

STEP 2 ENTER THE WAYWARD CAVE

RIGHT BELOW THE CYCLING ROAD is an entrance to the Wayward Cave. When you ride your Bicycle down to the south gate, dismount, then proceed towards Wayward Cave on foot. Chop down trees in your way using HM01 Cut. After a while you will get to the entrance of the cave.

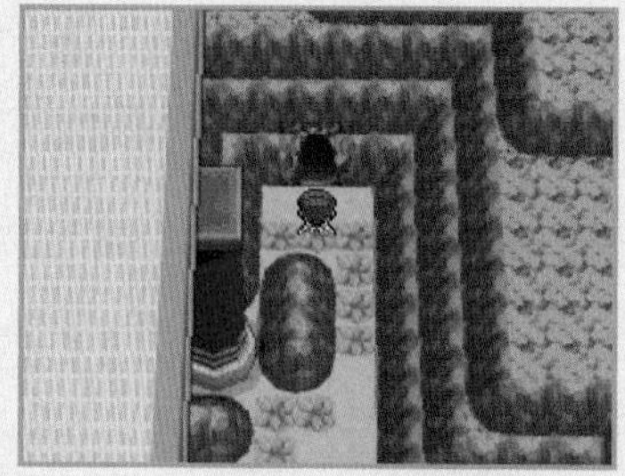

STEP 3 LIGHT UP THE CAVE WITH FLASH

THE CAVE IS DARK and mostly unnavigable. Use TM70 Flash and light up the cave. Now you can see more clearly and travel around in the cave more easily.

SHINX used Flash!

YOU CAN GET FLASH AT OREBURGH GATE

YOU'LL NEED TEACH your Pokémon Flash - which you can obtain at Oreburgh Gate. Remove rocks with HM06 Rock Smash, then go to the back of the passageway and find it.

STEP 4 HELP MIRA EXIT

IN THE TOP RIGHT SECTION of the 1 FL of the cave is a lost Pokémon Trainer named Mira. Travel with her and accompany her to the exit. She will heal your Pokémon's PP and HP, as well as special conditions, so battle as much as possible with her at your side.

Please!
Please take me to the exit!

MIRA WILL BATTLE WITH HER KADABRA

FOR SOMEONE LOST and scared, Mira proves to be a tough warrior. She and her Kadabra will prove to be a huge helping hand.

TAKE ROUTE 207 TO MT. CORONET

HEAD SOUTH ON ROUTE 206 and you will get to Route 207, which leads to Mt. Coronet. This is the place you couldn't access from the Oreburgh City side before because of the hill of shifting sand. You can now proceed if you have the Bicycle.

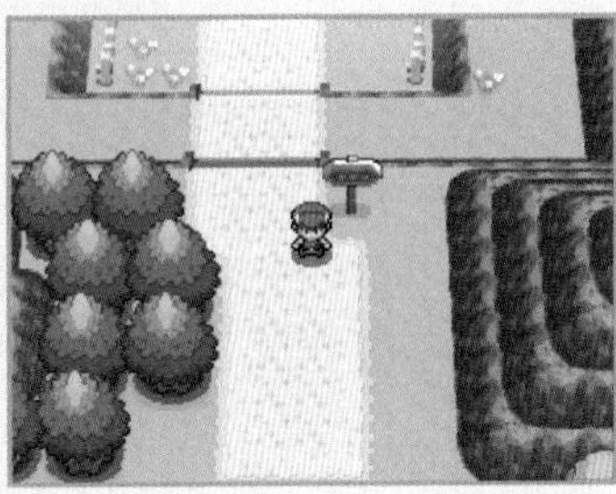

REST IN OREBURGH CITY

BEFORE HEADING to Mt. Coronet, go south on Route 207 and make a quick stop at Oreburgh City. You can heal your wounded Pokémon at the Pokémon Center there.

AFTER WINNING CANALAVE CITY GYM BATTLE
ENTER THE WAYWARD CAVE THROUGH A HIDDEN ENTRANCE

THERE IS ANOTHER HIDDEN ENTRANCE to Wayward Cave. Proceed north in an invisible place under Cycling Road and find the entrance. When you enter the cave, you'll see a rock blocking the path. Use HM04 Strength and remove it.

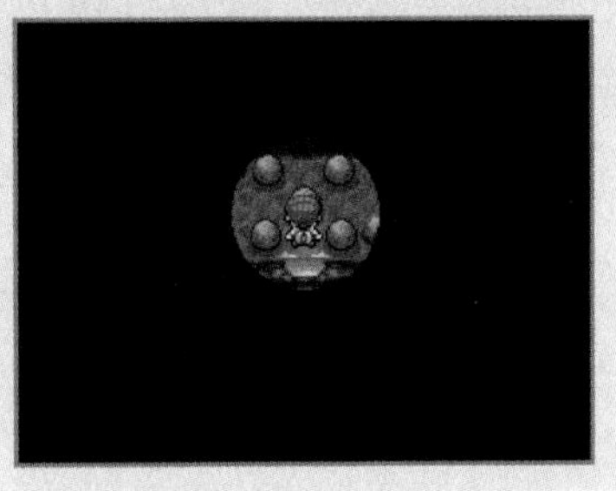

AFTER WINNING CANALAVE CITY GYM BATTLE
UTILIZE YOUR BIKE GEARS

ON THE B1F IN WAYWARD CAVE, you will proceed to the back by jumping over the jump stand on your Bicycle. The length of the jump is determined by which gear you're in. Setting it to third gear lets you jump for one length, while fourth gear lets you jump for two.

ROUTE 208

Route 208 consists of dangerous, steep mountain roads and a grassy path that is rich with thick green tree leaves. Go past Mt. Coronet and keep heading east, and eventually you'll reach Hearthome City. On your way, you'll come across the Berry Master's house, who'll give you one berry every day.

MOVES REQUIRED TO COMPLETE THIS AREA

- ROCK SMASH
- SURF
- ROCK CLIMB
- WATERFALL

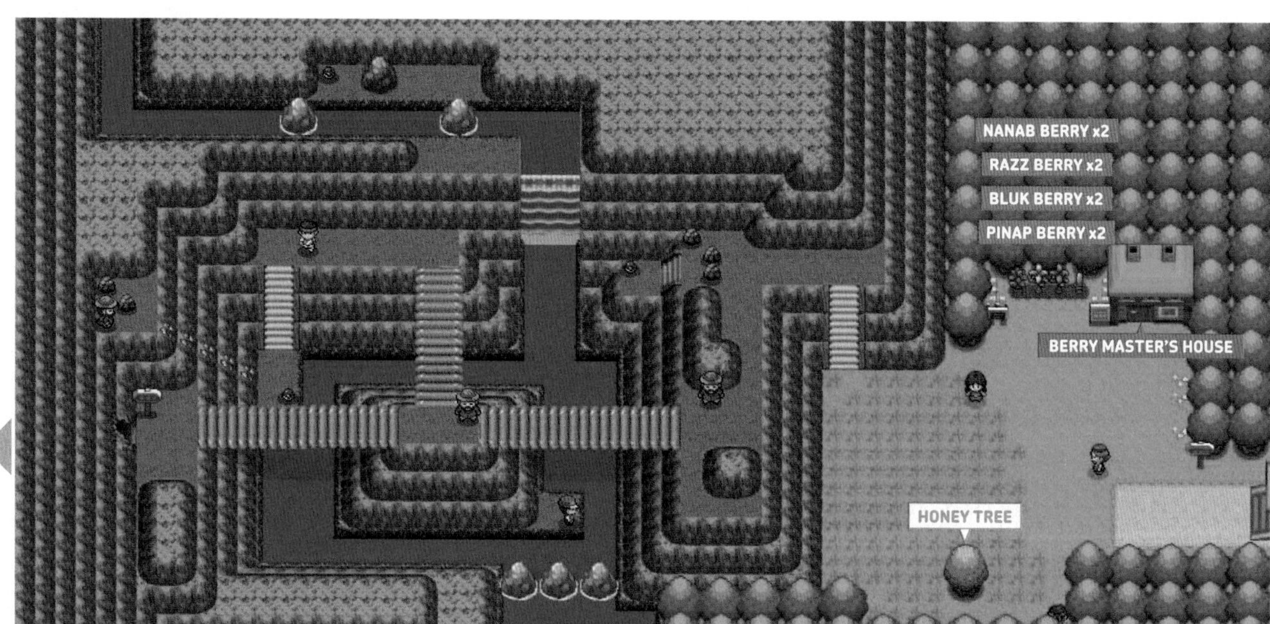

OBTAINABLE ITEMS

ON YOUR FIRST VISIT

☐ X Speed	☐ A Poké Ball
☐ Nanab Berry x2	☐ Razz Berry x2
☐ Bluk Berry x2	☐ Pinap Berry x2
☐ A Pokétch application: Berry Searcher	☐ Odd Keystone

AFTER WINNING SUNYSHORE CITY GYM BATTLE

☐ Carbos

BERRY MASTER'S HOUSE

Growth Mulch	200
Damp Mulch	200
Stable Mulch	200
Gooey Mulch	200

IN GRASS

POKÉMON	M	D	N
Psyduck	◎	◎	◎
Bidoof	○	○	○
Meditite	○	○	○
Machop	○	○	○
Bibarel	○	○	○
Zubat	✕	✕	○

ON WATER

POKÉMON	VARIABLE
Psyduck	◎
Golduck	○

FISHING

FISHING ROD	POKÉMON	VARIABLE
Old	Magikarp	◎
Good	Magikarp	◎
	Barboach	○

Bibarel
Normal-Water

Abilities:
- Simple
- Unaware

STEP 1 GET A POKÉTCH APPLICATION – BERRY SEARCHER

SPEAK TO A GIRL in the Berry Master's house. She'll ask you if you're the type that always forgets where you've buried your berries. If you answer yes, she'll give you the Berry Searcher. It's a Pokétch application that tells you where you've buried your berries.

I feel a sort of kinship with you!
You can have this Pokétch app!

GET BERRIES FROM BERRY MASTER

THE BERRY MASTER gives you one berry a day. Raise them in the soft soil – they will be very useful. You can equip them on your Pokémon and use them in battles, or use them to make Poffin to improve your Pokémon's condition.

STEP 2 BUY MULCH FOR YOUR BERRIES

THERE IS A WOMAN in the Berry Master's house who sells mulch, which can be used to regulate the berry growing process. Mulch can keep the soil from getting too dry, or it can also make the berries take longer to grow and ripe.

Um... Would you like some Mulch?

STEP 3 GET ODD KEYSTONE FROM A PERSON IN HIDING

THERE IS A MYSTERIOUS MAN who is hiding behind a tree south of the Berry Master's house. Speak to him and he'll give you the Odd Keystone. You can use this Odd Keystone on a broken stone tower on Route 209 (see p.118).

Obtained the Odd Keystone!

RESTORE THE BROKEN TOWER

WHEN YOU PUT the Odd Keystone on a broken stone tower on Route 209, it turns into a Spirit Tower. Who was the man who gave you the Odd Keystone? And what did he say about going to an underground passageway?

STEP 4 HEAD TO HEARTHOME CITY

HEAD EAST ON ROUTE 208 and you will come to Hearthome City. Hearthome City has facilities like the Pokémon Super Contest Hall and Amity Square where you can enjoy various activities with your Pokémon. Take your favorite Pokémon and participate in these events.

HEARTHOME CITY

Hearthome City is known as a friendly town where people and Pokémon congregate at fun places like the Contest Hall or Amity Square. If you don't know where those facilities are, ask a man for help. He'll show you around.

OBTAINABLE ITEMS

ON YOUR FIRST VISIT	
☐ Pokémon Egg	☐ Shell Bell
☐ Poffin Case	☐ Glitter Powder
☐ Tuxedo / Dress	☐ Mild Poffin
☐ TM43 Secret Power	☐ Spooky Plate
☐ TM45 Attract	

AFTER WINNING HEARTHOME CITY GYM BATTLE	
☐ Relic Badge	☐ TM65 Shadow Claw

POKÉMART	
Heart Mail	50
Heal Ball	300
Net Ball	1000
Nest Ball	1000

AMITY SQUARE

HEARTHOME CITY

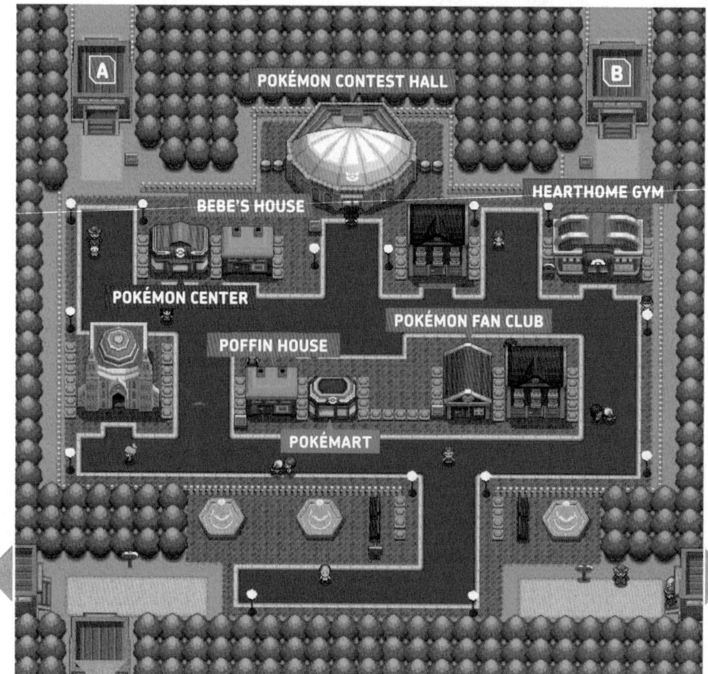

ROUTE 208 (TO MT. CORONET)

ROUTE 209 (TO SOLACEON TOWN)

ROUTE 212 (TO PASTORIA CITY)

CAPTURE KEIRA'S BUNEARY

ENTER THE TOWN from Route 208 and suddenly a Buneary comes running your way. It looks like it may have escaped from a Poké Ball. Capture it for its owner, Keira, who just so happens to be a Contest Judge. She'll thank you and leave, asking you to stop by the Contest Hall later.

Baby BUNEARY, back into the Poké
Ball you go!

GET A POKéMON EGG FROM A HIKER

BEFORE HEADING TO ROUTE 209 a hiker will give you a Pokémon Egg in front of the gate. He says he found it at a Pokémon Day Care in Solaceon Town. It contains a rare Pokémon called Happiny.

EGGS – THEY'RE WHAT'S GOOD FOR YOU

ADD THE POKéMON EGG to your party and continue with your adventure. As long as your party remains healthy and intact, the Egg will eventually hatch into a Pokémon.

WILL YOU STAY, BERRY POFFINS?

TALK TO THE PRESIDENT of the Pokémon Fan Club and he'll give you a Poffin Case. A Poffin case is a container that you store Poffin in. Poffin is a new type of Pokémon food that is made from berries. Go visit the Poffin House for details.

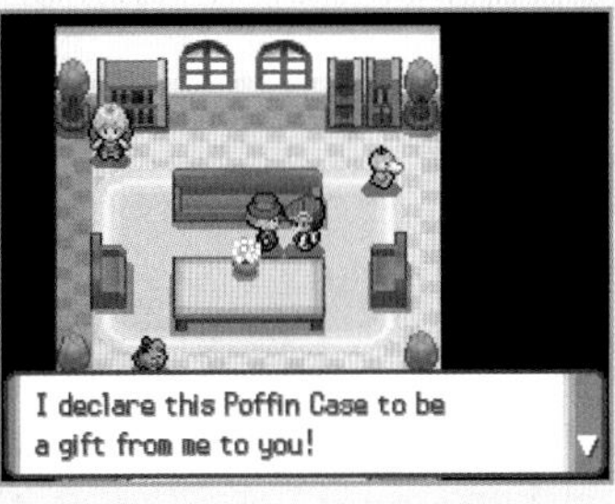

I declare this Poffin Case to be
a gift from me to you!

KNOW HOW HAPPY YOUR POKéMON ARE

SPEAK TO A WOMAN at the Pokémon Fan Club and she'll tell you how happy your Pokémon (the first one in the front of your party) is with you. It's helpful information if you have a Pokémon whose Evolution depends on its happiness. Check in with her from time to time.

MAKE POFFIN AT THE POFFIN COOKING HOUSE

YOU CAN MAKE a Pokémon's new favorite food, Poffin, at the Poffin House. Put your berries in the soup and stir it up – but be careful not to spill it or burn it.

Here you may cook Berries and
turn them into Poffins.

4 PLAYERS CAN POP SOME POFFINS

USING THE NINTENDO DS Wireless Connection, you can play with up to three people to cook Poffin together. With more ingredients, you and your friends can make Poffin of higher quality.

STEP 5 MEET BEBE, A PC ADMINISTRATOR

NEXT TO THE POKÉMON CENTER is the house of a PC administrator named Bebe, who is in charge of Pokémon Box. After you talk to her, the PC will now be shown as Bebe's PC (instead of Someone's PC) every time you access it.

That means you're using Pokémon

THE INITIAL PC WAS CREATED BY BILL

THE POKÉMON PC that Bebe has improved was originally invented by Bill of the Johto region. The two speak in a similar dialect so they may be from the same hometown.

STEP 6 GET ITEMS FROM MR. GOODS

THE NAME OF THE MAN you meet south of Bebe's house is Mr. Goods. He makes it his passion and life's purpose to discover all of the rare things in this world. When you speak to him after meeting certain conditions, he'll present you with a rare item (see p.119).

I'll find something rare for you,
so talk to me some other time.

THE SHELL BELL RESTORES HP

A WOMAN in a condominium next to the Pokémon Fan Club will give you the Shell Bell, a convenient battle item which slightly restores your Pokémon's HP after it causes some damage to your opponent.

STEP 7 YOU DON'T HAVE TO BE NASTY ABOUT IT

TALK TO FANTINA, the Gym Leader, in front of the Contest Hall, but she'll brush you off telling you to come back later when you get much better. Don't worry – you'll face her after your visit to Celestic Town. For now, just relax and take a stroll around the town.

You're questioning why, and the
answer is: she's not here.

STEP 8 GET CLOTHES FROM YOUR MOM

ENTER THE CONTEST HALL and you'll bump into Keira and your mom. Keira will give you Glitter Powder as a reward for catching her Buneary earlier. Your mom will give you a Tuxedo (or Dress, depending on who you chose to be) to wear for the contest.

MOM KNOWS HER STUFF

YOUR MOM is at the Contest Hall and it seems that she comes here to Hearthome City a lot. Actually, you can see from the way she talks to one of the judges, Keira, that she is very talented and skilled.

COMPETE IN A POKéMON SUPER CONTEST

AT THE CONTEST HALL, you can participate in a competition using your Pokémon. The contest consists of three different rounds which are Visual (appearance), Dance, and Performance. You should step aside from the tension of battling for a minute and enjoy this event.

OK! Your Pokémon has been accepted for entry!

THE MASTER MOM?

FANTINA, the Gym Leader of Hearthome Gym, and Jasmine, the Gym Leader from Johto region participate in the Masters' Rank of the Pokémon Super Contest. Surprise, surprise - your mom also competes in this rank! And, all three of them have amazing skills!

TAKE A STROLL THROUGH AMITY SQUARE

PROCEED TO THE NORTH of town where you'll come across two gates that lead to Amity Square. You can take the following Pokémon for a walk there: Pikachu, Clefairy, Psyduck, Pachirisu, Happiny, Buneary, or Drifloon. Enjoy the walk - you need a break.

POKéMON MAKE BERRY GOOD WALKERS

WHILE WALKING in Amity Square with your Pokémon, they may occasionally pick up accessories and berries. The berries they find are very rare ones that can only be found here (see p.277).

BATTLE YOUR RIVAL 2

Compared to the first battle on Route 203, your rival now has four Pokémon, all at Level 19 or higher.

IF YOUR STARTER WAS TURTWIG: YOUR RIVAL WILL CHOOSE:

POKéMON	LEVEL	TYPE
Starly ♂	Lv 19	Normal-Flying
Buizel ♂	Lv 20	Water
Roselia ♂	Lv 20	Grass-Poison
Monferno ♂	Lv 21	Fire-Fighting

IF YOUR STARTER WAS CHIMCHAR: YOUR RIVAL WILL CHOOSE:

POKéMON	LEVEL	TYPE
Starly ♂	Lv 19	Normal-Flying
Roselia ♂	Lv 20	Grass-Poison
Ponyta ♂	Lv 20	Fire
Prinplup ♂	Lv 21	Water

IF YOUR STARTER WAS PIPLUP: YOUR RIVAL WILL CHOOSE:

POKéMON	LEVEL	TYPE
Starly ♂	Lv 19	Normal-Flying
Buizel ♂	Lv 20	Water
Ponyta ♂	Lv 20	Fire
Grotle ♂	Lv 21	Grass

GO TO ROUTE 209 AND THE LOST TOWER

AFTER YOU'RE DONE with your rival, go under the gate on the east side of town and head to Route 209. There you'll find the Lost Tower where you obtain HM04 Strength. You'll also find the broken stone tower that needs the Odd Keystone.

AFTER VISITING HEARTHOME TOWN
FINALLY — FANTINA IS GOING DOWN

IN ORDER FOR YOU to be able to use HM03 Surf, you'll need to get the Relic Badge which belongs to the Hearthome City Gym. When you get back to Hearthome City from Celestic Town, the Gym Leader, Fantina is back in the Gym. Go challenge her.

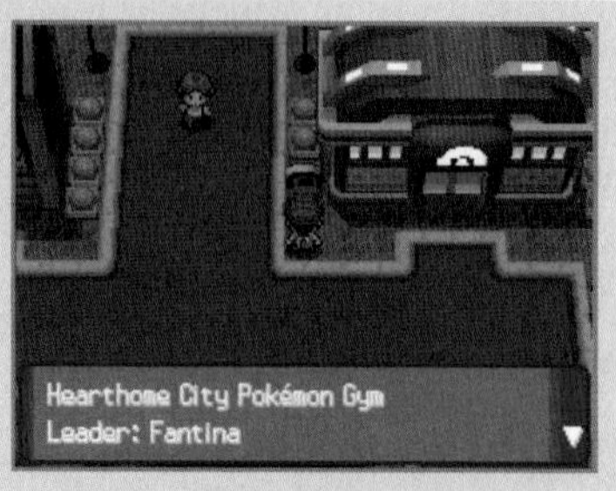

GYM BATTLE 5

FANTINA
HEARTHOME CITY GYM LEADER
POKÉMON TYPE: GHOST
RECOMMENDED TYPES:
GHOST, DARK

IN HEARTHOME CITY GYM, you'll be solving a quiz on each floor, proceed to the room of the correct answer and in the end face off against Fantina. There are 8 Trainers in the Gym but if you answer correctly to all the questions, you don't have to battle any of them. Fantina sends out Ghost-type Pokémon. Do her a huge damage by using Ghost- or Dark-type moves. When you win, you get the Relic Badge and also TM65 Shadow Claw.

RELIC BADGE:
You can use HM03 Surf.

POKÉMON IN THE PARTY

POKÉMON	LEVEL	TYPE
Drifblim ♀	Lv32	Ghost-Flying
Gengar ♀	Lv34	Ghost-Poison
Mismagius ♀	Lv36	Ghost

2FL

4FL

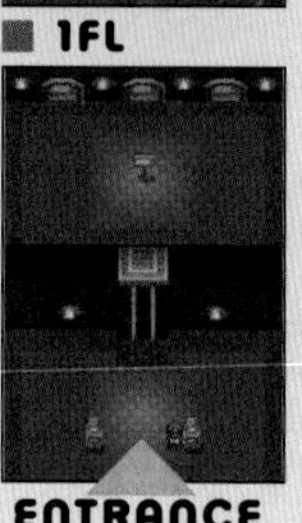

1FL

3FL

ENTRANCE

AFTER WINNING HEARTHOME CITY GYM BATTLE
TALK TO CYNTHIA, THEN HEAD TO CANALAVE CITY

WHEN YOU COME OUT OF THE GYM after you've defeated Fantina, Cynthia will approach you. She'll recommend that you go to a library in Canalave City, informing you that this will help complete your Pokédex. Take Route 218 to Canalave City.

Cynthia: I'm so glad to see you!
You're not very easy to track down.

TRAVEL AROUND USING HM03 SURF

WHEN YOU GET the Relic Badge from Fantina, you'll be able to use HM03 Surf in the field. Now you can travel across oceans and ponds that were inaccessible before. Make sure to check out all bodies of water as you come across them in your journeys.

POKÉMON THAT HAVE UNIQUE MOVES AND SPECIAL ATTRIBUTES

Amongst the new types of Pokémon inhabiting the Sinnoh region, there are ones that have unique moves. Chatot, for instance, speaks human languages and Cherrim blooms and shows a different face when the weather is sunny. Let's take a close look at these two Pokémon.

CHATOT

SPEAK HUMAN LANGUAGES WITH CHATTER!

Chatot learns a move called Chatter when it reaches Level 21. Every time you use this move Chatot speaks. Choose the move Chatter and talk into the Nintendo DS microphone. Chatot learns the words you speak, and from that point on, will speak every time you use the move.

HOW CHATOT LEARNS HOW TO SPEAK A LANGUAGE

CHOOSE THE MOVE CHATTER

TALK INTO A MICROPHONE

CHATOT SPEAKS!

CHERRIM

SUNNY DAY LETS CHERRIM BLOSSOM AND SHOW ITS FACE!

Cherrim normally is in bud and its face is hidden. But if you use the move Sunny Day, it bursts through the bud and shows its face. You can teach this move to Cherub when it reaches Level 22. After it's learned this move, level it up to Level 25 and let it evolve into Cherrim.

HOW CHERRIM BLOSSOMS

USE THE MOVE SUNNY DAY

THE SUNSHINE INTENSIFIES...

CHERRIM CHANGES ITS APPEARNACE!

ROUTE 209, THE LOST TOWER

MOVES REQUIRED TO COMPLETE THIS AREA

CUT SURF

On Route 209 where the river runs among meadows, forests, and a grassy field, you'll find the Lost Tower, which was dedicated to the spirits of Pokémon who have passed on. Head over there – it's rumored that Fantina trains there often.

OBTAINABLE ITEMS

ON YOUR FIRST VISIT

- ☐ Honey
- ☐ X Accuracy
- ☐ Chesto Berry
- ☐ TM47 Steel Wing
- ☐ Oval Stone
- ☐ TM27 Return
- ☐ HM04 Strength
- ☐ Good Rod
- ☐ Leppa Berry
- ☐ Razz Berry x2
- ☐ Calcium
- ☐ Revive
- ☐ Cleanse Tag

AFTER WINNING HEARTHOME CITY GYM BATTLE

- ☐ TM19 Giga Drain

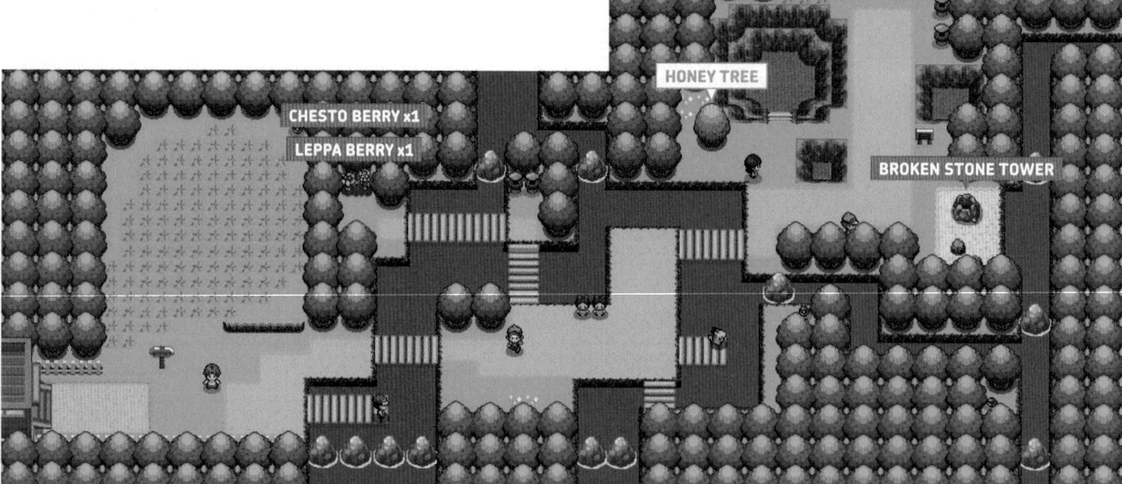

IN GRASS

POKÉMON	M	D	N
Bibarel	◎	◎	◎
Starly	○	○	○
Staravia	○	○	○
Mime Jr. ◆	○	△	△
Bonsly ●	○	△	△
Chansey	△	△	△
Gastly	⊗	⊗	○
Zubat	⊗	⊗	○

ON WATER

POKÉMON	VARIABLE
Psyduck	◎
Golduck	○

FISHING

FISHING ROD	POKÉMON	VARIABLE
Old	Magikarp	◎
Good	Magikarp	◎
	Goldeen	○

Chansey
Normal
Abilities:
- Natural Cure
- Serine Grace

THE LOST TOWER, 3 FL

THE LOST TOWER, 5 FL

Murkrow
Dark-Flying
Abilities:
• Insomnia
• Super Luck

THE LOST TOWER, 2 FL

THE LOST TOWER, 4 FL

Misdreavus
Ghost
Abilities:
• Levitate

THE LOST TOWER, 1 FL

ROUTE 209

THE LOST TOWER, 1 FL, 2 FL

IN GRASS

POKÉMON	M	D	N
Gastly	◎	◎	◎
Zubat	◎	◎	◎
Murkrow ♦	✕	✕	○
Misdreavus ●	✕	✕	○

THE LOST TOWER, 3 FL

IN GRASS

POKÉMON	M	D	N
Gastly	◎	◎	◎
Zubat	◎	◎	◎
Golbat	▲	▲	▲
Murkrow ♦	✕	✕	○
Misdreavus ●	✕	✕	○

THE LOST TOWER, 4 FL

IN GRASS

POKÉMON	M	D	N
Gastly	◎	◎	◎
Zubat	◎	◎	◎
Golbat	△	△	△
Murkrow ♦	✕	✕	○
Misdreavus ●	✕	✕	○

THE LOST TOWER, 5 FL

IN GRASS

POKÉMON	M	D	N
Gastly	◎	◎	◎
Zubat	◎	◎	◎
Golbat	○	○	○
Murkrow ♦	✕	✕	○
Misdreavus ●	✕	✕	○

STEP 1 GET THE GOOD ROD FROM A FISHERMAN

ON THE BRIDGE in the middle of Route 209 you'll meet a fisherman who'll give you the Good Rod. It catches more kinds of Pokémon than the Old Rod. Try to catch Goldeen near the fisherman.

Lucas obtained
the Good Rod!

PIKACHU, IS THAT YOU?

YOU'LL SEE Pikachu standing on the edge of a bridge on Route 209. Speak to it and it turns out to be a Pokémon Trainer pretending to be a Pokémon. Hmmm...some Trainers have some really special abilities!

STEP 2 USE THE ODD KEYSTONE

IN THE MIDDLE OF ROUTE 209 is a broken stone tower. Set the Odd Keystone that you got on Route 208 into the stone tower. It turns the broken stone tower into a Hallowed Tower.

The stone tower has been restored!
"Hallowed Tower" is written on it.

STEP 3 GO INTO THE LOST TOWER

NORTH OF ROUTE 209, there is the Lost Tower, in which the spirits of deceased Pokémon rest. This five story tower is inhabited by Ghost- and Dark-type Pokémon. Battle your way to the upper floors.

STEP 4 GET HM04 STRENGTH ON THE 5 FL

ON THE 5 FL of the tower you'll see an old lady who'll give you HM04 Strength. But you won't be able to use it in the field until you win the Canalave City Gym battle and obtain the Mine Badge.

Obtained the HM04!

GET CLEANSE TAG AND THEN GET HOME SAFE

YOU CAN GET the Cleanse Tag on the 5 FL of the Lost Tower, which will help you avoid encounters with wild Pokémon. If your Pokémon are hurt or weakened because of constant battling, let the first Pokémon in your party hold this before you start your way back outside.

STEP 5 LEAVE AND GO TO SOLACEON TOWN

AFTER YOU'VE OBTAINED HM04 STRENGTH, get out of the tower and head for Solaceon Town, where there are facilities like a Day Care where a rare Pokémon Egg was found, and caves like the Solaceon Ruins, which are inhabited by the Pokémon Unown - all of which are very important for the completion of the Sinnoh Pokédex.

BONSLY AND MIME JR. APPEAR!

YOU'LL COME ACROSS Bonsly and Mime Jr. in the bush on Route 209, but Bonsly only appears in Pokémon Diamond, and Mime Jr. appears only in Pokémon Pearl. Trade with your friends and get them both.

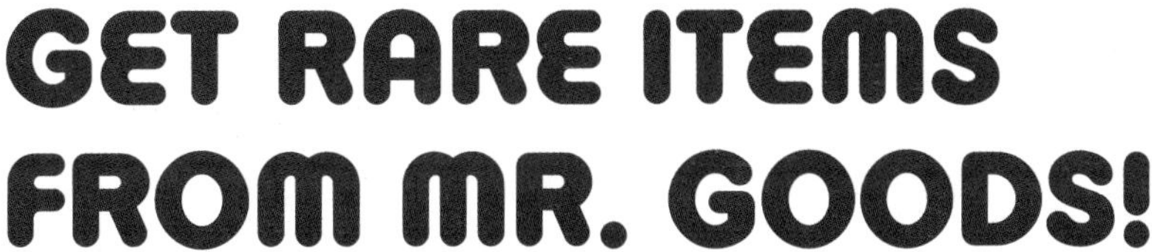

GET RARE ITEMS FROM MR. GOODS!

For progressing in your journey or your winning a grand prize in a contest, Mr. Goods in Hearthome City will reward you with decorative goods, very rare items that are only available there. There are 11 of them in total obtainable before you achieve the Hall of Fame. Work hard and get all of them.

DECORATE YOUR SECRET BASE WITH ITEMS MR. GOODS GIVES YOU

FIRST FULFILL CERTAIN CONDITIONS and talk to Mr. Goods. Then he will give you the items. Once you've obtained them, Use them to decorate your secret base and show them off to your friends.

For a Trainer like you, I have just the thing!

If there are more than 1 condition that you've fulfilled, talk to him as many times as possible until there is nothing left for him to give you.

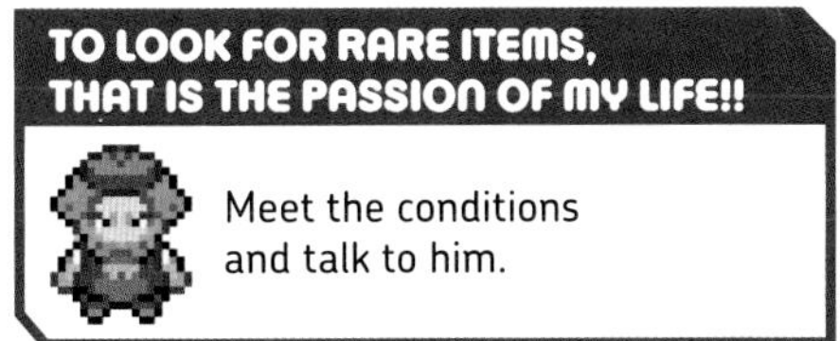

TO LOOK FOR RARE ITEMS, THAT IS THE PASSION OF MY LIFE!!

THE ITEMS AND CONDITIONS

BEFORE THE HALL OF FAME

ITEMS	CONDITIONS
GLOBE	Use Nintendo Wi-Fi Connection system at GTS in Jubilife City
GYM STATUE	Obtain all 8 Gym badges
CUTE CUP	Win a grand prize in Cute Contest in Super Contest Master Class
COOL CUP	Cool Contest
BEAUTY CUP	Beauty Contest
TOUGH CUP	Tough Contest
SMART CUP	Clever Contest
BLUE CRYSTAL	Greet 100 people in Underground
PINK CRYSTAL	Give decorative items to 100 people in Underground
RED CRYSTAL	Dig out 100 fossils (fossils & Rare Bone) in the Underground
YELLOW CRYSTAL	Trap 100 people in Underground

SOLACEON TOWN, SOLACEON RUINS

Solaceon Town has a very mild climate where both humans and Pokémon can have an easy, peaceful life. There is a Pokémon Day Care, a Pokémon newspaper company, and ahead past a thicket, is the Unown-filled Solaceon Ruins.

SOLACEON TOWN

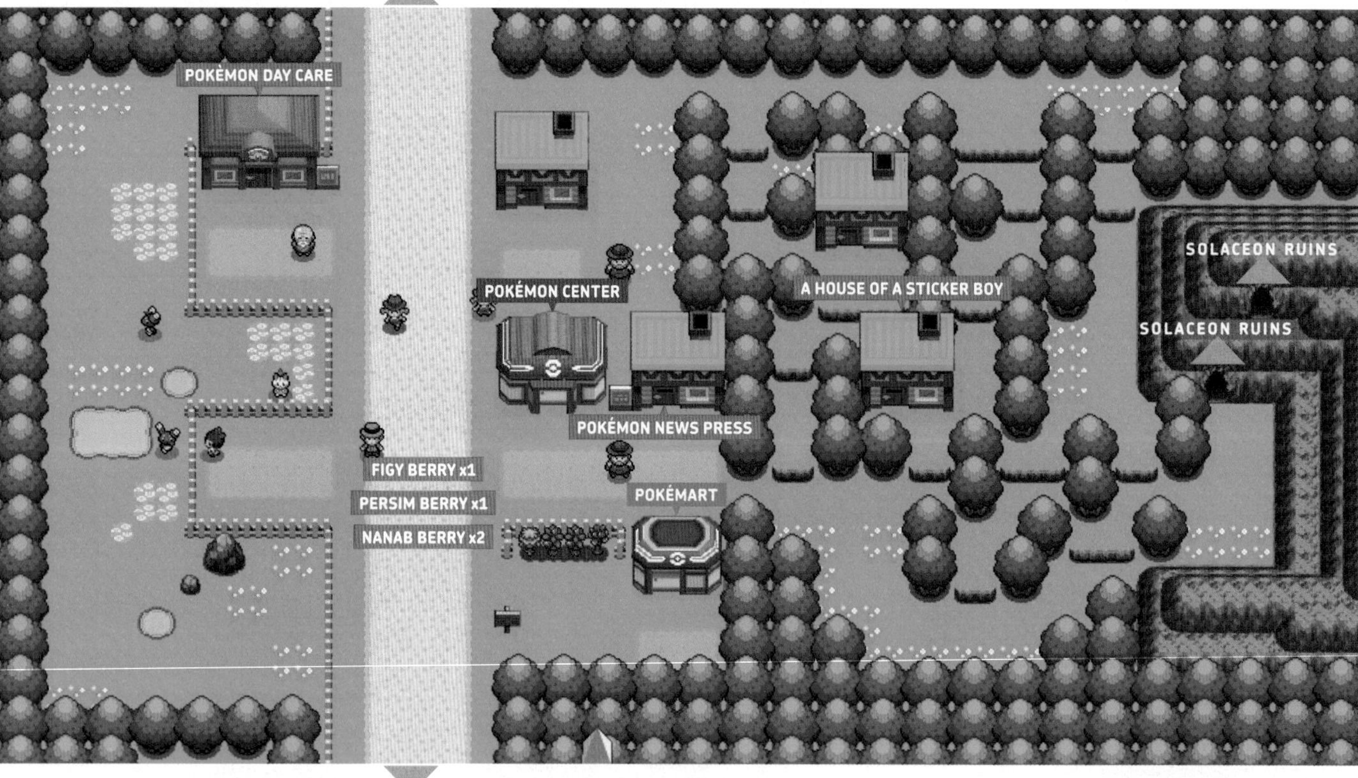

OBTAINABLE ITEMS

ON YOUR FIRST VISIT	
☐ Persim Berry	☐ Nanab Berry x2
☐ Figy Berry	☐ A Pokétch application Pokémon History
☐ A Pokétch application Day Care Checker	☐ Sticker Case
☐ Nugget	☐ Rare Candy
☐ Mind Plate	☐ Odd Incense

AFTER SHOWING YOUR UNOWN TO THE STICKER KID	
☐ A~Z Sticker x10	☐ ! Sticker x10
☐ ? Sticker x10	

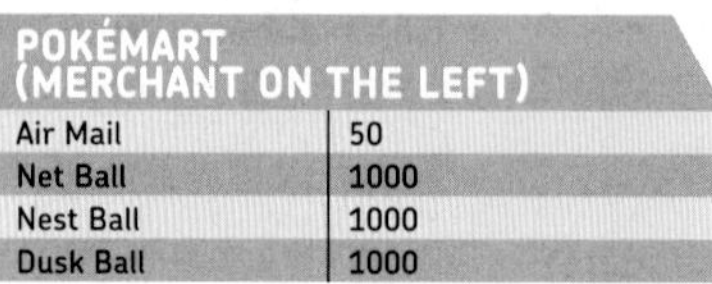

POKÉMART (MERCHANT ON THE LEFT)	
Air Mail	50
Net Ball	1000
Nest Ball	1000
Dusk Ball	1000

Unown
Psychic
Abilities:
• Levitate

SOLACEON RUINS

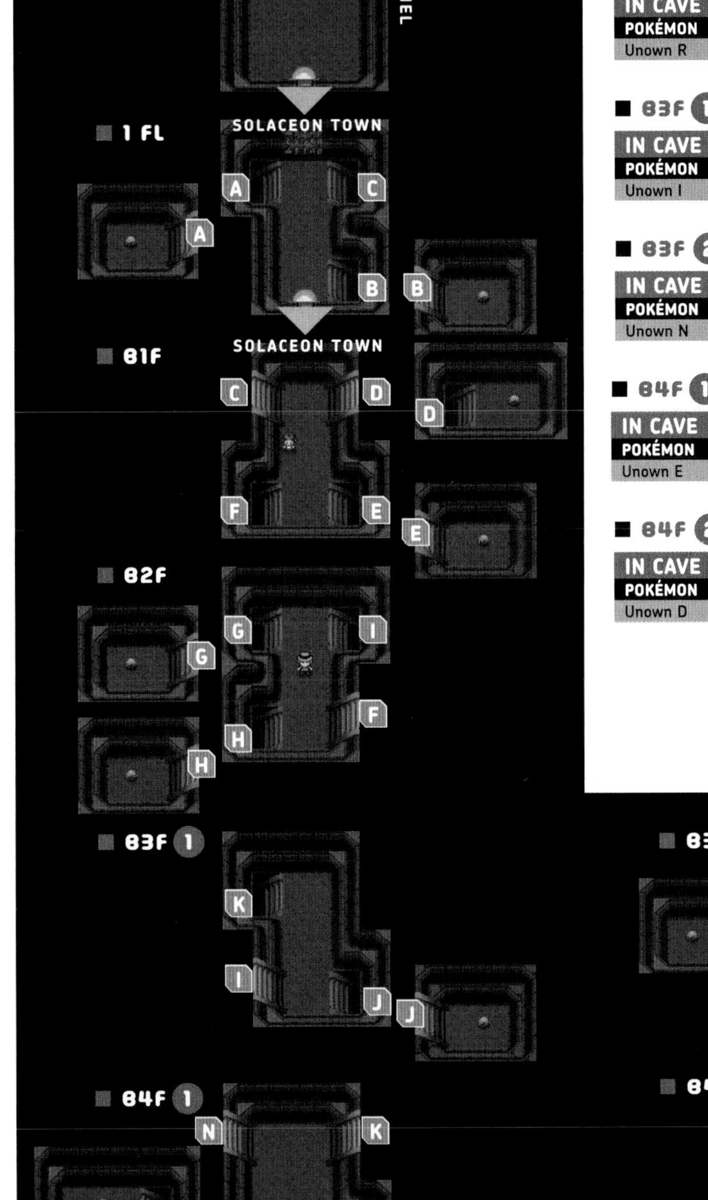

2 FL

IN CAVE

POKÉMON	M	D	N
Unown !	◎	◎	◎
Unown ?	◎	◎	◎

B1F

IN CAVE

POKÉMON	M	D	N
Unown F	◎	◎	◎

B2F

IN CAVE

POKÉMON	M	D	N
Unown R	◎	◎	◎

B3F 1

IN CAVE

POKÉMON	M	D	N
Unown I	◎	◎	◎

B3F 2

IN CAVE

POKÉMON	M	D	N
Unown N	◎	◎	◎

B4F 1

IN CAVE

POKÉMON	M	D	N
Unown E	◎	◎	◎

B4F 2

IN CAVE

POKÉMON	M	D	N
Unown D	◎	◎	◎

ALL DEAD END ROOMS

IN CAVE

POKÉMON	M	D	N
Unown A	◎	◎	◎
Unown B	◎	◎	◎
Unown C	◎	◎	◎
Unown G	◎	◎	◎
Unown H	◎	◎	◎
Unown J	◎	◎	◎
Unown K	◎	◎	◎
Unown L	◎	◎	◎
Unown M	◎	◎	◎
Unown O	◎	◎	◎
Unown P	◎	◎	◎
Unown Q	◎	◎	◎
Unown S	◎	◎	◎
Unown T	◎	◎	◎
Unown U	◎	◎	◎
Unown V	◎	◎	◎
Unown W	◎	◎	◎
Unown X	◎	◎	◎
Unown Y	◎	◎	◎
Unown Z	◎	◎	◎

STEP 1 POKÉTCH APPLICATION – POKÉMON HISTORY

YOU'LL MEET A MAN west of the Pokémon Center and he'll give you a Pokétch application called Pokémon History. This application shows you up to twelve of the last captured Pokémon in your party. Touch the Pokémon with the stylus and you'll hear their cries.

Lucas obtained the Pokétch
app POKéMON HISTORY.

STEP 2 LEAVE YOUR POKÉMON AT POKÉMON DAY CARE

THE POKÉMON DAY CARE facility raises your Pokémon for you. Check in Pokémon that you can't take with you, but still want to be raised during the time you're gone. They take in two Pokémon at a time.

Money
₽ 49328
I'm the Day-Care Lady.
We can raise Pokémon for you.

EGG-SCITING SURPRISES!

IF YOU LEAVE a pair of male and female Pokémon at a Day Care, they sometimes produce an Egg, which will be left with the elderly man outside.

STEP 3 POKÉTCH APPLICATION – DAY CARE CHECKER

WHEN YOU CHECK your Pokémon in at the Day Care, a man will appear and give you a Pokétch application called the Day Care Checker. With this device, you can always check on your Pokémon's development from afar.

Lucas obtained the Pokétch
app DAY-CARE CHECKER.

STEP 4 GET THE STICKER CASE

STEP OFF A SMALL HILL on the east side of town and you'll come to a house. There, a woman will give you an item called the Sticker Case. Stickers are used to deocarte your Poké Ball capsule (holder). See a kid in Solaceon Town or Sunyshore City for the stickers. (see p.125)

Oh, you don't have a Seal Case?
Well, here you go!

CUSTOMIZE YOUR CAPSULES

USE YOUR PC to edit your Ball Capsules. Use the stickers you obtain throughout the game to customize the Ball Capsules even more.

STEP 5 EXPLORE THE SOLACEON RUINS

HEAD EAST from Solaceon Town. Jump down from a small abutment and you'll find the entrance to Solaceon Ruins. This is a very mysterious ruin inhabited only by Unown. Check everywhere to find Unown.

DECIPHER THE LETTERS WRITTEN ON A FRESCO...

ON THE 1 FL and fourth level of the BF, you'll come across a message written in ancient letters on the walls. Observe the letters carefully and you'll notice that they look very much like Unown. Try and decode what is written here.

STEP 6 CAPTURE UNOWN

THERE ARE 28 KINDS of Unown altogether and every one of them is different in appearance. Entering Solaceon Ruins from Solaceon Town, you should be able to catch 26 different Unown that resemble the letters A through Z (there are also two Unown that resemble a "!" and "?"). In rooms that have stairs in them, you'll encounter six Unown which spell out F, R, I, E, N, D. There are twenty additional ones that you can find in a small dead-end rooms on each floor.

USE THE REPEAT BALL

TO TRY TO CAPTURE all of the Unown, it is recommended that you use the Repeat Ball which makes it easier to catch Pokémon that you have caught before (any Unown is considered one Pokémon – the group of all twenty eight is considered a repeat catch). Stock up on them at the Pokémart in Canalave City.

STEP 7 SHOW YOUR UNOWN TO THE BOY IN THE RUINS

TALK TO A BOY you meet on the B1F of the ruin and he'll tell you to come by his house later. After you get the Sticker Case from the woman, seek out the boy and he'll give you stickers that match Unown you have in the forefront of your party.

STEP 8 STOP THE PRESSES

NEXT TO A POKÉMON CENTER is Pokémon News Press that is popular in the Sinnoh region. Speak to the Editor-in-Chief and he'll ask you to bring certain Pokémon so that he can write an article about them. Bring it to him before the end of the day and he'll give you a Poké Ball in return.

RARE POKÉ BALLS

AT THE NEWSPAPER COMPANY, they have more than 10 kinds of Poké Balls, including the Premier Ball and Master Ball. This is an opportunity to obtain one for free.

STEP 9 HEAD TO VEILSTONE CITY

YOU'VE COME BACK to Hearthome City but the Gym Leader Fantina is not back yet. Go past Route 210 and Route 215 and head to Veilstone City first. In Veilstone City there are fun facilities like a department store and a Game Corner besides a Pokémon Gym.

AFTER OPENING OF MANIAC TUNNEL
COLLECT ALL 28 KINDS OF UNOWN

MANIAC TUNNEL ON ROUTE 214 connects to the 2 FL of Solaceon Town. Once you have caught Unown from A to Z, go to the 2 FL and catch the last two ("!" and "?") which will complete your collection.

UNOWN CHART

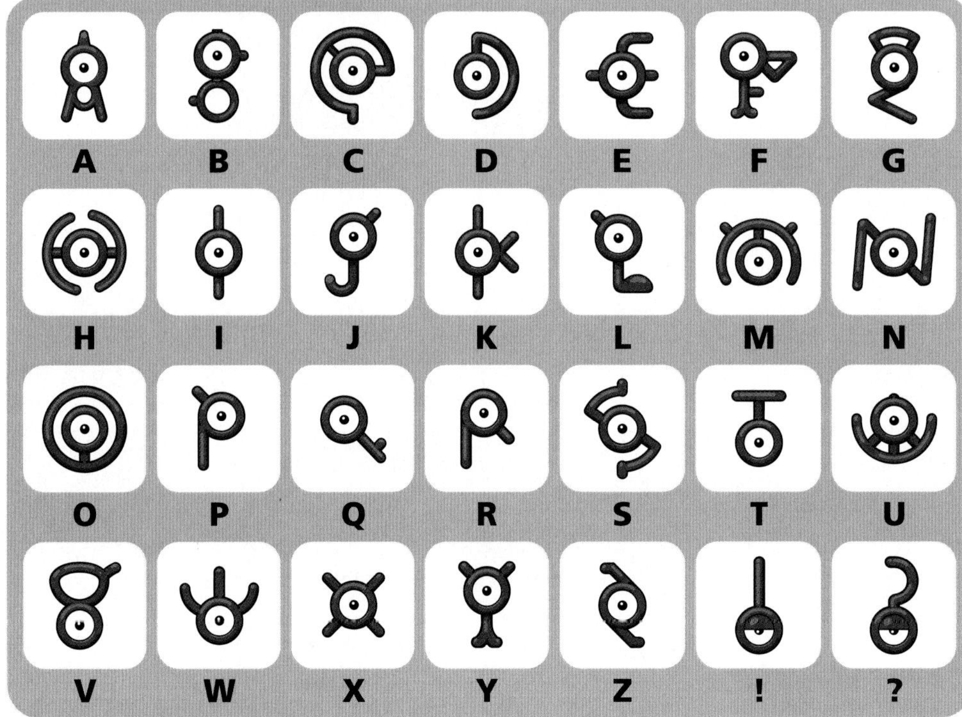

EDIT CAPSULES WITH COLLECTED STICKERS

A Ball Capsule is a clear capsule that wraps around a Poké Ball. Put a sticker on it and its pattern will appear as your Pokémon enters into a battle. Edit your Ball Capsules and produce your own entrance scene.

ACCESS YOUR PC AND EDIT YOUR BALL CAPSULES

YOU CAN EDIT YOUR BALL Capsules by accessing your PC. Choose a capsule you want to edit and put your favorite sticker(s) on it. The sticker(s) will appear quickly if it is close to the center of the capsule and less quickly if it's put farther out. Alphabetical patterns, however, all show up with the same timing.

PUT YOUR FAVORITE STICKER ON YOUR CAPSULE

You can put up to eight stickers on one capsule. Be particular about how you want to edit it.

EDITING EXAMPLES

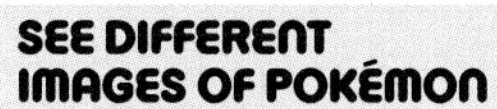

YOU CAN SHOW MESSAGES

SEE DIFFERENT IMAGES OF POKéMON

SPELL OUT POKéMON NAMES

COLLECT AS MANY STICKERS AS YOU CAN

YOU CAN GET stickers from a boy in Solaceon Town and at Sunyshore Market in Sunyshore City. The more stickers you obtain, the more creative, original and fun your capsule editing will be. Collect as many of them as you can and produce your own awesome effects!

1 SHOW YOUR UNOWN IN SOLACEON TOWN

Show your Unown to a boy in a house in Solaceon Town and he'll give you a corresponding alphabet sticker.

2 BUY THEM AT SUNYSHORE MARKET IN SUNYSHORE CITY

You can buy them from the man near the top left of the counter at Sunyshore Market. He sells different kinds of stickers on different days.

SEE P. 279 FOR THE LIST OF THE STICKERS.

ROUTE 210, ROUTE 215

Proceed north of Route 210, which is covered with tall grass, and venture past a foggy ravine, and eventually you will reach Celestic Town. Another town means another Gym, which means you should prepare for another battle. Go east of the Café Cabin, pass Route 215 and keep heading on to Veilstone City.

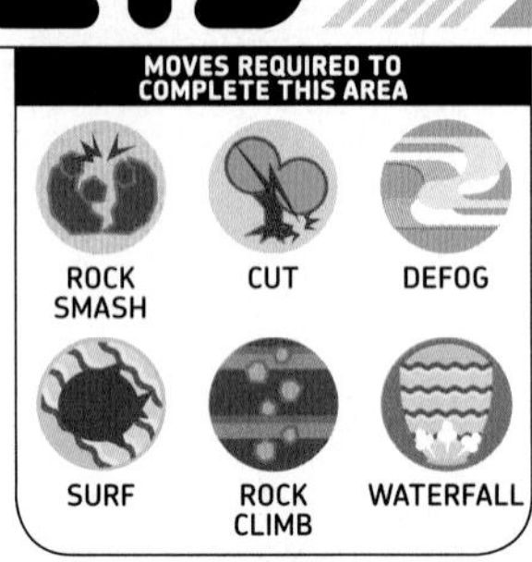

MOVES REQUIRED TO COMPLETE THIS AREA
ROCK SMASH
CUT
DEFOG
SURF
ROCK CLIMB
WATERFALL

ROUTE 210

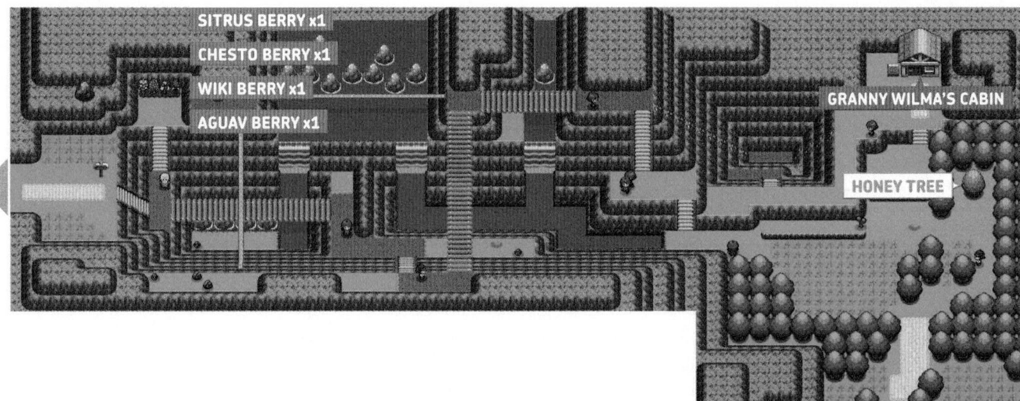

OBTAINABLE ITEMS

ON YOUR FIRST VISIT

☐ Aspear Berry x2	☐ Razz Berry
☐ Pinap Berry	☐ TM51 Roost
☐ Great Ball	☐ Ether
☐ TM66 Payback	☐ Fist Plate
☐ Pecha Berry x2	☐ Bluk Berry x2
☐ Guard Spec.	☐ TM34 Shock Wave
☐ Full Heal	☐ Wiki Berry
☐ Mago Berry	

AFTER OBTAINING SECRET POTION

☐ Old Charm	☐ Super Repel
☐ Hyper Potion	☐ TM30 Shadow Ball
☐ Smoke Ball	☐ Sitrus Berry
☐ Chesto Berry	☐ Wiki Berry
☐ Aguav Berry	

AFTER WINNING SUNYSHORE CITY GYM BATTLE

☐ Wave Incense

CAFÉ CABIN

Moomoo Milk	500

STEP 1 WALK IN THE GRASSY FIELD

ROUTE 210 on the side of Solaceon Town is covered with tall grass. It will tangle up in the spokes of your Bike, so you're forced to walk. Putting on the Running Shoes will be the best option here.

Mime Jr.
Psychic
Abilities:
• Soundproof
• Filter

Bonsly
Rock
Abilities:
• Sturdy
• Rock Head

Ponyta
Fire
Abilities:
• Run Away
• Flash Fire

■ ROUTE 215

VEILSTONE CITY

■ ROUTE 210 (SOLACEON TOWN SIDE)

IN GRASS

POKÉMON	M	D	N
Ponyta	◎	◎	◎
Geodude	◎	◎	◎
Kricketune	○	○	◎
Mime Jr. ♦	○	△	△
Bonsly ●	○	△	△
Chansey	△	△	△

■ ROUTE 215

IN GRASS

POKÉMON	M	D	N
Ponyta	◎	◎	○
Geodude	◎	○	○
Kricketune	○	○	◎
Abra	○	○	○
Kadabra	○	○	○

■ ROUTE 210 (CELESTIC TOWN SIDE)

IN GRASS

POKÉMON	M	D	N
Meditite	◎	◎	○
Psyduck	○	○	○
Bibarel	○	○	○
Machop	○	○	○
Machoke	○	○	○
Hoothoot	✕	✕	○
Noctowl	✕	✕	○

ON WATER

POKÉMON	VARIABLE
Psyduck	◎
Golduck	○

FISHING

FISHING ROD	POKÉMON	VARIABLE
Old	Magikarp	◎
Good	Magikarp	◎
	Barboach	○

STEP 2 BUY MOOMOO MILK AT CAFÉ CABIN

VISIT CAFÉ CABIN and enjoy battles with customers inside. Also they sell Moomoo Milk for 500 Poké Dollars. This milk restores HP by 100.

STEP 3 A GROUP OF PSYDUCK IS BLOCKING YOUR WAY

THERE ARE 4 PSYDUCK by the Café. Seems like they all have headaches and won't budge. At this time you can't go over to the other side so go east of Café Cabin towards Route 215.

STEP 4 GO PAST ROUTE 215 TO VEILSTONE CITY

IT'S ALWAYS POURING ON RAIN on Route 215 – and now is no exception. Rain raises the power of Water-type moves and weakens that of Fire-type moves. You are almost at Veilstone City.

ABILITY DETERMINES BATTLE RESULTS

SOME ABILITIES will give you an advantage in rainy weather. Use Pokémon that have Dry Skin, or Swift Swim. (see p.272)

AFTER OBTAINING SECRET POTION CURE PSYDUCK'S HEADACHE

GIVE THE PSYDUCK THE SECRET POTION you got from Cynthia at Valor Lakefront. It gets rid of their headaches and they all leave the area. Now the path is open for you to proceed on to Celestic Town.

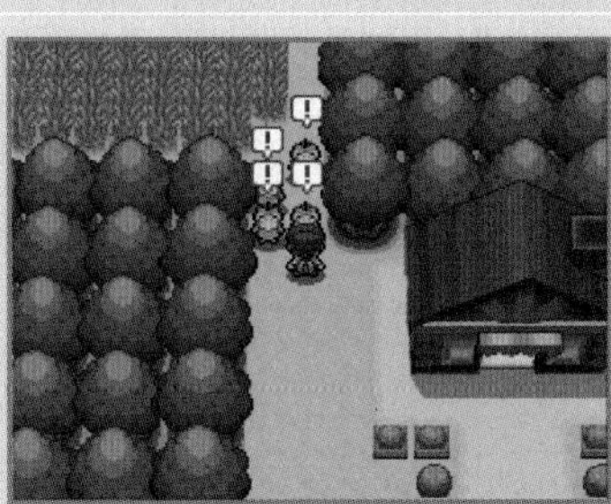

AFTER OBTAINING SECRET POTION
KEEP THE OLD CHARM FOR CYNTHIA

WHEN YOU RID THE PSYDUCK of their headaches and they are gone, Cynthia comes by. She will give you an Old Charm saying that she wants you to deliver it to her grandma. Do her a solid and head to Celestic Town.

I want you to deliver this Old Charm
to my grandma in Celestic Town.

THREE NINJAS, NO WAITING

SOMEWHERE in the tall grass field north of Café Cabin there are three Ninja Boys hiding. Look into the most suspicious spots and find all of them.

AFTER OBTAINING SECRET POTION
CLEAR THE FOG USING DEFOG

AS YOU PROCEED NORTH on Route 210, it becomes very foggy and you won't be able to see around you. Use HM05 Defog to clear the fog so that you will be able to see again. To reach Celestic Town, cross the bridge on the mountain path and proceed west.

If I could use the hidden move Defog,
I'd clear up the weather.

IN FOGGY WEATHER, ACCURACY GOES DOWN

IF YOU PROCEED without using HM05 Defog, you will end up battling wild Pokémon in foggy weather, and your accuracy will suffer. Make sure you clear the fog with HM05 Defog before you go on.

AFTER WINNING SNOWPOINT CITY GYM BATTLE
LEARN THE MOST POWERFUL DRAGON-TYPE MOVE

GO NORTH ON ROUTE 210 using HM08 Rock Climb, and you'll find Granny Wilma's cabin. Take a well-trained Dragon-type Pokémon with you and she will teach you Draco Meteor, the most powerful Dragon-type attack move.

YES
NO
Would you like me to teach that
move to one of your Pokémon?

GIBLE APPEARS IN THE WAYWARD CAVE

YOU WON'T ENCOUNTER Dragon-type Pokémon easily. Catch Gible on the first basement in the Wayward Cave and raise it until it becomes friendly with you. (see p.19)

PEOPLE WHO TAKE CARE OF POKÉMON

There are many people in Sinnoh region who take good care of Pokémon. Someone can change your Pokémon's nickname, and some can teach moves to them. When you don't know how to get to a particular person, refer to this page.

IF YOU'RE LOOKING FOR HELP, HERE'S A GUIDE!

CHANGE YOUR POKÉMON NICKNAME

LOCATION: NAME RATER IN ETERNA CITY

He will change your Pokémon's nickname. Pokémon that were given to you by other people cannot have their name changed here.

P. 090

YES
NO
Want me to rate the nicknames of your Pokémon?

TEACH YOUR POKÉMON MOVES

LOCATION: MOVE MANIAC (MOVE TUTOR) IN PASTORIA

Give him one Heart Scale and he will make your Pokémon learn moves, including moves that were forgotten.

P. 146

Let me guess, you want me to teach one of your Pokémon a move?

MAKE YOUR POKÉMON FORGET MOVES

LOCATION: MOVE DELETER IN CANALAVE CITY

He can make your Pokémon forget moves they have learned, including HMs that can't be deleted under normal circumstances.

P. 160

You've come to make me force your Pokémon to forget some moves?

HELP YOUR POKÉMON LEVEL UP

LOCATION: POKÉMON DAY CARE IN SOLACEON TOWN

Leave your Pokémon with them and they will raise them and level them up for you. They take in up to two Pokémon at a time.

P. 120

Money
₽222478
Ah, it's you! Good to see you.
Now, about your Pokémon...

RESTORE YOUR FOSSILS

LOCATION: OREBURGH MINING MUSEUM

Give them the Pokémon fossils you've dug out in the Underground, they will restore them to Pokémon in their original forms.

P. 064

TEACH YOUR DRAGON-TYPE THE MOST POWERFUL MOVE

LOCATION: GRANNY WILMA ON ROUTE 210

Show her your happy, friendly Dragon-type Pokémon and she will teach it the strongest Dragon-type move, Draco Meteor.

P. 126

YES
NO
Dragon-type move I know to one of your Pokémon?

VEILSTONE CITY

MOVES REQUIRED TO COMPLETE THIS AREA

ROCK CLIMB

Veilstone City was constructed in the face of a huge, steep mountain. It contains the Veilstone Dept. Store, which is always crowded with people, a Game Corner, a storage center, and Team Galactic's eerie headquarter building. First step - challenge the Gym Leader.

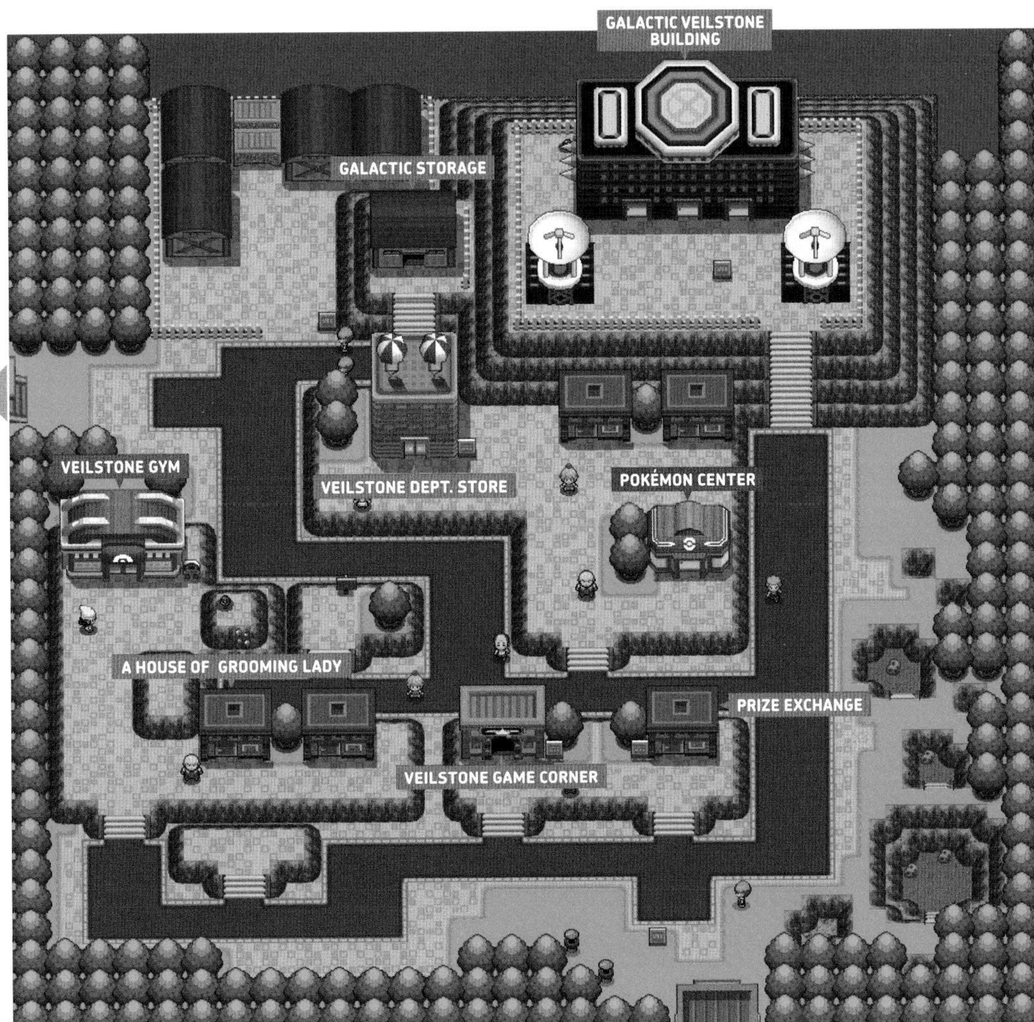

OBTAINABLE ITEMS

ON YOUR FIRST VISIT

- ☐ One of the following: Turtwig Mask Chimchar Mask or Piplup Mask
- ☐ PP Up
- ☐ Pokétch application: Counter
- ☐ Sticky Barb
- ☐ Coin Case
- ☐ TM63 Embargo

AFTER 10 CONSECUTIVE WINS ON A SLOT MACHINE

- ☐ TM64 Explosion

AFTER WINNING VEILSTONE CITY GYM BATTLE

- ☐ Cobble Badge
- ☐ HM02 Fly
- ☐ TM60 Drain Punch

AFTER VISITING LAKE ACUITY

- ☐ Storage Key

AFTER WINNING SNOWPOINT CITY GYM BATTLE

- ☐ Full Incense

ACCESSORIES YOU GET AFTER POKÉMON MASSAGES

Pretty Dewdrop	Glitter Powder
Sparks	Snow Crystal
Mystic Fire	Shimmering Fire
Determination	Peculiar Spoon
Puffy Smoke	Poison Extract
Wealthy Coin	Eerie Thing
Spring	Seashell
Humming Note	Shiny Powder

GET A POKÉTCH APPLICATION - COUNTER

A WOMAN AT THE COUNTER on the 2 FL of the Veilstone Dept. Store presents you with a Pokétch application called Counter. This is a device that counts up to 9999 that you can use for many different purposes.

We're giving away a Pokétch app for
free as a promotion.

TEAM GALACTIC GRUNTS ARE BLOCKING THE WAY

NEAR VEILSTONE DEPT. STORE there is a building called Galactic Storage. Try to enter it and Team Galactic Grunts will stop you. Come back after the Veilstone City Gym battle.

It ain't no playground for kids!

TEAM GALACTIC IS HIDING SOMETHING IMPORTANT

A MAN NEAR a Pokémon Center tells you that Team Galactic is hiding a HM in their Storage. You overhear some Team Galactic Grunts standing south of the Prize Exchange House that it is HM02 Fly.

GET COIN CASE FROM A CLOWN

IN A HOUSE WEST OF THE GAME CORNER is a clown who will play Guess Which Hand. Guess correctly which hand the coin is in, and he'll give you a Coin Case. Take it with you to the Game Corner.

For our winner, I have here...
A Coin Case!

SHELLOS DIFFER IN COLOR IN WEST AND EAST

SHELLOS LIVING on the west side of Mt. Coronet have different body color and form from the ones living on the other side of the mountain. Shellos in the west appear on Route 205, the ones in the east side appear on Route 213. Compare them both and see the difference.

TRY YOUR LUCK AT THE GAME CORNER

YOU PLAY SLOT MACHINES in the Game Corner using the game coins. Choose a machine you like and start playing. Stop all three reels and if their patterns match, you'll get a prize. (see p.136)

I'll explain how the slot machines
work at this Game Corner.

GET 70 COINS FOR FREE

AT THE GAME CORNER, talk to other players and they'll give you their coins for free. You can get up to 70 coins from them. Challenge the slot machine using these free coins.

STEP 5 TREAT YOUR POKÉMON TO A GOOD MASSAGE

IN A HOUSE south of Veilstone City Gym is a grooming lady who gives Pokémon one massage a day. When she is done, she will say your Pokémon had this with it and give you an accessory. There are 16 accessories in total. (see p.131)

Obtained the Seashell!

LOVE IS IN THE AIR

THE GROOMING LADY is dating the Scarf Guy in Pastoria City. They have their Pokémon deliver mails to each other.

STEP 6 GET A KEY TO GALACTIC VEILSTONE BUILDING

GALACTIC VEILSTONE BUILDING north of Pokémon Center, really, is Team Galactic's Headquarters. Here in this building they are doing research on how to produce new energy. You will need a special key to open the door to the upper floors.

The door is locked.
A special key is needed.

GYM BATTLE 3

MAYLENE

VEILSTONE GYM LEADER
POKÉMON TYPE: FIGHTING
RECOMMENDED TYPES:
FLYING, PSYCHIC

IN VEILSTONE CITY GYM, you work your way to the back where Maylene awaits by moving partitions to the right or left. There are four Trainers you have to clear. Maylene uses Pokémon with Fighting-type moves. Flying-type and Psychic-type moves will keep her in check. Defeat her to get the Cobble Badge and TM60 Drain Punch.

PARTY POKÉMON

POKÉMON	LEVEL	TYPE
Meditite ♀	Lv27	Fighting-Psychic
Machoke ♂	Lv27	Fighting
Lucario ♂	Lv30	Fighting-Steel

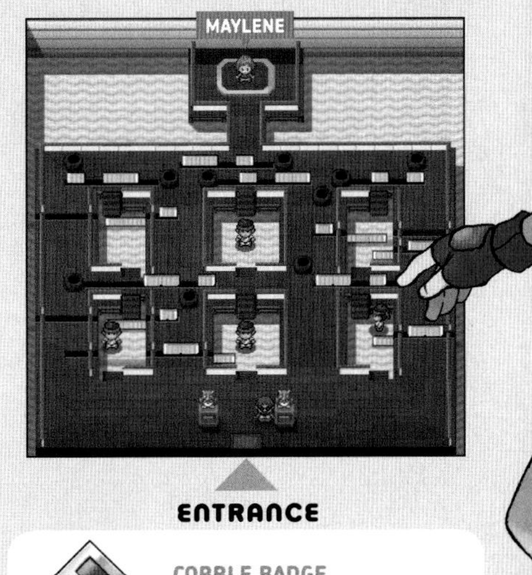

COBBLE BADGE
You can use field move HM02 Fly.

STEP 7 HELP THE ASSISTANT OUT OF TROUBLE

COME OUTSIDE AFTER the Gym battle and you will meet Rowan's assistant, who will ask for your help. The assistant claims that Team Galactic stole their Pokédex! Tag battle the Team Galactic Grunts in front of Galactic Storage and get the Pokédex back.

I dropped my Pokédex by accident,
and Team Galactic found it.

SO WHAT REALLY IS IN THE GALACTIC STORAGE?

THE TEAM GALACTIC Grunts on watch at the Storage entrance are overheard saying that something has been transferred to Pastoria already. Does this have anything to do with the new energy being researched in the Galactic Veilstone Building?

STEP 8 OBTAIN HM02 FLY

DEFEAT THE TEAM GALACTIC GRUNTS in front of Galactic Storage and you'll be able to enter the Storage. Inside, get HM02 Fly. There is a room that leads to the back of the Storage, but the door is locked and you can't proceed any further at this point.

Lucas put the HM02
in the TMs & HMs Pocket.

AFTER VISITING LAKE ACUITY
SEIZE STORAGE KEY FROM TEAM GALACTIC GRUNT

WHEN YOU GET BACK FROM LAKE ACUITY after chasing Jupiter, the Team Galactic grunt inside Galactic Storage blurts out that his colleague in front of the headquarter building has the Storage Key. Go to Galactic Veilstone Building and get the key from the Team Grunt.

I don't know anything about any

SHOP TILL YOU DROP!

A department store with something for everyone – the Veilstone Department Store!

THE BIGGEST DEPARTMENT STORE IN THE SINNOH REGION

THIS FIVE STORY DEPARTMENT STORE has everything – including TMs, useful battle items and lots of healing goods. This is the perfect place to be when you have to stock up for long trips. If you have trouble deciding what to get, go to the counter on the right side of each floor and ask for recommendations.

Go to the vending machine on the 5 FL. Sometimes you get lucky and get a free bottle of liquid refreshment.

VEILSTONE DEPARTMENT STORE DIRECTORY

5 FL – ROOFTOP PLAZA

VENDING MACHINE	
Fresh Water	200
Soda Pop	300
Lemonade	350

4 FL – GOODS AND DOLLS

Item	Price
Yellow Cushion	500
Cupboard	1000
TV	4500
Refrigerator	1000
Pretty Sink	3000
Munchlax Doll	2000
Bonsly Doll	2000
Mime Jr. Doll	2000
Mantyke Doll	3000
Buizel Doll	3000
Chatot Doll	3000

3 FL – TM COLLECTION

Item	Price
TM83 Natural Gift	2000
TM17 Protect	2000
TM54 False Swipe	2000
TM20 Safeguard	2000
TM33 Reflect	2000
TM16 Light Screen	2000
TM70 Flash	1000
TM38 Fire Blast	5500
TM25 Thunder	5500
TM14 Blizzard	5500
TM22 Solar Beam	3000
TM52 Focus Blast	5500
TM15 Hyper Beam	7500

2 FL – BATTLE PARTNERS

Item	Price
X Speed	350
X Attack	500
X Defend	550
Guard Spec.	700
Dire Hit	650
X Accuracy	950
X Special	350
X Sp. Def.	350
Protein	9800
Iron	9800
Calcium	9800
Zinc	9800
Carbos	9800
HP Up	9800

1 FL – TRAINERS' ZONE

Item	Price
Potion	300
Super Potion	700
Hyper Potion	1200
Max Potion	2500
Revive	1500
Antidote	100
Parlyz Heal	200
Burn Heal	250
Ice Heal	250
Awakening	250
Full Heal	600
Poké Ball	200
Great Ball	600
Ultra Ball	1200
Escape Rope	550
Clefairy Doll	1000
Repel	350
Super Repel	500
Max Repel	700
Grass Mail	50
Flame Mail	50
Bubble Mail	50
Space Mail	50

CHALLENGE THE SLOT MACHINES AT VEILSTONE GAME CORNER

Increase your coins, and increase your chances for rare TMs and items!

YOU CAN PLAY THE SLOTS at Veilstone Game Corner in Veilstone City using game coins. Try to stop the reels to get matching patterns to earn coins. Get as many coins as possible and exchange them for items or TMs at an exchange service corner.

GAME COINS	
50 Coins	1000
500 Coins	10000

WHAT YOU CAN EXCHANGE WITH YOUR COINS	
Silk Scarf	1000 Coins
Wide Lens	1000 Coins
Zoom Lens	1000 Coins
Metronome	1000 Coins
TM90 Substitute	2000 Coins
TM58 Endure	2000 Coins
TM75 Swords Dance	4000 Coins
TM32 Double Team	4000 Coins
TM44 Rest	6000 Coins
TM89 U-Turn	6000 Coins
TM10 Hidden Power	6000 Coins
TM27 Return	8000 Coins
TM21 Frustration	8000 Coins
TM35 Flamethrower	10000 Coins
TM24 Thunderbolt	10000 Coins
TM13 Ice Beam	10000 Coins
TM29 Psychic	10000 Coins
TM74 Gyro Ball	15000 Coins
TM68 Giga Impact	20000 Coins

SLOT RULE 1
MATCH THE PATTERNS AND INCREASE YOUR COINS

THE MOST BASIC RULE is, of course, to match the symbols on all three reels. The number of coins you get depends on which symbols you hit in a row. If you match the replay patterns, you will get to play again automatically.

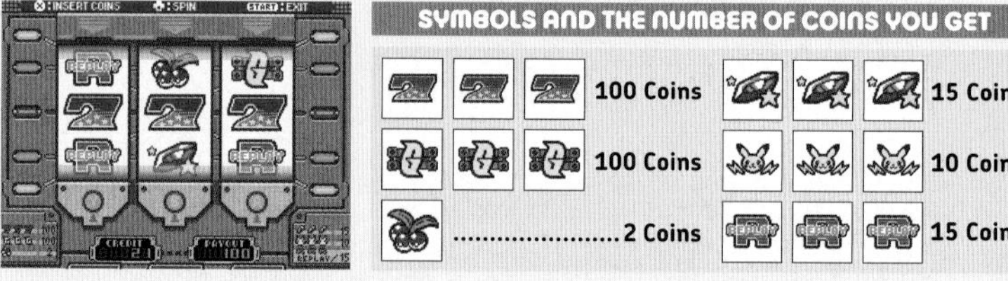

*IF YOU HIT REPLAY DURING CLEFAIRY'S BONUS, YOU WILL GET 15 COINS

SLOT RULE 2
WATCH CLOSELY TO STOP THE REELS

THERE ARE THREE REELS, left, middle and right. You can halt those three in any order but you are more likely to match Replay and Pikachu if you stop the reels from left to right in an orderly fashion. Watch carefully to see which symbol is coming.

STOP THE LEFT

STOP THE MIDDLE

STOP THE RIGHT

SLOT RULE 3
CHANGING THE MODES

A SLOT MACHINE CHANGES its mode from Normal Mode to Clefairy Mode, and then to Clefairy Bonus depending on the matched patterns. Different modes determines which patterns are more likely to match, and the graphics shown on the bottom monitor will change accordingly. Study the differences of each mode and master them before you start playing. Collect as many coins while in Clefairy bonus mode because Clefairy makes it easier for you to match those symbols.

THE THREE CHANGING MODES

MODE 1 : NORMAL MODE

Stop the reels from left to right in order to get Replay and Pikachu, Poké Ball and Moon Stone will be matched.

MODE 2 : CLEFAIRY MODE

Clefairy appears and makes 7's and G's more likely to match. 7 or G combination will change the mode to Clefairy Bonus.

MODE 3 : CLEFAIRY BONUS

Stop the reels in the order that Clefairy's pointing and Replay combination is guaranteed. The mode changes after you stop the reels 15 times.

SLOT RULE 4
PROBABILITIES FOR REPEAT ROLLS DEPENDS ON WHICH CLEFAIRY APPEARS

REPEAT MEANS THAT BONUS STILL CONTINUES after 15 times of playing. How probable this will be depends of what kind of Clefairy comes out of the Poké Ball. In addition, if Pikachu appears after the mode is over, it's more likely to repeat (it will be less likely to repeat if Clefairy appears again).

DITTO CLEFAIRY	CLEFAIRY	CLEFAIRY IN A DIFFERENT COLOR
LESS LIKELY TO REPEAT	LIKELY TO REPEAT	VERY LIKELY TO REPEAT

If Clefairy-faking Ditto appears, the mode is less likely to repeat.

If it's Clefairy that appears, Clefairy Bonus mode is likely to repeat.

If you get Clefairy in a different color, it's very likely to repeat with high probability.

SLOT RULE 5
WHEN THE MOON BECOMES RED, DON'T MATCH REPLAY

WHEN THE MOON BECOMES RED during the Clefairy Bonus Mode, don't follow Clefairy's direction for Replay combination because doing so will make the mode less likely to repeat. Defy Clefairy's direction and don't match the Replay symbols. On the other hand, when the moon becomes white, it almost guarantees repeat of the Bonus mode.

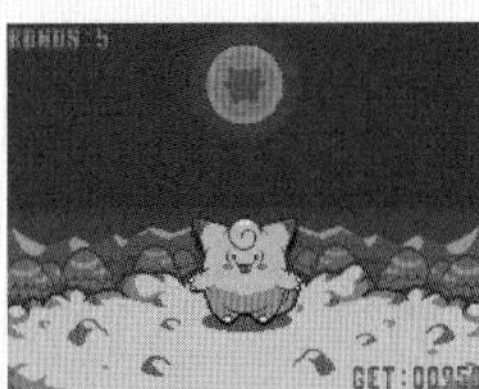

DON'T MATCH REPLAY COMBINATION WHEN THE MOON IS RED

If you Match Replay pattern when you have a red moon, It makes Clefairy very tired. When it's tired, the Bonus mode is less likely to continue.

ROUTE 214, VALOR LAKEFRONT, ROUTE 213

Route 214 is a fascinating place where nature is beautifully preserved. Valor Lakefront is near the lake of a mysterious legend, and Route 213 is home to a quiet and serene beach. Travel south of Veilstone City to Pastoria City along these places.

MOVES REQUIRED TO COMPLETE THIS AREA

ROCK SMASH
SURF
ROCK CLIMB

OBTAINABLE ITEMS

ON YOUR FIRST VISIT

- ☐ Cheri Berry
- ☐ Chesto Berry
- ☐ X Sp. Def.
- ☐ Big Root
- ☐ PP Up
- ☐ Red Shard
- ☐ Aguav Berry
- ☐ Iapapa Berry
- ☐ Sitrus Berry
- ☐ Pomeg Berry
- ☐ Max Potion
- ☐ Parlyz Heal
- ☐ TM92 Trick Room
- ☐ TM40 Aerial Ace
- ☐ Rawst Berry x2

WHEN YOUR PARTY-FRONT POKÉMON IS VERY HAPPY

- ☐ Footstep Ribbon

AFTER WINNING PASTORIA CITY GYM BATTLE

- ☐ Secret Potion

AFTER WINNING HEARTHOME CITY GYM BATTLE

- ☐ Rare Candy
- ☐ Max Revive
- ☐ Water Stone

AFTER WINNING SNOWPOINT CITY GYM BATTLE

- ☐ TM05 Roar
- ☐ Protein
- ☐ TM85 Dream Eater
- ☐ Pokétch application: Coin Toss

ROUTE 214

IN GRASS

POKÉMON	M	D	N
Ponyta	◎	◎	○
Geodude	○	○	○
Stunky ♦	○	○	○
Sudowoodo ●	○	○	○
Girafarig	○	○	○
Graveler	○	○	△
Kricketune	△	△	○

ON WATER

POKÉMON	VARIABLE
Psyduck	◎
Golduck	○

FISHING

FISHING ROD	POKÉMON	VARIABLE
Old	Magikarp	◎
Good	Magikarp	◎
	Goldeen	○

ROUTE 213

IN GRASS

POKÉMON	M	D	N
Buizel	◎	◎	◎
Shellos	◎	◎	◎
Wingull	○	○	○
Floatzel	○	○	○

ON WATER

POKÉMON	VARIABLE
Tentacool	◎
Wingull	○
Tentacruel	△
Pelipper	△

FISHING

FISHING ROD	POKÉMON	VARIABLE
Old	Magikarp	◎
Good	Magikarp	◎
	Remoraid	○

VALOR LAKEFRONT

IN GRASS

POKÉMON	M	D	N
Girafarig	◎	◎	◎
Geodude	○	○	○
Bibarel	○	○	○
Staravia	○	○	△
Graveler	○	○	△
Kricketune	△	△	○

Stunky
Poison-Dark
Abilities:
- Stench
- Aftermath

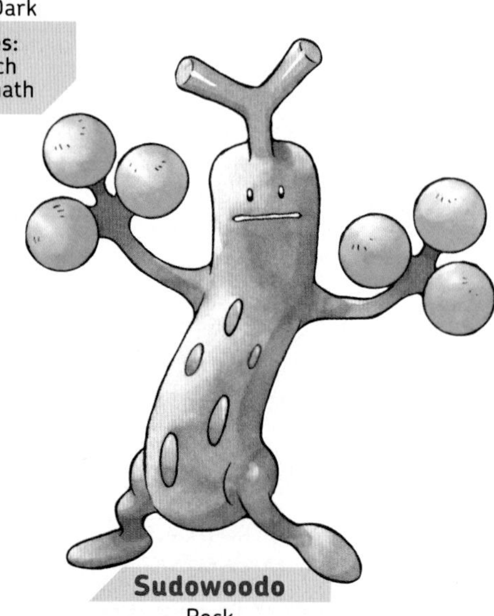

Sudowoodo
Rock
Abilities:
- Sturdy
- Rock Head

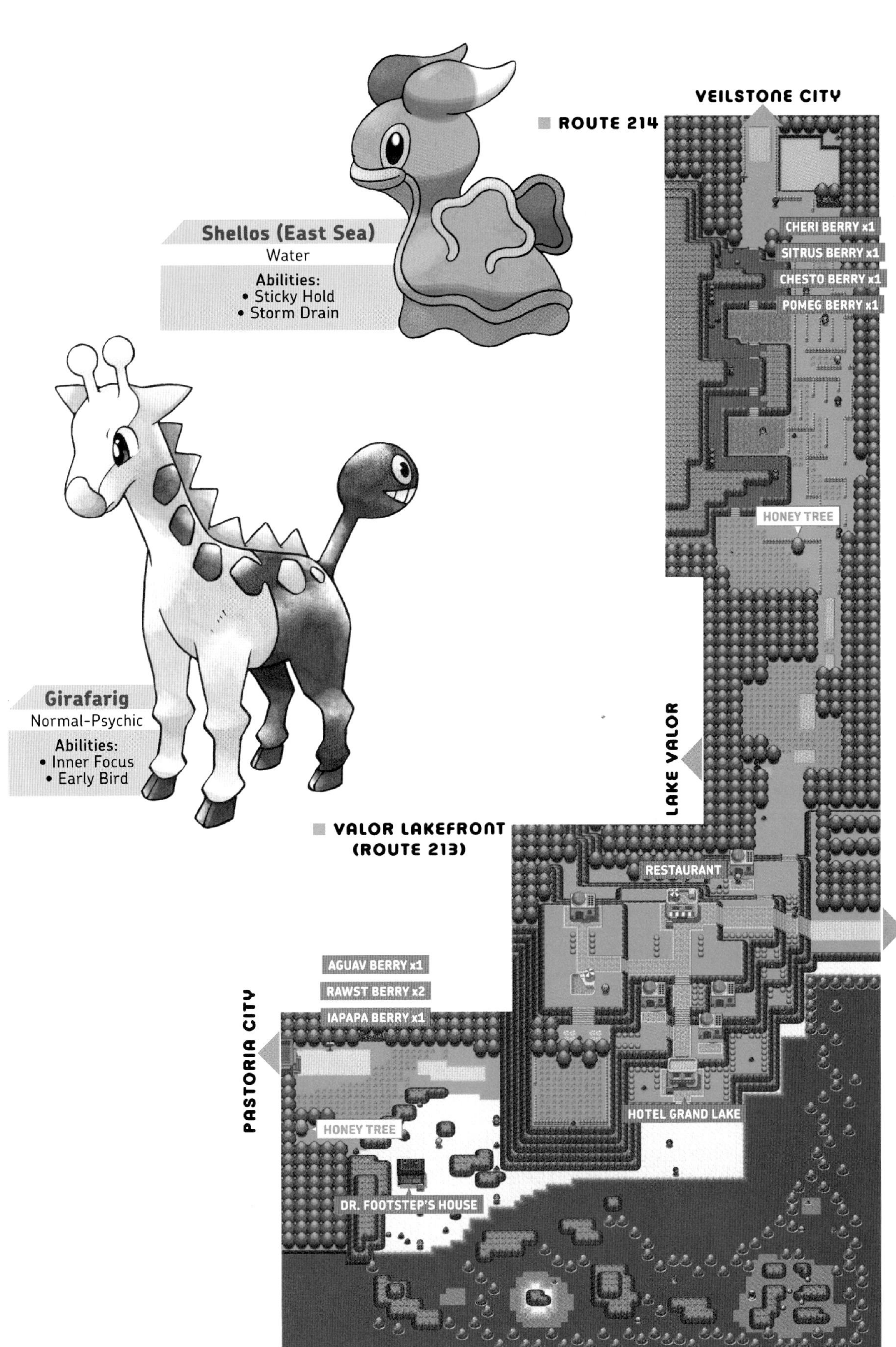
Shellos (East Sea)
Water
Abilities:
• Sticky Hold
• Storm Drain
Girafarig
Normal-Psychic
Abilities:
• Inner Focus
• Early Bird
VEILSTONE CITY
ROUTE 214
CHERI BERRY x1
SITRUS BERRY x1
CHESTO BERRY x1
POMEG BERRY x1
HONEY TREE
LAKE VALOR
VALOR LAKEFRONT (ROUTE 213)
RESTAURANT
ROUTE 222 (TO SUNYSHORE CITY)
AGUAV BERRY x1
RAWST BERRY x2
IAPAPA BERRY x1
PASTORIA CITY
HONEY TREE
HOTEL GRAND LAKE
DR. FOOTSTEP'S HOUSE

LAKE VALOR IS OFF LIMITS

THE ENTRANCE TO LAKE VALOR is blocked by guards who were told not to let anybody enter the lake. They say that the request was made by a man named Cyrus, who was trying to protect the lake. Head south for the Restaurant Seven Stars.

ROUTE 222 IS CLOSED UP

PROCEED EAST on Valor Lakefront and you will come to Route 222. Because of an earlier blackout in Sunyshore City, you can't go any further at this time. The situation will change after you visit the Spear Pillar.

BATTLING IS ON THE MENU

IN AN AREA SOUTH of Lake Valor is Restaurant Seven Stars. It's a unique place where you can enjoy Pokémon battles with other customers during the business hours between 9:00am and 11:00pm. A couple of customers will even want to have a Double Battle. Bring it.

CHALLENGE RESTAURANT CUSTOMERS EVERYDAY

BESIDES ENJOYING good food, you can challenge your fellow customers with Pokémon battles everyday at Restaurant Seven Stars. A certain Gentleman and a Madame are worth a try since they let you earn more prize money.

STEP 3

USING YOUR DOWSING MACHINE TO FIND KEY

IN FRONT OF A COTTAGE, you will see a woman who has lost her Suite Key. She says that she had it when she was at the reception. Using your Pokétch application Dowsing Machine, look around Hotel Grand Lake for it.

THE LAVA COOKIE IS A SPECIALTY OF HOENN

GIVE THE ROOM KEY back to the woman and she will thank you and give you a Lava Cookie which is a specialty of Hoenn region. Is that where she's from?

HEAL YOUR POKÉMON AT HOTEL GRAND LAKE

AT HOTEL GRAND LAKE ON ROUTE 213, they will heal your Pokémon. Go talk to the receptionist and she will let you and your Pokémon rest there for a while. After your Pokémon's recovery, head out and go west on Route 213.

WEATHER CHANGES DAILY

IN SOME PLACES, you experience a change of weather. For instance, when it is overcast, clouds appear and it gets dimmer on the screen. During your adventure, you should stop and check out the weather.

STEP 5 GET A RIBBON AT DR. FOOTSTEP'S HOUSE

ON ROUTE 213, you'll come across the house of a man called Dr. Footstep. Go speak to him and he'll take a look at the footsteps of the first Pokémon in your party and read its mind. If you and your Pokémon are well-bonded, he will give you the Footstep Ribbon.

Lucas received
the Footprint Ribbon.

YOU CAN'T READ MINDS WITHOUT FOOTSTEPS

IT'S HARD to read a Pokémon's mind without its footsteps - but if he analyzes your Pokémon and decides it is happy with you, he will give you the Footstep Ribbon.

STEP 6 HEAD TO PASTORIA CITY

PROCEED WEST on Route 213 and you will reach Pastoria City. There you will see the Pastoria Great Marsh where a lot of rare Pokémon can be found, and the house of the Move Tutor, who will teach moves to your Pokémon.

ARE TUBERS LOSERS?

A CERTAIN inner-tube boy and girl Trainer on the beach on Route 213 don't earn as much prize money as other Trainers. Do the bathing suits make them less worthy?

AFTER WINNING PASTORIA CITY GYM BATTLE
GO AFTER TEAM GALACTIC GRUNTS THAT RAN AWAY

THE TEAM GALACTIC grunt who ran away earlier is now taking a rest on the beach on Route 213. When you catch up with him, he yells out at you and starts running again towards Lake Valor.

AFTER WINNING PASTORIA CITY GYM BATTLE
CORNER HIM AND GET RIGHT INTO A BATTLE

WHEN YOU FINALLY catch up with the grunt near the restaurant, he then runs towards Lake Valor. Get him at the entrance of the lake then he'll give up running and come after you. When you win, he says something about giving this to the commander...and then leaves.

Aww, no...
You're still on my tail...?

AFTER WINNING PASTORIA CITY GYM BATTLE
GET SECRET POTION FROM CYNTHIA

AFTER BEATING UP THE GRUNT of Team Galactic, you run into Cynthia, who came to look into the folklore of the lake. Speak to her and she'll give you the Secret Potion, which will cure Psyduck's headaches. Go to Route 210 to find them.

Lucas obtained
the SecretPotion!

THE FOLKLORE OF THE LAKE

CYNTHIA SAYS she came here to research the folklore about an island in the lake where a Legendary Pokémon lives. It sounds as if it has something to do with Cyrus...

AFTER WINNING PASTORIA CITY GYM BATTLE
HEAD TO ROUTE 212 WHERE YOU HAVEN'T BEEN TO BEFORE

HEAD BACK TO ROUTE 210 via Route 212 to use the Secret Potion on Psyduck to alleviate their headaches. You've never been to Route 212 before. Stop by at the Pokémon Mansion which has a Trophy Garden where many Pokémon frequently appear – and is the pride and joy of its owner, Backlot.

Rt. 212
Pastoria City

AFTER WINNING HEARTHOME CITY GYM BATTLE
GO ON WATER USING SURF

ONCE YOU'RE ABLE TO USE HM03 SURF, get on the wave from the beach and literally surf around. You will find some valuable items out there as well as other Trainers who will be waiting to challenge you.

AFTER AN EARTHQUAKE IN CANALAVE CITY
GO TO LAKE VALOR TO DISCOVER THE LEGENDARY POKÉMON

GO TO LAKE VALOR to look for the Legendary Pokémon that Professor Rowan asked you to find. A sailor in Canalave City said that an explosion had taken place in Lake Valor. Does it have something to do with the Legendary Pokémon?

THE EARTHQUAKE IS TEAM GALACTIC'S FAULT

THE TREMOR YOU FELT in Canalave City came from an earthquake caused by an explosion caused by Team Galactic. They're up to something evil, and it has to do with that Legendary Pokémon in the middle of the lake...

AFTER WINNING SNOWPOINT CITY GYM BATTLE
COLLECT ITEMS USING ROCK CLIMB

AFTER WINNING ICICLE BADGE at Snowpoint Gym, you will be able to use HM08 Rock Climb in the field. Climb up on rocky cliffs and check out mountains on or around Route 213 and Valor Lakefront.

AFTER WINNING SNOWPOINT CITY GYM BATTLE
GET POKÉTCH APPLICATION - COIN TOSS

GO TO A COTTAGE SOUTH of Restaurant Seven Stars using HM08 Rock Climb. A man whose room was given to him by tossing a coin will give you a Pokétch application - Coin Toss. Use it when you want to test your luck.

Lucas obtained the Pokétch app COIN TOSS.

THERE ARE GOOD ITEMS IN THE TRASH SOMETIMES

AT THE COTTAGE of a man who gave you Coin Toss, you'll even discover an item in his trash. Look around some more and make sure you're not missing out on anything.

AFTER COMPLETING SINNOH POKÉDEX
SPEAK TO THE GAME DIRECTOR

AT A COTTAGE WEST of Restaurant Seven Stars, there is a man who calls himself a game director. Upon completion of the Sinnoh Pokédex, make sure you go to see him. He may have something for you.

I'm really impressed!
Let me give you an award!

THE GAME DIRECTOR IS FROM GAME FREAK

THE GAME DIRECTOR at the hotel cottage is really from Game Freak, the company that produces the Pokémon series.

RUIN MANIAC CAVE, MANIAC TUNNEL

The Maniac Tunnel is a cave dug through a mountain on Route 214 by a Ruin Maniac. Cave digging continues on according to the number of the kinds of Unown you will catch.

OBTAINABLE ITEMS

ON YOUR FIRST VISIT

☐ TM28 Dig

■ RUIN MANIAC CAVE 1ST TIME

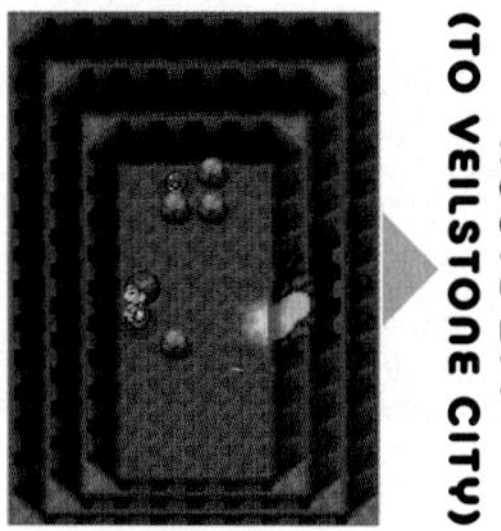

ROUTE 214 (TO VEILSTONE CITY)

■ RUIN MANIAC CAVE 1ST VISIT

IN CAVE

POKÉMON	M	D	N
Geodude	◎	◎	◎
Hippopotas	△	△	△

■ 2ND VISIT (STILL DIGGING) 3RD VISIT (MANIAC TUNNEL)

IN CAVE

POKÉMON	M	D	N
Geodude	◎	◎	◎
Hippopotas	○	○	○

Geodude
Rock-Ground
Abilities:
• Rock Head
• Sturdy

■ RUIN MANIAC CAVE 2ND TIME

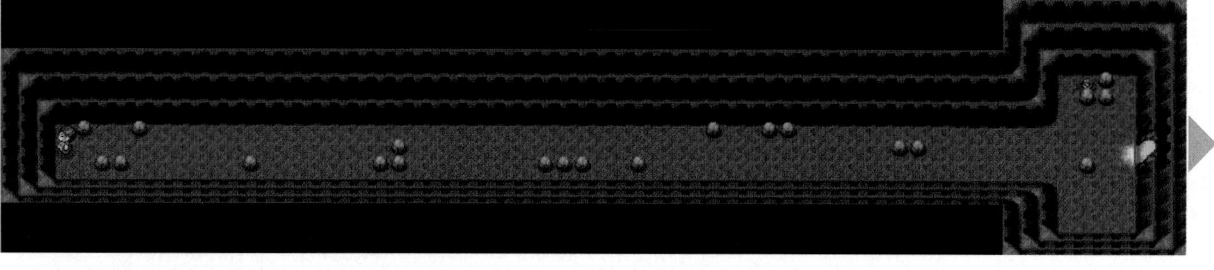

ROUTE 214 (TO VEILSTONE CITY)

■ MANIAC TUNNEL 3RD TIME

SOLACEON RUINS

STEP 1 COMPETE WITH THE RUIN MANIAC

THE RUIN MANIAC WHO DIGS in Maniac Tunnel loves Unown. He suggests that you go capture Unown while he digs on in his cave and wants to turn it into a competition. Go capture various kinds of Unown and report to the Ruin Maniac.

You go and catch the UNOWN,
and I'll keep digging away.

STEP 2 CHECK WITH THE RUIN MANIAC

ONCE YOU HAVE CAUGHT 10 KINDS of them or more, go check on the Ruin Maniac. Compared to how it was in the beginning, the cave now is dug much deeper. The next check point will be after you have collected 26 kinds of Unown. Go back to the ruin to find the rest of them.

Everyone calls me the Ruin Maniac.
Or they used to call me that.

AFTER CAPTURING ALL 26 KINDS OF UNOWN THE TUNNEL CONNECTS TO SOLACEON RUINS

WHEN YOU HAVE CAPTURED 26 kinds of Unown from A to Z, The Maniac Tunnel reaches the 3rd Stage and it finally connects to a hidden room in Solaceon Ruins. In this room you will catch the last 2 remaining ? and ! which will complete the collection of all 28 kinds of Unown.

Wow... My digging punched me through
to this weird place.

UNOWN ARE IN SOLACEON RUINS

THE UNOWN you'll need to capture in a competition with the Ruin Maniac are at Solaceon Ruins. Over there at the ruins, 26 kinds of them from A to Z are available for you to catch.

RUIN MANIAC IS A DIGGING MANIAC

WHEN THE MANIAC TUNNEL reaches the 2nd stage, People start calling the Ruin Maniac a Digging Maniac. Well, he has done all this digging all by himself, he well deserves people's admiration and adulation.

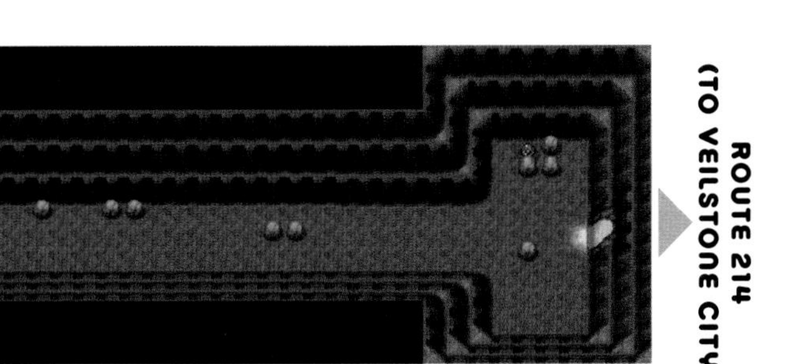

ROUTE 214 (TO VEILSTONE CITY)

Hippopotas
Ground
Abilities:
• Sand Stream

PASTORIA CITY, PASTORIA GREAT MARSH

Pastoria City was created to protect the Pastoria Great Marsh. From the safari observatory, you can enjoy a great command of Pastoria Great Marsh. After taking a tour, walk around the town and challenge Pastoria City Gym.

MOVES REQUIRED TO COMPLETE THIS AREA

SURF

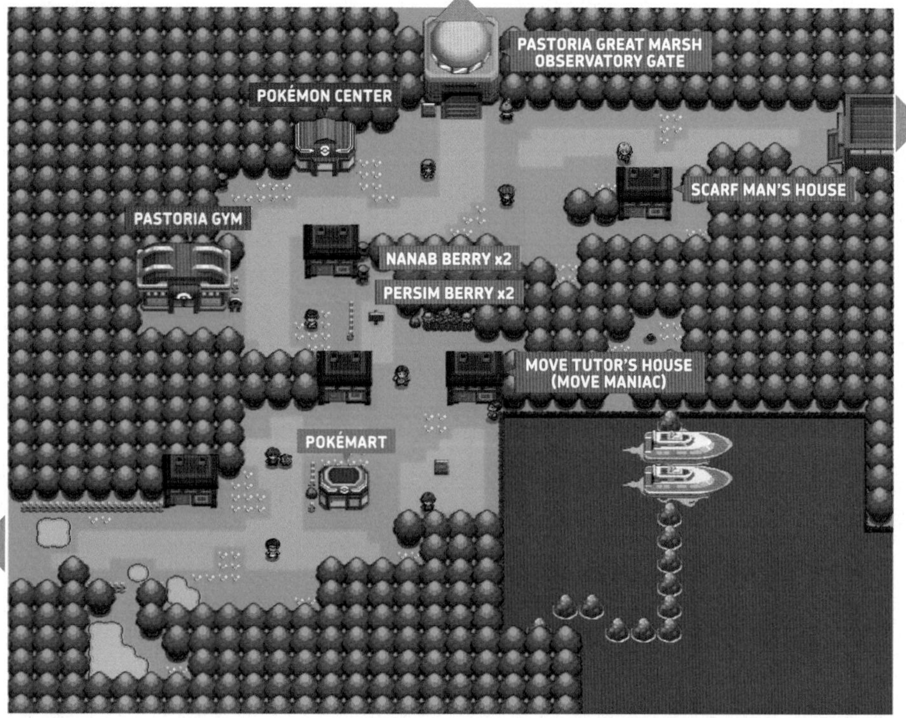

OBTAINABLE ITEMS

ON YOUR FIRST VISIT

☐ One of the following: Turtwig Mask Chimchar Mask or Piplup Mask	☐ Persim Berry x2
☐ Potion	☐ Nanab Berry x2
☐ Honey	☐ HM05 Defog
☐ Super Potion	☐ Super Repel
☐ Parlyz Heal	☐ Great Ball
	☐ Poké Ball
	☐ Antidote

AFTER SHOWING 3 KINDS OF BURMY TO A BOY

☐ Macho Brace

AFTER WINNING PASTORIA CITY GYM BATTLE

☐ Mystic Water

WHEN YOUR PARTY POKÉMON ARE IN A GREAT CONDITION

☐ Red Scarf	☐ Blue Scarf
☐ Pink Scarf	☐ Green Scarf
☐ Yellow Scarf	

AFTER WINNING HEARTHOME CITY GYM BATTLE

☐ Fen Badge	☐ TM55 Brine

POKÉMART (MERCHANT ON THE LEFT)

Item	Price
Air Mail	50
Nest Ball	1000
Dusk Ball	1000
Quick Ball	1000

ON WATER

POKÉMON	VARIABLE
Tentacool	◎
Wingull	◎
Tentacruel	△
Pelipper	△

FISHING

FISHING ROD	POKÉMON	VARIABLE
Old	Magikarp	◎
Good	Magikarp	◎
	Remoraid	○

STEP 1 GET DEFOG IN THE GREAT MARSH

YOU CAN GET HM05 Defog in the Pastoria Great Marsh. Defog is an invaluable field move that clears thick fog surrounding you. Go speak to a man near the gate of the Pastoria Great Marsh and ask him for the HM.

It's the Hidden Machine Defog, but
none of my Pokémon can learn it.

STEP 2 LEARN MOVES FROM A MOVE TUTOR

NEAR THE POKÉMART is the house of the Move Tutor who will teach moves to your Pokémon. Give him one Heart Scale and he will teach your Pokémon moves it has forgotten.

I'll do it if you'll trade me
a Heart Scale.

FIND HEART SCALE IN THE UNDERGROUND

YOU CAN FIND the Heart Scale that the Move Tutor wants to have by digging in the Underground. This is a rare item that is very hard to find, so keep digging until you find one. **(see p.248)**

GYM BATTLE 4

WAKE
PASTORIA GYM LEADER
POKÉMON TYPE: WATER
RECOMMENDED TYPES: GRASS, ELECTRIC

PASTORIA CITY GYM was designed and built as a water maze - in order for you to proceed inside you have to adjust the volume of water by pressing on three different kinds of buttons. Battle your way to the back where you finally face off against Wake. There are six Trainers in all who will challenge you. Wake will employ Water-type Pokémon - deal with him by using Grass- or Electric-type moves and you'll finsh him in no time. When you defeat him, he will give you the Fen Badge and TM55 Brine.

FEN BADGE
You can use HM05 Defog on the field. Make your Pokémon up to Lv50 obey your command.

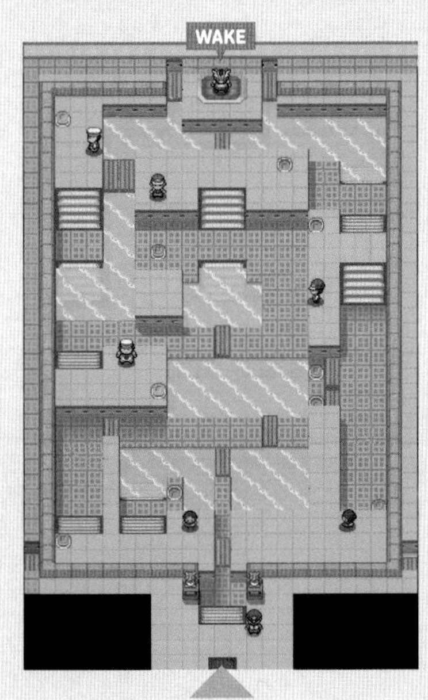

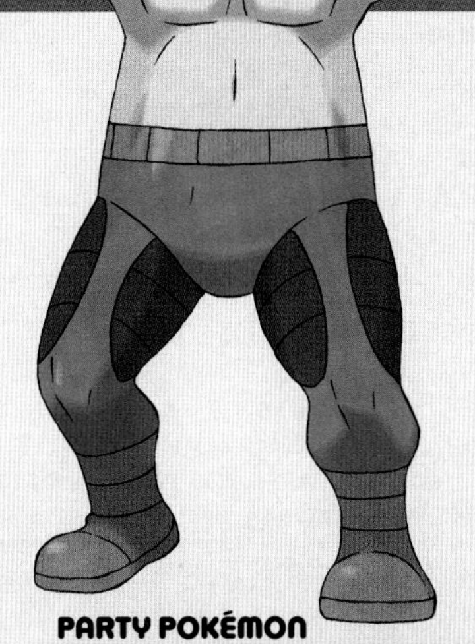

PARTY POKÉMON

POKÉMON	LEVEL	TYPE
Gyarados ♂	Lv27	Water-Flying
Quagsire ♂	Lv27	Water-Ground
Floatzel ♂	Lv30	Water

STEP 3 GET SCARVES FROM THE SCARF GUY

THERE IS A HOUSE NEAR A GATE leading to Route 213 where the Scarf Guy lives. Before you meet him, feed your Pokémon Poffin and have them in very good condition. He will give you five different Scarves based on your Pokémon's condition.

Let me examine your Pokémon to see if it's worthy of a scarf!

SHOW THREE KINDS OF BURMY TO A BOY

IN A HOUSE NORTH of the Pokémart is a boy who wants to see Burmy. Bring three Burmy (Plant Cloak, Sandy Cloak and Trash Cloak) and the boy will give you the Macho Brace.

AFTER WINNING PASTORIA CITY GYM BATTLE
TALK TO A TEAM GALACTIC GRUNT

AFTER YOU WIN THE GYM BATTLE, speak to a Team Galactic Grunt in front of the observatory. He will run towards Route 213 to deliver his mysterious "thing" to the lake. He will stop in front of the gate that leads to Route 213, so talk to him again.

So, now it's my job to deliver this to the lake!

GET ONE RARE BERRY PER DAY

AT A HOUSE WEST of the Pokémart a woman will give you one rare berry per day. The kinds she has are all very rare and unavailable anywhere else in this area. Go see her everyday and collect them all.

BATTLE YOUR RIVAL 3

Compared to the previous battle in Hearthome City, his Pokémon has leveled up several times!

IF YOUR STARTER WAS TURTWIG: YOUR RIVAL WILL CHOOSE:

POKÉMON	LEVEL	TYPE
Starly ♂	Lv26	Normal-Flying
Buizel ♂	Lv25	Water
Roselia ♂	Lv25	Grass-Poison
Monferno ♂	Lv28	Fire-Fighting

IF YOUR STARTER WAS CHIMCHAR: YOUR RIVAL WILL CHOOSE:

POKÉMON	LEVEL	TYPE
Starly ♂	Lv26	Normal-Flying
Roselia ♂	Lv25	Grass-Poison
Ponyta ♂	Lv25	Fire
Prinplup ♂	Lv28	Water

IF YOUR STARTER WAS PIPLUP: YOUR RIVAL WILL CHOOSE:

POKÉMON	LEVEL	TYPE
Starly ♂	Lv26	Normal-Flying
Buizel ♂	Lv25	Water
Ponyta ♂	Lv25	Fire
Grotle ♂	Lv28	Grass

AFTER WINNING PASTORIA CITY GYM BATTLE
HEAD TO ROUTE 213, CHASING THE TEAM GALACTIC GRUNT

THE GRUNT WHO RAN said that he was going to the lake to try and use the "thing". The lake that is in the same direction of Route 213 is Lake Valor. Chase after him towards to stop Team Galactic's evil plans.

SO WHAT WAS THAT THING?

THE THING THAT the Team Galactic Grunt was treating so secretively was brought over from their Storage in Veilstone City. It might be related to the energy they were researching in Galactic Veilstone Building.

CATCH POKéMON IN PASTORIA GREAT MARSH

Grab your Safari Ball and run wild in Pastoria Great Marsh!

IN PASTORIA GREAT MARSH, you can play Safari games for 500 Poké Dollars per turn. You'll get 30 Safari Balls to enjoy this all-you-can-catch game until you've either used up all your balls or taken 500 steps.

TIP 1
THROW FOOD OR MUD AT THEM

POKÉMON IN THE SAFARI GAME can be caught more easily by throwing food or mud at them - but it can also make them flee. Quickly capture them while they are either eating the food and being docile, or mad and preoccupied with the mud.

THROW FOOD	Makes it easier to catch them but once they eat it, they flee.
THROW MUD	Makes it easier to catch them but they get mad and run.

TIP 2
DOUBLE CHECK IN ADVANCE FROM THE OBSERVATORY

THERE IS ONE ADDITIONAL Pokémon-of-the-day in each area of the marsh and it changes every day. Look through the telescope at the observatory to double check all the Pokémon that are available in each area and see if you will be encountering the Pokémon you want to catch.

THE DAILY ADDITIONAL POKéMON	Croagunk, Skorupi, Carnivine, Golduck, Roselia, Staravia, Marill, Azurill, Wooper, Quagsire, Bidoof, Bibarel.

TIP 3
TRAVEL BETWEEN AREAS ON THE MARSH TRAIN

PASTORIA GREAT MARSH is divided into six different areas and you can travel between those areas on the marsh train, also known as the Quick Trams. It's crucial to use this service because you can save up on the limited number of walking steps you have per turn. Upon confirming the location of your target Pokémon at the observatory, hop on Quick Trams and shoot towards the area of your choice.

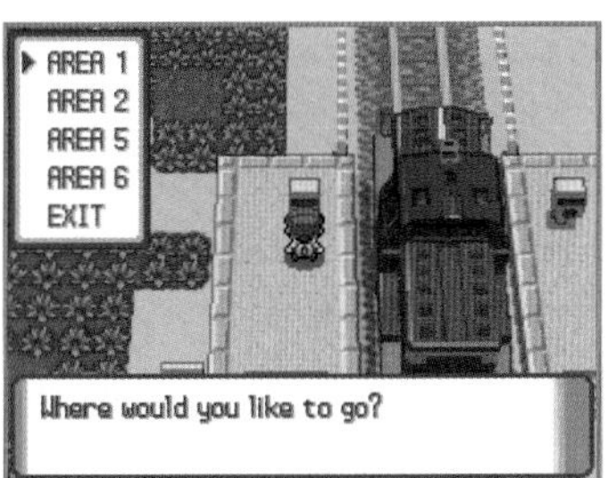

SINNOH ADVENTURE

PASTORIA GREAT MARSH MAP

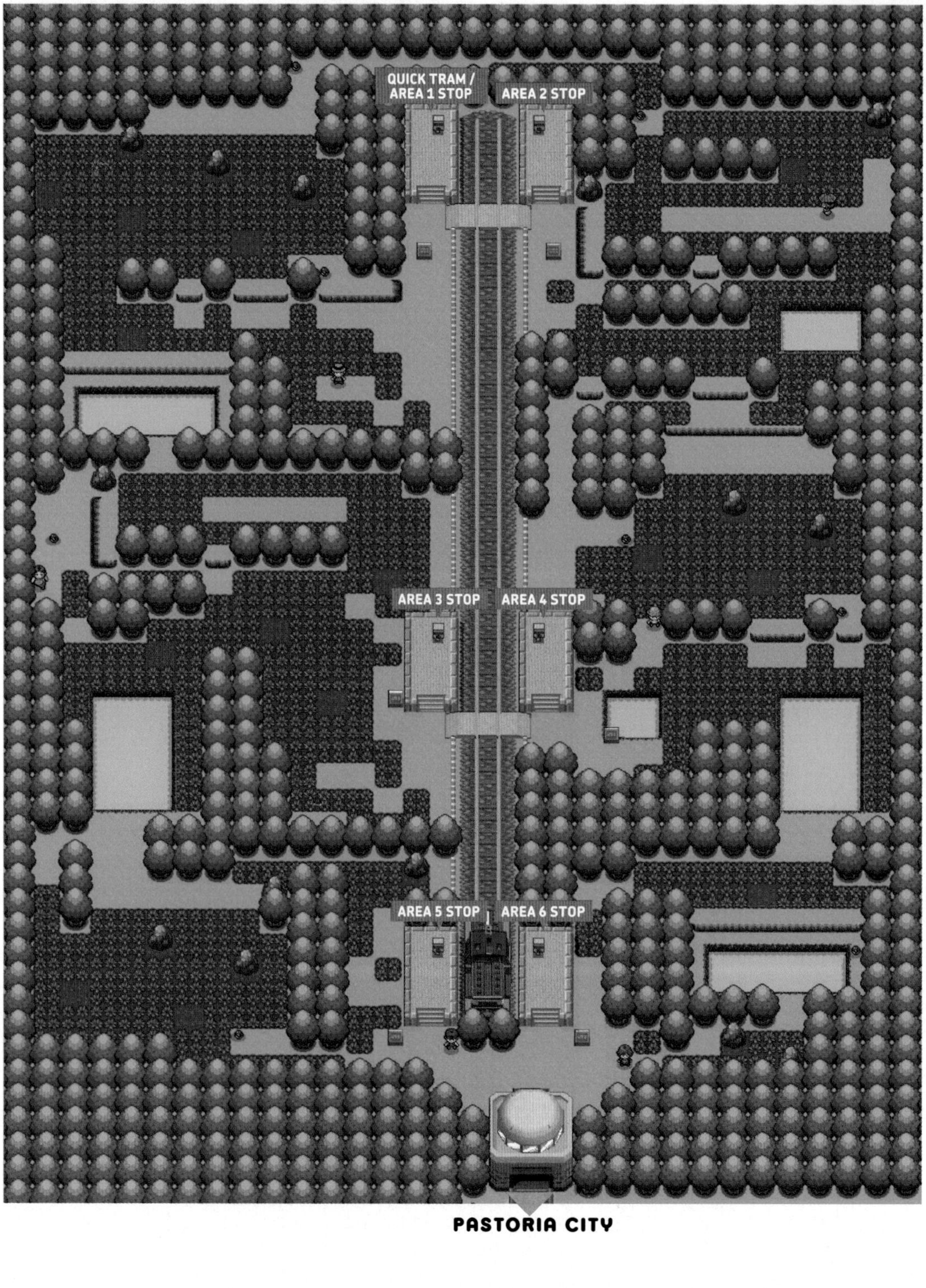

QUICK TRAM / AREA 1 STOP

AREA 2 STOP

AREA 3 STOP

AREA 4 STOP

AREA 5 STOP

AREA 6 STOP

PASTORIA CITY

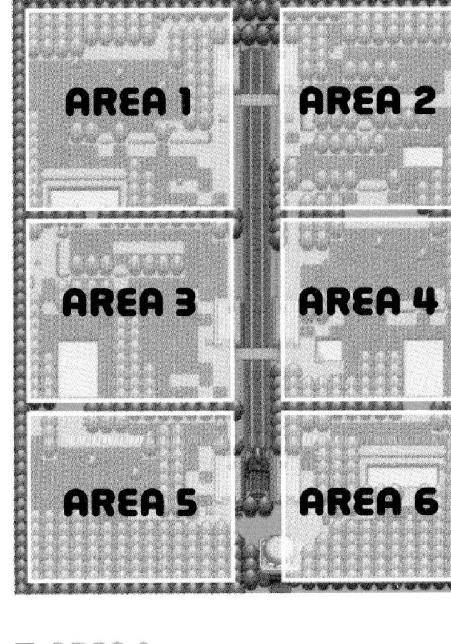

Croagunk
Poison-Fighting
Abilities:
• Anticipation
• Dry Skin

Carnivine
Grass
Ability:
• Levitate

Skorupi
Poison-Bug
Abilities:
• Battle Armor
• Sniper

AREA 1

IN GRASS

POKÉMON	M	D	N
Wooper	○	○	○
Bibarel	○	○	○
Budew	○	○	✕
Starly	○	○	✕
Noctowl	✕	✕	○
Hoothoot	✕	✕	○
Marill	○	○	○
Quagsire	○	○	○
Psyduck	△	△	△
Bidoof	▲	▲	▲
Azurill	▲	▲	▲

AREA 2

IN GRASS

POKÉMON	M	D	N
Wooper	○	○	○
Bibarel	○	○	○
Budew	○	○	✕
Starly	○	○	✕
Noctowl	✕	✕	○
Hoothoot	✕	✕	○
Marill	○	○	○
Quagsire	○	○	○
Psyduck	△	△	△
Bidoof	▲	▲	▲
Azurill	▲	▲	▲

AREA 3

IN GRASS

POKÉMON	M	D	N
Wooper	○	○	○
Bibarel	○	○	○
Budew	○	○	✕
Starly	○	○	✕
Hoothoot	✕	✕	○
Marill	○	○	○
Quagsire	○	○	○
Psyduck	△	△	△
Bidoof	▲	▲	▲
Azurill	▲	▲	▲

AREA 4

IN GRASS

POKÉMON	M	D	N
Wooper	○	○	○
Bibarel	○	○	○
Budew	○	○	✕
Starly	○	○	✕
Hoothoot	✕	✕	○
Marill	○	○	○
Quagsire	○	○	○
Psyduck	△	△	△
Bidoof	▲	▲	▲
Azurill	▲	▲	▲

AREA 5

IN GRASS

POKÉMON	M	D	N
Wooper	○	○	○
Bibarel	○	○	○
Budew	○	○	✕
Starly	○	○	✕
Hoothoot	✕	✕	○
Marill	○	○	○
Quagsire	○	○	○
Bidoof	△	△	△
Azurill	△	△	△

AREA 6

IN GRASS

POKÉMON	M	D	N
Wooper	○	○	○
Bibarel	○	○	○
Budew	○	○	✕
Starly	○	○	✕
Hoothoot	✕	✕	○
Marill	○	○	○
Quagsire	○	○	○
Psyduck	△	△	△
Bidoof	▲	▲	▲
Azurill	▲	▲	▲

ALL AREAS

ON WATER

POKÉMON	VARIABLE
Wooper	◎
Marill	◎
Quagsire	△
Psyduck	△

FISHING

FISHING ROD	POKÉMON	VARIABLE
Old	Magikarp	◎
Good	Magikarp	◎
	Barboach	○
	Gyarados	△

151

DAILY CHANGING POKÉMON

IN CAVE

POKÉMON	M	D	N
Croagunk	○	○	○
Skorupi	○	○	○
Carnivine	○	○	○
Golduck	○	○	○
Roselia	○	○	○
Staravia	○	○	○
Marill	○	○	○
Azurill	○	○	○
Wooper	○	○	○
Quagsire	○	○	○
Bidoof	○	○	○
Bibarel	○	○	○

Azurill
Normal
Abilities:
• Thick Fat
• Huge Power

Quagsire
Water-Ground
Abilities:
• Damp
• Water Absorb

ROUTE 212

Route 212 is a route of two faces, or places rather. One half is a lush property of green trees, green grass, and green with envy when you spy the luxurious Pokémon Mansion and its magnificent Trophy Garden. Then there's the other half of the route, which is full of rain, mud, and muddy puddles that will suck you in. Fun!

OBTAINABLE ITEMS

ON YOUR FIRST VISIT

- ☐ Pecha Berry
- ☐ Pinap Berry x3
- ☐ X Special
- ☐ Zinc
- ☐ Revive
- ☐ TM06 Toxic
- ☐ Great Ball
- ☐ Aspear Berry
- ☐ TM62 Silver Wind
- ☐ Antidote
- ☐ Elixir
- ☐ TM11 Sunny Day
- ☐ TM87 Swagger
- ☐ Soothe Bell
- ☐ Sitrus Berry

AFTER WINNING HEARTHOME CITY GYM BATTLE

- ☐ TM48 Poison Jab
- ☐ Lum Berry
- ☐ Tamato Berry
- ☐ Rose Incense

OBTAIN BY TRADING WITH SHARDS

- ☐ TM11 Sunny Day........................Red Shard x10
- ☐ TM18 Rain Dance.......................Blue Shard x10
- ☐ TM37 Sandstorm.....................Yellow Shard x10
- ☐ TM07 Hail.................................Green Shard x10

ROUTE 212 (PASTORIA CITY SIDE)

IN GRASS

POKÉMON	M	D	N
Budew	◎	◎	◎
Kricketune	○	○	◎
Starly	○	○	○
Staravia	○	○	△
Roselia	○	○	○

ON WATER

POKÉMON	VARIABLE
Psyduck	◎
Golduck	○

FISHING

FISHING ROD	POKÉMON	VARIABLE
Old	Magikarp	◎
Good	Magikarp	◎
	Goldeen	○

ROUTE 212 (HEARTHOME CITY SIDE)

IN GRASS

POKÉMON	M	D	N
Wooper	◎	◎	◎
Bibarel	◎	◎	○
Kricketune	○	○	◎
Roselia	○	○	○

ON WATER

POKÉMON	VARIABLE
Wooper	◎
Quagsire	○

FISHING

FISHING ROD	POKÉMON	VARIABLE
Old	Magikarp	◎
Good	Magikarp	◎
	Barboach	○

ROUTE 212
HEARTHOME CITY

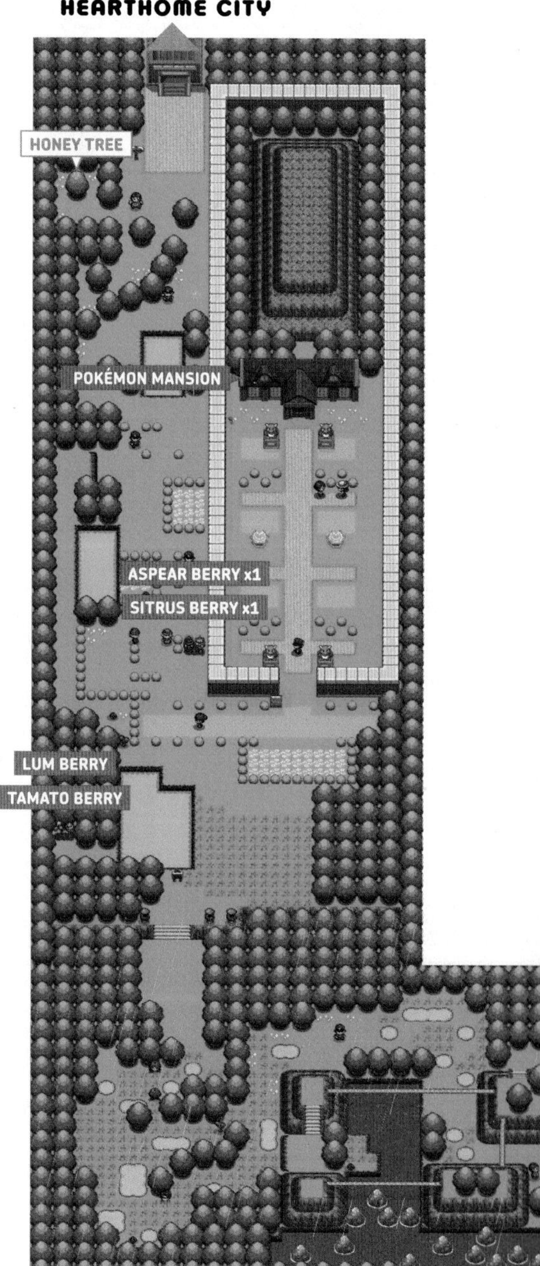

POKéMON MANSION THE TROPHY GARDEN

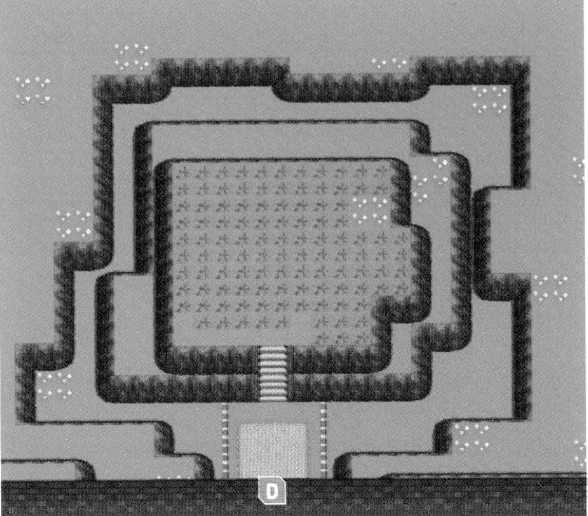

TROPHY GARDEN

IN GRASS

POKÉMON	M	D	N
Roselia	◎	◎	◎
Pichu	◎	◎	◎
Staravia	○	◎	○
Kricketune	○	○	◎
Pikachu	○	○	○

Pichu
Electric
Abilities:
- Static

Pikachu
Electric
Abilities:
- Static

POKéMON MANSION, 1 FL (MAIDS' ROOMS)

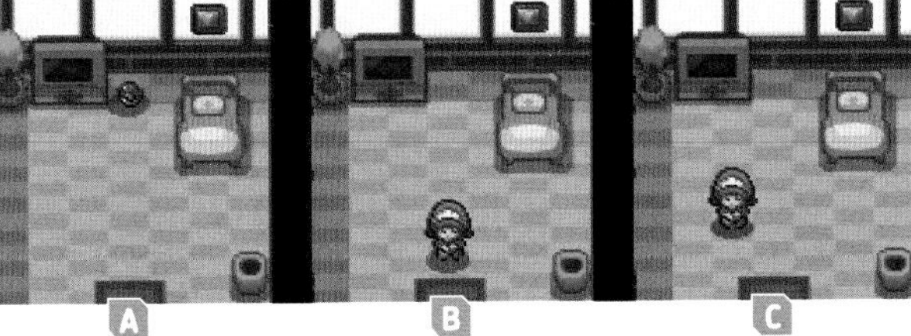

POKéMON MANSION 1 FL (BACKLOT'S ROOM)

POKéMON MANSION, 1 FL

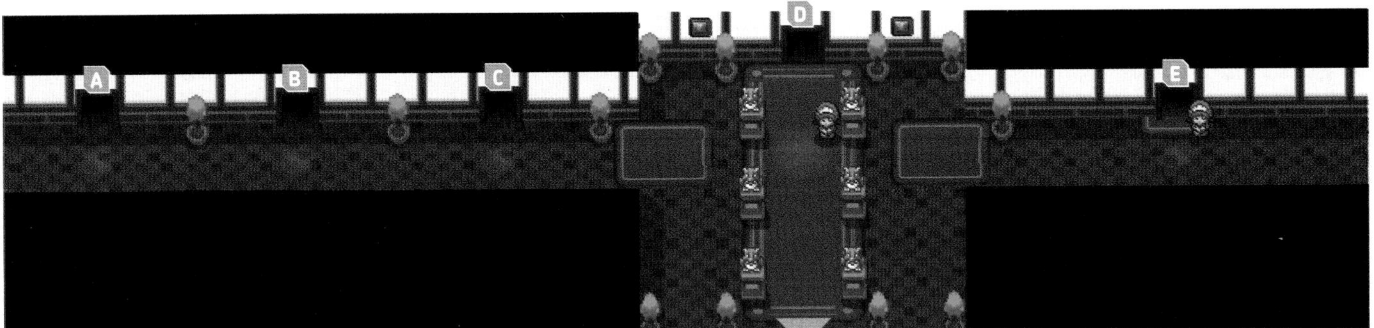

ROUTE 212

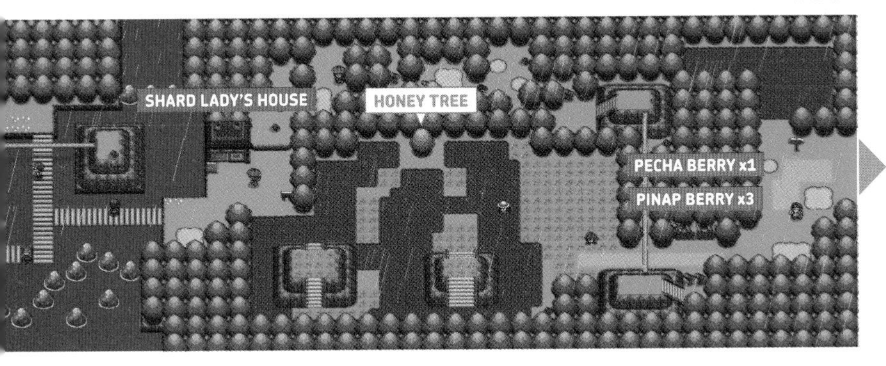

PASTORIA CITY

Budew
Grass-Poison
Abilities:
- Natural Cure
- Poison Point

STEP 1 STUCK IN A PUDDLE? JUST WIGGLE IT!

LET'S FACE IT, there's no way you're going to get across this route without getting a little dirty. Worst of all, you might get stuck in a deep mud puddle! It's not a problem – just hit the d-pad a few times and jimmy yourself out of this annoying mess.

STEP 2 THE TM TRADE

THERE'S A SMALL HOUSE just west of the water, and that's where the Shard Lady lives. This lovely lady will trade you a TM for every 10 of the same color shard that you bring her. These TMs can change the weather during battles, so you might want to do a little exploring to find shards to trade her.

DOWN TO THE UNDERGROUND

BUT WHERE WOULD YOU find shards to give to the Shard Lady? Why, in the Underground, of course. There are four different colors to dig up! (See pg 248)

STEP 3 COME ON AND KNOCK ON HIS DOOR...

BACKLOT IS VERY PROUD of his Trophy Garden, so might as well stop by to appreciate the unique landscaping, the beautiful foliage, and the wide variety of wild Pokémon to catch! He doesn't mind if you add a few to your collection, so build up that Pokédex with some unique catches.

WOW, WHAT A GREAT BRONZE STATUE!

EXCEPT THAT YOU CAN'T touch it, and the security guard standing watch will make sure it stays that way. He's got to take a break some time, right? Well, come back between 2am and 5am and you'll see. Stay awake, set an alarm, or pull some time-travel tricks to unlock this secret.

STEP 4 FLY FOR THE CURE

CYNTHIA GAVE YOU a Secret Potion to cure Psyduck's headaches, so it's time to put it to work. Head back to Route 210 using a shortcut, or use HM02 Fly to go from Hearthome City to Solaceon Town.

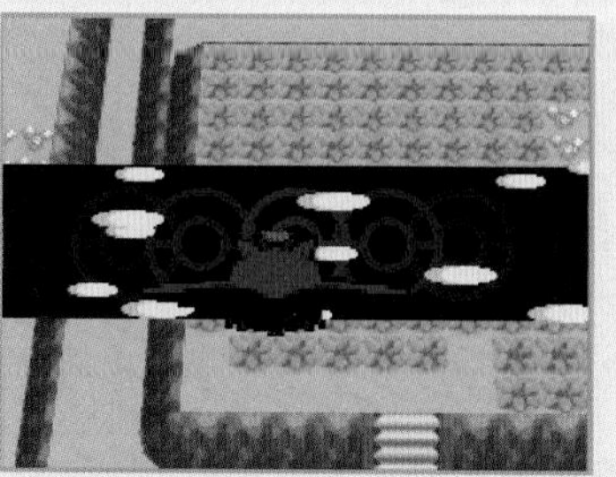

POLICE! FREEZE!

WANDERING AROUND the grounds of the Pokémon Mansion at night, well, that might look a little suspicious. If one of the security guards catches you, he won't hesitate to challenge you to a Pokémon battle.

YOUR GENEROUS BENEFACTORS

People who will give you stuff.

AS YOU TRAVEL through Sinnoh, you'll meet many people who will give you different items and accessories, but only if you show them your Pokémon or meet certain conditions. Who are these people and what do they want from you? Read this list to find out...

FIVE KINDS OF SCARVES

THE SCARF GUY IN PASTORIA CITY
Keep your Pokémon well-fed with Poffin, and this man will give you different scarves based on the condition of your party Pokémon.

P. 148

Let me examine your Pokémon to see if it's worthy of a scarf!

POKÉ BALL

NEWSPAPER OFFICE IN SOLACEON TOWN
The newspaper man will tell you what type of Pokémon he wants to see, so bring him what he wants the same day, he will give a Poké Ball. Don't show him the same Pokémon again – what he wants changes every day.

P. 123

You're just the Pokémon-searching expert we've been looking for!

SEVEN KINDS OF RIBBONS

JULIA IN SUNYSHORE CITY
Julia is a bit lonely, anxiously awaiting the return of her husband, a sailor at sea. She could really use some company, so if you talk to her a bit and answer her questions, she'll give you a different ribbon each day.

P. 195

I know! How about you visit me and tell me stories every so often?

SIXTEEN KINDS OF ACCESSORIES

YOUNG LADY IN A HOUSE IN VEILSTONE CITY
Visit this charming woman once a day so one of your Pokémon can receive a relaxing massage. As part of the experience, she will give you one accessory.

P. 133

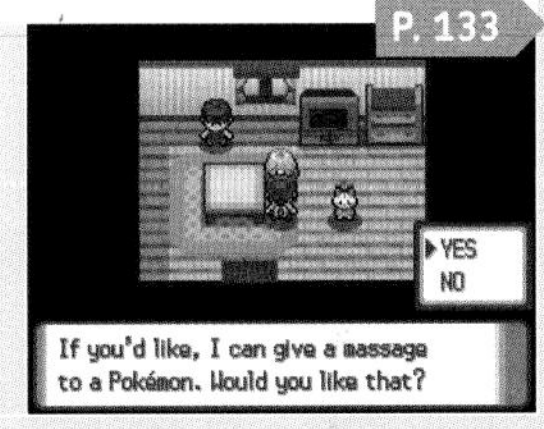

If you'd like, I can give a massage to a Pokémon. Would you like that?

EFFORT RIBBON

YOUNG LADY AT SUNYSHORE MARKET
If your lead Pokémon's stats have gone as high as they could go, this beautiful maiden will give you the Effort Ribbon as a reward to use on that Pokémon.

P. 195

As its reward, please give it this Effort Ribbon.

THREE KINDS OF ITEMS

AN OLD MAN IN A HOUSE ON ROUTE 221
The old man has a thing for strength and expertise, and so will ask to see a Pokémon of a certain level. In exchange, he will give you the Black Belt, the Expert Belt, or the Focus Sash. Come on three different days to collect all three.

P. 053

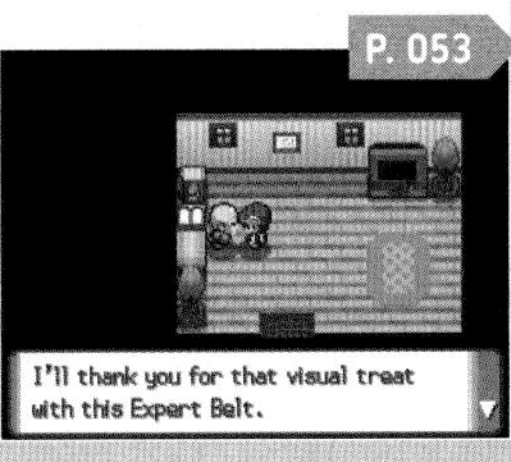

I'll thank you for that visual treat with this Expert Belt.

FOOTSTEP RIBBON

DR. FOOTSTEP ON ROUTE 213
As his name indicates, Dr. Footstep can tell a lot by looking at a Pokémon's footsteps. If your lead Pokémon is happy, he will reward you with a Footstep Ribbon.

P. 141

Lucas received the Footprint Ribbon.

MACHO BRACE

A BOY IN A HOUSE IN PASTORIA CITY
This kid really likes Burmy, so if you show him the three different kinds (Plant Cloak, Sandy Cloak, and Trash Cloak) he'll thank you with a Macho Brace.

P. 148

Since I feel so giddy, take this! Go ahead, take it!

CELESTIC TOWN

Celestic Town is a town of history and tradition, exemplified best by the fresco of ancient Pokémon in the center of town. But things aren't always so rosy, and it's up to you to rid the town of that pesky Team Galactic Grunt casting a pall over this revered landmark.

MOVES REQUIRED TO COMPLETE THIS AREA

SURF

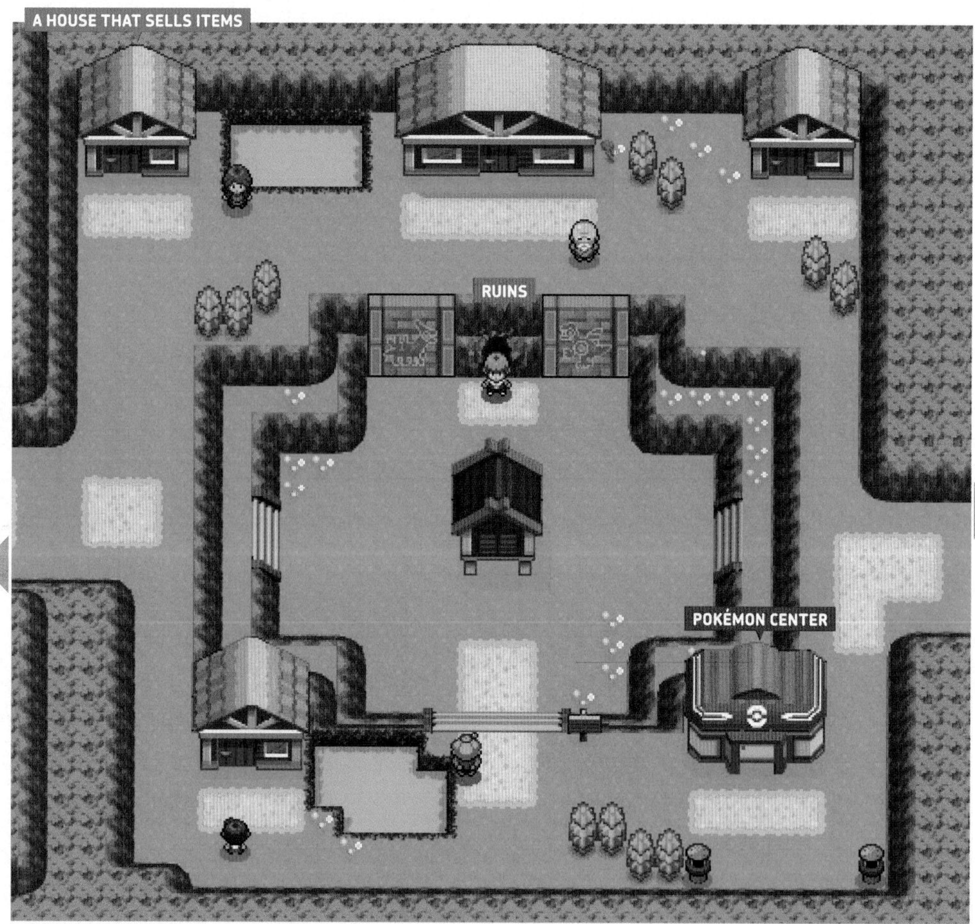

OBTAINABLE ITEMS

ON YOUR FIRST VISIT	
☐ Pokétch application: Analog Watch	☐ HM03 Surf

WHEN YOUR LEAD POKÉMON IS HAPPY
☐ Great Ball

OLD MAN IN HOUSE	
Air Mail	50
Dusk Ball	1000
Quick Ball	1000
Timer Ball	1000

HOUSE ON UPPER LEFT (ITEMS YOU CAN GET FROM MAN)	
4:00am - 10:00am	Choice Specs
10:00am - 8:00pm	Black Glasses
8:00pm - 4:00am	Wise Glasses

ON WATER

POKÉMON	VARIABLE
Psyduck	◎
Golduck	○

FISHING

FISHING ROD	POKÉMON	VARIABLE
Old	Magikarp	◎
Good	Magikarp	◎
	Barboach	○

STEP 1 WATCH YOUR POKÉTCH

THERE'S A SMALL HOUSE west of the Pokémon Center, and inside is a man with an upgrade for your Pokétch. He'll give you the Analog Watch – a timekeeper that indicates the hour and minute with long and short hands. You don't have to use it, but it's always nice to have a choice.

Lucas obtained the Pokétch
app ANALOG WATCH.

STEP 2 SHOP AT HOME

THERE MIGHT NOT BE a Pokémart in Celestic Town, but a couple living in the upper west side has got you covered. Head to this small residence to find an old lady on the right selling the usual Poké Balls and Potions, and an old man on the left selling mail.

There's no Pokémon Mart in this
town...

STEP 3 SEEING THINGS

YOU'RE NOT THE ONLY visitor to the small shop, and there's something to be gained from this man as well. Depending on when you talk to him, he will give you a pair of glasses. There are three different types of glasses – for morning, day, and night – so plan your shop visits accordingly.

STEP 4 GRAPPLE WITH A GRUNT

IT SEEMS SMALL town living doesn't agree with this crook – because there's nothing exciting for him to do, he's threatening to blow up the town and its ruins. Threats like that just won't stand with such a stalwart character as yourself, so teach this Grunt a lesson by defeating him soundly in a Pokémon battle, driving him away and clearing the path to the ruins.

If you try to mess with me, I'll shut
you down with a Pokémon battle.

MESPRIT AT LAKE VERITY?

IN THE ELDER'S HOUSE is an old man who speaks of a God of Emotion – Mesprit. Maybe your rival was right about that rare Pokémon after all...

THE MYTH OF CREATION

THERE'S A LOT TO BE SAID for the word on the street, but a boy you meet in town tells you that the Sinnoh region was created by Pokémon. Looks like those ruins in the center of town warrant further investigation...

ULTRA FRIENDLY

THE PEOPLE of Celestic Town certainly are a friendly lot – and a generous lot, if you approach them the right way. The man on the first floor of the Pokémon Center will give you an Ultra Ball if your lead Pokémon is friendly. You can come back for more as much as you want, but only once a day.

STEP 5 SPECIAL DELIVERY

AS THE HERO of the day, you'll be approached by an old lady who just happens to be Cynthia's grandmother. Good thing too – you still have that Old Charm that Cynthia asked you to pass along to her. After this pleasant exchange, the old woman will give you a tour of the ruins.

KNOWING IS HALF THE BATTLE

IF YOU HEAD back to the elder's house, you'll find a very interesting book on the desk. It's a record of the Sinnoh region, and talks about three very special Pokémon that ruled over Knowledge, Emotion, and Mind. How intriguing!

STEP 6 SURFIN' THE SINNOH REGION

CYNTHIA'S GRANDMOTHER will give you some of the scoop about the fresco and the history of Sinnoh, but she's got an even better gift for you – HM03 Surf. The only catch is that you can't use it yet, since you'll need to defeat Gym Leader Fantina in battle first. Better check to see if she's returned to the Gym in Hearthome City.

JUST WHAT WAS ON THAT FRESCO ANYWAY?

WELL, THERE WAS something about a God, and his three Pokémon. This isn't the first time you've heard about a trio of special Pokémon! Could they be the three Legendary Pokémon that Cynthia is researching?

STEP 7 SPEAKING WITH CYRUS

LEAVING THE RUINS, you'll find the blue-haired man you met back on Mt. Coronet waiting for you. You might not have known his name before, but you'll certainly remember it now, as he introduces himself as Cyrus, leader of Team Galactic! You might not have much to tell him now, but he wants a scoop should you find out about the power behind the legend...

I'VE SAID TOO MUCH

WHEN CYRUS TELLS YOU that Team Galactic is trying to find out the power of the legend in order to create a perfect world, it's not surprising. After all, we've seen his grunts and commanders mumbling about energy and power in our encounters with them.

STEP 8 HEARTHOME IS WHERE THE BADGE IS...

YOU NEED the Relic Badge in order to use HM03 Surf. And you need the Relic Badge in order to compete in the Sinnoh Pokémon League. So what are you waiting for? Time to head back to Hearthome City, where Gym Leader Fantina awaits.

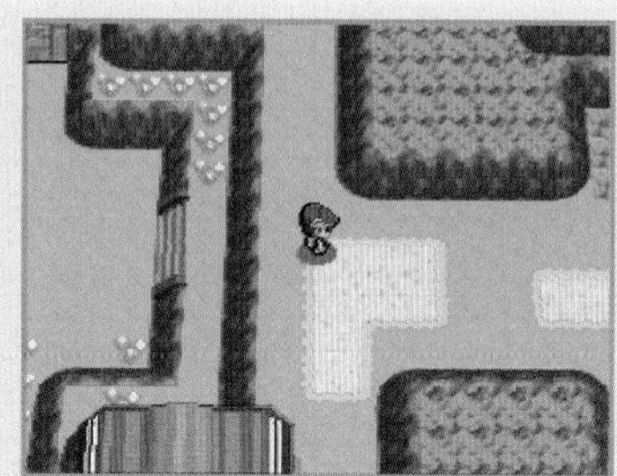

DAILY LIFE IN SINNOH

Events and battles that change every day

THE CLOCK NEVER STOPS TICKING in the region of Sinnoh, even when you're not playing. Monday to Sunday, and all the hours in between are present in the game, and there are activities for active Trainers every day of the week. Check out some of the daily events here.

NEW TRAINER TO BATTLE EVERY DAY

P. 056

1 FL OF JUBILIFE TV IN JUBILIFE CITY

Television is an exciting business, so it figures that there's a new Trainer to battle every single day in the studios of Jubilife TV. And to make it even more exciting, there's always an audience on hand to witness the action.

YES
NO
I've spotted a charismatic Trainer! Is it OK to go for the scoop?

NEW TRAINER TO BATTLE EVERY DAY

P. 140

THE SEVEN STARS RESTAURANT BY LAKE VALOR

Drop in during business hours (9am - 11pm) to check out some hot battles inside this trendy locale. The menu may not be different, but the Trainers change daily.

PLAY THE LOTTO FOR PRIZES

P. 056

1 FL OF JUBILIFE TV IN JUBILIFE CITY

While you're in the lobby at Jubilife TV, why not play the Pokémon Lotto? Prize items change daily, so it's always worth a second (and third) look.

YES
NO
Would you like to draw a Pokémon Loto Ticket?

PURCHASE STICKERS FOR YOUR POKÉ BALL

P. 195

SUNYSHORE MARKET IN SUNYSHORE CITY

Want to add a little flair to your Poké Balls? Head to the market and check out the ever-changing selection of stickers – from music to flowers to bubbles, there's a wide variety of designs, but the selection changes every day.

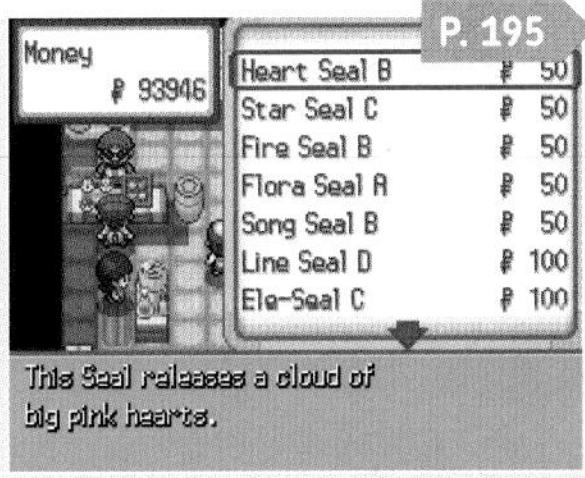

EXPAND YOUR VOCABULARY

P. 177

AN OLD MAN IN A HOUSE IN SNOWPOINT CITY

Ever wanted to bone up on those big, standardized-test-caliber words? This old man is willing to help you out once a day, with such vocabulary as "compulsory education" that is sure to leave rival Trainers' heads spinning.

YES
NO
Hello, hello. Would you like to hear a trendy saying?

FIVE KINDS OF BERRIES

P. 077

PICK A PECK OF COLORS FLOWER SHOP IN FLOAROMA TOWN

All these beautiful flowers, and there's yet another reason you might want to visit this store regularly. Talk to the woman with long black hair and she will give you one of five different kinds of berries every day.

Obtained the Aspear Berry!

SEVEN KINDS OF BERRIES

P. 148

A YOUNG LADY IN A HOUSE IN PASTORIA CITY

Pay this sweet young woman a visit and she'll be happy to give you a gift of a berry. Not only are there 17 different kinds that she gives out, but they're all rare, making the treat even sweeter.

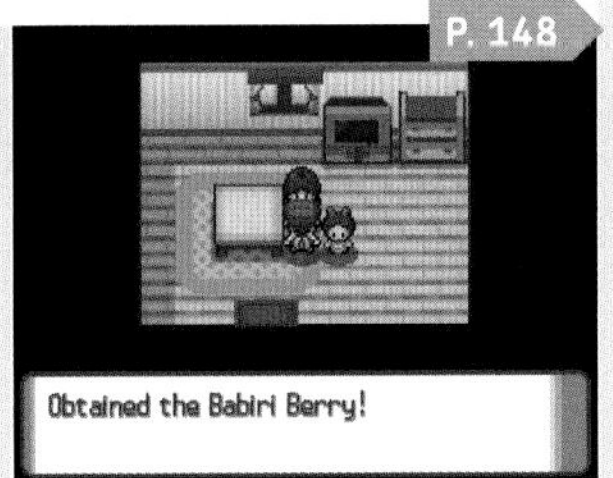

Obtained the Babiri Berry!

TWENTY SIX KINDS OF BERRIES

P. 109

BERRY MASTER ON ROUTE 208

The Berry Master knows a lot about berries and he would love to share that knowledge, along with the berries in his collection, 26 different kinds at all. Drop by each day for a new lesson in berryology!

Everyone seems to call me the Berry Master.

CANALAVE CITY

If you ever decided that it was a sailor's life for you, then Canalave City is the place to be. This exotic port town is home to numerous boats, a canal that splits the city in two, and the useful Canalave Library.

MOVES REQUIRED TO COMPLETE THIS AREA

SURF

OBTAINABLE ITEMS

ON YOUR FIRST VISIT
☐ TM48 Skill Swap

AFTER WINNING CANALAVE CITY GYM BATTLE	
☐ Mine Badge	☐ TM91 Flash Cannon

POKÉMART (MERCHANT ON THE LEFT)	
Air Mail	50
Quick Ball	1000
Timer Ball	1000
Repeat Ball	1000

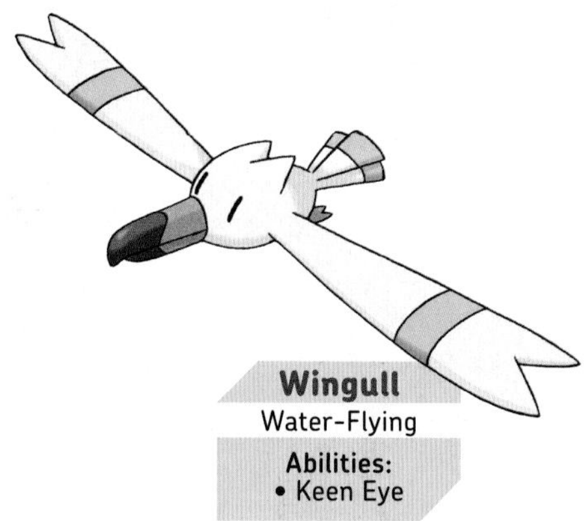

Wingull
Water-Flying

Abilities:
• Keen Eye

ROUTE 218 (TO JUBILIFE CITY)

ON WATER

POKÉMON	VARIABLE
Tentacool	◎
Wingull	◎
Tentacruel	△
Pelipper	△

FISHING

FISHING ROD	POKÉMON	VARIABLE
Old	Magikarp	◎
Good	Magikarp	◎
	Finneon	○

Finneon
Water

Abilities:
• Swift Swim
• Storm Drain

THE POWER TO FORGET

IT TAKES A LOT of time and patience to be really happy with your Pokémon's stats and moves. Until you reach that point, you'll find the services of the Move Deleter to be incredibly useful – he can make your Pokémon forget any move they've learned, even HMs! This is great for freeing up slots for new learned moves and TMs.

SORRY, WE'RE CLOSED

IT'S GREAT TO LIVE right next to the water, and someone in Canalave City is lucky enough to have their own lodge just north of the Pokémon Center. Unfortunately, you can't peer inside – the door's locked and there's no one around to let you in.

CROSS THAT BRIDGE

THE CANALAVE GYM is on the other side of the canal, so you'll have to use the bridge to get there. Alas, it seems your rival has beaten you there, and now you'll need to battle him if you want to progress any further. His Pokémon are much stronger than you remember, so best to stock up and heal up at the Pokémart and Pokémon Center before trying to cross.

BATTLE YOUR RIVAL 4

Not only have his Pokémon gone up by as much as seven levels, but he's also added another Pokémon to his team roster for a total of five.

IF YOUR STARTER WAS TURTWIG: YOUR RIVAL WILL CHOOSE:

POKÉMON	LEVEL	TYPE
Staravia ♂	Lv 31	Normal-Flying
Buizel ♂	Lv 32	Water
Heracross ♂	Lv 30	Bug-Fighting
Roselia ♂	Lv 32	Grass-Poison
Monferno ♂	Lv 35	Fire-Fighting

IF YOUR STARTER WAS CHIMCHAR: YOUR RIVAL WILL CHOOSE:

POKÉMON	LEVEL	TYPE
Staravia ♂	Lv 31	Normal-Flying
Roselia ♂	Lv 32	Grass-Poison
Heracross ♂	Lv 30	Bug-Fighting
Ponyta ♂	Lv 32	Fire
Prinplup ♂	Lv 35	Water

IF YOUR STARTER WAS PIPLUP: YOUR RIVAL WILL CHOOSE:

POKÉMON	LEVEL	TYPE
Staravia ♂	Lv 31	Normal-Flying
Buizel ♂	Lv 32	Water
Heracross ♂	Lv 30	Bug-Fighting
Ponyta ♂	Lv 32	Fire
Grotle ♂	Lv 35	Grass

SECRETS OF THE LOCAL LIBRARY

THE CANALAVE LIBRARY is well-known throughout the land and for good reason – they have a huge collection of books about the myths and legends of the Sinnoh region. Given your recent misadventures, you should check out every book on the 3 FL, where you can find out more about those Legendary Pokémon you keep hearing about.

STEP 4 BUILD UP AT IRON

IN A TOWN with so many boats, it would be a shame if you didn't get at least one ride. If you head to the harbor in the south of town, a sailor named Eldritch will offer you a ride to Iron Island, where you can train your Pokémon for the upcoming Gym battle.

WHAT A FAMILY!

FAMILY CONNECTIONS run deep in Sinnoh, as you'll see when you meet Byron. Roark - the Gym Leader of Oreburgh City - is his son! And it turns out that Underground Man of Eterna City is a relative as well.

GYM BATTLE 6

BYRON

CANALAVE CITY GYM LEADER
POKÉMON TYPE: STEEL
RECOMMENDED TYPES: FIRE, WATER

CANALAVE CITY GYM has four floors, but it's no straight-up climb. You'll need to take lifts up and down in order to navigate between the twisting walls until you finally reach Byron on the 4 FL. You way will be hampered by seven Trainers scattered throughout the floors. When you finally reach Byron, be prepared for a Steel-type barrage that is easily countered with Fire-, Water-, Ground-, and Fighting-type moves. For all your hard work, Byron will bestow upon you the Mine Badge and TM91 Flash Cannon.

The MINE BADGE allows use of HM04 Strength on the field, and ensures that all Pokémon up to level 70 will obey your commands.

2 FL

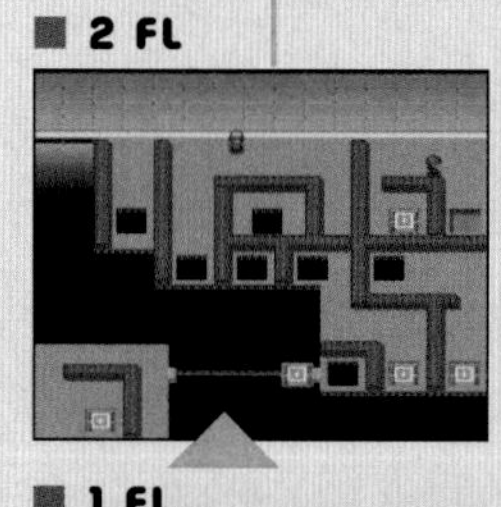

4 FL

1 FL

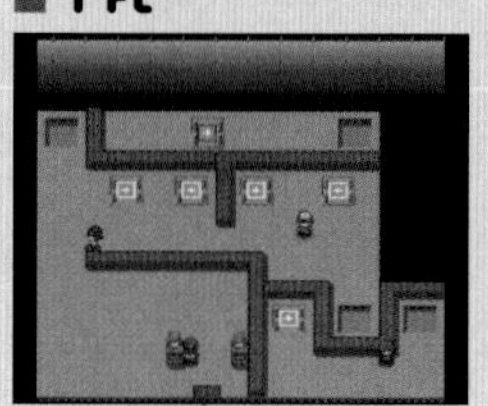

3 FL

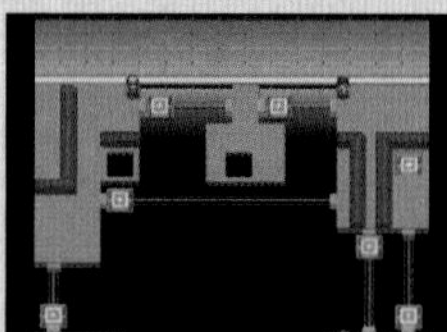

ENTRANCE

PARTY POKÉMON

POKÉMON	LEVEL	TYPE
Bronzor	Lv36	Steel-Psychic
Steelix ♂	Lv36	Steel-Ground
Bastiodon ♂	Lv39	Rock-Steel

AFTER WINNING CANALAVE CITY GYM BATTLE
WHAT DOES HE WANT NOW?

AS YOU COME OUT of the Canalave City Gym after you've won the battle against Byron, you'll see your rival at the exit who was waiting for you. Being always in a rush, he just tells you to come to the library and gets back on his way. Hurry up and go after him.

Anyways, Lucas, come with me to the library.

AFTER THE BATTLE AT CANALAVE CITY GYM
PROFESSOR ROWAN'S STORYTIME

HEAD TO THE 3 FL of Canalave Library again, where Professor Rowan and his assistant are waiting for you. Just when your rival thinks he has elsewhere to be, Professor Rowan tells him to stay – he's got some things to tell you about Pokémon Evolution.

AFTER THE BATTLE AT CANALAVE CITY GYM
PROFESSOR ROWAN'S REQUEST

THAT PROFESSOR ROWAN, always asking favors... well, not so much. But he wants the three of you (you, your rival, and his assistant) to go find the Legendary Pokémon that live in the three lakes in Sinnoh. So your rival is off to Lake Acuity, his assistant to Lake Verity, and you? To Lake Valor you go!

AFTER THE BATTLE AT CANALAVE CITY GYM
SHAKE, RATTLE, AND ROLL

AN EARTHQUAKE HITS! It's just a natural disaster, right? Nope. When you head outside, turns out the whole thing was caused by Team Galactic setting off explosives near Lake Valor. Is something wrong with the Legendary Pokémon there? Better get yourself to Lake Valor before it's too late.

FAMILY MATTERS

ELDRITCH IS PRETTY BUSY with his boat, taking passengers to Iron Island. But he's got a family waiting for him back home, and if you return to his house after earning the National Pokédex, you might see something special.

IRON ISLAND

Iron Island is just off the coast of Eterna City. It's long past its glory days of crystal mining but has experienced a second renaissance as a training ground for the Pokémon Trainers of Sinnoh.

1 FL

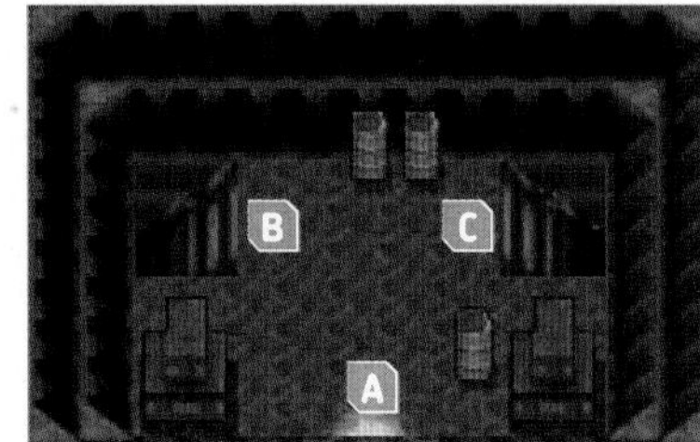

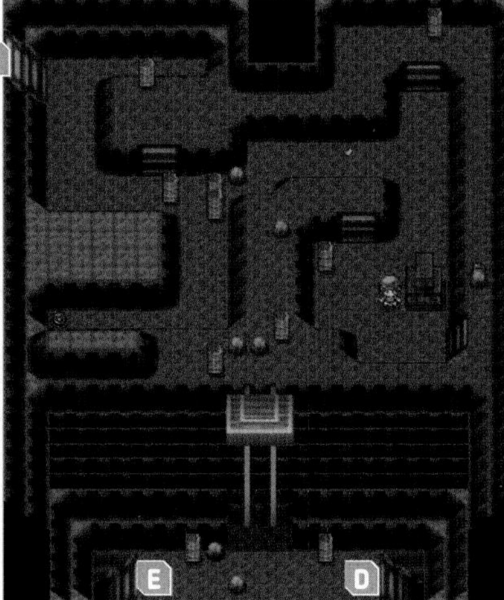

OUTSIDE

Pelipper
Water-Flying
Abilities:
• Keen Eye

OBTAINABLE ITEMS	
☐ Iron Ball	☐ Magnet
☐ Escape Rope	☐ Max Potion
☐ Super Repel	☐ HP Up
☐ Max Ether	☐ Pokémon Egg
☐ TM23 Iron Tail	☐ Shiny Stone
☐ Ultra Ball	

OUTSIDE

ON WATER

POKÉMON	VARIABLE
Tentacool	◎
Wingull	◎
Tentacruel	△
Pelipper	△

FISHING

FISHING ROD	POKÉMON	VARIABLE
Old	Magikarp	◎
Good	Magikarp	◎
	Finneon	○

1 FL

IN CAVE

POKÉMON	M	D	N
Geodude	◎	◎	◎
Graveler	◎	◎	◎
Zubat	○	○	○
Golbat	○	○	○
Onix	○	○	○

B1F 1 2

IN CAVE

POKÉMON	M	D	N
Graveler	◎	◎	◎
Golbat	○	○	○
Onix	○	○	○
Geodude	▲	▲	▲

■ B2F 2

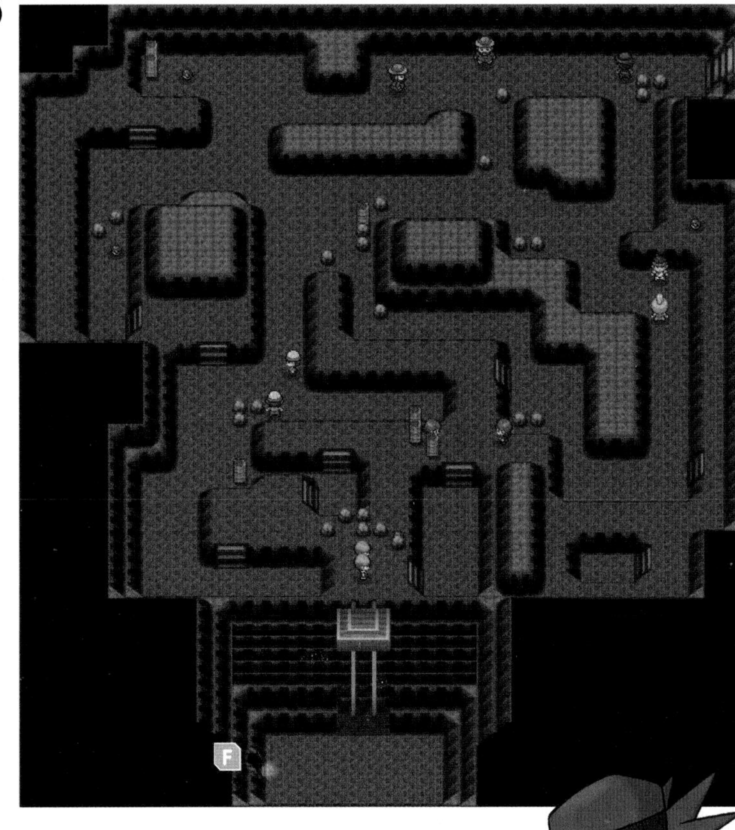

■ B3F

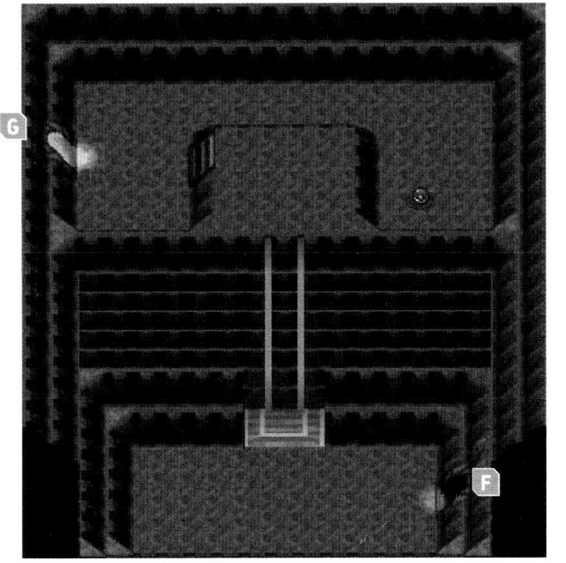

■ B2F 1

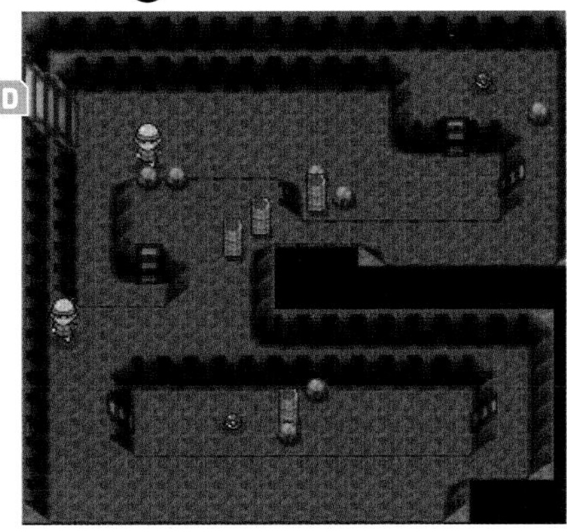

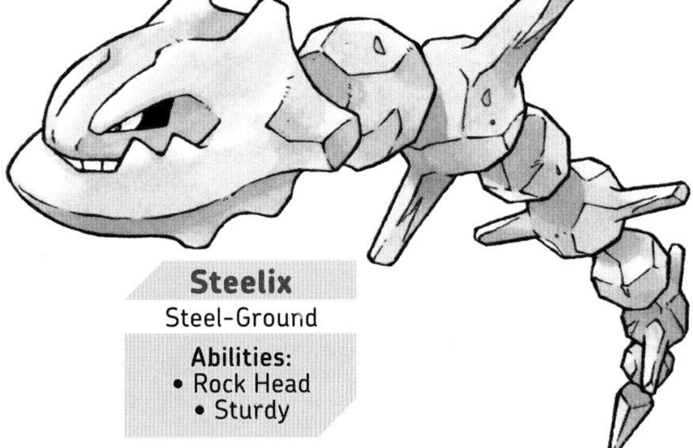

Steelix
Steel-Ground
Abilities:
• Rock Head
• Sturdy

Graveler
Rock-Ground
Abilities:
• Rock Head
• Sturdy

RILEY

■ B2F 1

IN CAVE

POKÉMON	M	D	N
Graveler	◎	◎	◎
Onix	◎	◎	◎
Golbat	○	○	○
Geodude	▲	▲	▲

■ B2F 2, B3F

IN CAVE

POKÉMON	M	D	N
Graveler	◎	◎	◎
Onix	◎	◎	◎
Golbat	○	○	○
Steelix	○	○	○
Geodude	▲	▲	▲

STEP 1 ALL ABOARD

TAKE THE BOAT out of Canalave City and head to Iron Island. Climb the stairs to the east, enjoying your last bit of sunshine here before you enter the cave. Looking north, you might notice the exit to the cave, but right now, your major concern is heading down into the depths...

EMPTY NEST?

CLIMB THE STAIRWAY near the harbor and you'll find a deserted house. Nothing special here, right? Well, not right now, but if you come back after getting the National Pokédex, you'll get something extra special.

STEP 2 WHAT'S UNDER THAT HAT?

HEAD DOWN to B2F to meet Riley, a dapper young man who makes as much time for Pokémon as he does for fashion. He's a bit concerned about all the commotion among the Pokémon 'round here, so the two of you will end up exploring the cave together. He certainly won't drag you down - after every battle, he heals your Pokémon's HP and PP!

If you'd like, we could team up.
The wild Pokémon here are restless.

STEP 3 TRAINER + TRAINER = DOUBLE BATTLE!

TAKE THE LIFT and you'll find the passage blocked by two Team Galactic Grunts. The odds might have been against you before, but with Riley and his Lucario on your side, it's all fair in love and Pokémon battling.

We're abducting all the Pokémon from
this rusted-out Iron Island!

STEP 4 HELLOS AND GOODBYES

YOU MUST HAVE MADE a good impression on Riley, because he decides to give you a Pokémon Egg as a present, one which will eventually hatch into Riolu if you carry it around. Unfortunately, it's a bittersweet present, as this is where you and this tailored Trainer will part.

YES
NO
Would you take it with you?

AND BABY MAKES SIX

YOU CANNOT ACCEPT the Egg from Riley if your Pokémon party is full. You'll need to head to the Pokémon Center in Canalave City and leave one of your Pokémon there for the time being. Don't worry about missing out - Riley will hang around with the Egg until you come back.

CARDED

Your Trainer Case and Trainer Card

SO MUCH TO DO, so much to say about you... luckily your Trainer Card is around to keep track of everything and say it all. It keeps the records of your adventure, like the Pokémon you've seen, and how long you've spent on the road. The Trainer Card changes from time to time, so check it occasionally to see your progress.

ALL ABOUT THIS BRAVE TRAINER

THE CARD KEEPS RECORDS of your allowance, how many Pokémon you've seen, how much time you've played, and even the date you started the game. On the back of the card (hit 'A') you'll see the results of any battles you've played over wireless, as well as any trades. The most notable part of the card is the score – which increases based on your activities in the game. The more you play, the higher the score will be.

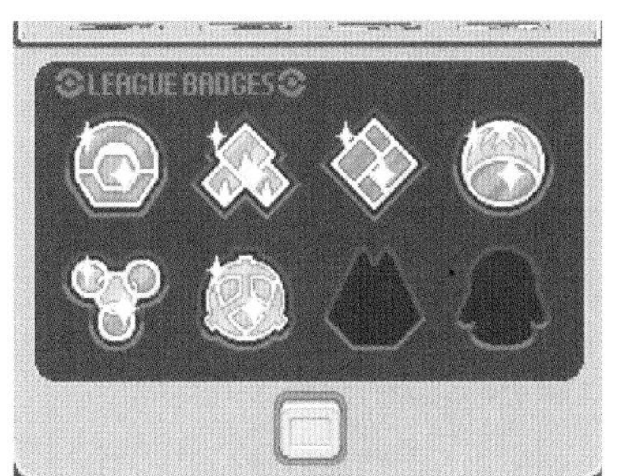

SPIT AND SHINE

WHILE YOU SHOULDN'T spit on your DS, you should tap the button on the bottom screen while the Trainer Card is on-screen to open your Trainer Case and see the Gym badges that you've earned. If you've never opened it before, your badges might look a little dull. Rub them with the stylus to shine them up until they sparkle.

There are 5 conditions to be met over the course of the game, each of which will upgrade your Trainer Card. The color will change and a star will be added, to indicate your skill level as a Pokémon Trainer. Work hard at the following goals to prove yourself a superb Trainer.

FIVE BY FIVE

THERE ARE 5 CONDITIONS to be met over the course of the game, each of which will upgrade your Trainer Card. The color will change and a star will be added, to indicate your skill level as a Pokémon Trainer. Work hard at the following goals to prove yourself a superb Trainer.

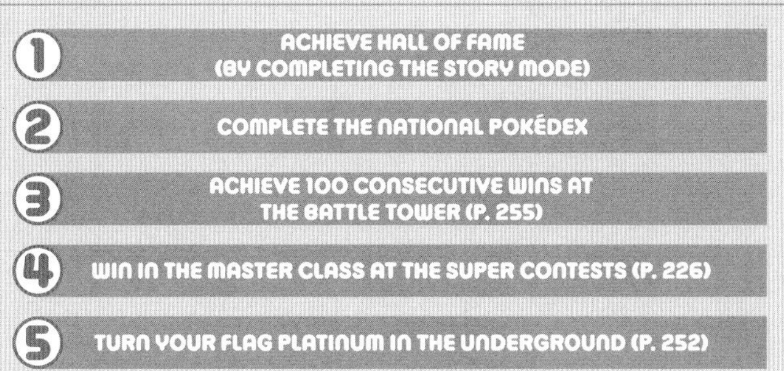

1. ACHIEVE HALL OF FAME (BY COMPLETING THE STORY MODE)
2. COMPLETE THE NATIONAL POKÉDEX
3. ACHIEVE 100 CONSECUTIVE WINS AT THE BATTLE TOWER (P. 255)
4. WIN IN THE MASTER CLASS AT THE SUPER CONTESTS (P. 226)
5. TURN YOUR FLAG PLATINUM IN THE UNDERGROUND (P. 252)

LAKE VALOR

Lake Valor has special significance in the water-abundant Sinnoh region because it is where the Legendary Pokémon Azelf lives. But now Team Galactic is causing some explosive trouble in the area, trying to seize this elusive Pokémon for themselves.

LAKE VALOR

VALOR LAKEFRONT

VALOR CAVERN

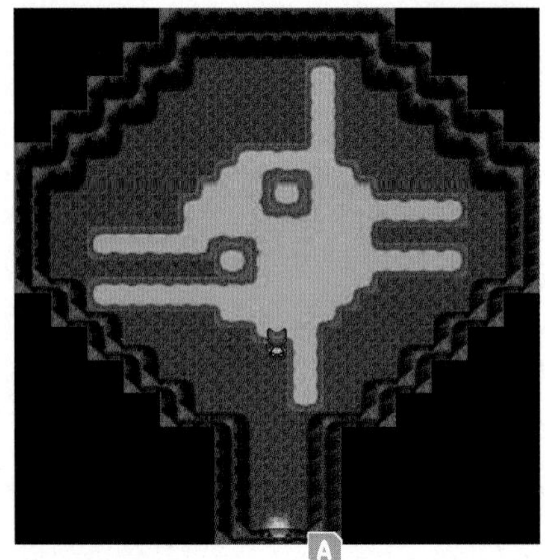

LAKE VALOR

AFTER VISITING SPEAR PILLAR

POKÉMON	M	D	N
Bibarel	◎	◎	◎
Psyduck	○	○	○
Chingling	○	○	○
Staravia	○	○	△
Noctowl	✕	✕	○

ON WATER

POKÉMON	VARIABLE
Psyduck	◎
Golduck	○

FISHING

FISHING ROD	POKÉMON	VARIABLE
Old	Magikarp	◎
Good	Magikarp	◎
	Goldeen	○

STEP 1 A DROUGHT OF MORE THAN IDEAS

YOU MIGHT NOT HAVE wasted time in heading over to Lake Valor, but it's too late – in addition to causing an earthquake in Canalave City, the Team Galactic explosives have completely dried up Lake Valor! Apparently they've stuck around to admire their handiwork, as Team Galactic Grunts are everywhere.

We set off the Galactic Bomb!
Its blast force was phenomenal!

POOR MAGIKARP!

WITH NO WATER to swim in, these poor Pokémon are just floundering around in what few puddles remain, unwanted by Team Galactic.

STEP 2 TOO LATE!

TEAM GALACTIC proudly declares that they already have their hands on the poor Legendary Pokémon. What are you going to do? Well, you're going to enter the cavern in the center of the lake, that's what. And you're going to challenge Saturn, a Team Galactic Commander. Bring it!

...Would you like to join the MAGIKARP
and flop around in the mud?

GALACTIC BATTLE 1

SATURN
TEAM GALACTIC COMMANDER

LIKE THE MULTIPLE RINGS of the planet, Saturn has many different types of Pokémon. You'll need to be flexible with your team. Lay the smackdown on Alakazam with Bug-, Ghost-, or Dark-type moves. Take out Toxicroak with Ground-, Flying-, or Psychic-type moves. And Bronzor? Well, some Fire-type moves should do the trick.

PARTY POKÉMON

POKÉMON	LEVEL	TYPE
Kadabra ♂	Lv 35	Psychic
Bronzor	Lv 35	Steel-Psychic
Toxicroak ♀	Lv 37	Poison-Fighting

STEP 3 VERIFY AT VERITY

EVEN AS YOU humiliate Saturn in battle, things are not looking rosier. It seems almost like you were a stalling tactic – his co-worker Mars is after another Pokémon at Lake Verity! That's where the Professor sent his assistant – are they alright?

By now, Mars should have captured
the Pokémon of Lake Verity...

LAKE VERITY (SECOND VISIT)

MOVES REQUIRED TO COMPLETE THIS AREA

SURF

Maybe it's too late, as Team Galactic has already arrived and taken over the lake, but it's not too late to save Professor Rowan and his assistant.

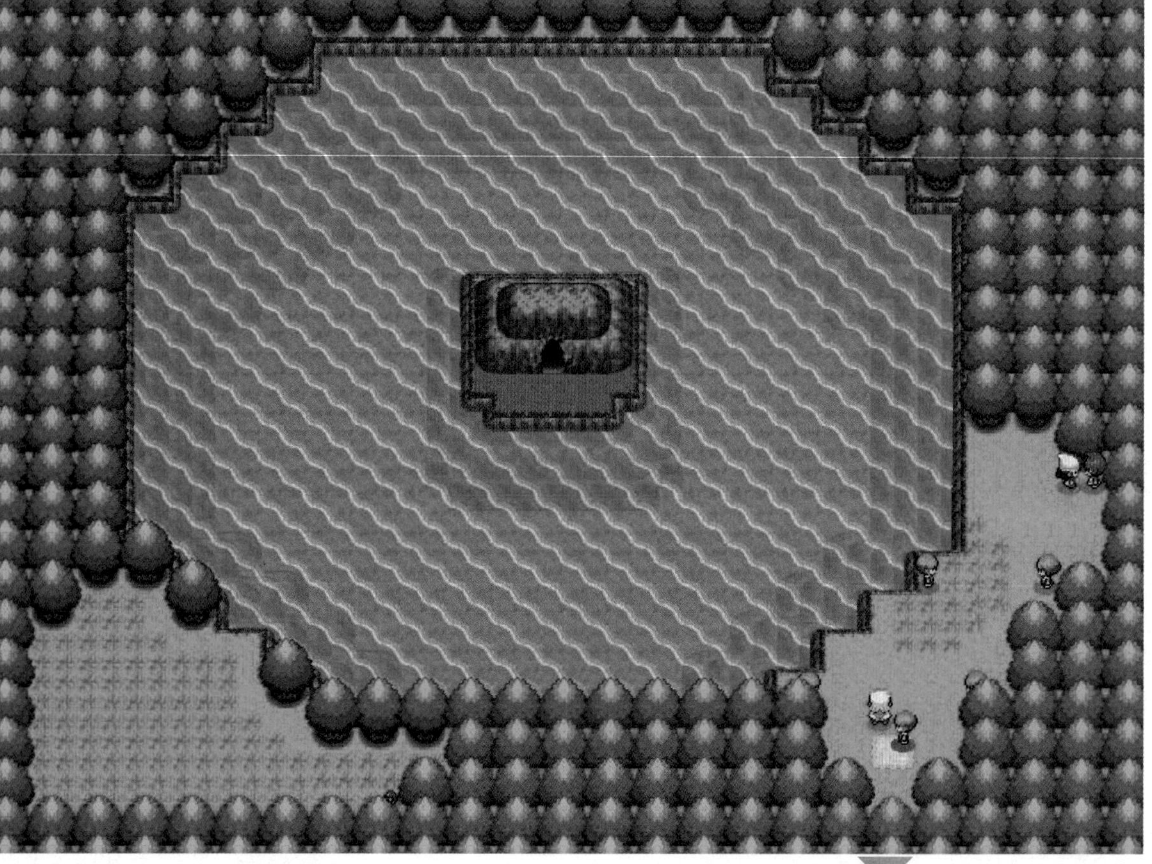

VERITY LAKEFRONT (TO TWINLEAF TOWN)

IN GRASS

POKÉMON	M	D	N
Starly	◎	◎	◎
Bidoof	◎	◎	◎

ON WATER

POKÉMON	VARIABLE
Psyduck	◎
Golduck	○

FISHING

FISHING ROD	POKÉMON	VARIABLE
Old	Magikarp	◎
Good	Magikarp	◎
	Goldeen	○

Psyduck
Water

Abilities:
• Damp
• Cloud Nine

IN THE NICK OF TIME

TEAM GALACTIC move pretty quickly, and when you arrive, Lake Verity's swarming with Grunts. Professor Rowan and his assistant are doing their best to fight them off, but the odds are against them. Maybe you can even the odds...

Those Team Galactic scoundrels are after the legendary Pokémon!

THE RIGHT TIME

IF YOU ARRIVE at Lake Verity before batting Commander Saturn, then you've gotten there way too early and nothing will ever happen. Make sure you battle Saturn first before heading to this next phase of the adventure.

ASSIST THE ASSISTANT!

PROFESSOR ROWAN'S assistant is doing their best, but things aren't looking good for this wily Trainer. Head out in the grass bush to find them battling desperately against Mars – if you talk to Mars, you'll swap places and end up in a truly cosmic battle.

So, what is it? Are you some lovey-dovey couple to the rescue?

GALACTIC BATTLE 2

MARS
TEAM GALACTIC COMMANDER

MARS IS A FIERCE combatant, with a mix of Pokémon that might present a problem to a less-prepared Trainer, but not to one with Electric-, Ice-, Psychic-, or Rock-type moves to take out her Golbat, Fighting-type moves for her Bronzor, and Fire-type moves to put her Bronzor (and her plans) to rest.

PARTY POKéMON

POKéMON	LEVEL	TYPE
Golbat ♀	Lv 37	Poison-Flying
Bronzor	Lv 37	Steel-Psychic
Purugly ♀	Lv 39	Normal

ACCELERATE TO ACUITY

YOU MAY HAVE defeated one of their commanders, but you haven't put the kibosh on Team Galactic's plans at all – they've spirited off with the Legendary Pokémon Mesprit. But all is not lost, as there's still one lake with a Legendary left. Best make your way to Lake Acuity post-haste.

Another legendary Pokémon was taken away by Team Galactic...

ROUTE 216, ROUTE 217, AND ACUITY LAKEFRONT

Snow falls from Mt. Coronet, blanketing the landscape in a thick white snow. As tempting as it is to avoid the blizzard by hiding inside with some hot chocolate, you have an important mission to undertake, and so you must make your way through the deep blankets of white.

MOVES REQUIRED TO COMPLETE THIS AREA

ROCK CLIMB

OBTAINABLE ITEMS

ON YOUR FIRST VISIT

- ☐ Ice Heal
- ☐ TM07 Hail
- ☐ Iron
- ☐ Spell Tag
- ☐ HM08 Rock Climb
- ☐ Icicle Plate
- ☐ Ultra Ball

AFTER WINNING SNOWPOINT CITY GYM BATTLE

- ☐ Mental Herb
- ☐ HP Up
- ☐ TM13 Ice Beam

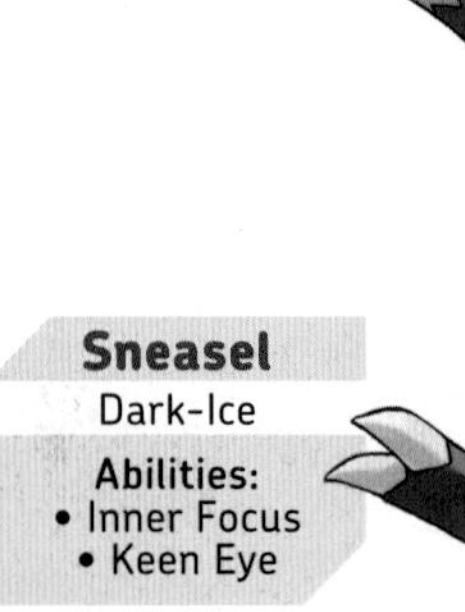

Sneasel
Dark-Ice
Abilities:
• Inner Focus
• Keen Eye

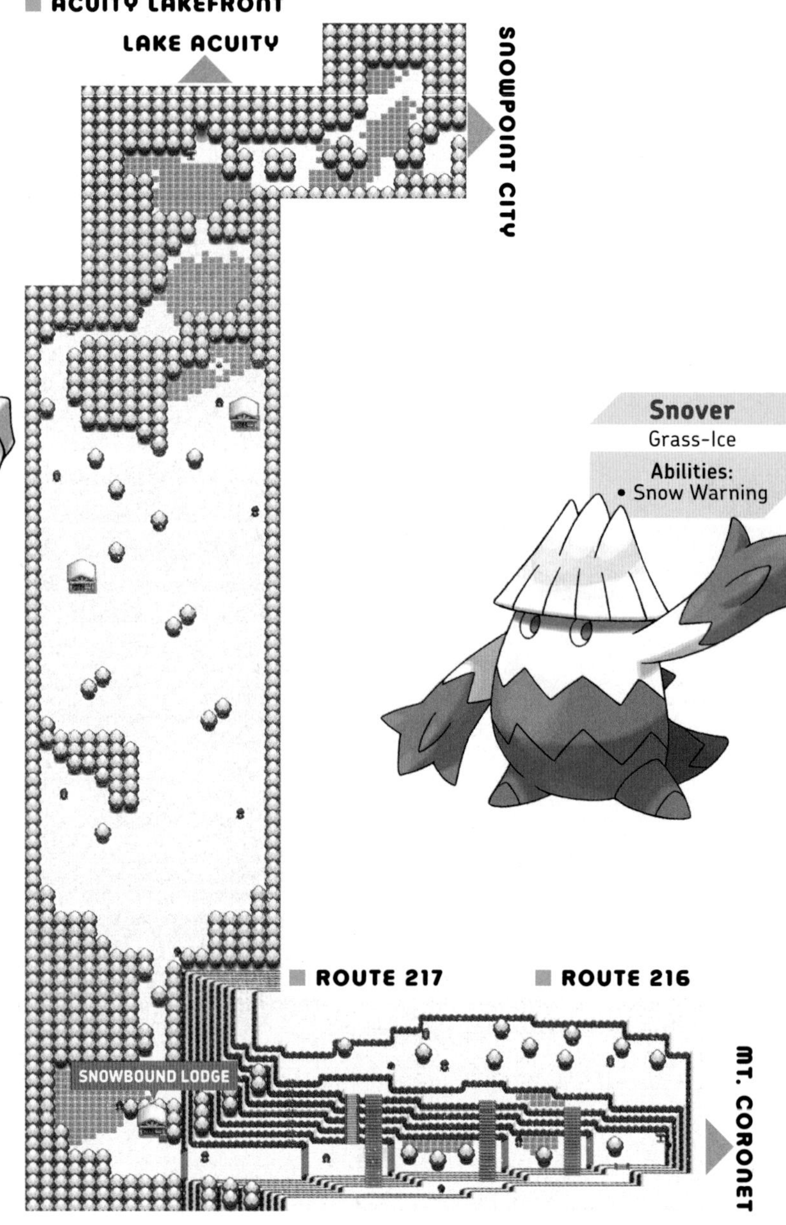

Snover
Grass-Ice
Abilities:
• Snow Warning

ROUTE 216

IN GRASS

POKÉMON	M	D	N
Snover	○	○	○
Sneasel	○	○	○
Meditite	○	○	○
Machoke	○	○	○
Graveler	○	○	○
Zubat	✕	✕	○
Noctowl	✕	✕	○

ROUTE 217

IN GRASS

POKÉMON	M	D	N
Snover	○	○	○
Sneasel	○	○	○
Machoke	○	○	○
Medicham	○	○	○
Meditite	○	○	✕
Zubat	✕	✕	○
Noctowl	✕	✕	○

THE WINTER WEATHER WALK

IT'S GOING TO BE a tough trek to Snowpoint City, since as the name indicates, it's snowing. Snowing enough that the routes on the way are completely covered and you might have a bit of trouble getting though the snow drifts. Just take your time, moving slowly, and you just might be able to avoid getting really stuck.

HAIL DROPS KEEP FALLING ON MY HEAD

IT'S NOT FUN to walk in, and it's certainly less fun to battle in this weather. Every battle from Route 216 to Snowpoint City will take place in Hail conditions, causing damage to all Pokémon except Ice-types. Plan ahead and be careful.

SETTLE DOWN FOR A SHORT WINTER'S NAP

WHAT A LOVELY little lodge, nestled here at the intersection of Route 216 and 217. Even lovelier is the cozy little bed in the room, especially when you need a rest. Walk up to the bed and press 'A' to completely restore all of your Pokémon's HP and PP. This is the only place to rest before Snowpoint City, so make the most of it.

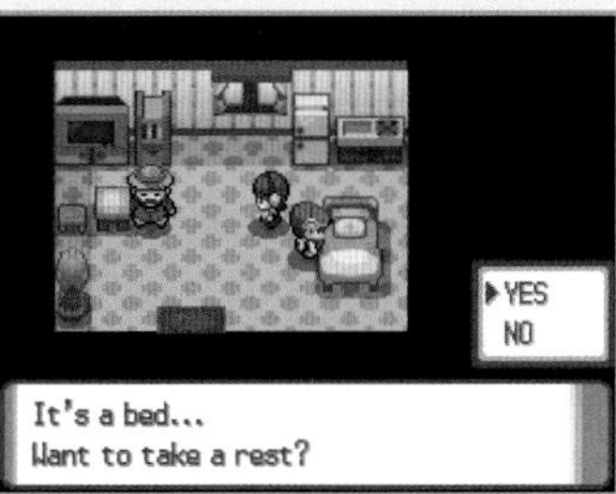

COVER UP

YOU'LL MEET (and battle) lots of Trainers on the way to Snowpoint City, but you won't get a good look at their usual stylish outfits – they're all bundled up to keep from the cold!

SENSE OF SNOW

BEHIND YOU it's white, in front of you it's white – the snow makes everything all white and hard to see! It's so thick and deep that you can't even use your Running Shoes or Bicycle. The only way to cope is to go through it slowly, and make sure you don't miss any good items.

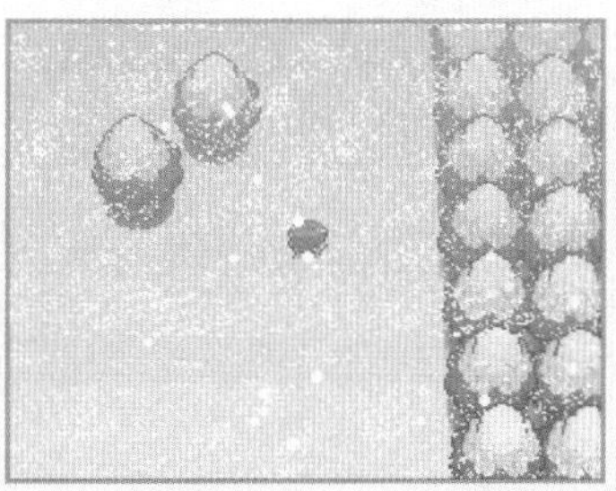

THE ICE COVERED ROCK MYSTERY

SPEAKING OF not missing anything, there's a grass bush hiding an item related to the Evolution of a certain Pokémon. Thing is, you won't meet this Pokémon until you've obtained the National Pokédex.

BE A MOUNTAIN CLIMBER

A FEW SOULS are brave enough to make their homes on this snowy route. And if you're brave enough to stand the cold, check the ground near the home on the east carefully for something hidden under the snow – you'll be rewarded with HM08 Rock Climb.

STEP 5 (DON'T) BREAK ON THROUGH TO THE OTHER SIDE

YOU WERE ALL SET to head to Lake Acuity, but unfortunately, your path is blocked by two Team Galactic Grunts. They can't be talked into moving, and you can't force your way past. What to do? Best to kill time by challenging the Gym Leader in Snowpoint City.

We're here to make sure Snowpoint's Gym Leader doesn't disturb us!

EVERYBODY LOVES... CLEFAIRY???

WHAT KEEPS **these Team Galactic Grunts so steadfast in their duty to keep people away from Lake Acuity? Apparently, it's the reward of their very own Clefairy. Go figure.**

AFTER THE BATTLE AT SNOWPOINT CITY GYM
ROCK CLIMB YOUR WAY TO NEW ITEMS

AFTER WINNING the Icicle Badge, you should be able to use the HM08 Rock Climb. And what use is that? Plenty, actually, since you can head back to Route 216 and climb up the craggy cliffs to access the TM13 Ice Beam – definitely a plus to have in battle.

AFTER THE BATTLE AT SNOWPOINT CITY GYM
FINALLY, LAKE ACUITY

APPARENTLY winning the Icicle Badge means some R-E-S-P-E-C-T for you, 'cause now the Team Galactic Grunts will move out of your way, allowing you to enter the lake. Your rival should be there – is he okay?

You're here to see the lake Pokémon, too?

POKÉMON TRAINER CATALOGUE 1

Remember when you battled those twins, or that cyclist? Here's a list of all of the types of Trainers you've encountered thus far on your quest throughout Sinnoh. How many do you recognize?

YOUNGSTER

LASS

SCHOOL KID (BOY)

SCHOOL KID (GIRL)

CAMPER

PICNICKER

WORKER

REPORTER

CAMERAMAN

CLOWN

INTERVIEWER

GUITARIST

POP IDOL

POKÉ KID

AROMA LADY

TWINS

HIKER

BATTLE GIRL

BUG CATCHER

PSYCHIC (MALE)

PSYCHIC (FEMALE)

P.I.

FISHERMAN

BEAUTY

NINJA BOY

BIRD KEEPER

CYCLIST (MALE)

CYCLIST (FEMALE)

SCIENTIST

COLLECTOR

RUIN MANIAC

BLACK BELT

ARTIST

POKÉMON BREEDER (MALE)

POKÉMON BREEDER (FEMALE)

RANCHER

COWGIRL

YOUNG COUPLE

ROUGH NECK

POKÉFAN (MALE)

POKÉFAN (FEMALE)

BELLE AND PA

WAITRESS

POLICEMAN

GENTLEMAN

SOCIALITE

EXPERT

SNOWPOINT CITY

What a beautiful world of silvery white snow! You might want to take a look around, but don't forget that you're here for one thing above all: your seventh Gym badge.

OBTAINABLE ITEMS

AFTER WINNING SNOWPOINT CITY GYM BATTLE	
☐ Icicle Badge	☐ TM72 Avalanche

PÓKEMART (SALES PERSON ON THE LEFT)	
Snow Mail	50
Dusk Ball	1000
Quick Ball	1000
Timer Ball	1000

SNOWPOINT TEMPLE

TRADE: HAUNTER (GIVE MEDICHAM)

HOUSE OF AN OLD MAN WHO TEACHES YOU "TRENDY SAYINGS"

SNOWPOINT GYM

POKÉMART

POKÉMON CENTER

ACUITY LAKEFRONT

STEP 1 NOT FOR TOURISTS

NORTH OF SNOWPOINT CITY GYM is Snowpoint Temple, and it looks like a pretty impressive place. Unfortunately, you cannot enter right now. A woman will stop you, because it's not open to the public. At least, not open until you receive the National Pokédex...

Only the chosen may enter
the Snowpoint Temple.

HOW'S YOUR VOCABULARY?

IT'LL GET A TURBO charge when you talk to a man in a house near the Gym. He'll teach you some nice brain-stretching words like "ubiquitous" and "omnibus" once every day.

GYM BATTLE 7

CANDICE

SNOWPOINT GYM LEADER
POKéMON TYPE: ICE
RECOMMENDED TYPES: FIRE, FLYING

WHEN YOU ENTER Snowpoint City Gym, you'll have to work your way around the Gym, sliding down and crushing snowballs until you finally reach Candice at the top. Six Trainers will block your path to this cute but clever Gym Leader. When you finally approach her on the dais, you'll find that the three f's will serve you best: Fire-, Flying-, and Fighting-types. For your own cunning efforts, you will be awarded a Icicle Badge and TM72 Avalanche.

The ICICLE BADGE will allow you to use HM08 Rock Climb on the field.

PARTY POKéMON

POKéMON	LEVEL	TYPE
Snover ♀	Lv38	Grass-Ice
Sneasel ♀	Lv38	Dark-Ice
Medicham ♀	Lv40	Fighting-Psychic
Abomasnow ♀	Lv42	Grass-Ice

STEP 2 BACK AGAIN

NOW THAT YOU'VE DEFEATED the Snowpoint City Gym, those Team Galactic Grunts are ready to give you the space you crave by getting out of your way and letting you proceed on to Lake Acuity. Time to check on that Legendary Pokémon!

ONLY THE TALENTED MAY BOARD

THERE'S A SAILOR by the water on the boat, but he has standards set for those who will ride on his boat. Come back after finishing the story mode, when you've entered the Hall of Fame.

LAKE ACUITY

MOVES REQUIRED TO COMPLETE THIS AREA

SURF

Lake Acuity is the last of the three lakes that represent Sinnoh, along with Lake Valor and Lake Verity. Each had its own Legendary Pokémon, but now it looks like you're too late to save the third...

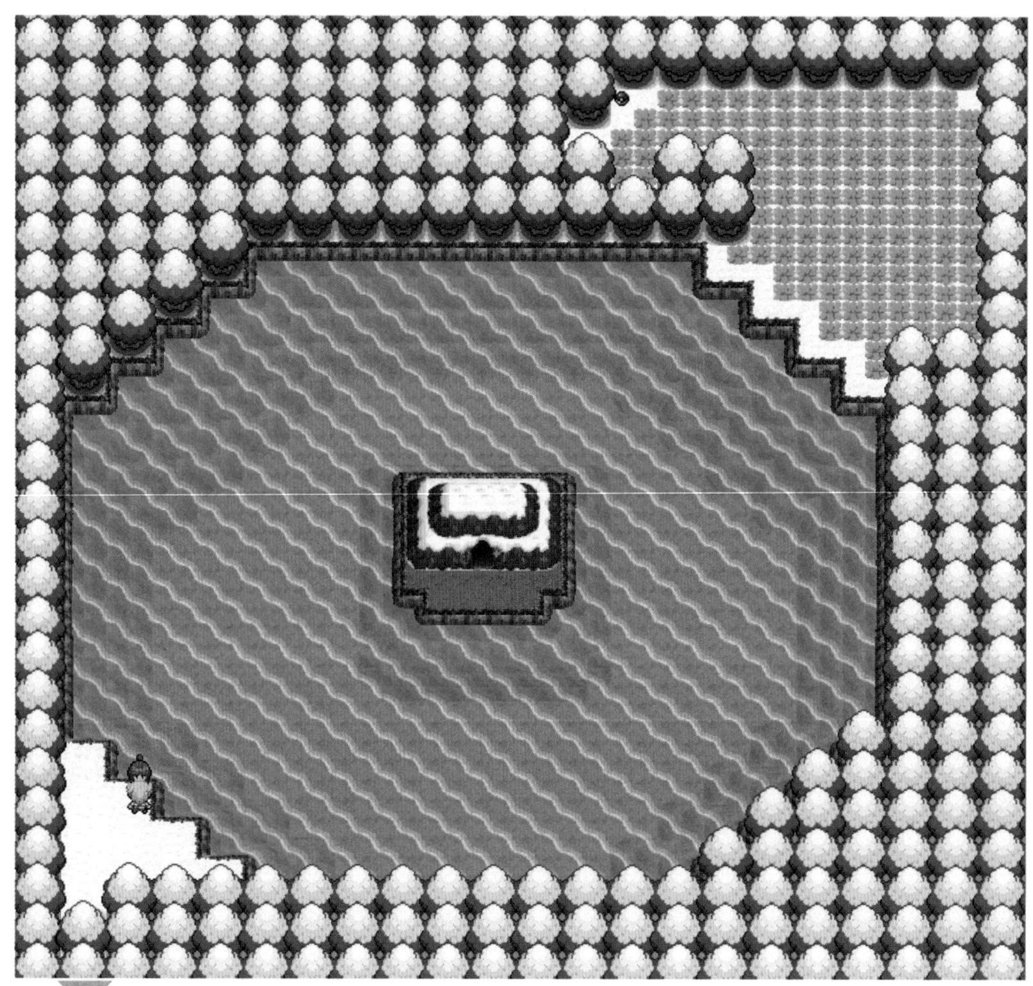

ACUITY LAKEFRONT (TO SNOWPOINT CITY)

IN GRASS

POKÉMON	M	D	N
Bibarel	◎	◎	○
Psyduck	◎	◎	○
Sneasel	○	○	○
Chingling	○	○	○
Noctowl	✕	✕	○

ON WATER

POKÉMON	VARIABLE
Psyduck	◎
Golduck	○

FISHING

FISHING ROD	POKÉMON	VARIABLE
Old	Magikarp	◎
Good	Magikarp	◎
	Goldeen	○

Chingling
Psychic
Abilities:
• Levitate

STEP 1 STEP ASIDE, STEP ASIDE

THE TEAM GALACTIC GRUNTS will allow you to pass now that you have an Icicle Badge in your possession. What were they guarding, pray tell? And what's happening now?

appear to be connected somehow.

STEP 2 RIBBING YOUR RIVAL

WHILE YOU WERE OFF defeating Candice, looks like your rival was engaged in a thrilling battle of his own, but with less successful results. He's been soundly beaten by Team Commander Jupiter, and he's feeling pretty bad about it. Of course, it's even worse when Jupiter is laughing right in his face.

You honestly thought you could save
the Pokémon of the lake?

STEP 3 OFF TO VEILSTONE!

IN A NOT-VERY-SUBTLE WAY, Jupiter lets you know that the Team Galactic headquarters are located in Veilstone City. She also tells you that there's not a thing you can do... but honestly, you don't even know what they're up to with those Legendary Pokémon! There's only one way to find out, and that's to head over to Veilstone City anyway and sneak into their base.

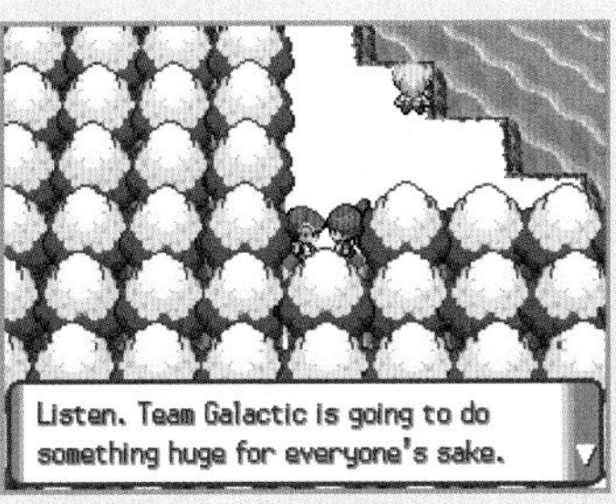

Listen. Team Galactic is going to do
something huge for everyone's sake.

POOR UXIE!

ALL THREE of the Legendary lake Pokémon are in the hands of Team Galactic now, and they've been taken to the Galactic Veilstone Building. You know they just aren't having a good time there. Time for a heroic rescue!

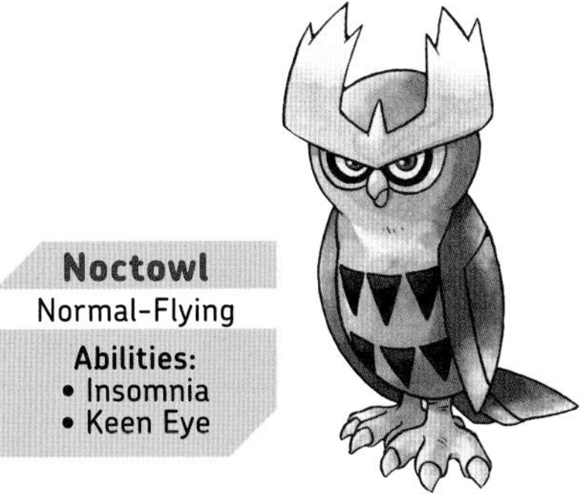

GALACTIC STORAGE AND THE GALACTIC VEILSTONE BUILDING

Team Galactic's headquarters is split between these two buildings in Veilstone City, which you only briefly glimpsed during your last visit here. The two are connected by an underground passageway, which what you'll need to sneak into to save the Legendary Pokémon trapped inside.

OBTAINABLE ITEMS

☐ Dusk Stone	☐ Zinc
☐ TM49 Snatch	☐ Galactic Key
☐ TM36 Sludge Bomb	☐ TM21 Frustration
☐ Max Revive	☐ Elixir
☐ Master Ball	

■ BUILDING 4 FL (2)

K

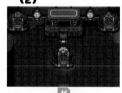

■ BUILDING 4 FL

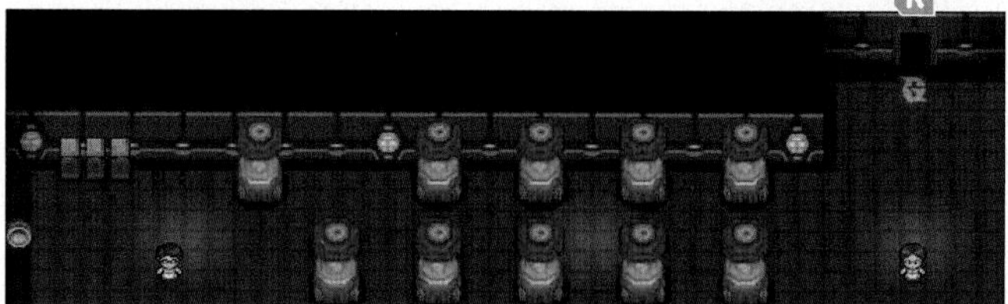

■ STORAGE

VEILSTONE CITY

■ BUILDING B1F

■ B2F

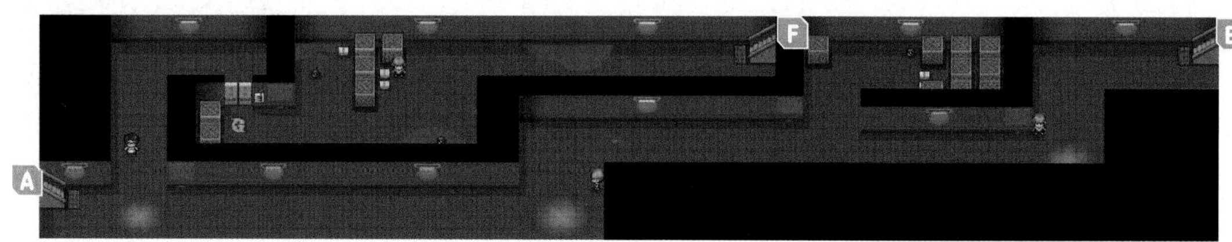

BUILDING 4 FL (1)

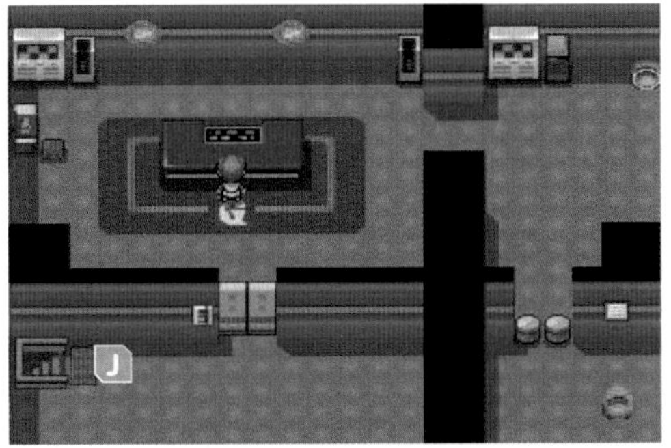

BUILDING 3 FL

BUILDING 2 FL

BUILDING 1 FL

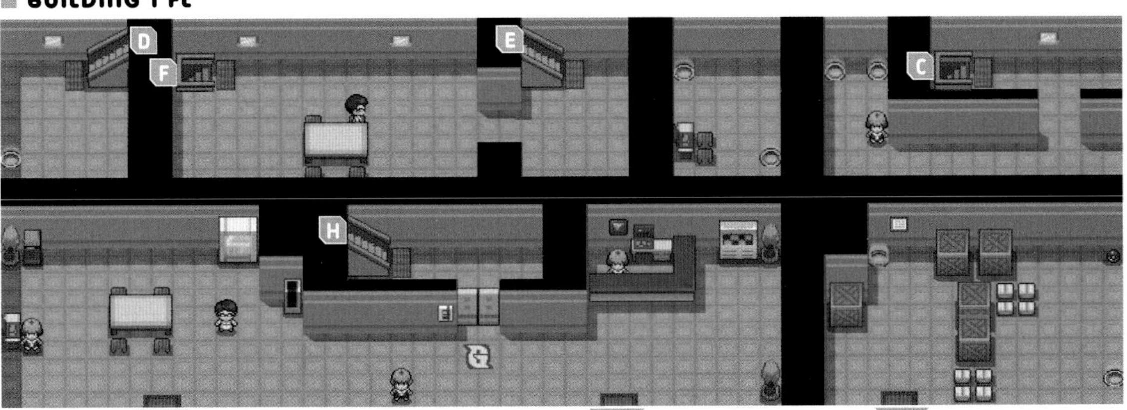

VEILSTONE CITY VEILSTONE CITY VEILSTONE CITY

STEP 1 THE KEY TO INFILTRATION IS A KEY

GOT THE STORAGE KEY? It's with the Team Galactic Grunt in front of the Galactic Veilstone Building, so finagle it out of him, because you need it to get into Galactic Storage, by way of the rusted door. Take the stairway to head further back.

The rusty door creaked open!

STEP 2 A NEW KEY

THE TEAM GALACTIC headquarters wasn't exactly designed for accessibility, so you'll make your way toward the back by using the stairs and warp panels. You'll need to get to the center of B2F, because there's another key you'll need if you hope to proceed further – the Galactic Key.

Lucas found
a Galactic Key!

EMPLOYEE HANDBOOK

THEY SAY "know your enemy," so what better way to know Team Galactic than by checking out the posters on the 2 FL and 3 FL detailing some of their rules and regulations?

STEP 3 UP AND AT THEM

NOW THAT YOU'VE GOT the Galactic Key clutched tightly in your hand, head to the Galactic Veilstone Building and enter though the left door or the one in the middle. In the center of the room is the locked door. Yep, now's the time to use the key. Open the door and proceed to the 4 FL where Cyrus awaits.

▶YES
NO
Use the Galactic Key?

THE DOOR TO NOWHERE

THERE ARE THREE DOORS that lead into the Galactic Veilstone Building, but only two will actually get you anywhere. The one on the far right cannot be used to go anywhere but right back out – it's really just an exit.

STEP 4 A LITTLE R-AND-R

IT LOOKS LIKE even Team Galactic needs to take a siesta once in a while, and they've got two little beds hidden away in the stairway between the 2 and 3 FL. Stand in front of one of the beds and hit 'A' to rest, restoring your Pokémon's HP and PP. The battles ahead are challenging, so don't be afraid to take advantage of this well-placed oasis.

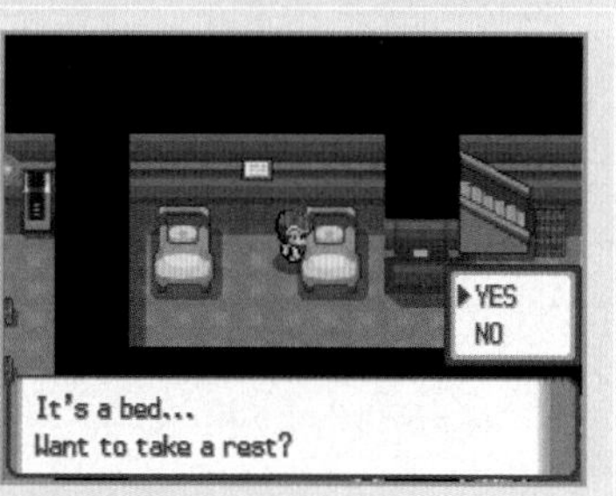
▶YES
NO
It's a bed...
Want to take a rest?

GALACTIC BOSS BATTLE 1

CYRUS
TEAM GALACTIC BOSS

CYRUS MAY look tough, but all of his Pokémon are vulnerable to Rock-type moves. And not only that, but you could always throw some Electric- or Ice-type moves at his Murkrow and Golbat, while taking down Sneasel with Fighting-, Fire-, Bug-, or Steel-type moves.

PARTY POKÉMON

POKÉMON	LEVEL	TYPE
Murkrow ♂	Lv 40	Dark-Flying
Golbat ♂	Lv 40	Poison-Flying
Sneasel ♂	Lv 43	Dark-Ice

STEP 5 HOW SWEET IT IS!

YOU'VE DEFEATED CYRUS, and now you're so close to rescuing the Legendary Pokémon. You even get a prize from the crushed Team Galactic Leader – a Master Ball! After presenting the goods, Cyrus will tell you where the three Legendaries are, up on the 4 FL. Head up there on a warp panel and save the day.

Obtained the Master Ball!

GALACTIC BATTLE 2

SATURN
TEAM GALACTIC COMMANDER

YOU MAY HAVE taken out Cyrus and found the Legendary Pokémon, but you're not in the clear just yet. Saturn is waiting for you, and he'll attack you with his trio of Pokémon. But no worries, as you take down his Psychic-type Kadabra with Bug-, Ghost-, or Dark-type moves. Against Toxicroak, use Ground-, Flying-, or Psychic-type moves, and for a big finish, use Fire-type moves on Bronzor.

PARTY POKÉMON

POKÉMON	LEVEL	TYPE
Kadabra ♂	Lv 38	Psychic
Bronzor	Lv 38	Steel-Psychic
Toxicroak ♀	Lv 40	Poison-Fighting

STEP 6 THE CHASE CONTINUES

EVEN THOUGH you defeated him, Saturn will let you know how to free the Legendary Pokémon. Just push the red button! They'll take off, and you've got places to be as well – Cyrus is headed to Mt. Coronet.

Press the button on that machine
to set them free.

MT. CORONET (SECOND VISIT)

Cyrus is up to no good – now that he's gathered the power of three Legendary Pokémon, he's got plans on Mt. Coronet. Don't let him get away!

■ 3 FL

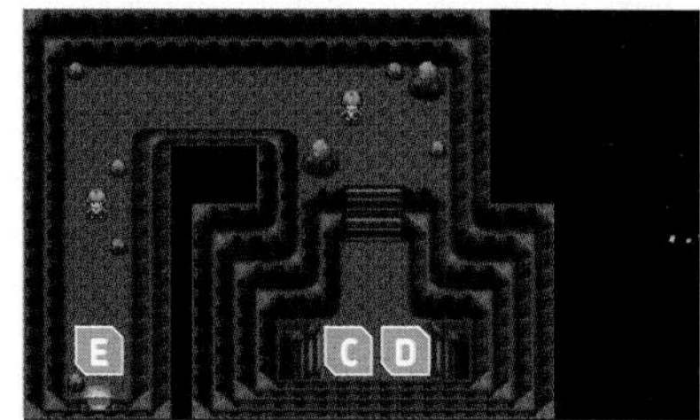

■ 2 FL

C D
B
B
A
ROUTE 207

■ SPEAR PILLAR

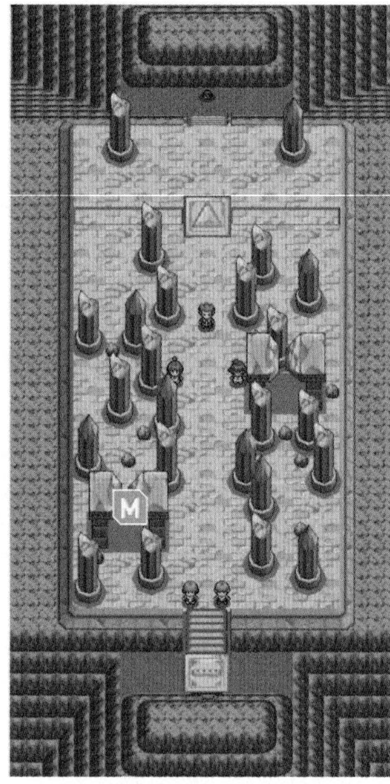

■ 1 FL

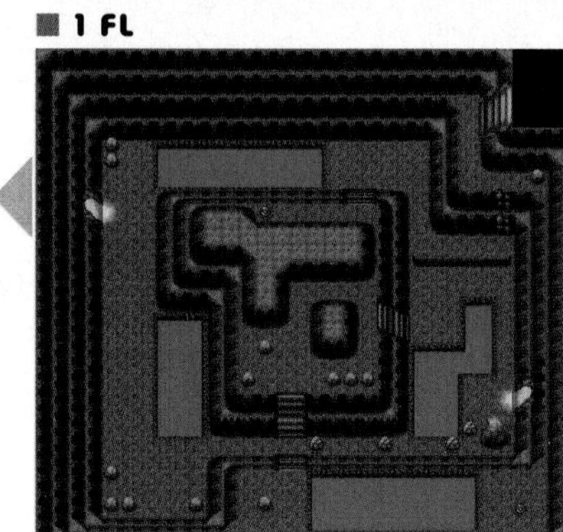

ROUTE 207 (TO OREBURGH CITY)

ROUTE 208 (TO HEARTHOME CITY)

OBTAINABLE ITEMS

ON YOUR FIRST VISIT	
☐ Dawn Stone	☐ Protein
☐ Max Potion	☐ Escape Rope
☐ Revive	☐ TM80 Rock Slide

AFTER VISITING SPEAR PILLAR	
☐ Adamant Orb (Diamond)	☐ Lustrous Orb (Pearl)
☐ TM02 Dragon Claw	

■ 1 FL ❶

IN CAVE

POKÉMON	M	D	N
Geodude	○	◎	◎
Machop	○	○	○
Meditite	○	○	○
Zubat	○	○	○
Chingling	○	○	○
Cleffa	○	△	△

■ 2 FL • 3 FL

IN CAVE

POKÉMON	M	D	N
Bronzong	○	○	○
Graveler	○	○	○
Machoke	○	○	○
Clefairy	○	○	○
Medicham	○	○	○
Golbat	○	○	○
Chingling	○	○	○
Bronzor	△	△	△

ON WATER

POKÉMON	VARIABLE
Zubat	◎
Golbat	○

FISHING

FISHING ROD	POKÉMON	VARIABLE
Old	Magikarp	◎
Good	Magikarp	◎
	Barboach	○

■ 6 FL ❷

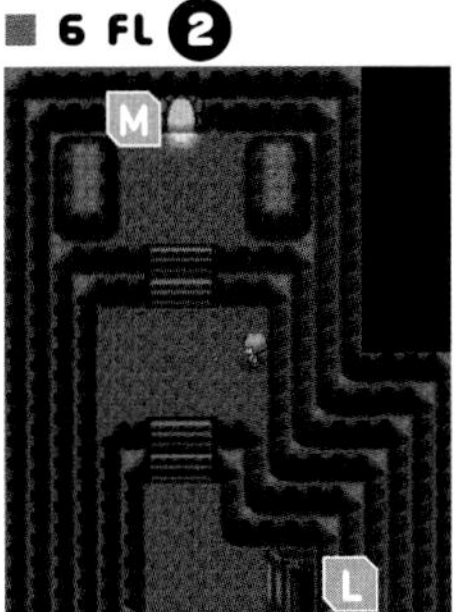

■ 4 FL ❸

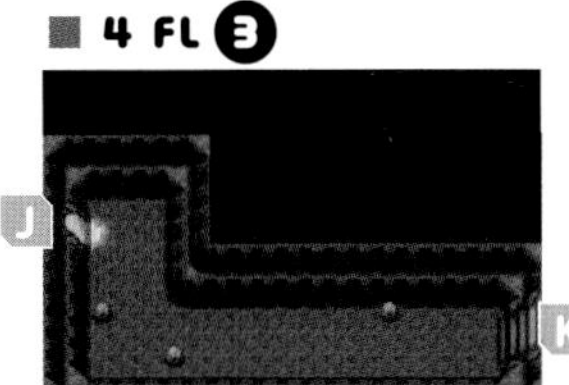

■ 5 FL

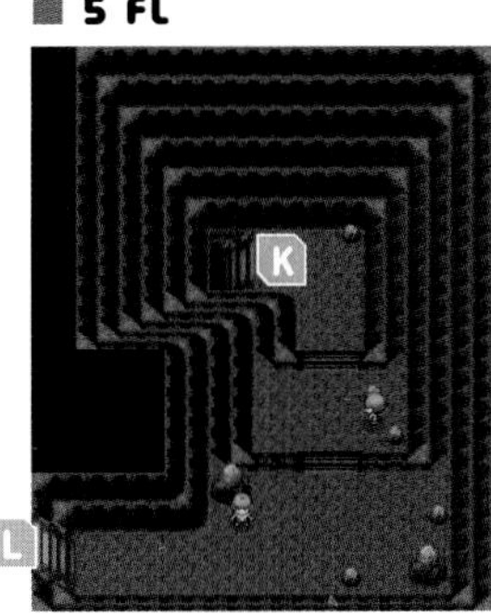

■ 1 FL ❷

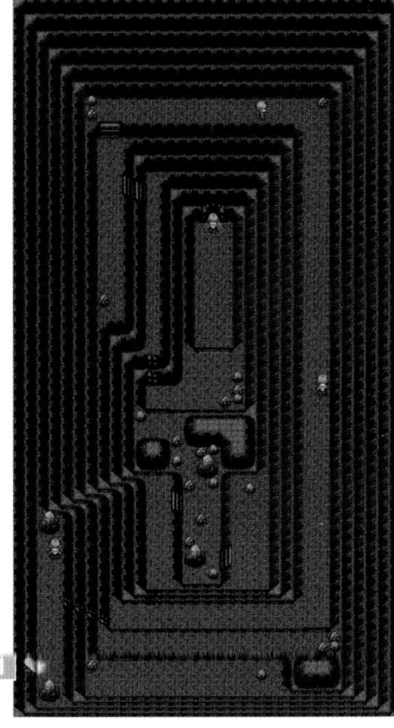

■ 4 FL ❷

■ SUMMIT 2ND AREA

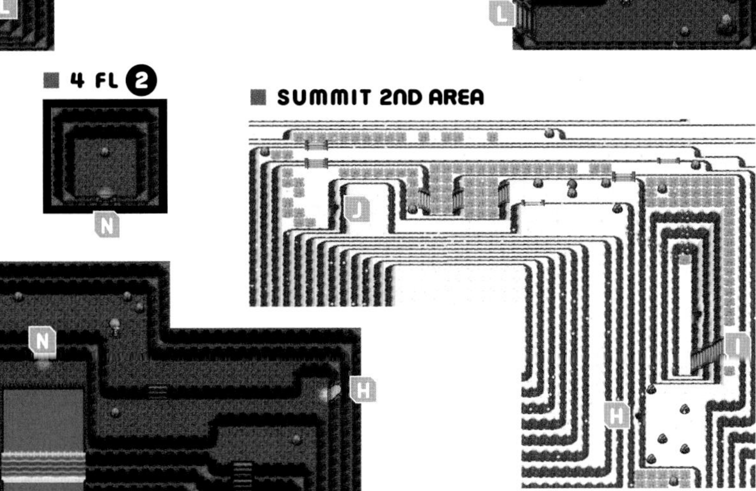

■ 4 FL ❶-2

■ SUMMIT 1ST AREA

■ SUMMIT 1ST AREA, 2ND AREA

IN GRASS

POKÉMON	M	D	N
Snover	○	○	○
Abomasnow	○	○	○
Medicham	○	○	○
Machoke	○	○	○
Chingling	○	○	○
Bronzong	△	△	△
Clefairy	△	△	△
Noctowl	✕	✕	○
Golbat	✕	✕	○

ON WATER

POKÉMON	VARIABLE
Zubat	◎
Golbat	○

FISHING

FISHING ROD	POKÉMON	VARIABLE
Old	Magikarp	◎
Good	Magikarp	◎
	Barboach	○

■ 1 FL ❷

IN CAVE

POKÉMON	M	D	N
Graveler	◎	◎	◎
Machoke	○	○	○
Clefairy	○	○	○
Medicham	○	○	○
Golbat	○	○	○
Chingling	○	○	○
Bronzong	△	△	△

■ 4 FL ❶-2

IN CAVE

POKÉMON	M	D	N
Bronzong	○	○	○
Graveler	○	○	○
Machoke	○	○	○
Clefairy	○	○	○
Medicham	○	○	○
Golbat	○	○	○
Chingling	○	○	○

Bronzong
Steel-Psychic

Abilities:
- Levitate
- Heatproof

■ 4 FL ❸

IN CAVE

POKÉMON	M	D	N
Bronzong	○	○	○
Graveler	○	○	○
Machoke	○	○	○
Clefairy	○	○	○
Medicham	○	○	○
Golbat	○	○	○
Chingling	△	△	△
Chimecho	△	△	△

■ 5 FL • 6 FL

IN CAVE

POKÉMON	M	D	N
Bronzong	○	○	○
Graveler	○	○	○
Machoke	○	○	○
Clefairy	○	○	○
Medicham	○	○	○
Golbat	○	○	○
Chimecho	○	○	○

STEP 1 FIELD MOVES ARE YOUR KEY THIS TIME

TO REACH the innermost sanctum of Mt. Coronet, you're going to need more field moves then ever – five, to be exact. Before you leave town make sure your team is up to the task. The going gets really rough when you reach the summit, where visibility is limited and you risk missing the rocky path where you need to use HM08 Rock Climb. Keep a sharp eye out, since so much is depending on you!

▶YES
NO
The wall is very rocky...
Would you like to use Rock Climb?

STEP 2 BLOCKED PATHS? NOT A PROBLEM!

THIS IS your second visit to Mt. Coronet, and you may notice that a path you've taken before is now blocked by a Team Galactic Grunt. Is there anything you can do? Ignore him, actually – this is not the way you need to go, anyway.

I'm hopelessly lost!

STURM AND DRANG

HAIL HITS your Pokémon hard in battle, so keep an eye on their HP here.

STEP 3 A SACRED CHARGE

STEP INTO the deepest area of Mt. Coronet, known as the Spear Pillar, to receive quite a shock. Sure, Cyrus is there, and so are the Team Galactic Commanders, but even more surprising is when Cyrus uses the power of the three Legendaries to resurrect an even more mysterious, more sacred Legendary Pokémon – Dialga (Pokémon Diamond) or Palkia (Pokémon Pearl).

DIALGA: Gugyugubah!

AFTER THE SPEAR PILLAR

WHILE THIS BLOCKED passage isn't very important now, it will be worth a look later. Come back after visiting the Spear Pillar to obtain TM02 Dragon Claw, which might come in handy for your final battles.

STEP 4 OUR POWERS COMBINED

CYRUS IS LOOKING for some of that world domination action, by using the power of the Legendary Pokémon he just raised. Of course, this just won't do, and it's up to you to stop him. You and your rival, that is, who arrives to back you up and take down Team Galactic.

Did you get any tougher since then?
We'll beat you two-on-two!

GALACTIC BATTLE

MARS AND JUPITER
TEAM GALACTIC COMMANDERS

You should be used to this pair and their Pokémon by now. Take out the Bronzor with Fire-type moves again, and either Electric-, Ice-, or Rock-type moves should do a number on the Golbat. As for Mars' Purugly? That's a job for Fighting-type moves, while Ground-type moves will put away Jupiter's Skuntank.

MARS' POKÉMON

POKÉMON	LEVEL	TYPE
Bronzor	Lv 41	Steel-Psychic
Golbat ♀	Lv 42	Poison-Flying
Purugly ♀	Lv 45	Normal

JUPITER'S POKÉMON

POKÉMON	LEVEL	TYPE
Bronzor	Lv 41	Steel-Psychic
Golbat ♀	Lv 41	Poison-Flying
Skuntank ♀	Lv 46	Poison-Dark

STEP 5 FOR THE COMMON GOOD

HEY, IT'S THE THREE Legendary Pokémon from the lakes – Uxie, Azelf, and Mesprit! What are they doing here? They give off a strange power, nullifying the force binding Palkia or Dialga. Uh oh, Cyrus doesn't look too happy about this...

GALACTIC BOSS BATTLE 2

CYRUS
TEAM GALACTIC BOSS

Cyrus may be angry, but that doesn't change the weaknesses of his Pokémon, even if they have leveled up. All of them are vulnerable to Rock-type attacks, while Electric-type moves will be very effective on Honchkrow, Gyarados, and Crobat. As for Weavile, try Fighting-, Fire-, Bug-, or Steel-type moves to end this battle.

CYRUS' POKÉMON

POKÉMON	LEVEL	TYPE
Honchkrow ♂	Lv 45	Dark-Flying
Crobat ♂	Lv 46	Poison-Flying
Gyarados ♂	Lv 45	Water-Flying
Weavile ♂	Lv 48	Dark-Ice

STEP 6 POKÉMON IN TROUBLE

RESURRECTED BY TEAM GALACTIC, then forced to use its power against it will, the least you can say is that Dialga or Palkia is having a bad day. A very bad day. As a result, it's gone wild, and that just won't do at all. You need to take Professor Rowan's advice and "see what's in its heart!" It's time to face your greatest challenge yet, as you step forward to battle this great creature.

Go on, Lucas.
Face up to DIALGA!

DIAMOND VERSION

CAPTURE DIALGA!

Dialga
Level 47
Steel-Dragon
Abilities:
- Pressure

Moves:
- Metal Claw
- Ancientpower
- Dragon Claw
- Roar of Time

TO CAPTURE this mighty Pokémon, you need to start out strong with Fighting- or Ground-type moves, causing 2x damage and reducing its HP by a lot. Then chip away at it with Normal-, Water-, Electric-, or Flying-type moves, which only do half damage. Grass-type moves are also good for hurting Dialga without completely knocking it out so you can capture it.

PEARL VERSION

CAPTURE PALKIA!

TO CAPTURE this impressive Pokémon, you need to deal a major blow to start by using Dragon-type moves for 2x damage. Then chip away with Fire- or Water-type moves, reducing HP slowly so that you can capture it.

Palkia
Level 47
Water-Dragon
Abilities:
- Pressure

Moves:
- Water Pulse
- Ancientpower
- Dragon Claw
- Spacial Rend

STEP 7 GET THE SHINY

AFTER CAPTURING the great Legendary, head back inside Mt. Coronet to the Spear Pillar. There you'll find a Held Item that intensifies the power of Pokémon moves – Adamant Orb for Dialga and Lustrous Orb for Palkia.

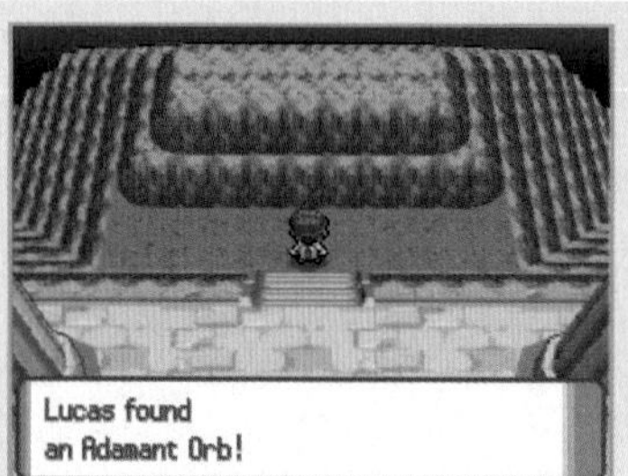
Lucas found
an Adamant Orb!

STEP 8 BACK TO THE THREE LAKES

NOW THAT EVERYTHING'S settled down, the three Legendary Pokémon of the lakes have gone back home. Now's your chance to meet these Pokémon and capture them for your Pokédex – Uxie at Lake Acuity, Azelf at Lake Valor, and Mesprit at Lake Verity.

NOW IT'S OK TO HEAD TO SUNYSHORE CITY

AFTER LEAVING Mt. Coronet, you can now go to Sunyshore City to obtain your eighth badge. If you want to save the excitement of capturing the three Legendary Pokémon for later, head to Sunyshore City first.

LAKE ACUITY, LAKE VALOR, LAKE VERITY

The three Legendary Pokémon have returned to the great lakes of Sinnoh. Now is your time to track them down and hopefully catch them all.

MOVES REQUIRED TO COMPLETE THIS AREA

SURF

UXIE AT ACUITY

TAKE THE QUICKEST route and Fly to Snowpoint City, from there heading toward Lake Acuity. Use Surf to reach the center of the lake, where Acuity Cavern awaits. You won't have to search long or far to find Uxie – it's right in the middle of the cavern.

LAKE ACUITY

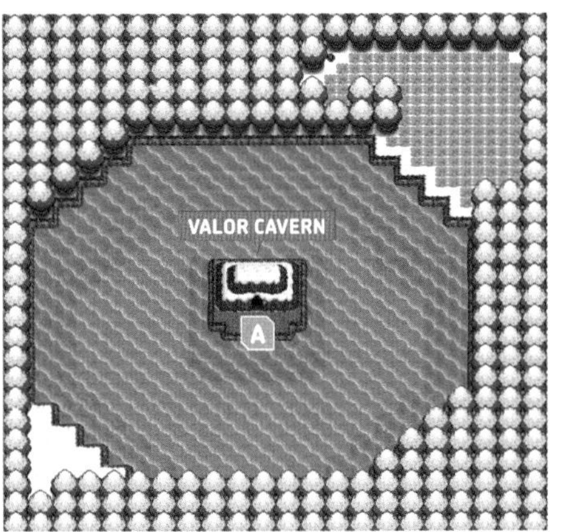

ACUITY CAVERN

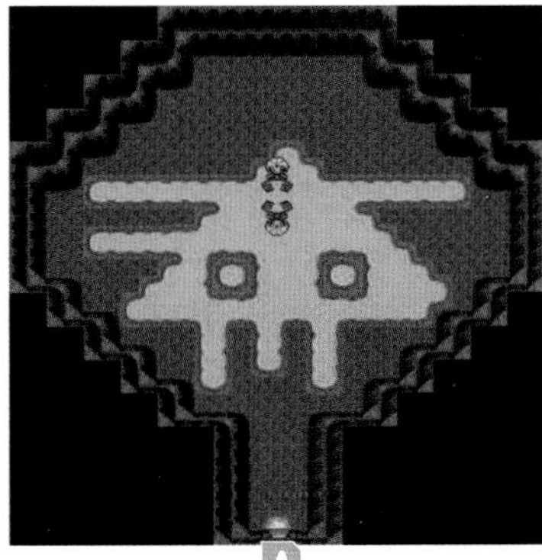

OBTAINABLE ITEMS

OUTSIDE

- ☐ TM14 Blizzard

CAPTURE UXIE!

DEAL A BLOW to Uxie's HP by using Bug-, Ghost-, or Dark-type moves, all of which it is weak against. Then pull out the Fighting- or Psychic-type moves, which will small amounts of damage that will eventually deplete the Pokémon enough so you can catch it. When Uxie uses the move Amnesia, it's raising its Special Defense. To counter, hit it with physical moves instead.

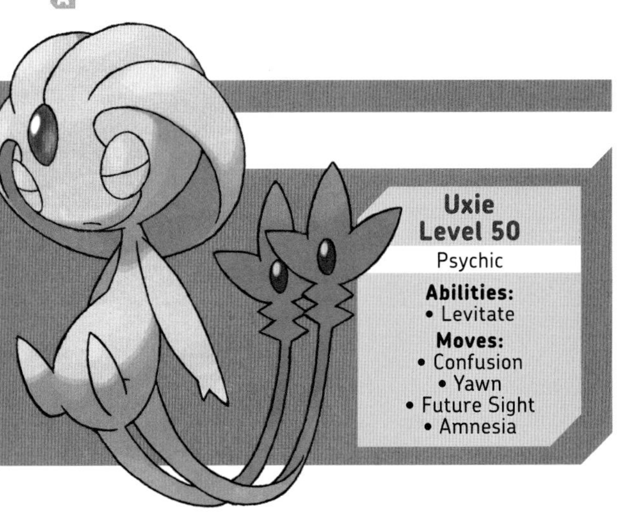

Uxie
Level 50
Psychic

Abilities:
- Levitate

Moves:
- Confusion
- Yawn
- Future Sight
- Amnesia

STEP 2 AZELF AT VALOR

YOUR NEXT FLIGHT OUT should be to Pastoria City, from which you can head out to Lake Valor. Use Surf to head out to the middle of the lake, where another cavern awaits you. In Valor Cavern, little Azelf is calmly waiting in the center of the room.

LAKE VALOR

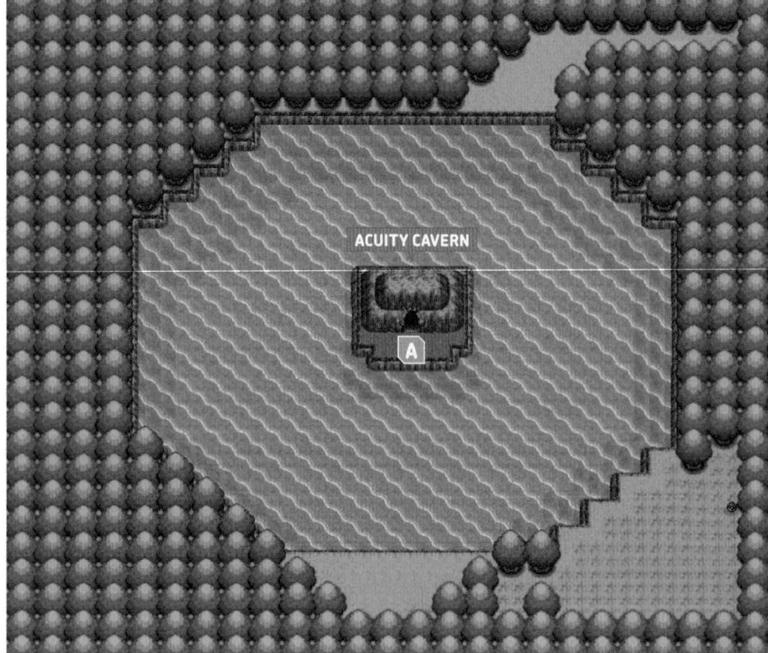

VALOR CAVERN

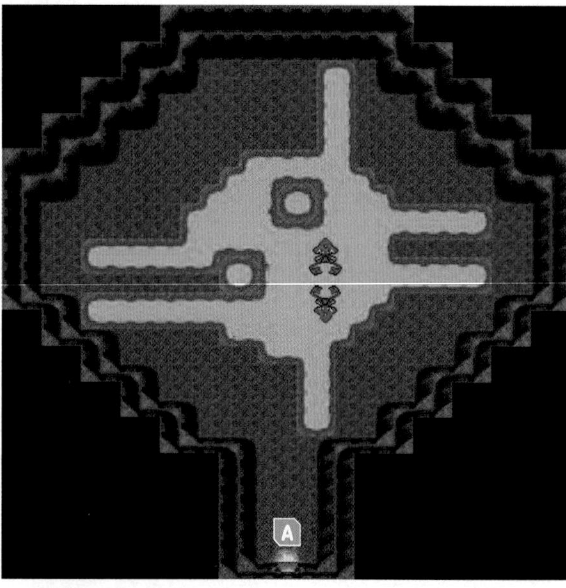

OBTAINABLE ITEMS

OUTSIDE

☐ TM25 Thunder

CAPTURE AZELF!

HIT IT HARD upfront with some Bug-, Ghost-, or Dark-type moves, then switch off to some move types that will decrease Azelf's HP slowly, like Fighting- or Psychic-type moves. The move Nasty Plot will increase its Special Attack, making Psychic a very powerful move for Azelf to use against you, so be careful.

Azelf
Level 50
Psychic

Abilities:
- Levitate

Moves:
- Confusion
- Uproar
- Future Sight
- Nasty Plot

3 MESPRIT AT VERITY BUT...

YOU CAN HEAD to Lake Verity to challenge Mesprit, crossing the lake with Surf and then entering the cavern to find Mesprit in the center. But when you approach, it's not a battle you'll find, but a chase! Mesprit will leave and start wandering all over the Sinnoh region, and your only hope for finding it is the Pokétch application Marking Map, which will show you where the little Pokémon has gone. However, you cannot fly as Mesprit did. Instead, you must approach carefully, either by walking or using the Bicycle.

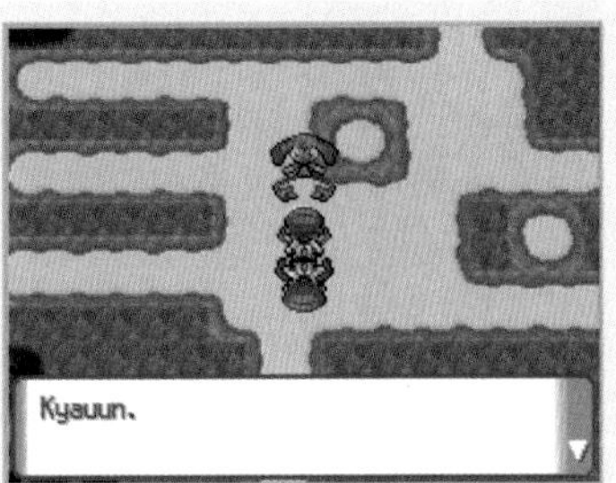

MOVE FOR YOUR POKéMON

WHAT DO YOU DO if you don't have the Marking Map? Well, just head to the Pokétch Company in Jubilife City. You'll be able to get one there if you have at least three Gym badges.

LAKE VERITY

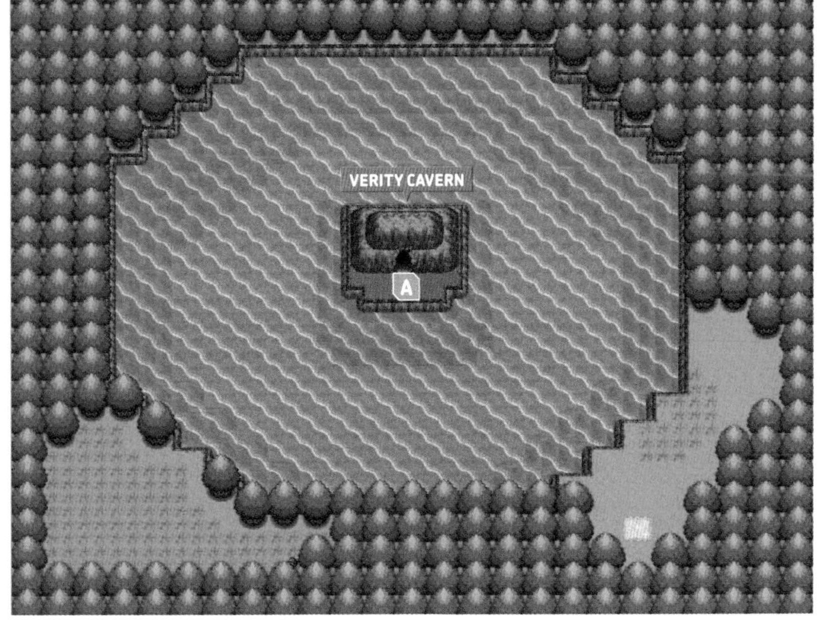

VERITY CAVERN

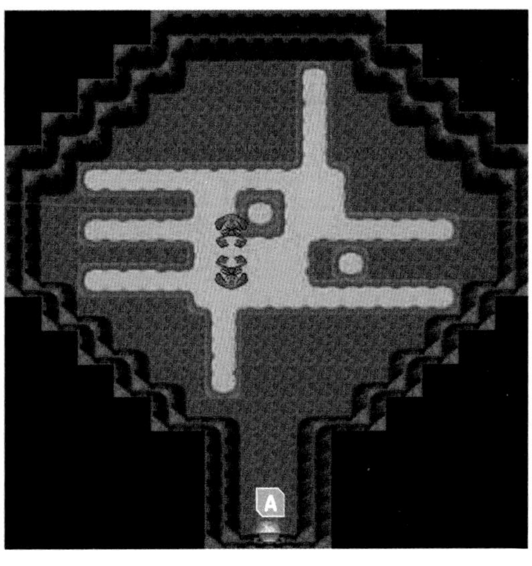

OBTAINABLE ITEMS

OUTSIDE

- ☐ TM38 Fire Blast

CAPTURE MESPRIT!

Mesprit
Level 50

Psychic

Abilities:
- Levitate

Moves:
- Confusion
- Charm
- Future Sight
- Lucky Chant

WALK THROUGH the tall grass or water shown on the Marking Map and Mesprit will come to you. Unfortunately, it won't give you much of a chance to catch it, escaping as soon as the battle starts. What to do? Use Mean Look or Block to keep Mesprit from fleeing and then bring out your power moves to wear it down and catch it.

ROUTE 222

What a lovely place to walk, relax, fish, and battle. But you have more pressing business in Sunyshore City nearby, as you try for your last badge!

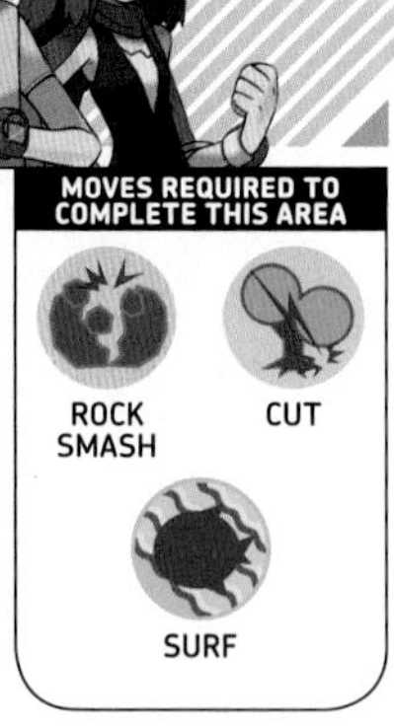

OBTAINABLE ITEMS

ON YOUR FIRST VISIT

- ☐ Honey
- ☐ Wiki Berry x2
- ☐ Aguav Berry x2
- ☐ TM56 Fling
- ☐ Carbos
- ☐ Mago Berry x2
- ☐ Qualot Berry

ON ACHIEVING A NEW RECORD IN THE REMORAID SIZE CONTEST

- ☐ Net Ball

IN GRASS

POKÉMON	M	D	N
Floatzel	○	○	◎
Gastrodon ♦	◎	◎	◎
Gastrodon ●	○	○	○
Mr. Mime ♦	○	○	○
Glameow ●	○	○	○
Purugly ●	○	○	○
Wingull	○	○	○
Chatot	○	○	✕

ON WATER

POKÉMON	VARIABLE
Tentacool	◎
Wingull	◎
Tentacruel	△
Pelipper	△

FISHING

FISHING ROD	POKÉMON	VARIABLE
Old	Magikarp	◎
Good	Magikarp	◎
	Remoraid	○

Chatot
Normal-Flying
Abilities:
- Keen Eye
- Tangled Feet

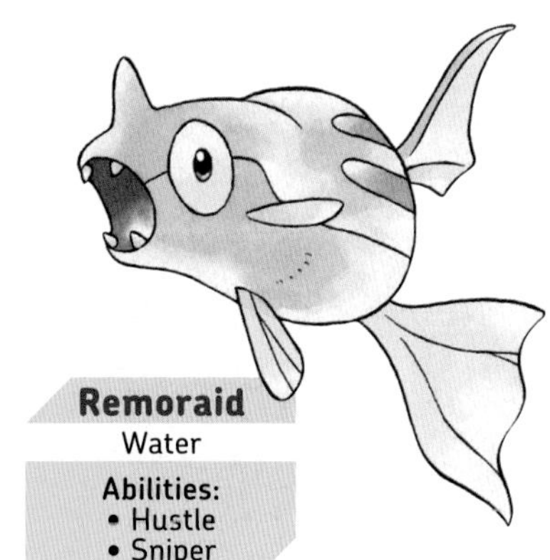

Remoraid
Water
Abilities:
- Hustle
- Sniper

STEP 1 FROM SHORE TO SHINING SHORE

YOU'LL NEED TO TAKE Route 213 or 214 to the Valor Lakefront, and then proceed east to Route 222. The road used to be blocked because of the Great Blackout in Sunyshore City – maybe they didn't want tourists stumbling around in the dark – but now it's all clear.

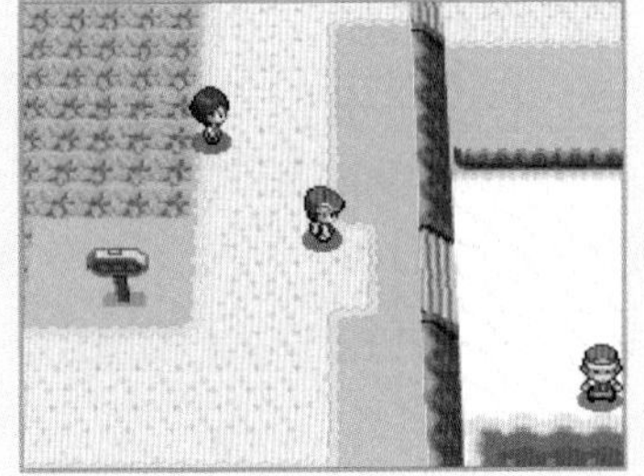

STEP 2 THE STRAIGHT SHOOT

THERE'S FEW TWISTS and turns to be found on Route 222, so you could just use those Running Shoes or the Bicycle to jet straight through. Of course, there are the usual cadre of Trainers who will challenge you, and there's a few houses to check out. Should you make the time? In one word, yes. You'll be quite busy once you get to town.

Pikapikapikah! Pikapika?

PIKA!

DO YOU LIKE PIKACHU? Because hey, there's a Pikachu Fan Club here, and a whole lot of Pikachu! But something isn't quite right with one of them. That's because it's not a Pikachu at all, but a Trainer pretending to be one. Can you spot the impostor?

STEP 3 THE BIGGER THE BETTER

THE HOUSE on the right near the beach is host to a Remoraid competition where Trainers try to impress the judge with the biggest one they can find. Good thing you're so close to the beach, right? Catch a big one and put it in your party – every time you break a record, he'll give you a Net Ball.

I dreamt that a Trainer would bring
me a giant REMORAID!

BIGGER THE BETTER

ROUTE 222 is a great place to fish, especially if you're fishing for Remoraid. Make some room in your party so you can bring them straight to the contest judge, and hopefully one of them will net you a Net Ball.

SUNYSHORE CITY

MOVES REQUIRED TO COMPLETE THIS AREA
CUT SURF

The sun and the sea rule in this intricately-designed port town, made up of small islands separated by water, and connected by footbridges that double as solar panels to power the town. Of course, you have a different power in mind, as you are here to earn your eighth and final badge from the Sunyshore Gym.

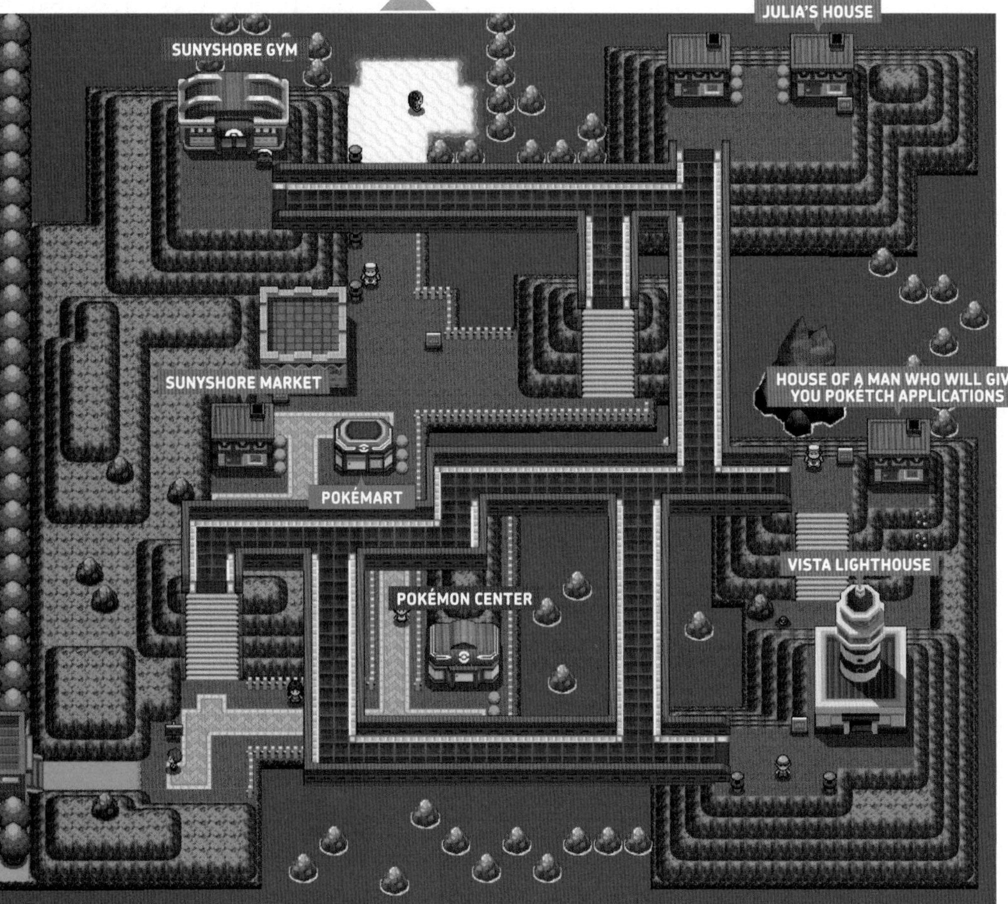

OBTAINABLE ITEMS

ON YOUR FIRST VISIT
- ☐ Thunderstone

WHEN YOUR LEAD POKÉMON IS STRONG
- ☐ Effort Ribbon

WHEN YOU SHOW THE MAN IN THE HOUSE A "SERIOUS" NATURE
- ☐ Pokétch application "Calendar"

WHEN YOU SHOW THE MAN A NAIVE POKÉMON
- ☐ Pokétch application "Dot Artist"

WHEN YOU SHOW THE MAN A QUIRKY POKÉMON
- ☐ Pokétch application "Roulette"

WHEN YOU TALK TO JULIA

☐ Mon: Alert Ribbon	☐ Fri: Relax Ribbon
☐ Tues: Shock Ribbon	☐ Sat: Snooze Ribbon
☐ Wed: Downcast Ribbon	☐ Sun: Smile Ribbon
☐ Thu: Careless Ribbon	

AFTER WINNING SUNYSHORE CITY GYM BATTLE

☐ Beacon Badge	☐ TM57 Charge Beam
☐ HM07 Waterfall	

ON WATER

POKÉMON	VARIABLE
Tentacruel	◎
Pelipper	◎
Mantyke	○

FISHING

FISHING ROD	POKÉMON	VARIABLE
Old	Magikarp	◎
Good	Magikarp	◎
	Remoraid	○

STEP 1 YOU WALK INTO TOWN...

HEY, YOU JUST GOT HERE, and already you've got people walking up to you, asking for things. A red-headed man will approach you, and don't worry, it's just Flint of the Elite Four! What could he possibly want from a regular Trainer like you? Well, turns out that the Gym Leader here in Sunyshore has lost the will to battle, and you're just the person to cheer him up!

The name's Flint! I'm one of
the Pokémon League's Elite Four!

STEP 2 ARE YOU WORKING HARD OR HARDLY WORKING?

IN THE SUNYSHORE MARKET you'll meet a nice lady with an eye for superior Pokémon. If you've really upped the stats of your lead Pokémon, she'll hand you an Effort Ribbon as a reward for your efforts.

Lucas received

STEP 3 RIBBONS THAT DON'T GO IN YOUR HAIR

JULIA IS SUCH A SWEET GIRL, and so generous too! When you visit her house and talk to her, she'll give you a ribbon for your Pokémon. She has seven different kinds in her possession, so you might want to visit her every day until you have at least one of each.

I know! How about you visit me and
tell me stories every so often?

STEP 4 BULK UP THE POKÉTCH

IN THE FAR EASTERN corner of Sunyshore City is a house that can only be reached using the Field move HM08 Rock Climb. Take the climb and talk to the man inside. He's looking for three Pokémon natures - Serious, Naive, and Quirky. Outfit your party with Pokémon of these natures, and he'll be pleased enough to give you three new Pokétch applications.

You've got Pokémon with different
natures, right? May I see them?

ABUSE OF POWER?

TO CAUSE a blackout in a town like this, well, that can't be too good. Especially if it happened to be caused by say, the Gym Leader? It looks like Volkner, the Sunyshore Gym Leader, went a little crazy with remodeling his Gym, consuming too much electricity in the act. It might be better for the town if he put that energy into Pokémon battling itself.

STICK 'EM ON

CHECK OUT the wares of the man at the upper left of the market - he'll sell you different stickers every day to decorate your Poké Balls with. There are a good variety of designs, so you're sure to eventually find something that fits you and your style.

PINT SIZE EXPERTS

THE UNDERGROUND can be a pretty big, overwhelming place. But in the house next to the Pokémart, there are three boys who seem to have the whole thing figured out. Visit them for some useful tips before making your own excursion into the Underground.

STEP 5 WHERE'S VOLKNER?

WELL, HE'S NOT at the Sunyshore City Gym... yet. Instead, check out the Vista Lighthouse, where Volkner is busy being mopey. You can change all that when you talk to him, as your sunny demeanor, high spirit and determination give him just the charge he needs to accept your challenge. Follow him back to the Gym, because it's time to rumble.

...So, you're the latest challenger
up against the Sunyshore Gym...

WHAT A VIEW!

HEY, IT SEEMS you can see pretty far from the Vista Lighthouse observatory. What's that big, church-like building in the distance? Why, it's the Pokémon League! And you'll be headed there soon, right after this next Gym battle.

GYM BATTLE 7

VOLKNER

SUNYSHORE GYM LEADER
POKÉMON TYPE: ELECTRIC
RECOMMENDED TYPES: GROUND, GRASS

THOSE RECENT renovations have really made Sunyshore Gym an impressive maze of passages that you must connect by pressing buttons. It'll be pretty tricky to figure out the right combinations to get to Volkner, though maybe not as tricky as the eight Trainers standing between you and the Gym Leader. As for handling Volkner, dish out some Ground-type moves on Raichu and Luxray, go for the Electric-type on Octillery, and then put Ambipom to rest with hard-hitting Fighting-type moves. The thrill of victory will include the Beacon Badge, and TM57 Charge Beam.

The BEACON BADGE allows you to use the HM07 Waterfall on the field, as well as ensuring that all of your Pokémon, regardless of their level, obey you.

PARTY POKÉMON

POKÉMON	LEVEL	TYPE
Raichu ♂	Lv 46	Electric
Ambipom ♂	Lv 47	Normal
Octillery ♂	Lv 47	Water
Luxray ♂	Lv 49	Electric

1 FL 2

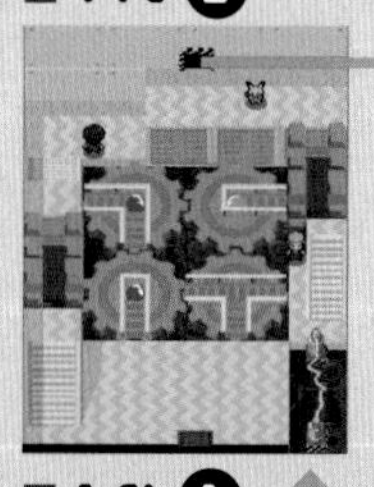

1 FL 1

ENTRANCE

1 FL 3

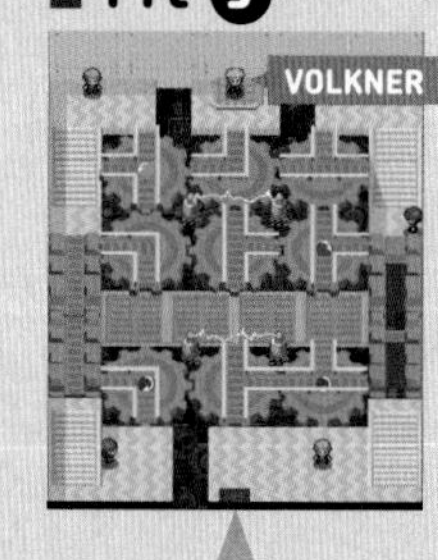

STEP 6 DON'T GO CHASING HM07 WATERFALL

IT'S GREAT THAT YOU CAN use HM07 Waterfall now, if only you actually had it. This is a problem easily solved, if you head to the beach to the north of town. A girl standing on the beach will come to talk to you – and it just happens to be Jasmine, a Gym Leader from the Johto region! She's not really a Water-type Pokémon Trainer, so maybe that's why she gives you HM07 Waterfall to teach to your Pokémon.

...Er...um...
P-please take this, too.

HOMETOWN BOY

LIVING NEXT DOOR to Julia is a nice elderly couple who remember that once upon a time, a little boy named Cyrus used to live in town. Could it be the same Cyrus of Team Galactic? Is that why they've never started trouble in Sunyshore City?

POKÉMON TRAINER CATALOGUE 2

You've met a few new types of Trainers since the last catalogue. Then there are a whole slew of people throughout the game who have inspired, challenged, and impressed you. Like the Gym Leaders, the Elite Four, your rival, and of course, the Pokémon League Champion. And let's not forget Team Galactic, and all the trials they put you through!

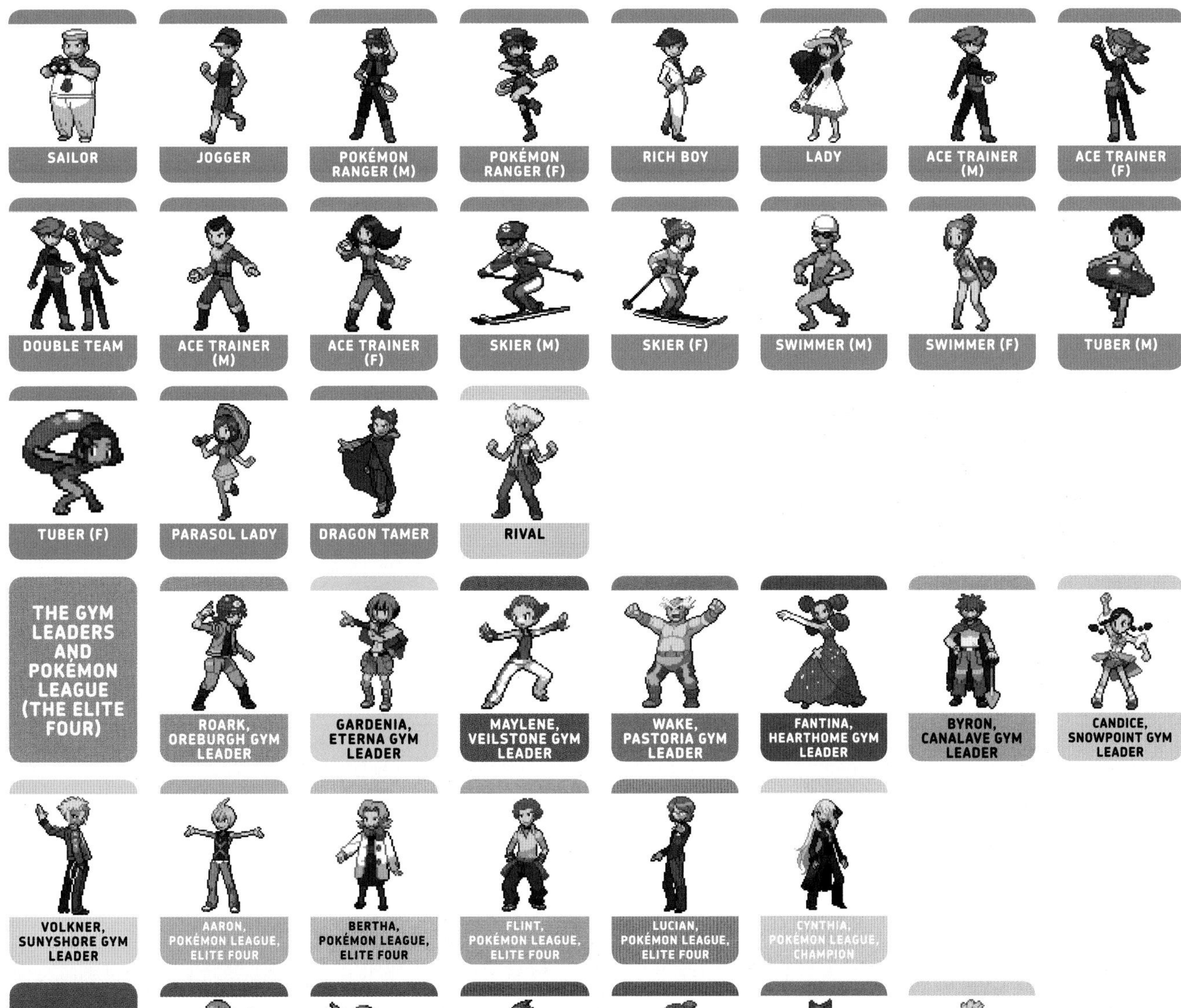

ROUTE 223

Route 223 is a bit tricky to navigate, what with all those rocks and shoals and twists and turns... and let's not forget all the Trainers just itching for a battle. Of course, this is all just a warm up as you head for your final goal, the Pokémon League.

MOVES REQUIRED TO COMPLETE THIS AREA

SURF | WATERFALL

OBTAINABLE ITEMS

☐ TM18 Rain Dance	☐ Pearl

ON WATER

POKÉMON	VARIABLE
Tentacruel	◎
Pelipper	◎
Mantyke	○

FISHING

FISHING ROD	POKÉMON	VARIABLE
Old	Magikarp	◎
Good	Magikarp	◎
	Remoraid	○

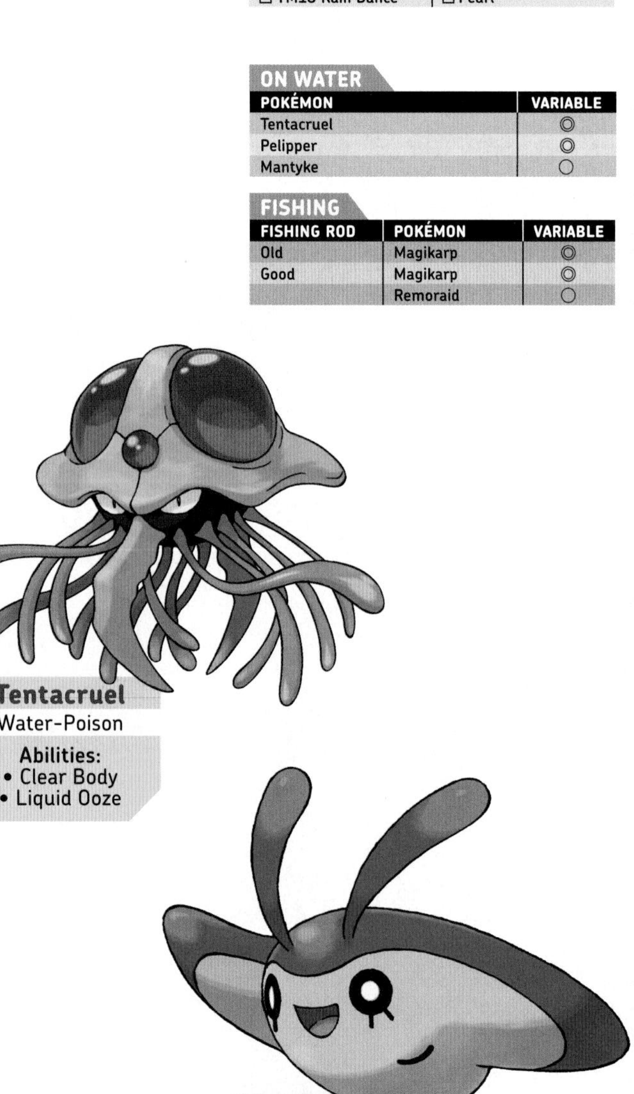

Tentacruel
Water-Poison
Abilities:
- Clear Body
- Liquid Ooze

Mantyke
Water-Flying
Abilities:
- Swift Swim
- Water Absorb

OVER THE WATER AND THROUGH THE ROCKS

A WHOLE LOT of water stands between you and your destination, and there's only one way to get there – Surf. Once you hop on board the Pokémon express, it's a straight shoot to the end of the route.

WHO NEEDS MORE EXPERIENCE?

THERE ARE QUITE A FEW Trainers here on Route 223, itching for a battle. While it may seem tempting to pass them by to get to Victory Road and the Pokémon League sooner, keep in mind that the battles ahead are much, much tougher. So take advantage of this opportunity to battle as many of the Trainers as possible, earning strength, skills, and experience points.

It might not look like it, but I'm traveling now.

MONEY MATTERS

WANDERING AROUND in bathing suits means the Trainers on Route 223 have a lot less pockets – and a lot less money as a result. To keep your prize money high, equip your lead Pokémon with Luck Incense.

AGAINST THE CURRENT

AT THE END of Route 223 is a huge waterfall. There's no other way to go – good thing Jasmine gave you HM07 Waterfall, then! Teach it to one of your Pokémon and climb on up. At the top of the waterfall is a Pokémon Center, so rest up, because there's a tough challenge just ahead in Victory Road.

YES
NO
It's a large waterfall.
Would you like to use Waterfall?

VICTORY ROAD

The Pokémon League is tough, so all Trainers seeking to take on the Elite Four and the Champion spend some time in Victory Road, bulking up their Pokémon by battling wild Pokémon – and other Trainers! Master Victory Road, and you're sure to succeed in your battles.

1 FL

POKÉMON LEAGUE (TO SUNYSHORE CITY)

2 FL

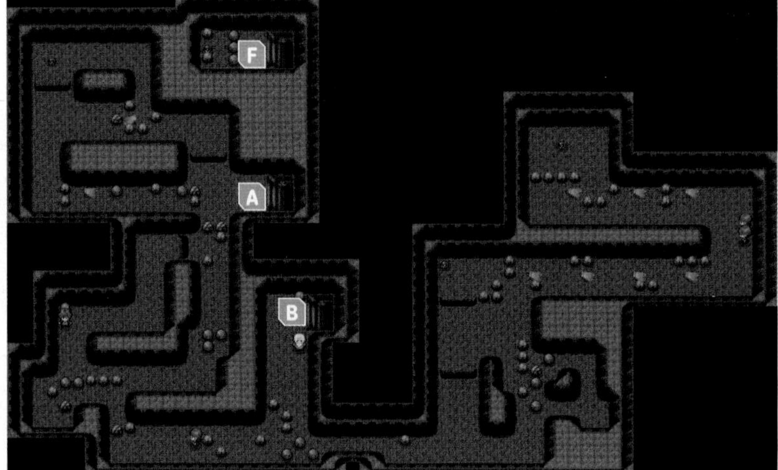

B1F

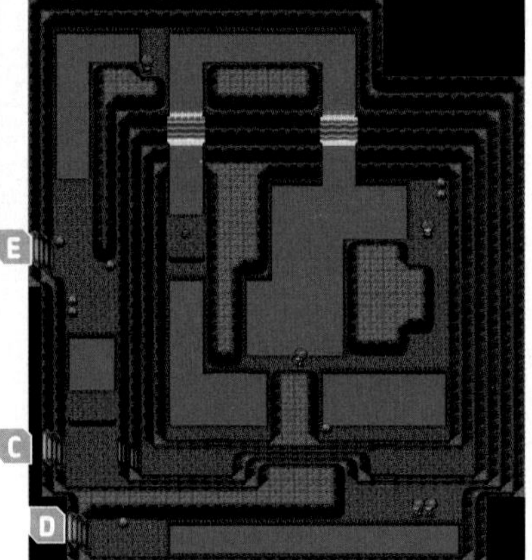

OBTAINABLE ITEMS

☐ TM41 Torment	☐ Full Heal
☐ Max Ether	☐ Full Restore
☐ TM71 Stone Edge	☐ TM59 Dragon Pulse
☐ Rare Candy	☐ Razor Claw
☐ TM79 Dark Pulse	☐ Zinc

1 FL

IN CAVE

POKÉMON	M	D	N
Machoke	○	○	○
Graveler	○	○	○
Medicham	○	○	○
Golbat	○	○	○
Onix	○	○	○
Steelix	○	○	○

2 FL

IN CAVE

POKÉMON	M	D	N
Kadabra	○	○	○
Graveler	○	○	○
Medicham	○	○	○
Golbat	○	○	○
Onix	○	○	○
Steelix	○	○	○

B1F

IN CAVE

POKÉMON	M	D	N
Floatzel	◎	◎	◎
Machoke	○	○	○
Medicham	○	○	○
Golbat	○	○	○
Steelix	○	○	○

ON WATER

POKÉMON	VARIABLE
Golbat	◎

FISHING

FISHING ROD	POKÉMON	VARIABLE
Old	Magikarp	◎
Good	Magikarp	◎

STEP 1 IN AND UP AND DOWN AND UP AND OUT

THE EXIT OF VICTORY ROAD may be on the same floor as the entrance, but it's not going to be a straight shoot escape from this crazy cavern. You'll need to travel down to both B1F and B2F before you see the light of day again, battling past other Trainers with their own dreams of Pokémon League glory.

Be warned, mortal!
I can see the future!

STEP 2 DO YOU HAVE THE POWER?

THE SECOND FLOOR just seems to be littered with large rocks, ones that block your path. Is this the time to turn around and go back? Of course not, as long as you have the HM04 Strength and a Pokémon who can use it. Move the boulders to solve the puzzles. If you make a mistake, don't sweat it. Just go to a different floor and come right back – the boulders will be restored to their original positions.

FINDING STUFF

BATTLING ISN'T the only thing you can do on Victory Road. Use the Dowsing Machine on the Pokétch to detect hidden items throughout the cavern.

STEP 3 YOU SHALL NOT PASS

ON THE RIGHT SIDE of the cave, not too far from the exit to the Pokémon League, is another exit blocked by a man. Curious about what could be in there? Well, you won't find out now. However, if you come back after getting the National Pokédex, the man will reconsider and let you pass.

Eventually, the world will grow
bigger to you!

Machoke
Fighting
Abilities:
- Guts
- No Guard

Medicham
Fighting-Psychic
Abilities:
- Pure Power

SURPRISES AND SECRETS OF POKÉMON

The field of Pokémon study is a rich one, since there are all sorts of things that continue to astonish even the most knowledgeable Pokémon expert. Two prime examples are unusual Pokémon coloring, and a strange Pokémon virus. Enlighten yourself a bit by reading below, and even you may feel like a Pokémon professor!

POKÉMON OF A DIFFERENT COLOR

POKÉMON ARE GENERALLY uniform in their color, but sometimes you'll find one with a color scheme completely unseen before. These are especially rare, and it's a special event when you do see one, in which stars will shine around their body and you'll hear a bright twinkle. It's like they're telling you to catch it! And you should – because they're incredibly rare, you may never have this opportunity again.

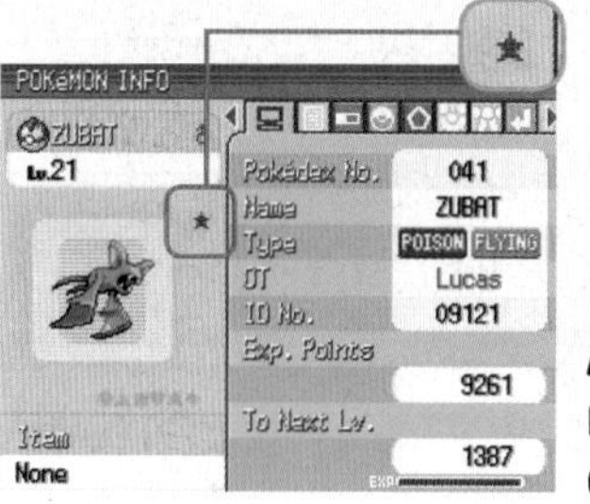

A STAR MARK WILL INDICATE THE COLOR DIFFERENCE

THE COLOR DOES NOT CHANGE WHEN THE POKÉMON EVOLVES

THE BENEFICIAL VIRUS

MICROSCOPIC TO THE EYE, you might not even notice that your Pokémon has Pokérus. But the clerk at the Pokémon Center will notice, since they're a Pokémon healing professional and all. But it's not like having a cold or the flu – in fact, the effects are only beneficial. It becomes easier for your Pokémon stats to increase, making it stronger and more effective in battle. Pokérus goes away in a few days, but the beneficial effects will last forever. You can spread it to your other Pokémon simply by having them all in the same party together. This is a virus that none of them will mind catching!

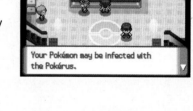

Your Pokémon may be infected with the Pokérus.

STATS WILL INCREASE WHEN THE POKÉMON HAS POKÉRUS

WHEN POKÉRUS PASSES, A SMALL SMILING FACE WILL APPEAR

POKÉMON LEAGUE

MOVES REQUIRED TO COMPLETE THIS AREA

SURF WATERFALL

This is it, the last stretch, the final showdown. This is where great Trainers are made. You've wanted this opportunity pretty badly, and now you must earn the right to call yourself the best by challenging the Elite Four and then the Champion...

ENTRANCE

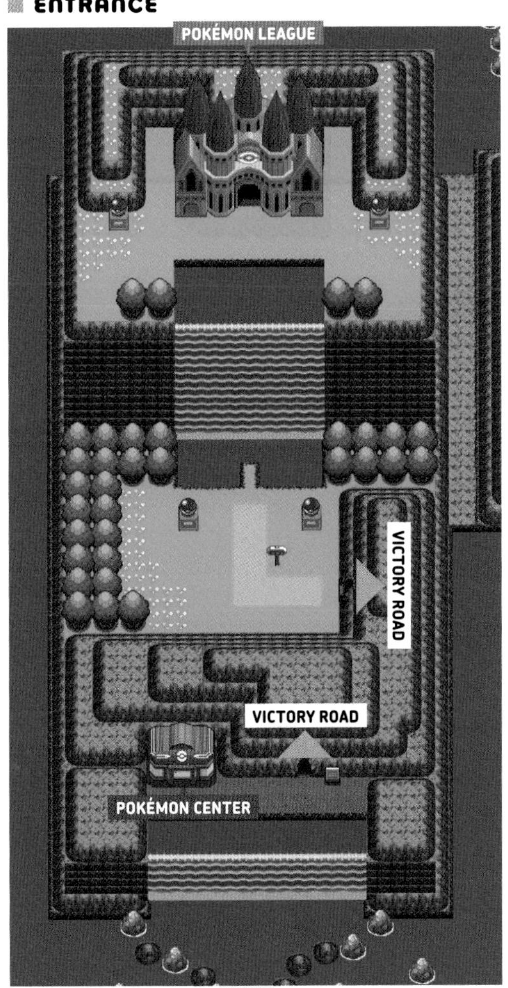

ROUTE 223 (TO SUNYSHORE CITY)

POKÉMON LEAGUE

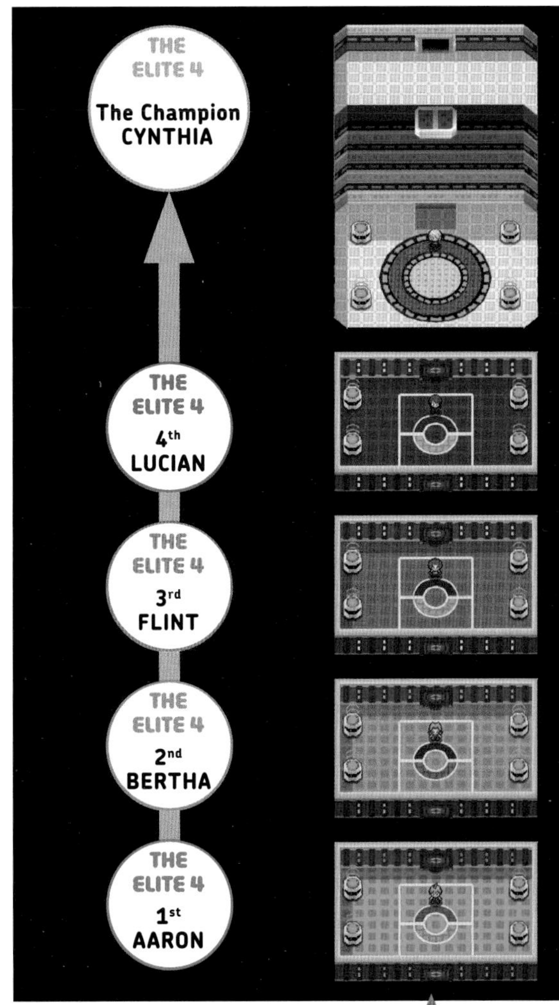

POKÉMON LEAGUE 1 FL

ENTRANCE

POKÉMART (MERCHANT ON THE RIGHT)	
Heal Ball	300
Net Ball	1000
Nest Ball	1000
Dusk Ball	1000
Quick Ball	1000
Timer Ball	1000
Repeat Ball	1000
Luxury Ball	1000

ON WATER

POKÉMON	VARIABLE
Tentacruel	◎
Pelipper	◎

FISHING

FISHING ROD	POKÉMON	VARIABLE
Old	Magikarp	◎
Good	Magikarp	◎
	Remoraid	○

STEP 1 ONE LAST TIME

YOU WALK UP TO the entrance, ready for your shot at the Elite Four, and who arrives? Your rival, also here to strut his stuff against the Pokémon League. Of course, he can't help but challenge you to one more battle. Take the challenge – if you can't take care of your rival, what chance do you have against the pros?

Let's see who's more worthy of making
the challenge with a battle!

BATTLE YOUR RIVAL 5

Looks like your rival's playing with a full deck of six Pokémon this time, with their levels higher by 17 or 18. You've got your work cut out for you here.

IF YOUR STARTER WAS TURTWIG: YOUR RIVAL WILL CHOOSE:

POKÉMON	LEVEL	TYPE
Staraptor ♂	Lv 48	Normal-Flying
Floatzel ♂	Lv 49	Water
Heracross ♂	Lv 50	Bug-Fighting
Roserade ♂	Lv 49	Grass-Poison
Snorlax ♂	Lv 51	Normal
Infernape ♂	Lv 53	Fire-Fighting

IF YOUR STARTER WAS CHIMCHAR: YOUR RIVAL WILL CHOOSE:

POKÉMON	LEVEL	TYPE
Staraptor ♂	Lv 48	Normal-Flying
Roserade ♂	Lv 49	Grass-Poison
Heracross ♂	Lv 50	Bug-Fighting
Rapidash ♂	Lv 49	Fire
Snorlax ♂	Lv 51	Normal
Empoleon ♂	Lv 53	Water-Steel

IF YOUR STARTER WAS PIPLUP: YOUR RIVAL WILL CHOOSE:

POKÉMON	LEVEL	TYPE
Staraptor ♂	Lv 48	Normal-Flying
Floatzel ♂	Lv 49	Water
Heracross ♂	Lv 50	Bug-Fighting
Rapidash ♂	Lv 49	Fire
Snorlax ♂	Lv 51	Normal
Torterra ♂	Lv 53	Grass-Ground

STEP 2 THE POWER OF PREPARATION

THE TIME HAS COME. Make you've got everything lined up and ready, including plenty of healing items like Full Restore and Max Potion, which can be purchased right there in the Pokémon League building.

ELITE FOUR BATTLE 1

AARON
ELITE FOUR
POKÉMON TYPE: BUG
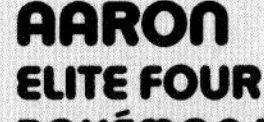
RECOMMENDED TYPES: FIRE, FLYING

AARON WILL send out mostly Bug-type Pokémon, with one Poison-and-Dark-type in the mix. Hit the Bug-types – Dustox, Heracross, Vespiquen, and Beautifly – with Fire- and Flying-type moves. Drapion, as a different type, will have a different weakness, so hit it with Ground-type moves to finish it. For ensured victory, it's best for your Pokémon to know moves like Flamethrower, Drill Peck, and Earthquake.

DUSTOX ♂
TYPE: Bug-Poison LV 53
EFFCTIVE MOVE TYPES: Fire, Flying, Psychic, Rock

BEAUTIFLY ♂
TYPE: Bug-Flying LV 53
EFFCTIVE MOVE TYPES: Rock, Fire, Electric, Ice, Flying

VESPIQUEN ♀
TYPE: Bug-Flying LV 54
EFFCTIVE MOVE TYPES: Rock, Fire, Electric, Ice, Flying

HERACROSS ♂
TYPE: Bug-Fighting LV 54
EFFCTIVE MOVE TYPES: Flying, Fire, Psychic

DRAPION ♂
TYPE: Poison-Dark LV 57
EFFCTIVE MOVE TYPES: Ground

ELITE FOUR BATTLE 2

BERTHA
ELITE FOUR
POKÉMON TYPE: GROUND
RECOMMENDED TYPES: GRASS, WATER

BERTHA HAS a strong collection of Pokémon, and the only weakness that her Quagsire and Whiscash have is Grass-type moves. Not only that, but those moves will deal 4x the damage! Pull out the Grass-, Water-, Fighting-, and Ground-type moves for Sudowoodo and Golem, while trying Grass, Water, and Ice on Hippowdon. If you need power against Bertha, then learn moves like Solarbeam and Surf to finish her Pokémon off.

QUAGSIRE ♀
TYPE: Water-Ground LV 55
EFFCTIVE MOVE TYPES: Grass

SUDOWOODO ♀
TYPE: Rock LV 56
EFFCTIVE MOVE TYPES: Grass, Water, Fighting, Ground, Steel

GOLEM ♀
TYPE: Rock-Ground LV 56
EFFCTIVE MOVE TYPES: Grass, Water, Fighting, Ground, Steel, Ice

WHISCASH ♀
TYPE: Water-Ground LV 55
EFFCTIVE MOVE TYPES: Grass

HIPPOWDON ♂
TYPE: Ground LV 59
EFFCTIVE MOVE TYPES: Grass, Water, Ice

ELITE FOUR BATTLE 3

FLINT

ELITE FOUR
POKéMON TYPE: FIRE
RECOMMENDED TYPES: WATER, GROUND

THOUGH HE'S labeled as a Fire-type user, the group of Pokémon that Flint uses are actually quite diverse. Fortunately, all of them are vulnerable to Ground-type moves, so make frequent use of moves like Earthquake and Magnitude. Lopunny is also weak to Fighting-type moves, and against Drifblim you have a choice of Electric-, Ice-, Rock-, Ghost-, or Dark-type moves.

RAPIDASH ♂
TYPE: Fire LV 58
EFFCTIVE MOVE TYPES: Water, Ground, Rock

STEELIX ♂
TYPE: Steel-Ground LV 57
EFFCTIVE MOVE TYPES: Fire, Water, Fighting, Ground

DRIFBLIM ♂
TYPE: Ghost-Flying LV 58
EFFCTIVE MOVE TYPES: Electric, Ice, Rock, Ghost, Dark

LOPUNNY ♂
TYPE: Normal LV 57
EFFCTIVE MOVE TYPES: Fighting

INFERNAPE ♂
TYPE: Fire-Fighting LV 61
EFFCTIVE MOVE TYPES: Water, Ground, Flying, Psychic

ELITE FOUR BATTLE 4

LUCIAN

ELITE FOUR
POKéMON TYPE: PSYCHIC
RECOMMENDED TYPES: BUG, GHOST, DARK

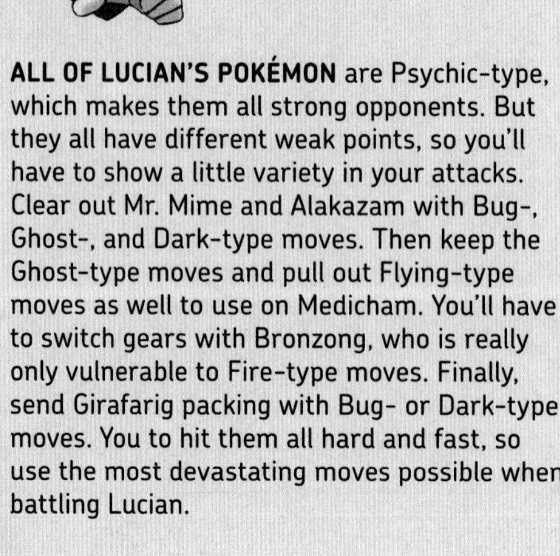

ALL OF LUCIAN'S POKéMON are Psychic-type, which makes them all strong opponents. But they all have different weak points, so you'll have to show a little variety in your attacks. Clear out Mr. Mime and Alakazam with Bug-, Ghost-, and Dark-type moves. Then keep the Ghost-type moves and pull out Flying-type moves as well to use on Medicham. You'll have to switch gears with Bronzong, who is really only vulnerable to Fire-type moves. Finally, send Girafarig packing with Bug- or Dark-type moves. You to hit them all hard and fast, so use the most devastating moves possible when battling Lucian.

Mr. Mime ♂
TYPE: Psychic LV 59
EFFCTIVE MOVE TYPES: Bug, Ghost, Dark

Girafarig ♂
TYPE: Normal-Psychic LV 59
EFFCTIVE MOVE TYPES: Bug, Dark

Medicham ♂
TYPE: Fighting-Psychic LV 60
EFFCTIVE MOVE TYPES: Flying, Ghost

Alakazam ♂
TYPE: Psychic LV 60
EFFCTIVE MOVE TYPES: Bug, Ghost, Dark

Bronzong
TYPE: Steel-Psychic LV 63
EFFCTIVE MOVE TYPES: Fire

CHAMPION BATTLE

CYNTHIA
POKÉMON LEAGUE CHAMPION

CYNTHIA DOESN'T specialize in one type of Pokémon, and as such, there's no one surefire type that will take out her entire team. Her Spiritomb has no weaknesses, in fact! You'll need to pull out your strongest, most powerful moves and just try to deal as much damage as possible. Gastrodon will be especially weak to Grass-type moves, while you should fight Lucario with Fire-, Ground-, or Fighting-type moves. Roserade and Garchomp are vulnerable to Ice-type moves, and to bring down the mighty Milotic, use Grass- or Electric-type moves.

The power you learned...
I can feel it emanating from you.

IF YOU LOSE, check your moves. Know when to switch your Pokémon – you want to distribute damage equally to avoid losing them.

Spiritomb ♀
TYPE: Ghost-Dark LV 61
EFFECTIVE MOVE TYPES: None

Roserade ♀
TYPE: Grass-Poison LV 60
EFFCTIVE MOVE TYPES: Fire, Ice, Flying, Psychic

Gastrodon ♀
TYPE: Water-Ground LV 60
EFFCTIVE MOVE TYPES: Grass

Lucario ♂
TYPE: Steel-Fighting LV 63
EFFCTIVE MOVE TYPES: Fire, Fighting, Ground

Milotic ♀
TYPE: Water LV 63
EFFCTIVE MOVE TYPES: Grass, Electric

Garchomp ♀
TYPE: Dragon-Ground LV 66
EFFCTIVE MOVE TYPES: Ice, Dragon

BEAT THE CHAMPION? WELCOME TO THE HALL OF FAME!

ONLY THE BEST OF THE BEST end up here. Your name will be forever immortalized, and all of your party Pokémon will receive Champion ribbons. The story is over... but the adventure continues! Turn the page to find out what awaits you next.

UPGRADE TO NATIONAL

Just because you've entered the Hall of Fame doesn't mean that there aren't still plenty of quests and adventures waiting for you! First, you might want to start on the path to recording all 150 kinds of Pokémon living in Sinnoh.

TWINLEAF TOWN
HOW MANY HAVE YOU SEEN?

LIKE YOU JUST HAD a wonderful dream, you'll find yourself back at home after achieving Hall of Fame status. Open up your Sinnoh Pokédex and check out the "seen" number of Pokémon. If you've been diligent about catching every Pokémon in Sinnoh thus far, it should be up to 149.

AND IF IT'S LESS THAN 149?

LOOKS LIKE there are Pokémon you haven't met yet. Check the Sinnoh Pokédex in the back of this book for their names and locations (pg 296) to get cracking on catching the rest!

TWINLEAF TOWN
A INVITATION

WHEN YOU GO downstairs your mother will have a message for you... from your rival! He wants you to take a boat out of Snowpoint City, to a place where you've never been before. How exciting! Better get your Pokédex upgraded ASAP.

Barry came looking for you
a little while ago.

SANDGEM TOWN
HELLO AGAIN

IT SEEMS YOU can't enter a town without someone bothering you. But no worries, it's just Professor Rowan's assistant. They have a message for you from the Celestic Town elder. Apparently he wants to show you something. Could be interesting...

ASSISTANT'S SIBLING

IF YOU HAPPEN to come back after your Pokédex gets upgraded, talk to the assistant again and they'll tell you all about their little sister. How cute! Head over to their house to talk to the little girl.

SANDGEM TOWN
THE STRONG BUT SILENT TYPE

ONCE YOU'VE obtained HM03 Surf by winning the Gym battle in Hearthome City, visit Sandgem Town and go east on the ocean. You'll encounter lot of Pokémon Trainers on the way, so be prepared – stock up on items and make sure you have leveled up your Pokémon.

You're not far from seeing every
Pokémon there is to see in Sinnoh!

CELESTIC TOWN
SOME LIGHT READING

IF YOU VISIT the house north of the small shrine there, you'll meet the elder, who just brought back a book that he found in the old shrine. It happens to have a drawing of a Pokémon you haven't seen yet... coincidentally, the one Pokémon that is missing from your Pokédex. In an awesome twist, seeing the Pokémon in this book will automatically add to the Pokédex, bringing your total to 150 Pokémon seen!

"PALKIA, the Pokémon that binds the
spatial dimensions," it is written...

SANDGEM TOWN
SHOW OFF YOUR ACCOMPLISHMENT

NOW THAT YOU have a completed Pokédex, head back to Professor Rowan to show it off. He'll give you his warmest congratulations, and then an unexpected visitor shows up... Professor Oak! Professor Oak is from the Kanto region, and is respected as a true expert on all things Pokémon. He'll congratulate you as well, in his own way.

You've recorded all the Pokémon of

SANDGEM TOWN
A NEW TASK, A NEW ADVENTURE

PROFESSOR OAK knows a lot about Pokémon from all over, including other regions. He'll upgrade your Pokédex to the National version, which will allow you to learn and know a lot about them too!

Rowan: Oh! If it isn't my old
colleague, Professor Oak!

FRIENDS AND COLLEAGUES

HEY, PROFESSOR ROWAN and Professor Oak seem to know each other pretty well. The study of Pokémon can really bring people together as friends...

EXTENDED STAY

THE KANTO REGION may be his home, but Professor Oak won't go running back any time soon. He's staying at a house in Eterna City, so visit him anytime after you go to the Pal Park so that he can check your Pokédex.

SECTION 3

POKÉDEX

COMPLETING THE SINNOH POKÉDEX

Discover the inhabitants of Sinnoh.

DEFEATING THE POKÉMON LEAGUE is all well and good, but it's not the only lofty goal that Sinnoh has to offer you. You might want to try the toughest challenge of all – completing the Sinnoh Pokédex. It'll be a tough journey, but well worth it for the satisfaction.

▸ FILL OUT THE SINNOH POKÉDEX

NOT TO CONFUSE YOU, but there are two versions of the Pokédex that you will encounter. The Sinnoh Pokédex covers only those Pokémon appearing in the Sinnoh region, while the National Pokédex is a bit more expansive, covering not just the Pokémon of Sinnoh, but Pokémon in other regions including Kanto and Hoenn. Before you think global, though, you'll need to act local by completing the Sinnoh Pokédex first.

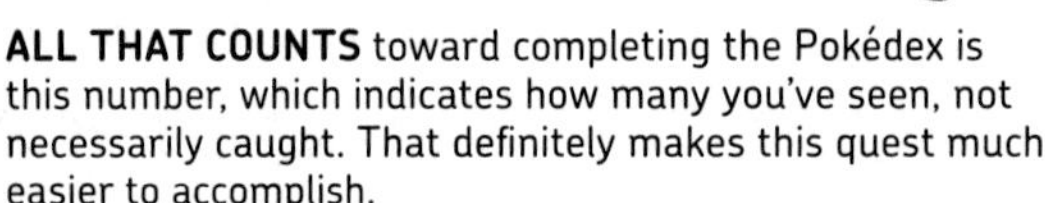

ALL THAT COUNTS toward completing the Pokédex is this number, which indicates how many you've seen, not necessarily caught. That definitely makes this quest much easier to accomplish.

▸ MR. DIRECTOR? MR. DIRECTOR?

ONCE YOU'VE SNEAKED A PEEK at every Pokémon to complete the Sinnoh Pokédex, head on over to the house at the Verity Lakefront. There you'll find the game director, who will reward you for having a completed Sinnoh Pokédex. I wonder which game he possibly could have directed, hmm?

I'm really impressed!
Let me give you an award!

▸ HOW TO LOCATE POKÉMON AND RECORD THEM IN THE POKÉDEX

THE ONLY WAY you're going to complete the Sinnoh Pokédex is by tracking down all 150 kinds of Pokémon in the Sinnoh region and recording them in your trusty Pokédex. It may sound intimidating, but there are a few basic methods that will make a huge impact on your "seen" Pokémon number.

IN THE WILD

THE BEST WAY TO BUILD up your collection is by catching wild Pokémon, but it's great for just doing some sightseeing to fill your Pokédex, too. Check tall grass, caves, or fish in ponds or at beaches – any encounter with a wild Pokémon will count toward having "seen" that Pokémon and adding it to the Pokédex.

WELL MET IN BATTLE

THERE ARE QUITE A NUMBER OF POKÉMON you will never meet in the wild – these tend to be evolved forms that require the expert hand of a Pokémon Trainer to help the Pokémon reach its full potential. These Trainers tend to be eager to battle, and you should be too, because simply having a Pokémon as your opponent adds it to your Pokédex.

STORIED ENCOUNTERS

SOME POKÉMON WON'T BE TOO HARD TO FIND, if you just follow the pull of the story and go where you're asked to go by other characters and circumstance. These mainly include Legendary Pokémon, like the three Legendaries of the lakes – Uxie, Azelf, and Mesprit – and the mighty Dialga (in Diamond) and Palkia (in Pearl).

FIRST SINNOH, THEN NATIONAL!

ONCE YOU'VE COMPLETED the Sinnoh Pokédex, it's time to aspire even higher by beginning work on the National Pokédex, the ultimate compendium of known Pokémon. It'll be much harder than completing the Sinnoh Pokédex, because you'll be expected to do a lot more than simply see every single Pokémon. You'll need to obtain every single Pokémon – even if it's only for a short time, the Pokémon need only register its information in your Pokédex – for the National Pokédex to be considered complete. Some Pokémon will require a little more effort than usual, like special methods or special knowledge. All in all, when you have an opportunity to capture a Pokémon, take it!

Lucas's Pokédex was upgraded with the National Mode!

001 TURTWIG

IN ACTIVITIES AND EVENTS: At Lake Verity, choose from Prof. Rowan's briefcase P. 047

OTHER TRAINERS (IN THEIR PARTY): Gardenia, Eterna City Gym Leader P. 092

002 GROTLE

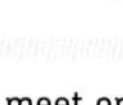

IN ACTIVITIES AND EVENTS: Make Turtwig level up to Lv.18 –

OTHER TRAINERS (IN THEIR PARTY): A Trainer you meet on Route 210 P. 126

003 TORTERRA

IN ACTIVITIES AND EVENTS: Make Grotle level up to Lv.32 –

OTHER TRAINERS (IN THEIR PARTY): A Trainer you meet on Victory Road P. 200

004 CHIMCHAR

IN ACTIVITIES AND EVENTS: At Lake Verity, choose from Prof. Rowan's briefcase P. 047

OTHER TRAINERS (IN THEIR PARTY): A Trainer you meet on Route 207 P. 070

005 MONFERNO

IN ACTIVITIES AND EVENTS: Make Chimchar level up to Lv.14 –

OTHER TRAINERS (IN THEIR PARTY): A Trainer you meet on Route 215 P. 126

006 INFERNAPE

IN ACTIVITIES AND EVENTS: Make Monferno level up to Lv.36 –

OTHER TRAINERS (IN THEIR PARTY): Flint, The Elite Four P. 206

007 PIPLUP

IN ACTIVITIES AND EVENTS: At Lake Verity, choose from Prof. Rowan's briefcase P. 047

OTHER TRAINERS (IN THEIR PARTY): A Trainer you meet on Route 205 P. 080

008 PRINPLUP

IN ACTIVITIES AND EVENTS: Make Piplup level up to Lv.16 –

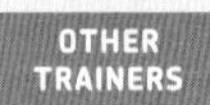

OTHER TRAINERS (IN THEIR PARTY): A Trainer you meet on Route 212 P. 152

009 EMPOLEON

IN ACTIVITIES AND EVENTS: Make Prinplup level up to Lv.36 –

OTHER TRAINERS (IN THEIR PARTY): A Trainer you meet on Victory Road P. 200

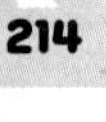

010 STARLY

ON THE FIELD (IN THE WILD): Tall grass on Route 201 P. 043

011 STARAVIA

ON THE FIELD (IN THE WILD): Tall grass on Route 209 P. 116

012 STARAPTOR

OTHER TRAINERS (IN THEIR PARTY): A Trainer you meet on Victory Road P. 200

013 BIDOOF

ON THE FIELD (IN THE WILD): Tall grass on Route 201 P. 043

014 BIBAREL

ON THE FIELD (IN THE WILD): Tall grass on Route 208 P. 108

015 KRICKETOT

ON THE FIELD (IN THE WILD): Tall grass on Route 202 P. 054

016 KRICKETUNE

ON THE FIELD (IN THE WILD): Tall grass on Route 206

P. 104

017 SHINX

ON THE FIELD (IN THE WILD): Tall grass on Route 202

P. 054

018 LUXIO

ON THE FIELD (IN THE WILD): Tall grass at Fuego Ironworks

P. 081

019 LUXRAY

OTHER TRAINERS (IN THEIR PARTY): Volkner, Sunyshore City Gym Leader

P. 196

020 ABRA

ON THE FIELD (IN THE WILD): Tall grass on Route 203

P. 060

021 KADABRA

ON THE FIELD (IN THE WILD): Tall grass on Route 215

P. 127

022 ALAKAZAM

OTHER TRAINERS (IN THEIR PARTY): A Trainer you meet in Victory Road

P. 200

023 MAGIKARP

ON THE FIELD (IN THE WILD): Fishing on Route 218 (Old Rod)

P. 072

024 GYARADOS

ON THE FIELD (IN THE WILD): Fishing in Pastoria Great Marsh (Good Rod)

P. 151

025 BUDEW

ON THE FIELD (IN THE WILD):

Tall grass on Route 204

P. 074

026 ROSELIA

ON THE FIELD (IN THE WILD): Tall grass on Route 212

P. 152

027 ROSERADE

OTHER TRAINERS (IN THEIR PARTY): Gardenia, Eterna City Gym Leader

P. 092

028 ZUBAT

ON THE FIELD (IN THE WILD): Oreburgh Gate, 1 FL

P. 062

029 GOLBAT

ON THE FIELD (IN THE WILD): Lost Tower, 5 FL

P. 117

030 CROBAT

OTHER TRAINERS (IN THEIR PARTY): Cyrus, Team Galactic Boss, when battling at Spear Pillar

P. 187

031 GEODUDE

ON THE FIELD (IN THE WILD) Oreburgh Gate, 1 FL P. 062

032 GRAVELER

ON THE FIELD (IN THE WILD) Tall grass on Valor Lakefront P. 138

033 GOLEM

OTHER TRAINERS (IN THEIR PARTY) A Trainer you meet in Victory Road P. 200

034 ONIX

ON THE FIELD (IN THE WILD) Oreburgh Coal Mine, B1F P. 068

035 STEELIX

ON THE FIELD (IN THE WILD) Iron Island, B2F P. 165

036 CRANIDOS

IN ACTIVITIES AND EVENTS Obtain Skull Fossil in the Underground (Diamond Version only) —

OTHER TRAINERS (IN THEIR PARTY) Roark, Oreburgh City Gym Leader P. 067

037 RAMPARDOS

OTHER TRAINERS (IN THEIR PARTY) A Trainer you meet in Victory Road P. 200

038 SHIELDON

IN ACTIVITIES AND EVENTS Obtain Armor Fossil in the Underground (Pearl Version only) —

OTHER TRAINERS (IN THEIR PARTY) A Trainer you meet on Route 215 P. 126

039 BASTIODON

OTHER TRAINERS (IN THEIR PARTY) Byron, Canalave City Gym Leader P. 162

040 MACHOP

ON THE FIELD (IN THE WILD) Tall grass on Route 207 P. 070

041 MACHOKE

ON THE FIELD (IN THE WILD) Tall grass on Route 210 P. 127

042 MACHAMP

OTHER TRAINERS (IN THEIR PARTY) A Trainer you meet in Victory Road P. 200

043 PSYDUCK

ON THE FIELD (IN THE WILD) Oreburgh Gate, B1F P. 062

044 GOLDUCK

ON THE FIELD (IN THE WILD) On the water on Route 208 P. 108

045 BURMY

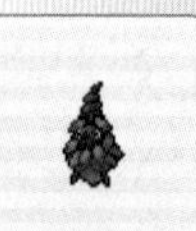

ON THE FIELD (IN THE WILD) Put Honey on a honey tree P. 089

046

WORMADAM

OTHER TRAINERS (IN THEIR PARTY) A Trainer you meet on Route 214 P. 139

047

MOTHIM

OTHER TRAINERS (IN THEIR PARTY) A Trainer you meet on Route 210 P. 126

048

WURMPLE

ON THE FIELD (IN THE WILD) Tall grass in Eterna Forest P. 086

049

SILCOON

ON THE FIELD (IN THE WILD) Tall grass in Eterna Forest (Diamond Version only) P. 086

OTHER TRAINERS (IN THEIR PARTY) A Trainer you meet in Eterna Forest (Diamond Version only) P. 086

050

BEAUTIFLY

ON THE FIELD (IN THE WILD) Tall grass in Eterna Forest (Diamond Version only) P. 086

OTHER TRAINERS (IN THEIR PARTY) A Trainer you meet in Eterna Forest (Diamond Version only) P. 086

051

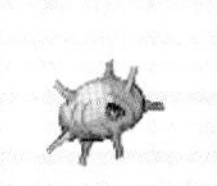

CASCOON

ON THE FIELD (IN THE WILD) Tall Grass in Eterna Forest (Pearl Version only) P. 086

OTHER TRAINERS (IN THEIR PARTY) A Trainer you meet in Wayward Cave P. 105

052

DUSTOX

ON THE FIELD (IN THE WILD) Tall Grass in Eterna Forest (Pearl Version only) P. 086

OTHER TRAINERS (IN THEIR PARTY) Gardenia, Eterna City Gym Leader P. 092

053

COMBEE

ON THE FIELD (IN THE WILD) Put Honey on a honey tree P. 089

054

VESPIQUEN

OTHER TRAINERS (IN THEIR PARTY) Aaron, the Elite Four P. 205

055

PACHIRISU

ON THE FIELD (IN THE WILD) Tall grass at Valley Windworks P. 084

056

BUIZEL

ON THE FIELD (IN THE WILD) Tall grass at Valley Windworks P. 084

057

FLOATZEL

ON THE FIELD (IN THE WILD) Tall grass on Route 213 P. 138

058

CHERUBI

ON THE FIELD (IN THE WILD) Put Honey on a honey tree P. 089

059

CHERRIM

OTHER TRAINERS (IN THEIR PARTY) A Trainer you meet on Route 221 P. 052

060

SHELLOS

ON THE FIELD (IN THE WILD) Tall grass at Valley Windworks P. 084

061 GASTRODON

ON THE FIELD (IN THE WILD)	Tall grass on Route 218

P. 072

062 HERACROSS

ON THE FIELD (IN THE WILD)	Put Honey on a honey tree

P. 089

063 AIPOM

ON THE FIELD (IN THE WILD)	Put Honey on a honey tree

P. 089

064 AMBIPOM

OTHER TRAINERS (IN THEIR PARTY)	A Trainer you meet on Route 216

P. 172

065 DRIFLOON

IN ACTIVITIES AND EVENTS	Go to the front door of Valley Windworks (Fridays only)

P. 085

066 DRIFBLIM

OTHER TRAINERS (IN THEIR PARTY)	Fantina, Hearthome City Gym Leader

P. 114

067 BUNEARY

ON THE FIELD (IN THE WILD)	Tall grass in Eterna Forest

P. 086

068 LOPUNNY

OTHER TRAINERS (IN THEIR PARTY)	A Trainer you meet on Route 216

P. 139

069 GASTLY

ON THE FIELD (IN THE WILD)	In Old Chateau

P. 087

070 HAUNTER

OTHER TRAINERS (IN THEIR PARTY)	A Trainer you meet on Route 214

P. 139

071 GENGAR

OTHER TRAINERS (IN THEIR PARTY)	Fantina, Hearthome City Gym Leader

P. 114

072 MISDREAVUS

ON THE FIELD (IN THE WILD)	Tall grass in Eterna Forest (Pearl version only)
OTHER TRAINERS (IN THEIR PARTY)	A Trainer you meet at the Lost Tower

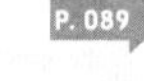
P. 089

P. 117

073 MISMAGIUS

OTHER TRAINERS (IN THEIR PARTY)	Fantina, Hearthome City Gym Leader

P. 114

074 MURKROW

ON THE FIELD (IN THE WILD)	Tall grass in Eterna Forest (Diamond version only)
OTHER TRAINERS (IN THEIR PARTY)	A Trainer you meet at the Lost Tower

P. 089

P. 117

075 HONCHKROW

OTHER TRAINERS (IN THEIR PARTY)	Cyrus, Team Galactic Boss, when battling at Spear Pillar

P. 187

076 GLAMEOW

ON THE FIELD (IN THE WILD): Tall grass on Route 218 (Pearl version only) P. 072

OTHER TRAINERS (IN THEIR PARTY): A Trainer you meet on Route 210 P. 126

077 PURUGLY

ON THE FIELD (IN THE WILD): Tall grass on Route 222 (Pearl version only) P. 192

OTHER TRAINERS (IN THEIR PARTY): Mars, Team Galactic Commander P. 085

078 GOLDEEN

ON THE FIELD (IN THE WILD): Fishing on Route 209 (Good Rod) P. 116

079 SEAKING

OTHER TRAINERS (IN THEIR PARTY): A Trainer you meet on Route 220 P. 052

080 BARBOACH

ON THE FIELD (IN THE WILD): Fishing on Route 208 (Good Rod) P. 108

081 WHISCASH

OTHER TRAINERS (IN THEIR PARTY): A Trainer you meet on Route 220 P. 052

082 CHINGLING

ON THE FIELD (IN THE WILD): Tall grass on Route 211 P. 096

083 CHIMECHO

ON THE FIELD (IN THE WILD): Mt. Coronet 4 FL (3) P. 185

084 STUNKY

ON THE FIELD (IN THE WILD): Tall grass on Route 206 (Diamond version only) P. 104

OTHER TRAINERS (IN THEIR PARTY): A Trainer you meet at the Lost Tower P. 117

085 SKUNTANK

ON THE FIELD (IN THE WILD): Tall grass on Route 221 (Diamond version only) P. 052

OTHER TRAINERS (IN THEIR PARTY): Jupiter, Team Galactic Commander P. 103

086 MEDITITE

ON THE FIELD (IN THE WILD): Tall grass on Route 208 P. 108

087 MEDICHAM

ON THE FIELD (IN THE WILD): Tall grass on Route 217 P. 172

088 BRONZOR

ON THE FIELD (IN THE WILD): Tall grass on Route 206 P. 104

089 BRONZONG

ON THE FIELD (IN THE WILD): Mt. Coronet, 2 FL P. 184

090 PONYTA

ON THE FIELD (IN THE WILD): Tall grass on Route 211 P. 096

091 RAPIDASH

OTHER TRAINERS (IN THEIR PARTY) — A Trainer you meet in Fuego Ironworks P. 081

092 BONSLY

ON THE FIELD (IN THE WILD) — Tall grass on Route 209 (Pearl version only) P. 116

OTHER TRAINERS (IN THEIR PARTY) — A Trainer you meet on Route 208 P. 108

093 SUDOWOODO

ON THE FIELD (IN THE WILD) — Tall grass on Route 214 (Pearl version only) P. 138

OTHER TRAINERS (IN THEIR PARTY) — A Trainer you meet on Route 210 P. 126

094 MIME JR.

ON THE FIELD (IN THE WILD) — Tall grass on Route 209 (Diamond version only) P. 116

OTHER TRAINERS (IN THEIR PARTY) — A Trainer you meet on Route 208 P. 108

095 MR. MIME

ON THE FIELD (IN THE WILD) — Tall grass on Route 218 (Diamond version only) P. 072

OTHER TRAINERS (IN THEIR PARTY) — A Trainer you meet on Route 210 P. 126

096 HAPPINY

IN ACTIVITIES AND EVENTS — Hatch an Egg you got from a Hiker in Hearthome City P. 111

097 CHANSEY

ON THE FIELD (IN THE WILD) — Tall grass on Route 209 P. 116

098 BLISSEY

OTHER TRAINERS (IN THEIR PARTY) — A Trainer you meet in Victory Road P. 200

099 CLEFFA

ON THE FIELD (IN THE WILD) — Mt. Coronet, 1 FL P. 099

100 CLEFAIRY

ON THE FIELD (IN THE WILD) — Mt. Coronet, 2 FL P. 099

101 CLEFABLE

OTHER TRAINERS (IN THEIR PARTY) — A Trainer you meet in Victory Road P. 200

102 CHATOT

ON THE FIELD (IN THE WILD) — Tall grass on Route 222 P. 192

103 PICHU

ON THE FIELD (IN THE WILD) — The Trophy Garden of Pokémon Mansion P. 153

104 PIKACHU

ON THE FIELD (IN THE WILD) — The Trophy Garden of Pokémon Mansion P. 153

105 RAICHU

OTHER TRAINERS (IN THEIR PARTY) — A Trainer you meet on Route 210 P. 126

106 HOOTHOOT

ON THE FIELD (IN THE WILD) Tall grass on Route 210 P. 127

107 NOCTOWL

ON THE FIELD (IN THE WILD) Tall grass on Route 210 P. 127

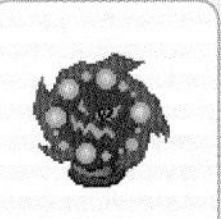

108 SPIRITOMB

OTHER TRAINERS (IN THEIR PARTY) Cynthia, Pokémon League Champion P. 207

109 GIBLE

ON THE FIELD (IN THE WILD) In Wayward Cave BIF P. 105

110 GABITE

OTHER TRAINERS (IN THEIR PARTY) A Trainer you meet in Victory Road P. 200

111 GARCHOMP

OTHER TRAINERS (IN THEIR PARTY) Cynthia, Pokémon League Champion P. 207

112 MUNCHLAX

ON THE FIELD (IN THE WILD) Put Honey on a honey tree P. 089

113 SNORLAX

OTHER TRAINERS (IN THEIR PARTY) Your rival when battling at the Pokémon League P. 204

114 UNOWN

ON THE FIELD (IN THE WILD) Solaceon Ruins P. 121

115 RIOLU

IN ACTIVITIES AND EVENTS Hatch an Egg you got from Riley on Iron Island P. 166

116 LUCARIO

OTHER TRAINERS (IN THEIR PARTY) Maylene, Veilstone City Gym Leader P. 133

117 WOOPER

ON THE FIELD (IN THE WILD) Tall grass in Pastoria Great Marsh P. 151

118 QUAGSIRE

ON THE FIELD (IN THE WILD) Tall grass in Pastoria Great Marsh P. 151

119 WINGULL

ON THE FIELD (IN THE WILD) Tall grass on Route 213 P. 138

120 PELIPPER

ON THE FIELD (IN THE WILD) On the water on Route 213 P. 138

121 GIRAFARIG

ON THE FIELD (IN THE WILD): Tall grass on Route 214

P. 138

122 HIPPOPOTAS

ON THE FIELD (IN THE WILD): The Maniac Tunnel

P. 144

123 HIPPOWDON

OTHER TRAINERS (IN THEIR PARTY): A Trainer you meet in Victory Road

P. 200

124 AZURILL

ON THE FIELD (IN THE WILD): Tall grass in Pastoria Great Marsh

P. 151

125 MARILL

ON THE FIELD (IN THE WILD): Tall grass in Pastoria Great Marsh

P. 151

126 AZUMARILL

OTHER TRAINERS (IN THEIR PARTY): A Trainer you meet on the water on Route 213

P. 139

127 SKORUPI

ON THE FIELD (IN THE WILD): Tall grass in Pastoria Great Marsh

P. 151

128 DRAPION

OTHER TRAINERS (IN THEIR PARTY): Aaron, the Elite Four

P. 205

129 CROAGUNK

ON THE FIELD (IN THE WILD): Tall grass in Pastoria Great Marsh

P. 151

130 TOXICROAK

OTHER TRAINERS (IN THEIR PARTY): Saturn, Team Galactic Commander

P. 169

131 CARNIVINE

ON THE FIELD (IN THE WILD): Tall grass in Pastoria Great Marsh

P. 151

132 REMORAID

ON THE FIELD (IN THE WILD): Fishing on Route 213 (Good Rod)

P. 138

133 OCTILLERY

OTHER TRAINERS (IN THEIR PARTY): Volkner, Sunyshore City Gym Leader

P. 196

134 FINNEON

ON THE FIELD (IN THE WILD): Fishing on Route 205 (Good Rod)

P. 081

135 LUMINEON

OTHER TRAINERS (IN THEIR PARTY): A Trainer you meet on Route 223

P. 198

136 TENTACOOL

ON THE FIELD (IN THE WILD) — On the water on Route 205

P. 081

137 TENTACRUEL

ON THE FIELD (IN THE WILD) — On the water on Route 205

P. 081

138 FEEBAS

OTHER TRAINERS (IN THEIR PARTY) — A Trainer you meet on Route 222

P. 192

139 MILOTIC

OTHER TRAINERS (IN THEIR PARTY) — Cynthia, Pokémon League Champion

P. 207

140 MANTYKE

ON THE FIELD (IN THE WILD) — On the water in Sunyshore City

P. 194

141 MANTINE

OTHER TRAINERS (IN THEIR PARTY) — A Trainer you meet on Route 223

P. 198

142 SNOVER

ON THE FIELD (IN THE WILD) — Tall grass on Route 216

P. 172

143 ABOMASNOW

ON THE FIELD (IN THE WILD) — Tall grass on the summit of Mt. Coronet

P. 185

144 SNEASEL

ON THE FIELD (IN THE WILD) — Tall grass on Route 216

P. 172

145 WEAVILE

OTHER TRAINERS (IN THEIR PARTY) — Cyrus, Team Galactic Boss, when battling at Spear Pillar

P. 187

146 UXIE

IN ACTIVITIES AND EVENTS — At Lake Acuity (After visiting Spear Pillar)

P. 189

147 MESPRIT

IN ACTIVITIES AND EVENTS — At Lake Verity (After visiting Spear Pillar)

P. 191

148 AZELF

IN ACTIVITIES AND EVENTS — At Lake Valor (After visiting Spear Pillar)

P. 190

149 DIALGA

IN ACTIVITIES AND EVENTS — At Spear Pillar (Diamond version only)

P. 188

IN ACTIVITIES AND EVENTS — A ancient book the elder in Celestic Town shows you (Pearl version only)

P. 209

150 PALKIA

IN ACTIVITIES AND EVENTS — At Spear Pillar (Pearl version only)

P. 188

IN ACTIVITIES AND EVENTS — A ancient book the elder in Celestic Town shows you (Diamond version only)

P. 209

SECTION 4

CONTESTS

THE CONTEST CHALLENGE

In Hearthome City is a different kind of Pokémon competition for you to take on – the Pokémon Super Contest. Instead of battling another Trainer, this will be a test of your Pokémon's skills and talents. You will be judged in three divisions: appearance, dancing, and performance. Four contestants will face off, but which one will ultimately win the favor of the judges and the crowd?

THE BASICS  THERE ARE FOUR CLASSES IN EACH OF 5 DIVISIONS

THE CONTEST HAS FIVE DIVISIONS – that is, five different types of Contests that you can compete in, all judging a different attribute. Within each division are four ranks. The starting rank, the Normal Rank, can be entered by anyone, but to proceed into higher, more competitive ranks, a Trainer must first win the previous rank.

COOL CONTEST	COMPETE TO SHOW POKÉMON'S "COOLNESS" 	NORMAL RANK → GREAT RANK → ULTRA RANK → MASTER RANK
BEAUTY CONTEST	COMPETE TO SHOW POKÉMON'S "BEAUTY" 	NORMAL RANK → GREAT RANK → ULTRA RANK → MASTER RANK
CUTE CONTEST	COMPETE TO SHOW POKÉMON'S "CUTENESS" 	NORMAL RANK → GREAT RANK → ULTRA RANK → MASTER RANK
SMART CONTEST	COMPETE TO SHOW POKÉMON'S "SMARTNESS" 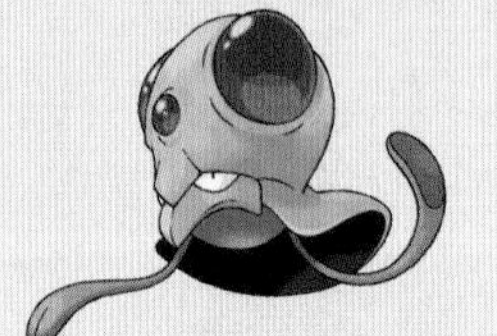	NORMAL RANK → GREAT RANK → ULTRA RANK → MASTER RANK
TOUGH CONTEST	COMPETE TO SHOW POKÉMON'S "TOUGHNESS" 	NORMAL RANK → GREAT RANK → ULTRA RANK → MASTER RANK

THE BASICS  WINNING HAS GENEROUS REWARDS

WINNING A SUPER CONTEST is about more than just prestige, it also means earning prizes such as ribbons and other accessories according to your division and rank. And these aren't just any items, as they are only available to winners of the Contests. How many can you win for your collection?

I'm Dexter, and I'll be serving as the MC and as one of the Judges!

COOL CONTEST

NORMAL RANK	GREAT RANK	ULTRA RANK	MASTER RANK
 COOL RIBBON	COOL RIBBON GREAT	 COOL RIBBON ULTRA	 COOL RIBBON MASTER
RED BARETTE 	RED BALLOON 	TOP HAT 	GOLD PEDESTAL 

BEAUTY CONTEST

NORMAL RANK	GREAT RANK	ULTRA RANK	MASTER RANK
 BEAUTY RIBBON	 BEAUTY RIBBON GREAT	  BEAUTY RIBBON ULTRA	BEAUTY RIBBON MASTER
BLUE BARETTE	BLUE BALLOON	SILK VEIL 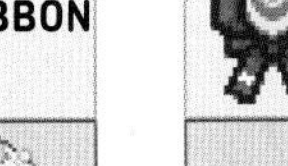	GLASS STAGE 

CUTE CONTEST

NORMAL RANK	GREAT RANK	ULTRA RANK	MASTER RANK
 CUTE RIBBON	  CUTE RIBBON GREAT	 CUTE RIBBON ULTRA	 CUTE RIBBON MASTER
PINK BARETTE	PINK BALLOON	LACE HEADDRESS	FLOWER STAGE 

SMART CONTEST

NORMAL RANK	GREAT RANK	ULTRA RANK	MASTER RANK
 GENIUS RIBBON	 GENIUS RIBBON GREAT	 GENIUS RIBBON ULTRA	 GENIUS RIBBON MASTER
GREEN BARETTE	GREEN BALLOON	PROFESSOR HAT	CUBE STAGE 

TOUGH CONTEST

NORMAL RANK	GREAT RANK	ULTRA RANK	MASTER RANK
 POWERFUL RIBBON	  POWERFUL RIBBON GREAT	 POWERFUL RIBBON ULTRA	POWERFUL RIBBON MASTER
YELLOW BARETTE	YELLOW BALLOON	HEROIC HEADBAND 	AWARD PODIUM 

THE BASICS 3 THREE ROUNDS: VISUAL, DANCE AND ACTING

THERE ARE THREE ROUNDS, which require different skills and will be judged separately. These are visual, dance, and acting. All three scores will be combined at the end, with the winner being the Pokémon with the highest total. The pressure can be a bit much for your Pokémon, so it's best to familiarize yourself with the Contest procedures for a smooth and worry-free Contest experience.

STEP 1 CHOOSE A RANK AND DIVISION

SPEAK TO THE RECEPTIONIST in the Contest Hall and she will ask you to choose your rank, followed by division.

STEP 2 PICK YOUR CONTESTANT POKéMON

OUT OF THE POKéMON currently in your party, select the Pokémon most suited for the division you have chosen.

STEP 3 ROUND 1 - APPEARANCE

EACH OF THE FOUR contestants steps forward in front of the audience, using their appearance to attract them. To raise the Pokémon's condition and charm, wear accessories that correspond to that round's theme.

STEP 4 ROUND 2 - DANCE

ALL FOUR CONTESTANTS will have to line up on stage together and then dance for the audience. One will take the lead and the other three must follow; to be fair, all four Pokémon will have a turn at being the lead dancer.

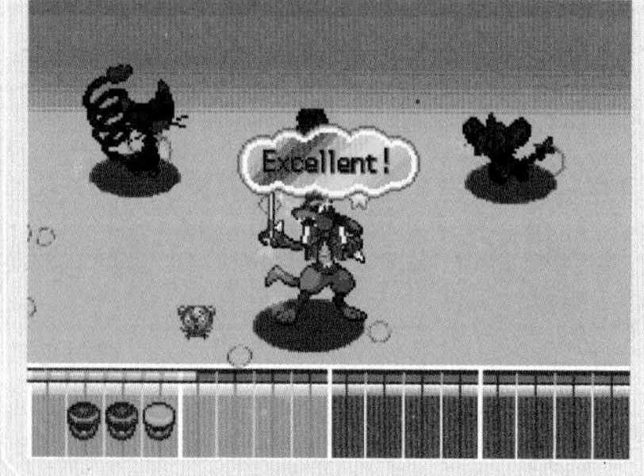

STEP 5 ROUND 3 - ACTING

EACH POKéMON gets a turn in front of the judges to perform their moves. They come out front, and you must pick a judge to perform for and a move to perform. The Pokémon gets four performances.

STEP 6 RESULTS

WHEN ALL ROUNDS are completed, the result will be announced. The contestant with the highest total of points is the winner.

PRACTICE, PRACTICE, PRACTICE

IN THE RECEPTION AREA in the upper right of the Contest Hall, you can rehearse your performance. This practice session will let you take it a bit easy, as you can practice each round separately. It's a valuable tool in figuring out what will work for you and what won't, so practice early and often, especially before your first Contest.

APPEARANCE

Attract and dazzle the audience with your appearance.

DRESS TO IMPRESS. The most important thing when you enter the first round is your Pokémon's appearance. Raise its condition and really work with the accessories to create a stunning look that fits the Contest theme and dazzles the audience.

ROUND 1

TIPS & TRICKS 1

RAISE YOUR POKéMON'S CONDITION WITH POFFIN

THE FIVE DIVISIONS that the Contests are divided into all correspond to different attributes, or conditions, that your Pokémon has. These conditions that your Pokémon will be judged on are Coolness, Beauty, Cuteness, Smartness, and Toughness. The level of these conditions can be improved by feeding your Pokémon Poffin. However, the amount you can feed them is not unlimited - once their fur-sheen meter maxes out, that's it for improving their conditions. Make the most of your Poffin feeding!

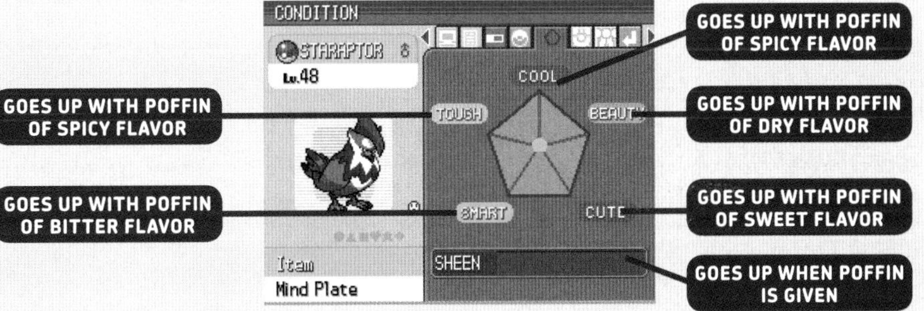

TIPS & TRICKS 2

CHOOSE YOUR POFFIN WISELY

BECAUSE EACH CONTEST DIVISION corresponds to one of the five conditions, you need to focus on improving one particular condition in the Pokémon you wish to enter. If you compete in the Cool Contest, then you should be feeding your Pokémon Poffin that raises its coolness - in this case, spicy Poffin.

PLAN AHEAD

BEFORE YOU START feeding your Pokémon Poffin, decide what division you would like to enter first, in order to better specialize.

THE CONDITIONS THAT AFFECT THE CONTEST RESULTS IN EACH DIVISION

DIVISION	MAJOR EFFECTS	MINOR EFFECTS	EFFECTIVE POFFIN
COOL	Coolness	Beauty, Toughness, Fur	Spicy
BEAUTY	Beauty	Cuteness, Coolness, Fur	Dry
CUTE	Cuteness	Smartness, Beauty, Fur	Sweet
SMART	Smartness	Cuteness, Toughness, Fur	Bitter
TOUGH	Toughness	Smartness, Coolness, Fur	Spicy

TIPS & TRICKS 3

YOU ARE WHAT YOU EAT

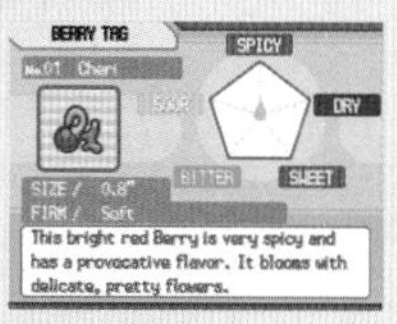

POFFIN MAY improve your Pokémon's conditions based on its flavor, but that's not the whole story. How much Poffin improves the conditions depends on how good the Poffin is – flavor and richness. Better food means a better Pokémon.

THE FLAVORS OF POFFIN

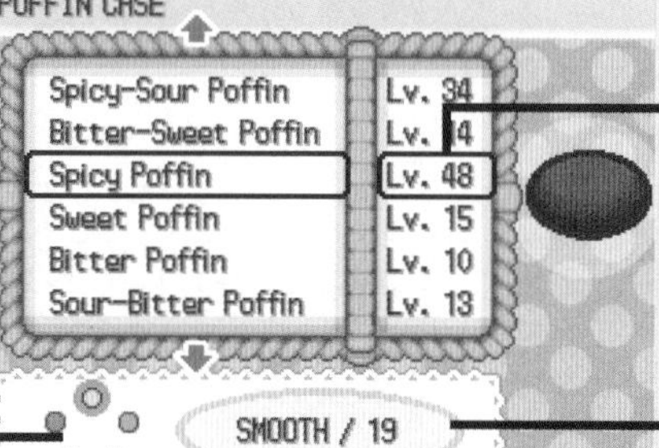

Level is an indication of how rich the Poffin is – the higher the level, the richer the flavor.

Flavors are determined by what berries are used to make the Poffin, and sometimes it ends up with more than two flavors.

Smoothness determines how much it affects your Pokémon's fur meter. Since Poffin can no longer affect a Pokémon once its fur meter is full, it's better to feed them Poffin that doesn't raise the fur meter much. That means lower smoothness.

TIPS & TRICKS 4

CREATE POFFIN WITH BERRIES

POFFIN IS MADE by cooking berries. So using different berries will of course, create different-flavored Poffin, with varied richness and smoothness. Gathering a wide variety of berries will allow you to create good Poffin rich in flavor, low on smoothness.

HEARTH AND HEARTHOME

IF YOU WANT to make Poffin, gather up your berries and head on over to the Poffin House in Hearthome City.

STEP 1 CHOOSE THE INGREDIENTS

Choose your berries carefully, because those will determine the flavor of your Poffin.

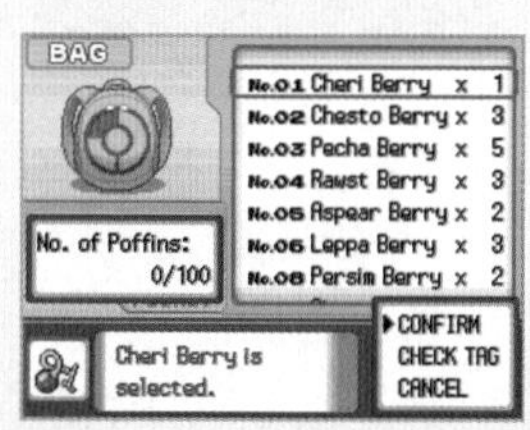

STEP 2 STIR THE MIX

Your Poffin starts out as a liquid that you must stir slowly to avoid spilling any.

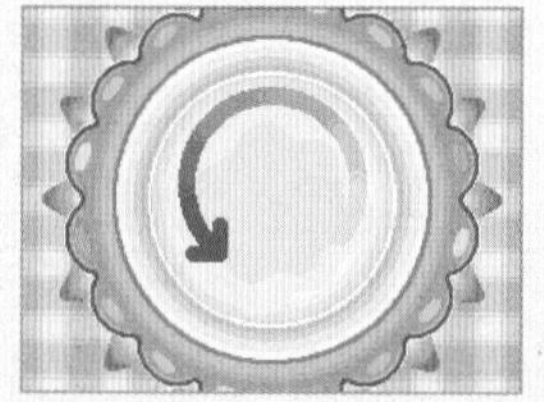

STEP 3 STIR A LITTLE FASTER

As you continue to stir, the Poffin will begin to thicken. Stir a little more briskly to avoid the mixture sticking to the pan and burning.

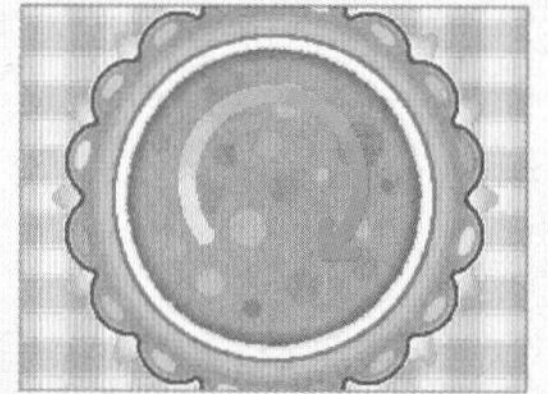

STEP 4 DONE AND DONE

Once finished, you will get a display with the cooking time, the kind of Poffin, and its level.

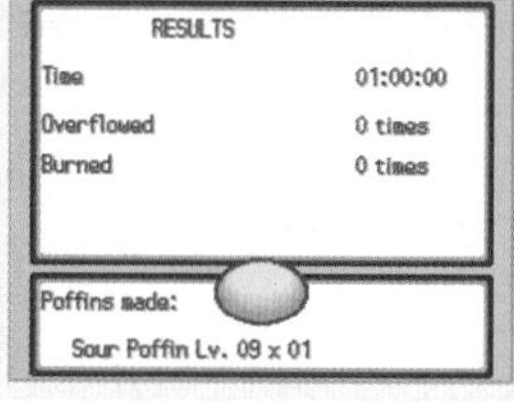

YOU GOT THE LOOK

Your EMPOLEON's looking good!
I'd say it's pretty impressive!

IN PASTORIA CITY is a Scarf Man who will give you five different kinds of scarves. Not only do they look good on your Pokémon, but they'll help it earn a high score in the Contests.

ITEMS YOU EARN BY IMPROVING THE CONDITIONS OF YOUR POKÉMON:

- RED SCARF
- BLUE SCARF
- PINK SCARF
- GREEN SCARF
- YELLOW SCARF

TIPS & TRICKS 5

COMBINE FLAVORS TO CREATE SUPERB POFFIN

USING THE NINTENDO DS Wireless Connection, you can make Poffin with your friends! A variety of people means a variety of ingredients, allowing you to make higher-level Poffin. There are five different berry flavors – some of which can cancel each other out. Dry flavor can weaken Spicy flavor, for example. You and your friends will need to put on your thinking caps and coordinate with each other in order to avoid ruining your group Poffin.

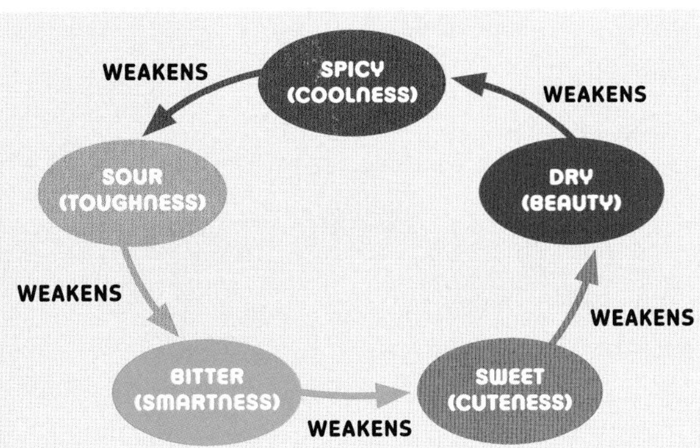

TIPS & TRICKS 6

FAVORITE FLAVORS, BETTER CONDITIONS

EVERY POKÉMON has their own personal preferences when it comes to Poffin, based on their nature. Feeding them what they like will make them healthier and more content, which in turn will raise the appropriate condition even higher.

Check the Poffin feeding screen or strength-lookup screen to find out your Pokémon's taste for Poffin.

Feed your Pokémon the Poffin they like to bring up their condition even higher than usual.

NATURE AND POFFIN TASTE

NATURE	LIKE	DISLIKE
Hardy	none	
Adament	Spicy	Dry
Brave	Spicy	Sweet
Naughty	Spicy	Bitter
Lonely	Spicy	Sour
Modest	Dry	Spicy
Bashful	none	
Quiet	Dry	Sweet
Rash	Dry	Bitter
Mild	Dry	Sour
Timid	Sweet	Spicy
Jolly	Sweet	Dry
Serious	none	
Naive	Sweet	Bitter
Hasty	Sweet	Sour
Calm	Bitter	Spicy
Careful	Bitter	Dry
Sassy	Bitter	Sweet
Quirky	none	
Gentle	Bitter	Sour
Bold	Sour	Spicy
Impish	Sour	Dry
Relaxed	Sour	Sweet
Lax	Sour	Bitter
Docile	none	

TIPS & TRICKS 7

DRESS FOR THE THEME

THE FIRST ROUND is all about making your Pokémon look good, and part of that is dressing the part with the right accessories. There are 12 possible themes, and in every Contest one of those will be named as the one to aim for. Show off your keen fashion sense and score high by choosing the right accessories for the theme.

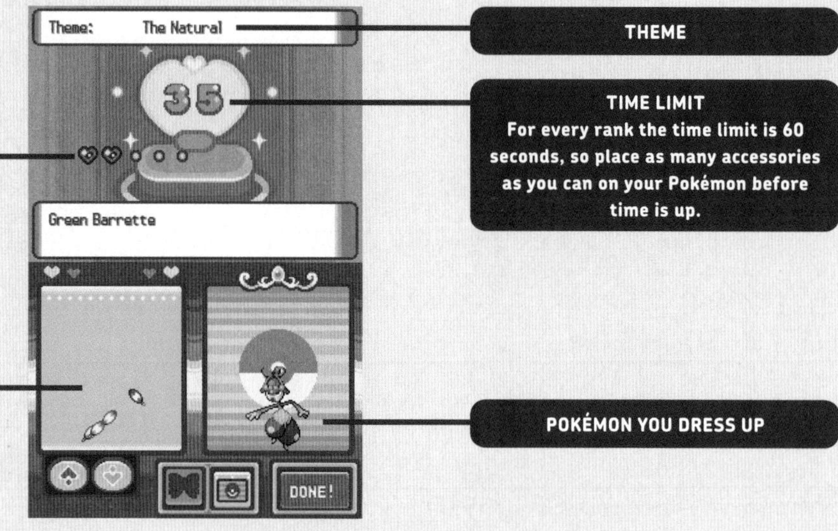

THEME

TIME LIMIT
For every rank the time limit is 60 seconds, so place as many accessories as you can on your Pokémon before time is up.

THE NUMBER OF ACCESSORIES YOU ARE PERMITTED TO USE:
Normal Rank = 5, Great Rank = 10, Ultra Rank = 15, Master Rank = 20

ACCESSORY CASE
Your accessories are automatically organized and sorted in your accessory case. Use your stylus to place them on your Pokémon.

POKÉMON YOU DRESS UP

THEMES AND SAMPLES OF ACCESSORIES

THE COLORFUL

- Yellow Fluff
- Pink Fluff
- Blue Scale
- Green Scale
- Red Flower
- Orange Flower
- Flag etc.

SHARPNESS

- Narrow Scale
- Big Scale
- Blue Feather
- Red Feather
- Shed Horn
- Thin Mushroom
- Spring
  etc.

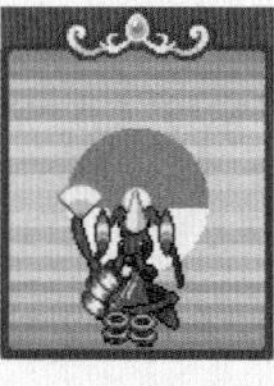

NATURE

- White Fluff
- Brown Fluff
- Snaggy Pebble
- Shed Claw
- Thick Mushroom
- Pretty Dewdrop
- Snow Crystal
  etc.

THE CREATED

- Black Moustache
- White Moustache
- Spring
- Glitter Powder
- Googly Specs
- Black Specs
- Confetti etc.

SHAPELY

- Round Pebble
- Jagged Boulder
- White Flower
- Pink Flower
- Turtwig Mask
- Chimchar Mask
- Piplup Mask etc.

INTANGIBLE

- Glitter Powder
- Shimmering Fire
- Puffy Smoke
- Humming Note
- Confetti
- Spotlight
- Flag

RELAXATION

- Brown Fluff
- Black Fluff
- Jagged Boulder
- Black Pebble
- Blue Scale
- Thin Scale
- Black Beard

BRIGHTNESS

- Yellow Fluff
- White Fluff
- Glitter Boulder
- Big Scale
- Yellow Feather
- White Beard
- Shed Horn

THE SOLID

- Jagged Boulder
- Mini Pebble
- Thin Scale
- Shed Horn
- Peculiar Spoon
- Black Specs
- Sweet Candy

FLEXIBILITY

- Orange Fluff
- Black Moustache
- Small Leaf
- Pretty Dewdrop
- Comet
- Poison Extract
- Confetti

THE GAUDY

- Round Pebble
- Mini Pebble
- Green Scale
- Purple Scale
- Red Feather
- Glitter Powder
- Spotlight

THE FESTIVE

- Glitter Boulder
- Pretty Dewdrop
- Snow Crystal
- Mystic Fire
- Glitter Powder
- Gorgeous Specs
- Colored Parasol

TIPS & TRICKS 8

LOAD UP ON ACCESSORIES

HOW WELL YOU DO in Round 1 depends on how many different accessories you have on hand. Make sure you have a number of accessories of each kind so you are equipped to handle whatever theme they throw at you. Here, we present three ways to find accessories.

1 AMBLE AMIABLY IN AMITY SQUARE

AMITY SQUARE is a lovely location in Hearthome City where you can take a walk with seven different kinds of Pokémon from your collection. Not only is it a pleasant experience, but your Pokémon will sometimes pick up accessories there. Each Pokémon picks up a different accessory (P. 280) so take one of each out at some point to collect every item.

Take some time to walk, though you can always run if you prefer.

BUNEARY is holding something!

Stand in front of your Pokémon and press 'A' to obtain the accessory they've picked up on their walk.

POKÉMON YOU CAN TAKE FOR A WALK
PIKACHU
CLEFAIRY
PSYDUCK
PACHIRISU
HAPPINY
BUNEARY
DRIFLOON

2 A RELAXING MASSAGE

HEAD TO VEILSTONE CITY and climb the stairs north of the Game Corner to find a house in which lives a lovely lady who will give your Pokémon one massage a day. As proof that your Pokémon was massaged, she will give you an accessory. You can go back to her again and again for accessories, but only once a day.

If you'd like, I can give a massage to a Pokémon. Would you like that?

The lady will massage any Pokémon, so choose one from your party.

3 TRADE BERRIES FOR ACCESSORIES

AT THE PICK A PECK OF COLORS Flower Shop in Floaroma Town, you can exchange your berries for their accessories. But they won't just take a handful – you need a lot! Bury your berries in soft, loamy soil and water them with the Sprayduck to grow more berries in a short period of time (P. 288).

If you need flower accessories, this is the place to get stuff like Red Flower and White Flower.

USE MULCH TO INCREASE YOUR BERRIES

Berries will grow more plentiful if you use mulch that you can purchase on Route 208. There are four different kinds, so pick the one that fits your need the most.

FERTILIZE
PLANT BERRY

It's soft, earthy soil.

See the list of accessories on page 282.

DANCE

Move to the music to get a high score.

JUST MOVE IT AND GROOVE IT. Round 2 is less about style and more about skill – you'll have to dance precisely and harmoniously to the music played. As opposed to the other two rounds, which require more preparation, this round will require the player's attention and focus as it happens. Use the castanets on the bottom screen to tap a great performance out of your Pokémon!

ROUND 2

TIPS & TRICKS 1

TAKE THE LEAD OR PROVIDE BACKUP

ALL FOUR CONTESTANT POKÉMON will dance together, with one taking the role of lead while the other three following along. To be fair, all four Pokémon get a shot at being the lead at least once in the round.

BACKUP DANCER

CLICK YOUR CASTANETS JUST LIKE THE LEAD DANCER DID

1 THE LEAD DANCER

The lead dancer will step in front and start a dance, the steps of which the other three Pokémon must imitate. As you progress in rank the lead Pokémon's dancing will become harder and harder.

2 THE BACKUP DANCERS

In the role of backup dancer, you must click your castanets exactly as the lead dancer did. Their moves will be indicated on the blue bar at the lower left of the top screen. For higher points, click on the castanets at the same exact beat. To increase accuracy, memorize the location of the castanets.

LEAD DANCER

DANCE TO THE MUSIC ACCORDING TO YOUR OWN RHYTHM

1 YOUR DANCING

When dancing in the lead, your goal is to make the other Pokémon fail to follow you. To do so, you need to come up with more complicated steps that will be hard to imitate. Improvisation is your greatest ally.

2 THE BACKUP DANCERS

The backup dancers will dance the same dance that your lead Pokémon is doing. As you go up in rank, they will make fewer mistakes.

TIPS & TRICKS 2

MARCH TO YOUR OWN BEAT

YOU MIGHT DANCE a pretty dance, but what you're really aiming for is to make the other Pokémon screw up. To do this, there has to be opportunity for mistakes, which means making your dance as complex and difficult as possible.

You can try each of the different patterns, but your dance will be far more effective if you combine techniques.

HOW TO TAKE ON AND TAKE OUT YOUR BACKUP

PATTERN 1

USE ALL FOUR PAIRS OF CASTANETS

Though it might be tempting for simplicity's sake, sticking to the same castanets makes it too simple for your rival contestants to dance along with you. You'll get three pairs of castanets in Normal and Great Rank, and four in Ultra and Master Rank – use them all to make complicated combinations of moves that will trip up your backup dancers, even on a simple rhythm.

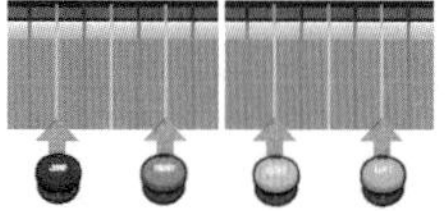

PATTERN 2

CLICK LONG INTERVALS IN THE CASTANET PLAYING

At the start of your session, click on your castanets, and then hold for a few seconds, clicking toward the end of the music. Creating a long interval between clicks breaks your opponents' concentration, causing them to make more mistakes.

PATTERN 3

CLICK YOUR CASTANETS INTO THE PALE BLUE AREA

When you play along with the music, a mark appears in the white area of the music score, linking it directly to the rhythm. However, if you're off-beat by a half note, the mark will appear in the blue area of the score, much harder for the backup dancers to keep up with.

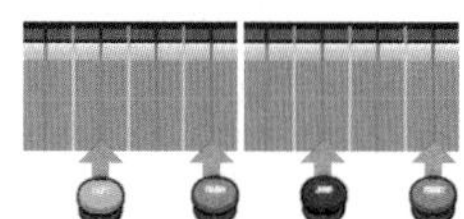

PATTERN 4

CLICK ON THE BLUE CASTANETS

At the beginning of the music, click on the blue castanets. Then click them again at the end of the music. Your Pokémon will step to the front, briefly obscuring the pink score. If the backup dancers have short memories, they will have trouble keeping up.

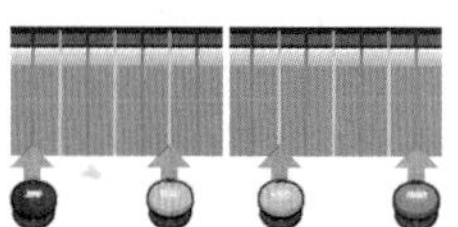

ACTING

Show off your moves for a high score.

TURN HEADS WITH AN IMPRESSIVE SET OF MOVES. The final round of the Contest is where your Pokémon will perform their battle moves for the judges. Points are indicated with hearts – the more hearts appear, the more impressed the judges. Of course, you want to get as many as possible.

ROUND 3

TIPS & TRICKS 1

GO OVER THE MOVES YOUR POKÉMON WILL USE

EVERY POKÉMON MOVE has a specific effect in a Contest. Before the Contest, it's best to check your Pokémon's move on the status screen to see how they can help you out in performance.

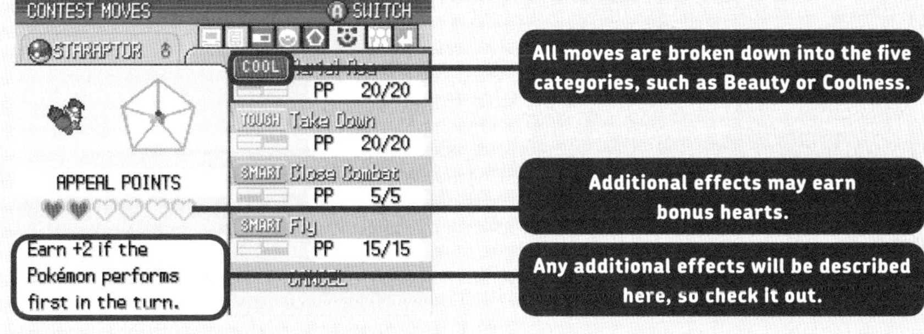

You will have to perform four times, so make sure you have a nice inventory of moves available.

TIPS & TRICKS 2

SELECT YOUR JUDGE

THERE ARE three judges watching the performance round, and you will have to choose one judge to perform for. If you don't choose the same judge as the other contestant, you'll have the entirety of their attention – and all of their affection, earning you three additional hearts.

You don't know which judge your opponents will choose, but hopefully you won't pick the same one.

JORDAN
One of the regular judges.

DEXTER
The head judge and also the MC.

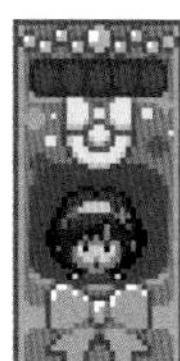

KEIRA
One of the regular judges.

THE NUMBER OF HEARTS YOU EARN FROM THE JUDGES

CONDITIONS	THE NUMBER OF HEARTS YOU EARN
You have your own judge	Heart +3
Your share your judge with one contestant	Heart +2 each
Your share your judge with two contestants	Heart +1 each
Your share your judge with three contestants	0

TIPS & TRICKS 3

COMBINE THE SAME DIVISION AND MOVE FOR HIGH VOLTAGE

THE VOLTAGE indicates the zeal of the audience watching the Contest. If you use like kind moves in the appropriate Contest – like Cool moves in the Cool Contest – then the Voltage of your judge will go up by one and a star appears above the judge's head. Unfortunately, some moves can also bring down the voltage.

HOW MOVES AFFECT THE VOLTAGE

DIVISIONS	MOVES THAT RAISE THE VOLTAGE	MOVES THAT LOWER THE VOLTAGE
Cool Contest	Coolness	Cuteness/Smartness
Beauty Contest	Beauty	Smartness/Toughness
Cute Contest	Cuteness	Toughness/Coolness
Smart Contest	Smartness	Coolness/Beauty
Tough Contest	Toughness	Beauty/Cuteness

TIPS & TRICKS 4

RAISE THE VOLTAGE TO GET A LOT OF HEARTS

WHEN YOUR selected judge's voltage reaches stage 5, you receive a bonus number of hearts. Dexter will give you 8 hearts, while Jordan and Keira will give you 5. You need to choose the judge with high Voltage and reach stage 5 as soon as possible.

Once a judge's Voltage reaches stage 5, the arena is filled with zeal and star marks will line up above the judge's head.

In addition to your usual bonus hearts, 8 or 5 extra hearts will be granted as a bonus.

VOLTAGE BONUS HEARTS

JUDGE	BONUS HEARTS
Dexter	+8
Jordan/Keira	+5

TIPS & TRICKS 5

MASTER YOUR MOVES

THE MOVES YOU USE in performance have many different effects. The ones with a high chance of success won't earn as many hearts, while the ones with a low chance of success with earn a lot of hearts. You'll need to teach your Contest Pokémon as many moves as possible for a wide selection that can add up to a high score.

EARNS YOU A REGULAR AMOUNT OF HEARTS

No additional effects, will always secure you 3 hearts.

EARNS DIFFERENT AMOUNT OF HEARTS BASED ON VOLTAGE

The number of hearts will change based on the Voltage.

EARNS DIFFERENT AMOUNT OF HEARTS BASED ON THE ORDER OF YOUR PERFORMANCE

When you perform in relation to the other Contestants will change the number of hearts.

EARNS DIFFERENT AMOUNT OF HEARTS BASED ON SPECIAL CIRCUMSTANCES

Special situations can alter the number of hearts you earn.

WHO WANTS TO BE A WINNER?

Select the best Pokémon to take into each division.

WHEN PICKING YOUR CONTEST POKÉMON, the biggest factor will be what moves they possess. Imagine your Pokémon performing in front of a judge. How well will they do them? Here are a few recommendations for Pokémon that really shine in each division.

COOL CONTEST

GET CHATOT TO LEVEL 33 and teach it the moves Taunt and Roost. Taunt earns a lot of hearts when the Voltage is low, while Roost will earn a lot of hearts when the Voltage is high. Which one you should use depends on the judge you're performing for.

NATURES:	MOVES:
Adamant	Taunt
Brave	Roost
Naughty	Peck
Lonely	Mimic

BEAUTY CONTEST

BRING REMORAID TO LEVEL 36 without evolving it and teach it the move Signal Beam. This will raise the judge's Voltage, earning 2 additional hearts for a total of four in performance.

NATURES:	MOVES:
Modest	Signal Beam
Quiet	Frustration
Rash	BubbleBeam
Mild	Water Gun

CUTE CONTEST

RAISE KRICKETUNE TO LEVEL 34 and teach it the move Bug Buzz. This move will earn additional hearts if you raise the Voltage. Unless your opponents use a move that prevents the Voltage from going up, you are guaranteed 4 hearts.

NATURES:	MOVES:
Timid	Bug Buzz
Jolly	Sleep Talk
Naive	X-Scissor
Hasty	Sing

SMART CONTEST

GET TENTACOOL TO LEVEL 34 without evolving it and teach it the move Poison Jab. Raise your judge's Voltage to earn 4 hearts. If you're the only one performing to that judge, this move will net you 7 hearts.

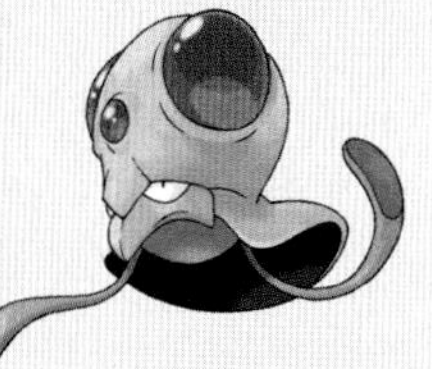

NATURES:	MOVES:
Calm	Acid
Careful	Poison Jab
Sassy	BubbleBeam
Gentle	Wrap

TOUGH CONTEST

BRING GEODUDE TO LEVEL 39 without evolving it and teach it both the moves Earthquake and Stone Edge. Stone Edge earns 4 hearts if the judge's Voltage goes up, and Earthquake will earn 4 hearts if it's the last performance in a turn.

NATURES:	MOVES:
Bold	Stone Edge
Impish	Earthquake
Relaxed	Rock Throw
Lax	Rock Polish

SECTION 5

WIRELESS FUNCTION

GET THE MOST OUT OF YOUR GAME WITH CONNECTION PLAY

Have fun with friends and family!

POKÉMON DIAMOND AND POKÉMON PEARL now feature special communication functions that allow you to trade and battle in whole new ways – they're easy, and most important of all, fun!

8 WAYS TO CONNECT IN DIAMOND AND PEARL

POKÉMON DIAMOND AND POKÉMON PEARL are compatible with both the Nintendo DS wireless connection and the Nintendo Wi-Fi Connection, with 8 different games and activities to try. The DS wireless connection requires no additional hardware to try, though you will need additional equipment to try the Nintendo Wi-Fi Connection.

NINTENDO DS WIRELESS CONNECTION

1. BATTLE WITH NEARBY FRIENDS ON THE 2 FL OF THE POKÉMON CENTER.
2. BATTLE, TRADE AND MIX RECORDS WITH FRIENDS IN UNION ROOM.
3. PLAY WITH YOUR FRIENDS IN THE UNDERGROUND.
4. MAKE POFFIN WITH YOUR FRIENDS.
5. PARTICIPATE IN CONNECTION CONTEST.

NINTENDO WI-FI CONNECTION

6. TRADE POKÉMON WITH PEOPLE FROM AROUND THE COUNTRY WITH GTS.
7. IN THE POKÉMON WI-FI CLUB, BATTLE OR TRADE WITH PLAYERS WHO LIVE FAR AWAY FROM YOU.
8. DOWNLOAD PLAYER DATA IN THE WI-FI BATTLE ROOM OF THE BATTLE TOWER.

WHAT IS THE NINTENDO WI-FI CONNECTION?

IT'S THE WORLD'S FIRST wireless Internet service that allows you to play games with friends anywhere – in your country, and even across the world. It's safe, and best of all, free! Players who have corresponding software can play together, bypassing the constraints of space and time (zones). To connect, you need a computer with Internet access, and either a wireless router or the Nintendo Wi-Fi USB Connector.

FOR MORE DETAILS, SEE: WWW.NINTENDOWIFI.COM

POKÉMON COMMUNICATION CLUB COLOSSEUM

Take your Pokémon on some exciting connection battles.

THERE'S A POKÉMON CENTER in every town, and a Colosseum on the 2 FL of every Pokémon Center. If you want to experience the thrill of battle with friends and family, stop on by for some action.

BATTLES FOR TWO
SINGLE BATTLE
DOUBLE BATTLE
MIX BATTLE
BATTLES FOR FOUR
MULTI BATTLE
INFO
EXIT
Which Battle Mode would you like to play?

FEARSOME FOURSOME

WHEN SIGNING UP in the Pokémon Communication Colosseum you have the choice of single battle or double battle, for two or four players. Try them all out, or stick with the one you like the most.

SINGLE BATTLE

IT'S JUST YOU versus one opponent with a Pokémon apiece. It's basic, simple, though not always easy.

The foe's ALAKAZAM used
Calm Mind!

DOUBLE BATTLE

THIS TIME it's two players, two Pokémon on the field apiece. The Pokémon will have to work together with the right combinations of moves to achieve victory.

VESPIQUEN used
Power Gem!

MIX BATTLE

TWO PLAYERS enter the arena with two Pokémon on the field and one in reserve for a total of three on their teams.

GYARADOS used
Aqua Tail!

MULTI BATTLE

FOUR PLAYERS pair off with Pokémon apiece, for the ultimate Double Battle that requires a deal of team work and skill.

GARCHOMP used
Dragon Rage!

6 CUPS OF POKÉMON CONNECTION COLOSSEUM

CUP	SUPER CUP	STANDARD CUP	FANCY CUP	LITTLE CUP	LIGHT CUP	DOUBLE CUP
No. of Pokémon	6	3	3	3	3	4
Upper Limit of Level	No Upper Limit	Lv 50	Lv 30	Lv 5	Lv 50	Lv 50
Level In Total	No Limit	No Limit	Lv 80	No Limit	No Limit	No Limit
Height	No Limit	No Limit	6ft and under	No Limit	No Limit	No Limit
Weight	No Limit	No Limit	44lbs and under	No Limit	219lbs and under	No Limit
Evolving Pokémon	Qualified	Qualified	Not Qualified	Not Qualified	Not Qualified	Qualified
Same Pokémon	Qualified	Not Qualified	Not Qualified	Not Qualified	Not Qualified	Not Qualified
Same Items	Allowed	Not Allowed	Not Allowed	Not Allowed	Not Allowed	Not Allowed

UNION ROOM

Enjoy the numerous functions of the wondrous Union Room.

IN EVERY POKÉMON CENTER in Sinnoh is a Union Room located on the second floor. You can trade, battle, and chat with friends in the same room in the real world.

SIX DEGREES OF UNION ROOM FUN

UP TO FIVE players can gather in the Union Room, to trade or to battle. You can invite any of your friends who have a copy of Pokémon Diamond or Pokémon Pearl to come on in and join the fun.

SIX GAMES YOU CAN PLAY

GREETINGS

SHOW OFF your Trainer Card! The card you show will be the one you designed at the Pokémon Center in Oreburgh City.

DRAWING

ALL OF THE PEOPLE in the room can work together on the canvas to create pretty pictures with lines and colors.

BATTLES

SELECT TWO Pokémon at level 30 or below for a single battle, low on stress and great for practice sessions.

TRADE

YOU CAN TRADE Pokémon with the other people in the room. Simply select "Trade (Up for a Trade)" and off you go!

RECORDS

SET YOUR PLAY data loose by mixing records with a friend, creating some rather interesting occurrences that will appear throughout the game.

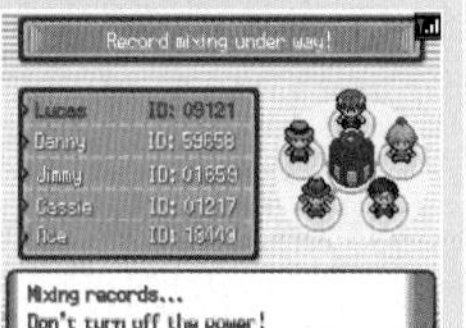

CHAT

SEND A MESSAGE to everyone in the room by pressing the 'X' button and selecting "Chat" to begin Easy Chat.

MIX RECORDS

You can exchange game information with friends.

YOU ARE NOT ALONE in your journey across Sinnoh, as you'll see when you mix records with friends. With this function, details about your journey will find their way into your friends' games and vice versa, allowing you glimpses into each other's activities.

MIX IT UP

YOUR RECORD CONSISTS of a smattering of information about your adventure. When you mix records, you'll start to see your friends featured in television programs, and the images of their Pokémon will be displayed at Jubilife TV. And some of the effects are more subtle, like the timing for catching Feebas will be the same, or you'll all have the same chance of winning the slot machines.

HOW TO MIX

STEP 1 GO THE UNION ROOM

ENTER THE UNION ROOM from the Pokémon Wireless Club on the 2 FL of any Pokémon Center. You must speak to the woman at the info counter in the center and start up a Nintendo DS Wireless Connection before you step inside.

YOU CAN ACCESS the Union Room any time between Sandgem Town and the Pokémon League.

STEP 2 TALK TO A FRIEND

YOUR FRIEND will walk into the room as well, bearing the appearance that they chose for themselves at the Pokémon Center in Oreburgh City when asked who their favorite Trainer was. Speak to your friend and select "Record".

IF THE OTHER player agrees by selecting "yes", then you will switch to the Mix Records screen.

STEP 3 EVERYONE CAN MIX TOO

IF THE PERSON responds in the positive, then they will participate in the record mixing. All of the participants will have their records mixed, and if you and a friend are in the same group, you will end up having the same experiences in your respective journeys.

UP TO FIVE people can participate at a time, making it even more fun to mix records.

MIXING RECORDS 1 YOUR FRIEND WILL APPEAR ON TV

AS YOU TRAVEL, you may occasionally find programs on the televisions in your house or other people's houses. These generally aren't much, until you mix records. You will start seeing your friends in interviews and other programming. After mixing records, keep an eye on the televisions you encounter – there'll be lots of new things to see.

Today, we dropped in to check up on the Trainer Lucas.

Keeping up with your friends' journey is easy when you watch television regularly.

PROGRAMMING GUIDE – SHOWS YOU MIGHT SEE YOUR FRIENDS ON

YOUR POKÉMON

INTRODUCING your friend's Pokémon

EGG HATCHING

YOUR FRIEND had a Pokémon Egg – where did it hatch and what came out?

THREE CHEERS FOR POFFIN

JOIN THE Poffin Maniac for an overview of Poffin your friends made.

PERSONALITY CHECK UP

LOOK INTO your friend's inner psyche based on the type of Pokémon they chose.

CATCH THAT POKÉMON SHOW

FEATURING THE BATTLE data of your friends, this program shows how many times they threw their Poké Balls and the end results.

RIGHT ON PHOTO

TALK SHOW about your friend's Pokémon and the photos at Jubilife TV.

AMITY SQUARE WATCH

WHAT KIND of items did your friend's Pokémon find in Amity Square?

CONTEST!

LIVE COVERAGE of Pokémon Super Contests, with contest results and your friend's comments.

DISCOVERING GROUPS

WHAT GROUP do your friends belong to and what type of Pokémon do they have?

SMILE FOR THE CAMERA AND GET INTERVIEWED

THE COMMENTS featured in the television programs don't come from thin air – they actually are from the interviews done by the TV reporters located throughout Sinnoh, like the Contest Hall and the Poffin House in Hearthome City. Talk to them to create interviews that will appear on your friends' televisions as well. If you really want to impress, have the man in Snowpoint City teach you some difficult words to make your interviews a little intellectually stimulating.

So, may I hear about your Contest challenge?

MIXING RECORDS 2 PHOTO DISPLAY AT JUBILIFE TV

HEAD TO THE 2 FL of Jubilife TV in Jubilife City to check out photos of dressed up Pokémon. After mixing records, the photos displayed will be that of your friends' Pokémon, with up to 10 photos being displayed. If you've always been curious about what accessories your friends are fond of using on their Pokémon, now's the time to check 'em out.

Check out the titles your friends gave the portraits of their beloved Pokémon.

MIXING RECORDS 3 SHARING EXPERIENCES

IF YOU AND YOUR FRIENDS are in the same group, then you can share information that will lead to you sharing the same experiences. Events and activities in some parts of the game will end up being the same, allowing you to collaborate on things like the Pastoria Great Marsh and the slot machines.

ALL TOGETHER

YOU CAN FORM or join a group by speaking to a man in Jubilife City.

THE DETAILS SHARED BY GROUPS

THE POKÉMON APPEARING AT THE PASTORIA GREAT MARSH

THE POKÉMON encountered at the Pastoria Great Marsh change daily, but members of the same group will have the same Pokémon, allowing them to coordinate and strategize together on how to catch them all.

FEEBAS' LOCATION

THOUGH FEEBAS is always located at Mt. Coronet, where exactly it will appear changes daily. Friends in the same group will always find Feebas at the same location as each other, so they can work together to find and catch Feebas quickly.

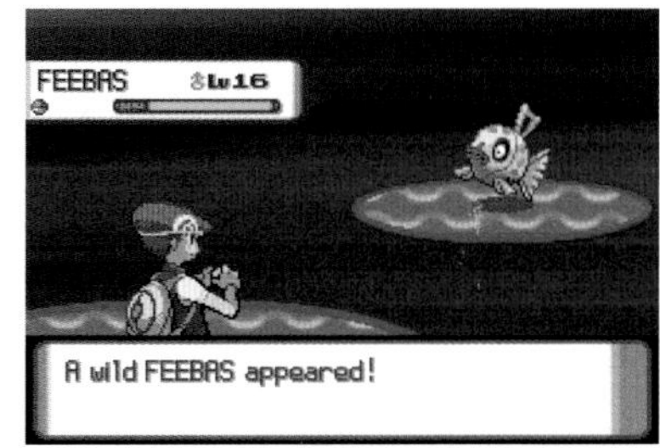

SLOT MACHINE PROBABILITY

EVERY SLOT MACHINE in the Veilstone Game Corner has a different chance of winning big. If you mix records, all of the members in your group will share the same probabilities – if you find one that looks promising, you can tell them about it!

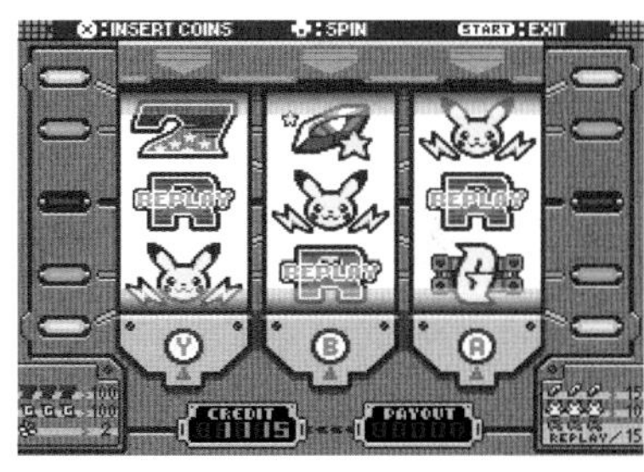

BATTLE TOWER TRAINERS

THE BATTLE ROOM of the Battle Tower has different Trainers in it. When you mix records the kinds of Trainers and the order of their appearence is shared between the group, allowing a little competition to see who does better.

GROUP RECORDS AND RANKINGS

ON THE 3 FL of Jubilife TV is a Group Ranking section where you can compare the stats of the group members, such as Pokémon Super Contest or Battle Tower results, number of captured Pokémon, and much more.

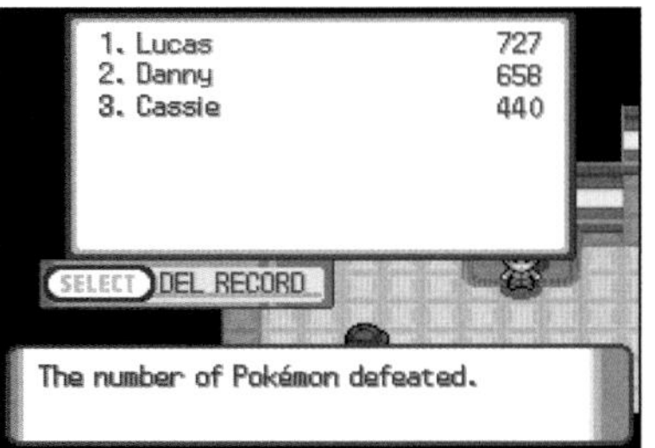

POKÉMON GATHERINGS

ONCE YOU obtain the National Pokédex, the professor's assistant will tell you about a massive gathering of Pokémon somewhere in Sinnoh – a location that will be the same for other members of your group. Cooperate with each other to take care of the situation.

EXPLORE THE UNDERGROUND!

Check out the Sinnoh region's Underground with some friends.

DEEP DOWN below the surface of Sinnoh is a vast underground filled with treasure hunting and fun activities for up to eight players.

WHAT IS WAITING FOR YOU AND YOUR FRIENDS?

WELL, THREE ACTIVITIES are waiting for you down in the Underground: the Fossil Dig, Secret Bases, and the rousing game of Capture the Flag. They may seem like simple enough games on the surface, but once you get into them with some friends, things can get pretty crazy and challenging, but fun. Just the kind of break that every Trainer needs while on their Pokémon journey.

THE ACTIVITIES OF THE UNDERGROUND

FOSSIL DIG

USE A HAMMER and pick to dig at the walls in the Underground, locating valuable items like spheres which can be traded for Secret Base items, fossils that can be restored into Pokémon, and useful Battle items. Unfortunately, you can't take your time, since the walls could crumble at any time!

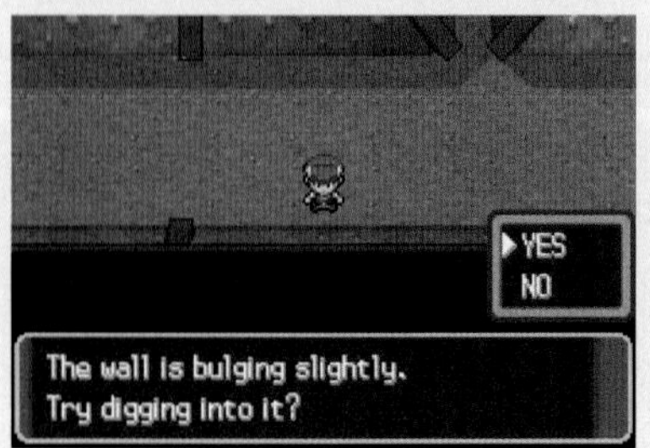

SECRET BASES

INSIDE THE UNDERGROUND players can build Secret Bases that they can decorate to their liking, using furniture, dolls, and other items found throughout Sinnoh. Collect as many items as you can to personalize your own little piece of Sinnoh.

CAPTURE THE FLAG

YOU CAN INFILTRATE other player's Secret Bases to seize their flags, bringing the small symbol back to your base. Beware – other players can take your flag as well, forcing you to run after them to get them back. Luckily, you can place traps on the floor in advance so the thief won't get very far.

UNDERGROUND RULE 1: GET AN EXPLORER KIT FROM UNDERGROUND MAN

TO BE ABLE to travel to the Underground at all, you need to get a kit from Underground Man. Just speak to him in Eterna City, and you'll get a kit that you can use any outdoor place in Sinnoh.

I am! I am the first to have gone underground and dug some tunnels.

A TO-DO LIST

UNDERGROUND MAN will assign you six missions. Complete them successfully for great rewards.

UNDERGROUND RULE 2: THE UNDERGROUND IS EVERYWHERE IN SINNOH

SINNOH GETS a whole lot bigger when you enter the Underground, a huge area stretched out over the entire region. A radar on the upper screen will indicate your location, the location of your secret base, and the location of hidden treasures. Keep an eye on this radar, and you'll have no worries about getting lost.

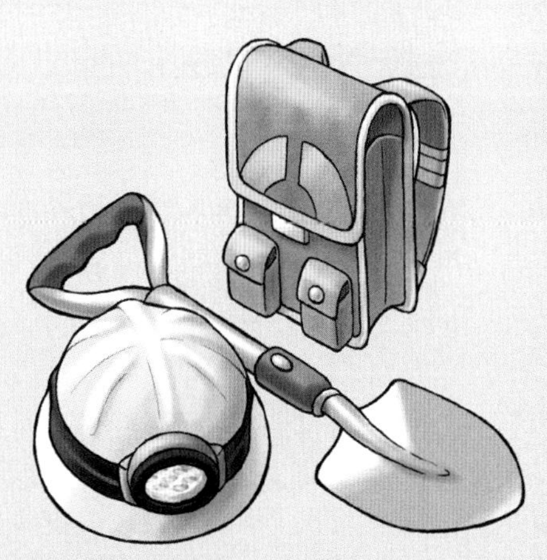

UNDERGROUND RULE 3: GET A RESPONSE BY TOUCHING THE BOTTOM SCREEN

FOLLOW THE RADAR to the treasure, and then touch the bottom screen with the stylus. Treasures in the wall and traps in the ground will respond by glowing. With this method, all you need in the Underground is the radar and stylus.

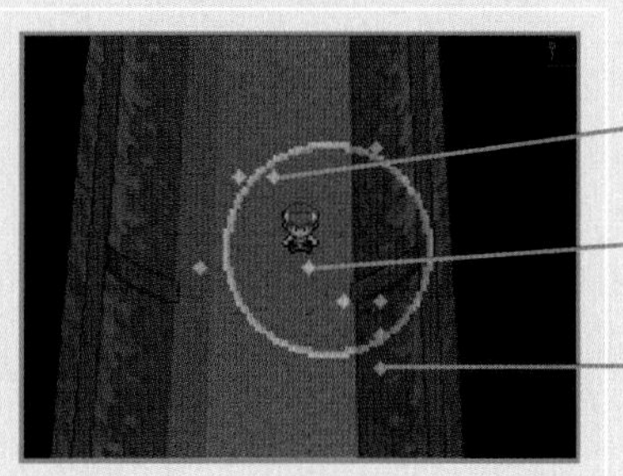

FOSSIL DIG

Items of different types are hidden in the walls.

UNDERNEATH all those glowing spots on the walls are many kinds of treasures like spheres, shards, and Pokémon fossils. Using your hammer and pick, you can dig these treasures out of the walls before they collapse.

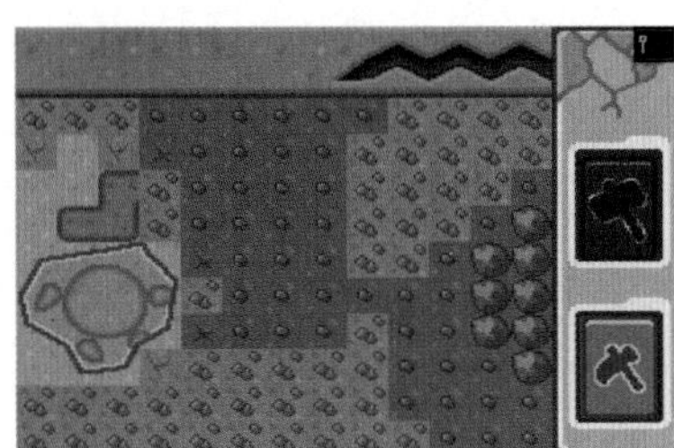

TAP ON THE WALL TO DIG OUT TREASURE

YOU HAVE TWO tools with which to dig items out of the walls: the hammer and the pick. These items have different levels of power, which affects the stability of the wall. The hammer lets you dig large areas quickly, but it clefts the wall quickly. The pick lets you work at small areas carefully, only increasing the cleft in the wall a bit each time. The cleft meter will let you know how big the cleft in the wall is – once the meter is at the left end of the screen, the wall collapses. Work with both tools to dig out items quickly and successfully.

ITEMS YOU CAN DIG OUT OF THE WALL

SPHERES

THESE CAN BE traded for Secret Base items. If you manage to dig all of them out before the walls collapse, you will be rewarded with a big sphere at the end.

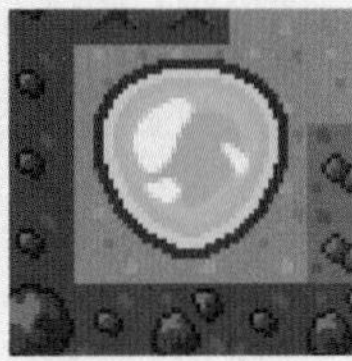

SHARDS

COLLECT 10 and obtain a TM. Four different colored shards exist: red, blue, yellow, and green.

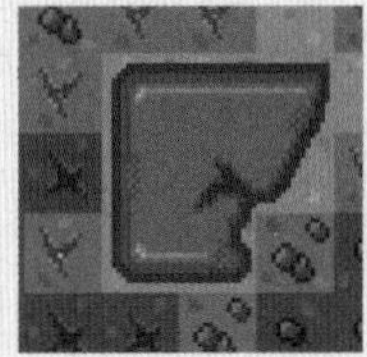

POKÉMON FOSSILS

ANCIENT POKÉMON may be gone, but their fossils remain buried in the Underground. Once your obtain the National Pokédex, more fossils will become available to dig up.

EVOLUTION ITEMS

LOTS OF RARE stones that make Pokémon evolve can be found here, like the Moon Stone and the Thunderstone.

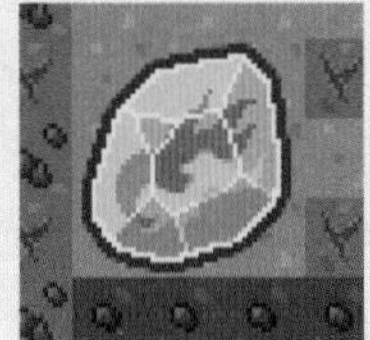

BATTLE ITEMS

LOTS OF ITEMS that can't be found in stores are buried in the Underground, like Max Revive, a invaluable item that you'll be glad to have for your toughest battles.

HEART SCALES

COLLECT THESE and give them to the Move Tutor in Pastoria City, who will teach your Pokémon a new move for every scale.

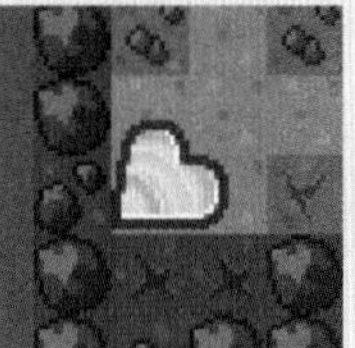

SEE P. 287 FOR A COMPLETE LIST OF ITEMS THAT CAN BE FOUND IN THE UNDERGROUND.

EXCHANGE YOUR LOOT FOR POKÉMON AND ITEMS

THE STUFF YOU DIG out of the walls might be pretty, but rather than holding on to them, you should trade them in for Secret Base items or revive the fossils into living, breathing Pokémon. Check out the examples below for reasons why you should keep digging for treasure.

PLACES TO TRADE IN YOUR FINDINGS

SPHERES: THREE TRADERS IN THE UNDERGROUND

HAND OVER YOUR SPHERES and they will give you items based on what they trade in. There are three kinds of traders: goods traders, trap traders, and loot traders. If you want items for your Secret Base, track down a goods trader. Of course, if you want traps, you go to a trap trader.

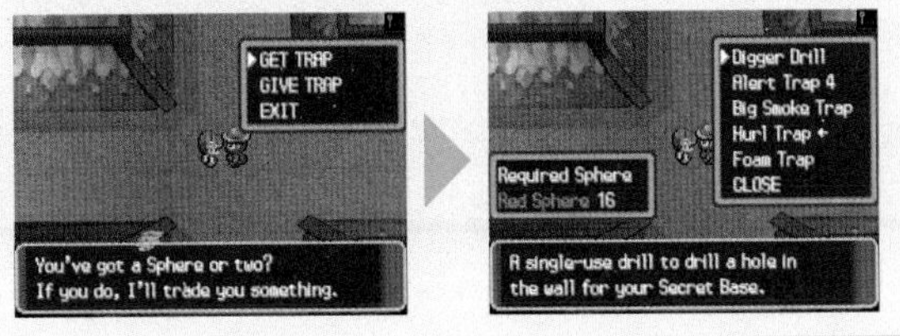

FOSSILS: OREBURGH MINING MUSEUM

BRING YOUR FOSSILS to the Oreburgh Mining Museum to witness the miraculous – they will restore the fossils to Pokémon! Just leave your fossils at reception and come back a little later to pick up your newly-revived friends.

SHARDS: HOUSE ON ROUTE 212

IF YOU COLLECT 10 of the same color shard, bring them to the lady living on Route 212, because she will give you a TM in exchange. Red shards will gain you Sunny Day, blue shards grant Rain Dance, yellow shards mean Sandstorm, and green shards will gain you Hail.

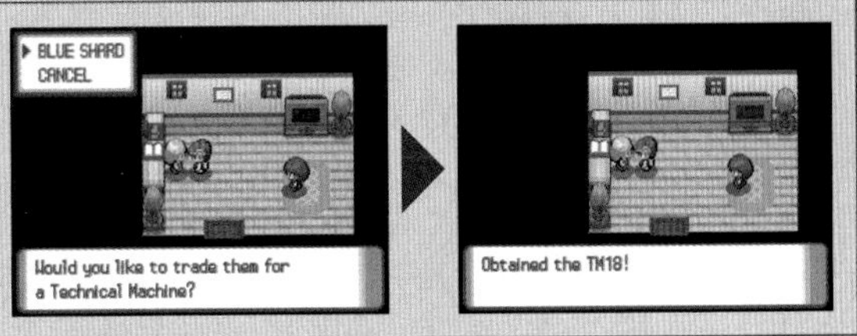

MAKE SURE ITEMS ARE IN YOUR BAG

ITEMS YOU FIND in the Underground are deposited into a loot sack, which you can't take with you back to the surface. So make sure to transfer items into your bag, so you don't lose items like the Skull Fossil or Max Revive when you head back into the sunlight. A loot sack can only hold so much, so once it's full you won't be able to put anything else in it. Make sure to transfer items into your bag often.

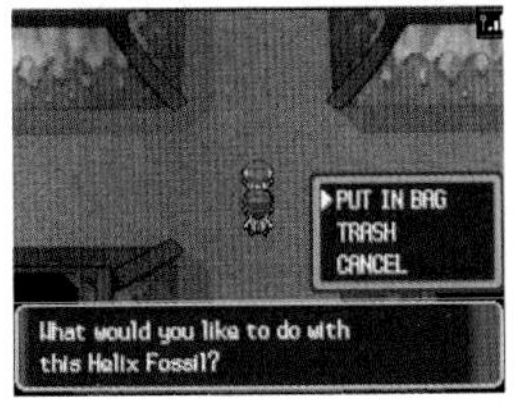

BUILD A SECRET BASE

YOUR SECRET BASE in the Underground is your own personal space to arrange as you will. Trade the spheres you find for furniture items and use them to decorate your base. With enough work, it'll become the special hideaway you dreamed of.

MAKE IT ORIGINAL, MAKE IT ONE-OF-A-KIND

TO REARRANGE YOUR SECRET Base, you use your PC. When you get an item, place it in the PC, where you can then arrange it wherever you want in the base, as long as a rock is not blocking the area. The only way to remove those rocks is to steal the flag out of your friend's Secret Base.

TRADE SPHERES TO THE TRADERS

THERE ARE THREE DIFFERENT kinds of traders wandering through the Underground: the goods traders, the trap traders, and the loot traders. They aren't scarce, either – you'll find as many as eight trap traders alone – and they always remain in the same spots. Remember their locations well, so you always know where to go to trade specific items.

THE THREE TRADERS

GOODS TRADERS

THESE TRADERS are looking for spheres, for which they will trade you items for your Secret Base. The variety of goods changes daily. You can also trade them good in exchange for spheres.

TRAP TRADERS

THESE GUYS will trade you traps in exchange for spheres of different colors and sizes. Stock changes every day. You can also trade traps back to them in exchange for spheres.

LOOT TRADERS

YOU CAN give these guys any assorted items you find in the Underground, like fossils, Evolution items, or battle items, and they will trade you spheres in return. The color and sizes of their spheres varies by trader.

COLLECT GOODS TO DECORATE YOUR SECRET BASE

THERE ARE MORE THAN 80 different items for your Secret Base that can be obtained before the end of the story mode. The majority can be gotten from the goods traders, but you can buy some on the 4 FL of the Veilstone Department Store or get some as gifts from Mr. Goods in Hearthome City by fulfilling certain requirements.

You can use your PC to decorate your Secret Base any way you want.

GOODS FOR YOUR SECRET BASE

TABLES

THESE COME IN different styles and sizes, like Big Table and Small Table.

CHAIRS

THESE HAVE DIFFERENT sizes and materials, like Wood Chair and Blue Cushion.

SHELVES

THIS CONSISTS OF various storage items, like Cupboard and Bike Rack.

DOLLS

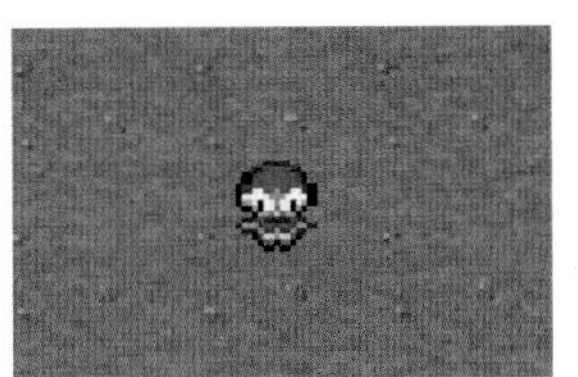

LOTS OF POKÉMON represented as cute plush, like Munchlax and Bonsly.

MACHINES

GREAT GADGETS of all kinds, like Game System and Vending Machine.

MAZE GOODS

THERE ARE FIVE kinds of these, which you can arrange to trap friends who try to steal your flag.

TROPHIES

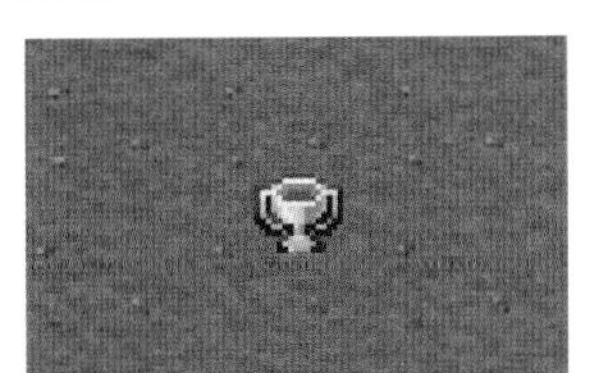

THIS IS A VARIETY of cups and trophies, like Cute Cup and Shiny Gem.

FLOWERS

THESE COME IN various sizes and colors, like Lavish Flowers and Bonsai.

SEE COMPLETE LIST OF GOODS ON P. 286

BURY SPHERES TO MAKE THEM BIGGER

YOU MIGHT LOVE DIGGING spheres out of the wall, but there's a huge advantage to reburying them in the ground. The longer they're buried, the larger they grow. You can even bury spheres of the same color together such that they fuse together to make an even bigger sphere. Check the chart for how the spheres grow do you can earn all the goods you want.

SPHERES AND THEIR GROWING TENDENCIES

PRISM SPHERE	HARD TO GROW
PALE SPHERE	HARD TO GROW
RED SPHERE	EASY TO GROW
BLUE SPHERE	EASY TO GROW
GREEN SPHERE	EASY TO GROW

CAPTURE THE FLAG

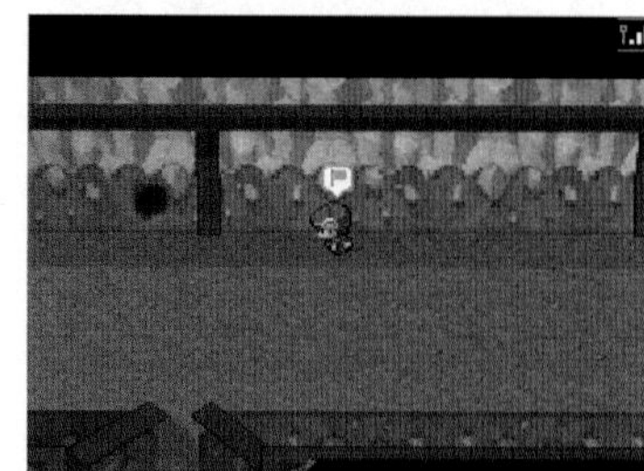

TAKE YOUR FRIEND'S FLAG BACK TO YOUR SECRET BASE FOR SWEET VICTORY!

UTILIZING THE Nintendo DS Wireless Connection, you can play a frenzied game with friends where you try to grab each other's flags. With all the capturing and recapturing, it's like the Sinnoh version of tag.

RUN AS FAST AS YOU CAN

You've obtained the Flag
from Danny's Base!

GRAB HOLD of your friend's flag from their Secret Base and carry it back to your base. Your own flag will upgrade, allowing you to move more rocks from your base and place your goods even more to your liking. If you want the perfect Secret Base, this is the only way to go.

THE FLAG RANKS AND WHAT YOU CAN DO

NORMAL FLAG

- You have never obtained a flag yet.
- You can place up to 10 goods in your base.
- You can't remove any rocks.

BRONZE FLAG

- You've obtained 1 flag.
- You can place up to 12 goods in your base.
- You can remove 1 rock.

SILVER FLAG

- You've obtained 3 flags.
- You can place up to 14 goods in your base.
- You can remove up to 5 rocks.

GOLD FLAG

- You've obtained 10 flags.
- You can place up to 15 goods in your base.
- You can remove up to 10 rocks.
- You can use fossils, spheres and trap radar.

PLATINUM FLAG

- You've obtained 50 flags.
- You can place up to 15 goods in your base.
- You can remove all the rocks.

PLACE TRAPS TO PROTECT YOUR FLAG

WHEN YOU TRY to steal flags from your friend's Secret Bases, you aren't alone in your thievery. While you're headed to their base, they're headed to your base to steal your flag. Protect your base with traps to keep them away from your flag. Should they avoid your traps and run off with your flag, go after them – you need simply touch them to end the chase.

THE TRICK OF TRAPS

MOVE TRAP

WILL THROW you one of four directions. A Hurl Trap will throw you even further.

ROCK TRAP

A ROCK falls on top of you, which you can break by tapping it with the stylus. Rockfall Trap is harder to break.

SMOKE TRAP

SMOKE COVERS the screen. You can push it away with the stylus. The Big Smoke Trap has an even bigger amount of smoke.

FOAM TRAP

FOAM WILL COME OUT. You can dispel it with the stylus. A Bubble Trap will give you even more bubbles.

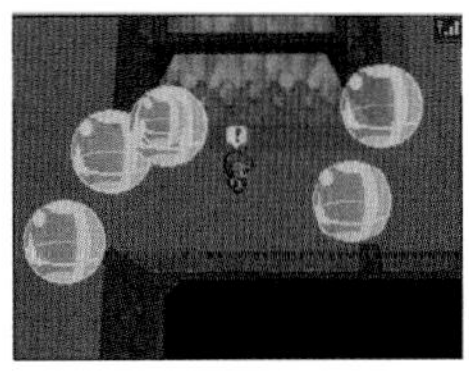

FLOWER TRAP

FLOWER PETALS will whirl up on the screen. You can blow on them to make them disappear.. A Leaf Trap will have a similar effect.

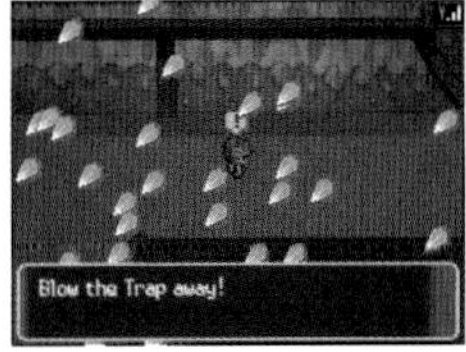

EMBER TRAP

FIRE ATTACKS you. You can put the fire out by blowing on it. A Fire Trap is harder to extinguish.

SEE FULL LIST OF TRAPS ON PAGE 287 

BE MORE EFFECTIVE BY COMBINING TRAPS

SIMPLY THROWING the traps when your opponents approach you will do no good. The best use you could make of traps is to combine their effects to baffle and hinder your opponent. With six different types of traps, you have a number of effective combinations to try out with dastardly results.

MOVE TRAP | RIGHT

Throw your friend to the right.

MOVE TRAP | UP

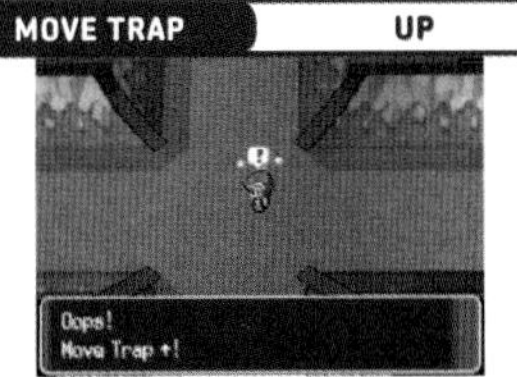

Throw your friend in an upwards direction

ROCKFALL TRAP

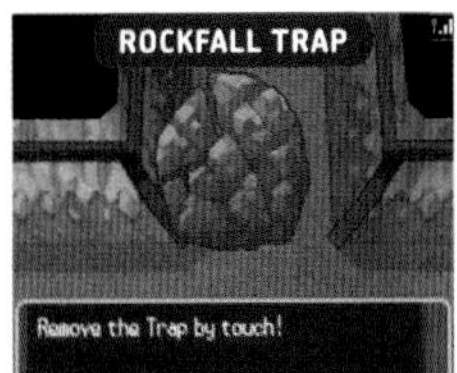

Drop a big rock on them to completely block them.

WI-FI COMMUNICATION

Use the Nintendo Wi-Fi Connection to connect with other Pokémon players across the land!

THE NINTENDO WI-FI CONNECTION lets you interact with other Pokémon Diamond and Pokémon Pearl players through the Global Trade System, Pokémon Wi-Fi Club, and Wi-Fi Battle room, all found in the Pokémon Center. Now you can battle and trade with Trainers from near and far!

GLOBAL TRADE STATION (GTS)

ACROSS GREAT DISTANCES

AT GLOBAL TRADE STATION in Jubilife City, you can trade Pokémon with Trainers that you've never even met. In order to complete your Pokédex, take advantage of this worldwide trade.

YOU CAN ALWAYS GET WHAT YOU WANT

YOU CAN USE the Global Trade Station to trade Pokémon with other Trainers, even ones you've never met before! You can set your own conditions for a trade or search for other Trainers who are want to trade the Pokémon you want. Since you don't have to deal directly with the person you're trading with, you don't have to worry about being on Wi-Fi at the same time.

THE TWO OPTIONS AT GTS:

PUTTING YOUR POKÉMON UP FOR TRADE

TO MAKE A POKÉMON AVAILABLE for trade, first set the trading conditions for your target Pokémon. Then, leave your Pokémon with the GTS. If someone has agreed to your conditions by the next time you connect to the GTS, the trade will go through.

SEARCHING FOR A POKÉMON

YOU CAN ALSO VISIT THE GTS to search for a particular species of Pokémon. You can limit your search by gender and level. If it's available, you can see up to 7 Trainers who can trade with you.

POKÉMON WI-FI CLUB

CONNECT WITH YOUR FRIENDS

AT THE POKÉMON WI-FI CLUB, you trade and battle with registered friends over the Nintendo Wi-Fi Connection! To register friends, receive the Pal Pad item the first time you visit the Pokémon Wi-Fi Club, then use it to register Friend Codes. You can directly input your friends' Friend Codes or register Friend Codes of Trainers you've connected with in the Union Room.

A FILE OF FRIENDS

WITH YOUR PAL PAD, you'll be able to write down the Friend Codes of people you've met in the Union Room, or codes that are given to you elsewhere. You come to rely on this tool when communicating with people, and you'll get the Pal Pad the first time you visit the Wi-Fi Club.

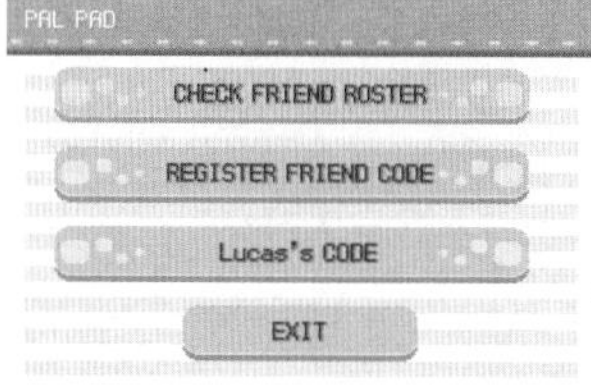

THE SINNOH CONNECTION

THERE ARE FOUR activities you can do at the Pokémon Wi-Fi Club: Single Battle, Double Battle, Trade, or See Records. If your friends are online, you can also chat with your friends.

FOUR ACTIVITIES TO ENJOY

SINGLE BATTLE

There are three different divisions for single battles: Lv.50, Lv.100, and Free.

DOUBLE BATTLE

Each player selects two Pokémon to battle with. There are three different divisions: Lv 50, Lv 100, and Free.

TRADE

You can trade Pokémon with your friends.

SEE RECORDS

Check your friend's records! You can view information such as your friend's battle results, number of trades completed, and the last time they connected.

WI-FI BATTLE ROOM: THE BATTLE TOWER

DOWNLOAD DATA AND BATTLE IN THE WI-FI BATTLE ROOM

CHALLENGE TRAINERS from across the world in the magnificent Battle Tower. Face off against opponents you've never met before and prove your might!

HOW TO REACH THE BATTLE TOWER

- Defeat the Pokémon League Champion.
- Take the boat from Snowpoint City.

TAKE ON THE TOWER

ONCE YOU complete the game by defeating Cynthia, take the boat from Snowpoint City to access the Battle Tower. There you'll find a Wi-Fi Battle Room where you can get info on other Trainers and challenge them. By beating your rivals, you can move up in the ranks as well! The Pokémon you'll face there will be limited to Lv 50.

SEVEN TO SERENADE SAVAGELY

TO START your climb through the ranks, you'll have to defeat the Trainers who have conquered the Wi-Fi Battle Room. Seven of those Trainers will form your first challenge. You can download their data to check your opposition beforehand, too.

You are challenged by
Cowgirl Shawna!

RUMBLE FOR YOUR RANK

AS YOU CONTINUE to beat these champions, you'll move up to higher ranks and challenge tougher Trainers in other battle rooms. You start at rank 1 and advance by winning battles, but losing battles can drop you back down the ranks as well. Do well and you may see your own name on the list of champions!

KEEP GOING
REST
RETIRE
You will be facing opponent no. 2.
Are you ready?

SECTION 6

CHARTS & INFO

BATTLE MOVES

MOVES	TYPE	CLASS	POWER	ACC	PP	RANGE	DA	EFFECT
Absorb	Grass	Special	20	100	25	Normal		Restores your HP by half of the damage inflicted on your opponent.
Acid	Poison	Special	40	100	30	Enemy 2		Lowers your opponent's Special Defense by 1 with a 10% probability. (*2-P263)
Acid Armor	Poison	Status			40	Self		Raises your Defense by 2.
Acupressure	Normal	Status			30	Ally 1		Randomly raises one of your Stats by 2.
Aerial Ace	Flying	Physical	60		20	Normal	○	Makes your attack land without fail.
Agility	Psychic	Status			30	Self		Raises your Speed by 2
Air Cutter	Flying	Special	55	95	25	Enemy 2		Makes it easier to produce a critical hit. (*2-P263)
Air Slash	Flying	Special	75	95	20	Normal		Makes your opponent Flinch with a 30% probability (Disables the opponent's move during that turn).
Amnesia	Psychic	Status			20	Self		Raises your Special Defense by 2.
Ancientpower	Rock	Special	60	100	5	Normal		Raises your Attack, Defense, Speed, Special Attack, Special Defense by 1 with a 10% probability.
Aqua Jet	Water	Physical	40	100	20	Normal	○	Attack hits first without fail (if used by both, it works for one with higher Speed).
Aqua Ring	Water	Status			20	Self		Recovers your HP gradually each turn.
Aqua Tail	Water	Physical	90	90	10	Normal	○	Normal Attack.
Aromatherapy	Grass	Status			5	All Allies		Cures status conditions of all allies.
Assist	Normal	Status			20	DoM		Randomly use moves of your party Pokémon.
Assurance	Dark	Physical	50	100	10	Normal	○	Doubles the move's strength if your opponent is already damaged in that turn.
Astonish	Ghost	Physical	30	100	15	Normal	○	Makes your opponent Flinch with a 30% probability (Disables the opponent's move during that turn).
Attack Order	Bug	Physical	90	100	15	Normal		Makes it easier to produce a critical hit.
Attract	Normal	Status		100	15	Normal		Makes your opponent unable to attack opposite gender. Not effective on the same gender opponent.
Aura Sphere	Fighting	Special	90		20	Normal		Makes your attack land without fail.
Aurora Beam	Ice	Special	65	100	20	Normal		Lowers your opponent's Attack by 1 with a 10% probability.
Avalanche	Ice	Physical	60	100	10	Normal	○	Doubles the strength of the move if your Pokémon received damage in the same turn.
Barrier	Psychic	Status			30	Self		Raises your Defense by 2.
Baton Pass	Normal	Status			40	Self		When changes out to another ally, the new Pokémon inherits all the stat changes cast over your retiring Pokémon.
Beat Up	Dark	Physical	10	100	10	Normal		Allows you to have the numbers of attacks equals to the numbers of your party Pokémon. (Excluding the ones that fainted or affected by status conditions.
Belly Drum	Normal	Status			10	Self		Decreases your HP to half of your max HPs but instead maxes out your Attack.
Bide	Normal	Physical			10	Self	○	Doubles the damage inflicted during the 2 turns after using the move and return it back to your opponent.
Bind	Normal	Physical	15	75	20	Normal	○	Keeps inflicting damage on your opponent for 2-5 turns during which the opponent can't flee.
Bite	Dark	Physical	60	100	25	Normal	○	Makes your opponent Flinch with a 30% probability. (Disables the opponent's move during that turn).
Blizzard	Ice	Special	120	70	5	Enemy 2		Inflicts Freeze condition on an opponent with a 10% probability. (*2-P263)
Block	Normal	Status			5	Normal		Prevents your opponent from fleeing. Trainers can't switch Pokémon.
Body Slam	Normal	Physical	85	100	15	Normal	○	Inflicts Paralyze condition on an opponent with a 30% probability.
Bone Rush	Ground	Physical	25	80	10	Normal		Lets you attack 2-5 consecutive times in one turn.
Bounce	Flying	Physical	85	85	5	Normal	○	Bounces into the air on the 1st turn and attack on the 2nd turn. Inflicts Paralyze condition on an opponent with a 30% probability.
Brave Bird	Flying	Physical	120	100	15	Normal	○	Receive 1/3 of the damage inflicted on your opponent.
Brick Break	Fighting	Physical	75	100	15	Normal	○	Makes you immune to the move Reflect. Destroys Reflect and Light Screen.
Brine	Water	Special	65	100	10	Normal		Doubles the power if the opponent's HP is less than half of its max point.
Bubble	Water	Special	20	100	30	Enemy 2		Lowers your opponent's Speed with a 10% probability. (*2 -P263)
BubbleBeam	Water	Special	65	100	20	Normal		Lowers your opponent's Speed by 1 with a 10% probability.
Bug Buzz	Bug	Special	90	100	10	Normal		Lowers your opponent's Special Defense by 1 with a 10% probability.
Bulk Up	Fighting	Status			20	Self		Raises your Attack and Defense by 1.
Bullet Seed	Grass	Physical	10	100	30	Normal		Lets you attack 2-5 consecutive times in one turn.
Camouflage	Normal	Status			20	Self		Changes your Pokémon type according to the battlefield terrain. (*26-P263)
Captivate	Normal	Status		100	20	Enemy 2		Lowers your opposite-gender opponent's Special Attack by 2. Has no effect on the same gender opponent.
Charge	Electric	Status			20	Self		Doubles the power of your next Electric-type move. Raise your Special Defense by 1.
Charge Beam	Electric	Special	50	90	10	Normal		Raises your Special Attack by 1 with a 70% probability.
Charm	Normal	Status		100	20	Normal		Lowers your opponent's Attack by 2.
Chatter	Flying	Special	60	100	20	Normal		Confuses your opponent with a probability that corresponds to the volume of the recorded sound. (Chatot only)
Close Combat	Fighting	Physical	120	100	5	Normal	○	Lowers your Defense and Special Defense by 1.
Comet Punch	Steel	Physical	100	85	10	Normal	○	Raises your Attack by 1 with a 20% probability.
Confuse Ray	Ghost	Status		100	10	Normal		Makes your opponent confused.
Confusion	Psychic	Special	50	100	25	Normal		Inflicts Confuse condition on an opponent with a 10% probability.
Constrict	Normal	Physical	10	100	35	Normal	○	Lowers your opponent's Speed by 1 with a 10% probability.
Copycat	Normal	Status			20	DoM		Attacks with a previously used move.
Cosmic Power	Psychic	Status			20	Self		Raises your Defense and Special Defense by 1.
Counter	Fighting	Physical		100	20	Self	○	Makes you attack second but inflicts twice as much damage as the opponent's Physical Attack.
Cross Chop	Fighting	Physical	100	80	5	Normal	○	Makes it easier to produce a critical hit.
Cross Poison	Poison	Physical	70	100	20	Normal	○	Makes it easier to produce a critical hit. Inflicts the Poison condition with a 10% probability.
Crunch	Dark	Physical	80	100	15	Normal	○	Lowers your opponent's Defense by 1 with a 20% probability.
Curse	???	Status			10	Norm/Self		Lowers your Speed by 1, raises your Attack and Defense by 1. (*22-P263)
Cut	Normal	Physical	50	95	30	Normal	○	Normal Attack.
Dark Pulse	Dark	Special	80	100	15	Normal		Makes your opponent Flinch with a 20% probability. (Disable your opponent's moves during that turn).
Defend Order	Bug	Status			10	Self		Raises your Defense and Special Defense by 1.
Defense Curl	Normal	Status			40	Self		Raises your Defense by 1.
Defog	Flying	Status			15	Normal		Lowers your opponent's Evasiveness by 1. (*8-P263)
Detect	Fighting	Status			5	Self		Defends against your opponent's current attack. Success ratio is lowered if used consecutively.
Dig	Ground	Physical	80	100	10	Normal	○	Goes underground on the 1st turn, attacks on the 2nd turn.
Disable	Normal	Status		80	20	Normal		Prevents your opponent from using the last used move for several turns.
Discharge	Electric	Special	80	100	15	Enemy 2 / Ally 1		Inflicts Paralyze condition on an opponent with a 30% probability. (*2-P263)
Dive	Water	Physical	80	100	10	Normal	○	Dives into the water on the 1st turn and attack on the 2nd turn.
Dizzy Punch	Normal	Physical	70	100	10	Normal	○	Inflicts Confuse condition on an opponent with a 20% probability.
Double Edge	Normal	Physical	120	100	15	Normal	○	Receives 1/3 of the damage inflicted on your opponent.
Double Hit	Normal	Physical	35	90	10	Normal	○	Lets you attack 2 consecutive times in one turn.
Doubleslap	Normal	Physical	15	85	10	Normal	○	Lets you attack 2-5 times consecutively in 1 turn.
Double Team	Normal	Status			15	Self		Raises your Evasiveness by 1.

DA......Direct Attack
DoM......Depends on Move

BATTLE MOVES, CONT.

MOVES	TYPE	CLASS	POWER	ACC	PP	RANGE	DA	EFFECT
Draco Meteor	Dragon	Special	140	90	5	Normal		Lowers your Special Attack by 2.
Dragon Claw	Dragon	Physical	80	100	15	Normal	○	Normal Attack.
Dragon Dance	Dragon	Status			20	Self		Raises your Attack and Speed by 1.
Dragon Pulse	Dragon	Special	90	100	10	Normal		Normal Attack.
Dragon Rage	Dragon	Special		100	10	Normal		Cause fixed damage of 40.
Dragon Rush	Dragon	Physical	100	75	10	Normal	○	Makes your opponent Flinch with a 20% probability. (Disables the opponent's move during that turn.)
Dragonbreath	Dragon	Special	60	100	20	Normal		Inflicts Paralyze condition on an opponent with a 30% probability.
Drain Punch	Fighting	Physical	60	100	5	Normal	○	Restores your HP for up to 1/2 of damage inflicted on the opponent.
Dream Eater	Psychic	Special	100	100	15	Normal		Recovers your HP for 1/2 of the damage inflicted on your opponent. Effective only when the opponent's Sleeping.
Drill Peck	Flying	Physical	80	100	20	Normal	○	Normal Attack.
Dynamic Punch	Fighting	Physical	100	50	5	Normal	○	Inflicts Confuse condition on an opponent with a 100% probability.
Earth Power	Ground	Special	90	100	10	Normal		Lowers your opponent's Special Defense by 1 with a 10% probability.
Earthquake	Ground	Physical	100	100	10	Enemy 2 / Ally 1		Normal Attack. (*11-P263)
Egg Bomb	Normal	Physical	100	75	10	Normal		Normal Attack.
Embargo	Dark	Status		100	15	Normal		Prevents your opponent from using items for 5 turns. Its Trainer can't use items on that Pokémon, either.
Ember	Fire	Special	40	100	25	Normal		Inflicts Burn condition on an opponent with a 10% probability. If your opponent's Frozen, it'll melt the ice.
Encore	Normal	Status		100	5	Normal		Makes your opponent repeat the last used move for 2-6 turns.
Endeavor	Normal	Physical		100	5	Normal	○	Inflicts damage equal to your foes HP minus your HP.
Endure	Normal	Status			10	Self		Lets you survive with 1 HP regardless of the attack. The success rate decreases with repeated use.
Energy Ball	Grass	Special	80	100	10	Normal		Lowers your opponent's Special Defense by 1 with a 10% probability.
Explosion	Normal	Physical	250	100	5	Enemy 2 / Ally 1		After using this move, you will faint. (*12-P263)
Extrasensory	Psychic	Special	80	100	30	Normal		Makes your opponent Flinch with a 10% probability. (Disables the opponent's move during that turn).
Extreme Speed	Normal	Physical	80	100	5	Normal	○	Attack hits first without fail. (If used by both, it works for one with higher Speed.)
Façade	Normal	Physical	70	100	20	Normal	○	Doubles the power if used when you're inflicted with Poison, Paralyze, or Burn.
Faint Attack	Normal	Physical	50	100	10	Normal		Makes your attack land without fail.
Fake Out	Dark	Physical	60		20	Normal	○	You attack first. Makes your opponent Flinch with a 100% probability. Succeed only in your first turn.
Fake Tears	Normal	Physical	40	100	10	Normal	○	Lowers your opponent's Special Defense by 2.
False Swipe	Dark	Status		100	20	Normal		Always leaves your opponent with 1 HP even after causing him huge damage that would make him faint.
Featherdance	Normal	Physical	40	100	40	Normal	○	Lowers your opponent's Attack by 2.
Feint	Flying	Status		100	15	Normal		Attacks only on opponent who's using Protect and Detect and disables each move.
Fire Blast	Fire	Special	120	85	5	Normal		Inflicts the Burn condition on an opponent with a 10% probability. If your opponent is Frozen, it melts the ice.
Fire Fang	Fire	Physical	65	95	15	Normal	○	Inflicts Burn condition on an opponent or Flinch with a 10% probability. If your opponent's Frozen, it melts the ice.
Fire Punch	Fire	Physical	75	100	15	Normal	○	Inflicts Burn condition on an opponent with a 10% probability. If your opponent's Frozen, it melts the ice.
Fire Spin	Fire	Special	15	70	15	Normal		Causes damage to your opponent and makes him unable to flee for 2-5 turns. It melts the ice when your opponent is Frozen.
Fissure	Ground	Physical		30	5	Normal		Makes your opponent faint with just one hit. (*14-P263)
Flail	Normal	Physical		100	15	Normal	○	The lower your HP is, the more damage this move will do to your opponent.
Flame Wheel	Fire	Physical	60	100	25	Normal	○	Inflicts Burn condition on an opponent with a 10% probability. (*5 -P263)
Flamethrower	Fire	Special	95	100	15	Normal		Inflicts Burn condition on an opponent with a 10% probability. If your opponent's Frozen, it'll melt the ice.
Flare Blitz	Fire	Physical	120	100	15	Normal	○	Receive 1/3 of the damage inflicted on your opponent. Inflicts Burn condition on an opponent with a 10% probability. (*5)
Flash	Normal	Status		100	20	Normal		Lowers your opponent's Accuracy by 1.
Flash Cannon	Steel	Special	80	100	10	Normal		Lowers your opponent's Special Defense by 1 with a 10% probability. (*2-P263)
Flatter	Dark	Status		100	15	Normal		Inflicts the Confuse condition on an opponent, but also raises its Special Attack by 1.
Fling	Dark	Physical		100	10	Normal		Attack by throwing your items at your opponent. Effectiveness depends on an item you use.
Fly	Flying	Physical	90	95	15	Normal	○	Flies up in the air on the 1st turn and Attack on the 2nd turn.
Focus Blast	Fighting	Special	120	70	5	Normal		Lowers your opponent's Special Defense by 1 with a 10% probability.
Focus Energy	Normal	Status			30	Self		Makes it easier for your next move to produce a critical hit.
Focus Punch	Fighting	Physical	150	100	20	Normal	○	Makes you attack second. When you take damage from your opponent by your next attack, you will Flinch and can't attack.
Follow Me	Normal	Status			20	Self		Makes your attack first and receive all of your opponent's attacks.
Force Palm	Fighting	Physical	60	100	10	Normal	○	Inflicts Paralyze condition on an opponent with a 30% probability.
Foresight	Normal	Status			40	Normal		Makes your attack a hit regardless of your opponent's Evasiveness. Makes your Normal- and Fighting-type moves land on Ghost-type Pokémon.
Frustration	Normal	Physical		100	20	Normal	○	The less the user Pokémon likes you, the stronger the attack.
Fury Attack	Normal	Physical	15	85	20	Normal	○	Attacks 2-5 consecutive times in one turn.
Fury Cutter	Bug	Physical	10	95	20	Normal	○	Doubles the strength of the move with every hit. (Up to 5 times.) Once missed, the strength will return to normal.
Future Sight	Psychic	Special	80	90	15	Normal		Attacks the opponent after 2 turns. Causes damage regardless of the opponent's type.
Giga Drain	Grass	Special	60	100	10	Normal		Recovers your HPs by half the damage this move inflicts on your opponent.
Giga Impact	Normal	Physical	150	90	5	Normal	○	Prevents you from taking any action in the next turn after using this move.
Grass Knot	Grass	Special		100	20	Normal	○	The heavier your opponent is, the stronger this move is.
Grasswhistle	Grass	Status		55	15	Normal		Inflicts the Sleep condition on an opponent.
Gravity	Psychic	Status			5	All		Raises Accuracy of all battling Pokémon for 5 turns. (*13-P263)
Growl	Normal	Status		100	40	Enemy 2		Lowers your opponent's Attack by 1.
Growth	Normal	Status			40	Self		Raises your Special Attack by 1.
Grudge	Ghost	Status			5	Self		Nullifies the PP of your opponent's move that made you faint.
Guard Swap	Psychic	Status			10	Normal		Swaps your stats change in Defense and Special Defense with your opponent's.
Gunk Shot	Poison	Physical	120	70	5	Normal		Inflicts the Poison condition with a 30% probability.
Gust	Flying	Special	40	100	35	Normal		Normal Attack. (*6-P263)
Gyro Ball	Steel	Physical		100	5	Normal	○	The lower your Speed is, the stronger this attack gets. (Up to 1502)
Hail	Ice	Status			10	All		Summons a hail storm that lasts for 5 turns. In each turn, causes damage to all opponents that are not Ice-type.
Hammer Arm	Fighting	Physical	100	90	10	Normal	○	Raises your Speed by 1.
Harden	Normal	Status			30	Self		Raises your Defense by 1.
Haze	Ice	Status			30	All		Restores the stats change between you and you opponent.
Headbutt	Normal	Physical	70	100	15	Normal	○	Makes your opponent Flinch with a 30% probability. (Disables the opponent's move during that turn.)
Head Smash	Rock	Physical	150	80	5	Normal	○	Receives 1/2 of damage you inflicted on your opponent.
Heal Bell	Normal	Status			5	All Allies		Cures status conditions of all allies.
Heal Block	Psychic	Status		100	15	Enemy 2		Prevents your opponent from healing by using its moves for 5 turns.
Heal Order	Bug	Status			10	Self		Restores your HP by 1/2 of the max points.
Healing Wish	Psychic	Status			10	Self		Makes you faint but completely heals HPs and cures status conditions of your next entering ally.

BATTLE MOVES, CONT.

MOVES	TYPE	CLASS	POWER	ACC	PP	RANGE	DA	EFFECT
Heart Swap	Psychic	Status			10	Normal		You and your opponent swap all the stats changes.
Helping Hand	Normal	Status			20	Ally 1		Multiplies your ally's move strength by 1.5.
Hi Jump Kick	Fighting	Physical	100	90	20	Normal	○	If missed, receive 1/2 of damage if would have caused the opponent.
Hidden Power	Normal	Special		100	15	Normal		Changes type and power based on the user Pokémon.
Horn Attack	Normal	Physical	65	100	25	Normal	○	Normal Attack.
Horn Drill	Normal	Physical		30	5	Normal	○	Knocks out your opponent in one hit.
Hydro Pump	Water	Special	120	80	5	Normal		Normal Attack.
Hyper Beam	Normal	Special	150	90	5	Normal		Prevents you from making any action on your next turn after using this move.
Hyper Fang	Normal	Physical	80	90	15	Normal	○	Makes your opponent Flinch with a 10% probability. (Disable opponent's moves during that turn.)
Hyper Voice	Normal	Special	90	100	10	Enemy 2		Normal Attack. (*2-P263)
Hypnosis	Psychic	Status		70	20	Normal		Inflicts the Sleep condition on an opponent.
Ice Beam	Ice	Special	95	100	10	Normal		Inflicts the Freeze condition on an opponent with a 10% probability.
Ice Fang	Ice	Physical	65	95	15	Normal	○	Inflicts the Freeze condition on an opponent or Flinch with a 10% probability.
Ice Punch	Ice	Physical	75	100	15	Normal	○	Inflicts the Freeze condition on an opponent with a 10% probability.
Ice Shard	Ice	Physical	40	100	30	Normal		Attack hits first without fail. (If used by both, it works for one with higher Speed.)
Icy Wind	Ice	Special	55	95	15	Enemy 2		Lowers your opponent's Speed by 1 with a 100% probability. (*2-P263)
Imprison	Psychic	Status			10	Self		Prevents your opponent from using learned moves.
Ingrain	Grass	Status			20	Self		Restores your HP gradually each turn, The user of the move can't switch out. (*20-P263)
Iron Defense	Steel	Status			15	Self		Raises your Defense by 2.
Iron Head	Water	Physical	40	100	20	Normal	○	Attack hits first without fail. (If used by both, it works for one with higher Speed.)
Iron Tail	Steel	Physical	100	75	15	Normal	○	Lowers opponent's Defense by 1 with a 30% probability.
Jump Kick	Fighting	Physical	85	95	25	Normal	○	If missed, receive 1/2 of damage if would have caused the opponent.
Karate Chop	Fighting	Physical	50	100	25	Normal	○	Makes it easier to produce a critical hit.
Kinesis	Psychic	Status		80	15	Normal		Lowers your opponent's Accuracy by 1.
Knock Off	Dark	Physical	20	100	20	Normal	○	Takes opponents held items during the battle. The items return after the battle.
Last Resort	Normal	Physical	130	100	5	Normal	○	Won't succeed unless you've used each of your other moves once.
Leaf Storm	Grass	Special	140	90	5	Normal		Lowers your Special Attack by 2.
Leech Life	Bug	Physical	20	100	15	Normal	○	Recovers your HPs by a half of the damage this move inflicts on your opponent.
Leech Seed	Grass	Status		90	10	Normal		Recovers your HPs every turn for the amount of your opponent's HPs you absorbed. Effect continues even after opponent Pokémon switches out.
Leer	Normal	Status		100	30	Enemy 2		Lowers your opponent's Defense by 1.
Lick	Ghost	Physical	20	100	30	Normal	○	Inflicts the Paralyze condition on an opponent with a 30% probability.
Light Screen	Psychic	Status			30	Ally 2		Decreases the damage of your opponent's Special Attack by half for 5 turns. (*23-P263)
Lock-On	Normal	Status			5	Normal		Makes your attack in the next turn land without fail.
Low Kick	Fighting	Physical		100	20	Normal	○	The heavier your opponent is, the stronger this move is.
Lucky Chant	Normal	Status			30	Ally 2		Prevents your opponent from producing critical hits for 5 turns.
Mach Punch	Fighting	Physical	40	100	30	Normal	○	Lets you strike first without fail. (If used by both, it works for one with higher Speed.)
Magic Coat	Psychic	Status			15	Self		Reflects effects of moves like Poison, Paralysis, Confuse, and Leech Seed.
Magical Leaf	Grass	Special	60		20	Normal		Attack always hits the opponent without fail.
Magnitude	Ground	Physical		100	30	Enemy 2 / Ally 1		Attack strength randomly changes (10, 30, 50, 70, 90, 110). (*11-P263)
Me First	Normal	Status			20	DoM		Lets you attack more powerfully with your opponent's next move. Won't succeed if you fail to attack first.
Mean Look	Normal	Status			5	Normal		Prevents your opponent from fleeing. In battles with Trainers, prevents swapping between Pokémon.
Meditate	Psychic	Status			20	Self		Raises your Special Attack and Special Defense by 1.
Meditate	Psychic	Status			40	Self		Raises your Attack by 1.
Mega Drain	Grass	Special	40	100	15	Normal		Restore your HP by a half of the damage inflicted on your opponent.
Megahorn	Bug	Physical	120	85	10	Normal	○	Normal Attack.
Memento	Dark	Status		100	10	Normal		Makes you faint but lowers your opponent's Attack and Special Attack by 2.
Metal Burst	Steel	Physical		100	10	Self		Returns 1.5x of the damage you took at the end of the turn.
Metal Claw	Steel	Physical	50	95	35	Normal	○	Raises your Defense by 1 with a 10% probability.
Metal Sound	Steel	Status		85	40	Normal		Lowers your opponent's Special Defense by 2.
Metronome	Normal	Status			10	DoM		Randomly executes one move out of all.
Mimic	Normal	Status			10	Normal		Allows you to copy your opponent's last used move for the duration of the battle. (PP of copied move is 5.)
Mind Reader	Normal	Status			5	Normal		Makes your Attack in the next land without fail.
Minimize	Normal	Status			20	Self		Raises your Accuracy by 1.
Miracle Eye	Psychic	Status			40	Normal		Makes your Attack a hit regardless of your opponent's Evasiveness. Makes your Psychic-type moves land on Dark-type Pokémon.
Mirror Coat	Psychic	Special		100	20	Self		Returns 2x the damage of your opponent's Special Attack. Always makes you strike second.
Mirror Move	Flying	Status			20	DoM		Makes you repeat the same move your opponent has just used on you.
Mirror Shot	Steel	Special	65	85	10	Normal		Lowers your opponent's Accuracy by 1 with a 30% probability.
Mist	Ice	Status			30	Ally 2		Makes you immune to Stat changes.
Moonlight	Normal	Status			5	Self		Restores your HP. Effectiveness depends on weather. (*1-P263)
Morning Sun	Normal	Status			5	Self		Recovers your HP. Effectiveness changes depending on weather. (*1-P263)
Mud Bomb	Ground	Special	65	85	10	Normal		Lowers your opponent's Accuracy by 1 with a 30% probability.
Mud Shot	Ground	Special	55	95	15	Normal		Lowers your opponent's Speed by 1 with a 100% probability.
Mud Slap	Ground	Special	20	100	10	Normal		Lowers your opponent's Accuracy by 1 with a 100% probability.
Mud Sport	Ground	Status			15	All		Halves the strength of Electric-type moves.
Muddy Water	Water	Special	95	85	10	Enemy 2		Lowers your opponent's Accuracy by 1 with a 30% probability. (*2-P263)
Nasty Plot	Dark	Status			20	Self		Raises your Special Attack by 2.
Natural Gift	Normal	Physical		100	15	Normal		Your held berry determines the type and strength of your move. Once used you lose the berry.
Night Shade	Ghost	Special		100	15	Normal		Inflicts fixed damage equal to your Pokémon's level.
Night Slash	Dark	Physical	70	100	15	Normal	○	Makes it easier to produce a critical hit.
Nightmare	Ghost	Status		100	15	Normal		Reduces your opponent's HP by 1/4 of its max HP each turn. Effective only when opponent's sleeping.
Octazooka	Water	Special	65	85	10	Normal		Lowers your opponent's Accuracy by 1 with a 50% probability.
Odor Sleuth	Normal	Status			40	Normal		Makes your attacks hit regardless of your opponent's Evasiveness. Makes Normal- and Fighting-type moves hit Ghost-type Pokémon.
Ominous Wind	Ghost	Special	60	100	5	Normal		Raises Attack, Defense, Speed, Special Attack, Special Defense by 1 with a 10% probability.
Overheat	Fire	Special	140	90	5	Normal		Raises Attack but sharply lowers your Special Attack by 2. When your opponent is frozen, it will melt the ice.

BATTLE MOVES, CONT.

MOVES	TYPE	CLASS	POWER	ACC	PP	RANGE	DA	EFFECT
Pain Split	Normal	Status			20	Normal		Combines your HP with your opponent's and splits them between both.
Payback	Dark	Physical	50	100	10	Normal	○	Doubles the power of your move when you attack after your opponent.
Peck	Flying	Physical	35	100	35	Normal	○	Normal Attack.
Perish Song	Normal	Status			5	All		Makes all Pokémon in the battle at the time of use of this move faint after 3 turns.
Petal Dance	Grass	Special	90	100	20	Random 1	○	Attack consecutively for 2-3 turns. When effectiveness wears off, you suffer Confusion.
Pin Missile	Bug	Physical	14	85	20	Normal		Attacks 2-5 consecutive times in one turn.
Pluck	Flying	Physical	60	100	20	Normal	○	If your opponent has berries effective in battles, takes that berry and applies it to you.
Poison Fang	Poison	Physical	50	100	15	Normal	○	Causes your opponent to be Badly Poisoned with a 30% probability. Damage increases with each turn.
Poison Gas	Poison	Status		55	40	Normal		Inflicts Poison condition on an opponent.
Poison Jab	Poison	Physical	80	100	20	Normal	○	Inflicts Poison condition on an opponent with a 30% probability.
Poisonpowder	Poison	Status		75	35	Normal		Inflicts Poison condition on an opponent.
Poison Sting	Poison	Physical	15	100	35	Normal		Inflicts Poison condition on an opponent with a 30% probability.
Pound	Normal	Physical	40	100	35	Normal	○	Normal Attack.
Powder Snow	Ice	Special	40	100	25	Enemy 2		Inflicts the Freeze condition on an opponent with a 10% probability. (*2-P263)
Power Gem	Rock	Special	70	100	20	Normal		Normal Attack.
Power Swap	Psychic	Status			10	Normal		Switches your Attack and Special Attack stats changes with your opponent.
Power Trick	Psychic	Status			10	Self		Switches your Attack and Special Attack with your opponent. (Stats changes won't be switched.)
Power Whip	Grass	Physical	120	85	10	Normal	○	Normal Attack.
Protect	Normal	Status			10	Self		Defends against your opponent's current attack. Success ratio is lowered if used consecutively.
Psybeam	Psychic	Special	65	100	20	Normal		Inflicts Confuse condition on an opponent with a 10% probability.
Psych Up	Normal	Status			10	Normal		Casts on yourself the stats change caused to your opponent.
Psychic	Psychic	Special	90	100	10	Normal		Lowers your opponent's Special Defense by 1 with a 10% probability.
Psycho Cut	Psychic	Physical	70	100	20	Normal		Makes it easier to produce a critical hit.
Psycho Shift	Psychic	Status		90	10	Normal		Cures your own status conditions (Poison, Fatal Poison, Sleep, Paralysis, Burn) by shifting the condition to your opponent.
Psywave	Psychic	Special		80	15	Normal		Randomly causes damage (0.5-1.5) multiplied by your level.
Punishment	Dark	Physical		100	5	Normal	○	The higher your opponent's stats, the stronger your Pokémon becomes.
Pursuit	Dark	Physical	40	100	20	Normal	○	When your opponent retires and its ally enter, causes 2x damage to the retiring Pokémon.
Quick Attack	Normal	Physical	40	100	30	Normal	○	Attack hits first without fail. (If used by both, it works for one with higher Speed.)
Rage	Normal	Physical	20	100	20	Normal	○	Raises the strength of your moves every time you're hit by your opponent's Attack.
Rain Dance	Water	Status			5	All		Summons a rain storm that lasts for 5 turns and raises the strength of Water-type moves.
Razor Leaf	Grass	Physical	55	95	25	Enemy 2		Makes it easier to produce a critical hit. (*2-P263)
Razor Wind	Normal	Special	80	100	10	Enemy 2		Makes you gather up strength on the 1st turn and attack on the 2nd turn. Makes it easier to do a critical hit.
Recover	Normal	Status			10	Self		Restores your HP by up to a half of your max point.
Recycle	Normal	Status			10	Self		Allows you to reuse your items in the same battle.
Reflect	Psychic	Status			20	Ally 2		Halves the damage of your opponent's Physical Attack for 5 turns. (*23-P263)
Refresh	Normal	Status			20	Self		Cures the status conditions Poison, Paralyze, and Burn.
Rest	Psychic	Status			10	Self		Restores all your HP and Sleep for 2 turns.
Return	Normal	Physical		100	20	Normal	○	The more emotionally attached your battling Pokémon is to you, the more powerful it becomes.
Revenge	Fighting	Physical	60	100	10	Normal	○	Doubles the strength of the move if receive damage in the current turn.
Reversal	Fighting	Physical		100	15	Normal	○	The lower your HP is, the more damage this move will do on your opponent.
Roar	Normal	Status		100	20	Normal		Ends battles against wild Pokémon. Forces your opponent Trainer to change Pokémon.
Roar of Time	Dragon	Special	150	90	5	Normal		Prevents your opponent from making any action in the next turn after using this move.
Rock Blast	Rock	Physical	25	80	10	Normal		Attacks 2-5 consecutive times in one turn.
Rock Climb	Normal	Physical	90	85	20	Normal	○	Confuses your opponent with a 20% probability.
Rock Polish	Rock	Status			20	Self		Raises your Speed by 2.
Rock Slide	Rock	Physical	75	90	10	Enemy 2		Makes your opponent Flinch with a 30% probability. (Disables the opponent's move during that turn.) (*2-P263)
Rock Smash	Fighting	Physical	40	100	15	Normal	○	Lowers your opponent's Defense by 1 with a 50% probability.
Rock Throw	Rock	Physical	50	90	15	Normal		Normal Attack.
Rock Tomb	Rock	Physical	50	80	10	Normal		Lowers your opponent's Speed by 1 with a 100% probability.
Role Play	Psychic	Status			10	Normal		Copies your opponent's Ability. (Can't copy Wonder Guard.)
Rollout	Rock	Physical	30	90	20	Normal	○	Allows consecutive attacks for up to 5 turns until you miss. Damage increases with each hit. (*10-P263)
Roost	Flying	Status			10	Self		Restores your HP by 1/2 of your max HPs but prevents you to be a Flying-type during that turn.
Safeguard	Normal	Status			25	Ally 2		Protects you against status conditions for 5 turns. Effect lasts when you change Pokémon.
Sand Attack	Ground	Status		100	15	Normal		Lowers your opponent's Accuracy by 1.
Sand Tomb	Ground	Physical	15	70	15	Normal		Causes damage to your opponent for 2-5 turns during which the opponent can't flee.
Sandstorm	Rock	Status			10	All		Creates Sandstorm that lasts for 5 turns. Damages all Pokémon each turn except for Rock-, Steel- and Ground-type.
Scary Face	Normal	Status		90	10	Normal		Lowers your opponent's Speed by 2.
Scratch	Normal	Physical	40	100	35	Normal	○	Normal Attack.
Screech	Normal	Status		85	40	Normal		Lowers your opponent's Defense by 2.
Secret Power	Normal	Physical	70	100	20	Normal		Adds extra effects that corresponds to the battlefield's terrain. (*24-P263)
Seismic Toss	Fighting	Physical		100	20	Normal	○	Inflicts the fixed damage equivalent to your level points.
Selfdestruct	Normal	Physical	200	100	5	Enemy 2 / Ally 1		Makes you faint after using this move. (*12-P263)
Shadow Ball	Ghost	Special	80	100	15	Normal		Lowers your opponent's Special Defense by 1 with a 20% probability.
Shadow Claw	Ghost	Physical	70	100	15	Normal	○	Makes it easier to produce a critical hit.
Shadow Punch	Ghost	Physical	60		20	Normal	○	Makes your attack land without fail.
Shadow Sneak	Ghost	Physical	40	100	30	Normal	○	Attack hits first without fail. (If used by both, it works for one with higher Speed.)
Sheer Cold	Ice	Special		30	5	Normal		Knocks out your opponent in one hit. (*14-P263)
Shock Wave	Electric	Special	60		20	Normal		Makes your attack land without fail.
Signal Beam	Bug	Special	75	100	15	Normal		Inflicts Confuse condition on an opponent with a 10% probability.
Silver Wind	Bug	Special	60	100	5	Normal		Raises your Attack, Defense, Speed, Special Attack, Special Defense by 1 with a 10% probability.
Sing	Normal	Status		55	15	Normal		Inflicts the Sleep condition on an opponent.
Skill Swap	Psychic	Status			10	Normal		You and your opponent switch Abilities.
Sky Attack	Flying	Physical	140	90	5	Normal		Makes you gather up strength on the 1st turn and attack on the 2nd turn. Makes your opponent Flinch with a 30% probability. (*9-P263)
Slack Off	Normal	Status			10	Self		Restores your HP for up to 1/2 of your max HPs.
Slam	Normal	Physical	80	75	20	Normal	○	Normal Attack.
Slash	Normal	Physical	70	100	20	Normal	○	Makes it easier to produce a critical hit.

BATTLE MOVES, CONT.

MOVES	TYPE	CLASS	POWER	ACC	PP	RANGE	DA	EFFECT
Sleep Talk	Normal	Status			10	DoM		Randomly use moves you have. Effective only when you are asleep.
Sludge Bomb	Poison	Special	90	100	10	Normal		Cause your opponent to be Poisoned with a 30% probability.
Smokescreen	Normal	Status		100	20	Normal		Lowers your opponent's Accuracy by 1.
Snatch	Dark	Status			10	DoM		Steals the effects of your opponent's stats changing moves and HP recovering moves.
Snore	Normal	Physical	40	100	15	Normal		Makes your opponent Flinch with a 30% probability. Effective only when you're sleeping.
Softboiled	Normal	Status			10	Self		Restores your HP for up to 1/2 of your max HPs.
Solarbeam	Grass	Special	120	100	10	Normal		Gathers up strength on the 1st turn and attack on the 2nd turn. (*15-P263)
Sonicboom	Normal	Special		90	20	Normal		Causes 20 points of damage regardless of your opponent's Attack of Defense strength.
Spacial Rend	Dragon	Special	100	95	5	Normal		Makes it easier to produce a critical hit.
Spark	Electric	Physical	65	100	20	Normal	○	Inflicts Paralyze condition on an opponent with a 30% probability.
Spit Up	Normal	Special		100	10	Normal		The damage will increase by the number of times you use Stockpile. (*21-P263)
Spite	Ghost	Status		100	10	Normal		Reduces the PP by 4 of the last move used by opponent.
Splash	Normal	Status			40	Self		No effect.
Stealth Rock	Rock	Status			20	Enemy 2		Inflicts damage to your opponent every time he changes Pokémon. The amount of damage will be determined by the type compatibility.
Steel Wing	Steel	Physical	70	90	25	Normal	○	Raises your Defense by 1 with a 30% probability.
Stockpile	Normal	Status			20	Self		Raises your Defense and Special Defense by 1. Use up to 3 times to build up on your moves.
Stomp	Normal	Physical	65	100	20	Normal	○	Makes your opponent Flinch with a 30% probability. (Disable opponent's moves during that turn.) (*25-P263)
Stone Edge	Rock	Physical	100	80	5	Normal		Makes it easier to produce a critical hit.
Strength	Normal	Physical	80	100	15	Normal	○	Normal Attack.
String Shot	Bug	Status		95	40	Enemy 2		Lowers your opponent's Speed by 1.
Struggle	Normal	Physical	50		1	Normal	○	Hits opponent, but takes 1/4 max HP - only available when you lose PP for all moves.
Stun Spore	Grass	Status		75	30	Normal		Inflicts Paralyze condition on an opponent.
Submission	Fighting	Physical	80	80	15	Normal	○	Receives 1/4 of the damage inflicted on your opponent.
Substitute	Normal	Status			10	Self		Builds the Pokémon's own alter-ego using 1/4 of its max HPs.
Sucker Punch	Dark	Physical	80	100	5	Normal	○	If your opponent uses a physical attack, this attack attacks first and damages the opponent. If the opponent did not use a physical attack, this move will fail.
Sunny Day	Fire	Status			5	All		Creates Sunny weather that lasts for 5 turns and raises the strength of Fire-type moves.
Super Fang	Normal	Physical		90	10	Normal	○	Reduces your opponent's HP by 50%.
Superpower	Fighting	Physical	120	100	5	Normal	○	Lowers your Attack and Defense by 1.
Supersonic	Normal	Status		55	20	Normal		Inflicts Confuse condition on an opponent.
Surf	Water	Special	95	100	15	Enemy 2 / Ally 1		Normal Attack. (*19-P263)
Swagger	Normal	Status		90	15	Normal		Inflicts Confuse condition on an opponent, but also raises its Attack by 2.
Swallow	Normal	Status			10	Self		The more you use Stockpile, more HP you recover. (*21-P263)
Sweet Kiss	Normal	Status		75	10	Normal		Inflicts Confuse condition on an opponent.
Sweet Scent	Normal	Status		100	20	Enemy 2		Lowers your opponent's Evasiveness by 1.
Swift	Normal	Special	60		20	Enemy 2		Makes your attack land without fail. (*2-P263)
Swords Dance	Normal	Status			30	Self		Raises your Attack by 2.
Synthesis	Grass	Status			5	Self		Restores your HP. Effectiveness depends on weather. (*1-P263)
Tackle	Normal	Physical	35	95	35	Normal	○	Normal Attack.
Tail Glow	Bug	Status			20	Self		Raises your Special Defense by 2.
Tail Whip	Normal	Status		100	30	Enemy 2		Lowers your opponent's Defense by 1.
Tailwind	Flying	Status			30	Ally 2		Double both your and opponent's Speed for 3 turns.
Take Down	Normal	Physical	90	85	20	Normal	○	Receive 1/4 of damage inflicted on your opponent.
Taunt	Dark	Status		100	20	Normal		Your opponents can only use attack moves for 2-4 turns.
Teleport	Psychic	Status			20	Self		Ends battles against wild Pokémon.
Thief	Dark	Physical	40	100	10	Normal	○	Allows you to steal your opponent's items when you don't have any.
Thrash	Normal	Physical	90	100	20	Random 1	○	Attack consecutively for 2-3 turns. When effectiveness wears off, you suffer Confusion.
Thunder	Electric	Special	120	70	10	Normal		Inflicts the Paralyze condition on an opponent with a 30% probability. (*7-P263)
Thunder Fang	Electric	Physical	65	95	15	Normal	○	Makes your opponent Flinch or inflicts the Paralyze condition with a 10% probability.
Thunder Punch	Electric	Physical	75	100	15	Normal	○	Inflicts the Paralyze condition on an opponent with a 10% probability.
Thundershock	Electric	Special	40	100	30	Normal		Inflicts Paralyze condition on an opponent with a 10% probability.
Thunder Wave	Electric	Status		100	20	Normal		Inflicts Paralyze condition on an opponent.
Thunderbolt	Electric	Special	95	100	15	Normal		Inflicts Paralyze condition on an opponent with a 10% probability.
Tickle	Normal	Status		100	20	Normal		Lowers your opponent's Attack and Defense by 1.
Torment	Dark	Status		100	15	Normal		Prevents your opponent from using the same move twice in a row.
Toxic	Poison	Status		85	10	Normal		Causes your opponent to be Badly Poisoned. Damage increases with each turn.
Toxic Spikes	Poison	Status			20	Enemy 2		Causes your entering opponent to be Poisoned. (*17-P263)
Trick	Psychic	Status		100	10	Normal		You and your opponent switch items you carry.
Trick Room	Psychic	Status			5	All		For 5 turns, one with less Speed gets to attack first. (*18-P263)
Twister	Dragon	Special	40	100	20	Enemy 2		Makes your opponent Flinch with a 20% probability. (Disables the opponent's move during that turn.)
Uproar	Normal	Special	50	100	10	Random 1		Makes you keep making noise for 2-5 turns during which both you and your opponent won't be put to Sleep.
U-Turn	Bug	Physical	70	100	20	Normal	○	Lets you switch to your stand-by ally Pokémon after this attack.
Vine Whip	Grass	Physical	35	100	15	Normal	○	Normal Attack.
Vital Throw	Fighting	Physical	70		10	Normal	○	You attack second but your attack hits without fail.
Volt Tackle	Electric	Physical	120	100	15	Normal	○	Receives 1/3 of the damage inflicted on your opponent. Inflicts Paralyze condition on an opponent with a 10% probability.
Wake-Up Slap	Fighting	Physical	60	100	10	Normal	○	Causes 2x damage to the Sleeping opponent but it cures his status condition.
Water Gun	Water	Special	40	100	25	Normal		Normal Attack.
Water Pulse	Water	Special	60	100	20	Normal		Inflicts Confuse condition on an opponent with a 20% probability.
Water Sport	Water	Status			15	All		Halves the strength of Fire-type moves during the time the user is in battle.
Water Spout	Water	Special	150	100	5	Enemy 2		Inflicts less damage if your HP is weaker.
Waterfall	Water	Physical	80	100	15	Normal	○	Makes your opponent Flinch with a 20% probability. (Disables the opponent's move during that turn).
Weather Ball	Normal	Special	50	100	10	Normal		Changes the type of the move to correspond with weather and doubles its power. (*3-P263)
Whirlpool	Water	Special	15	70	15	Normal		Inflicts damage to your opponent for 2-5 turns. During this time the opponent can't flee. (*4-P263)
Whirlwind	Normal	Status		100	20	Normal		Ends battles against wild Pokémon. Forces your opponent Trainer to change Pokémon.
Will-O-Wisp	Fire	Status		75	15	Normal		Inflicts Burn condition on an opponent.
Wing Attack	Flying	Physical	60	100	35	Normal	○	Normal Attack.
Wish	Normal	Status		100	10	Self		Restores half of max HP on next turn. Effect transfers if you switch Pokémon.

DA......Direct Attack DoM......Depends on Move

BATTLE MOVES, CONT.

MOVES	TYPE	CLASS	POWER	ACC	PP	RANGE	DA	EFFECT
Withdraw	Water	Status			40	Self		Raises your Defense by 1.
Wood Hammer	Grass	Physical	120	100	15	Normal	○	The caster receives 1/3 of the damage inflicted on its opponent.
Worry Seed	Grass	Status		100	10	Normal		Changes opponent's Ability to Insomnia. Not effective on opponent's Pokémon that have Truant.
Wrap	Normal	Physical	15	85	20	Normal	○	Causes damage to your opponent and makes him unable to flee for 2-5 turns.
Wring Out	Normal	Special		100	5	Normal	○	The higher your opponent's HP, the stronger the attack. (Up to 120)
X-Scissor	Bug	Physical	80	100	15	Normal	○	Normal Attack.
Yawn	Normal	Status			10	Normal		Inflicts the Sleep condition on an opponent at the end of the next turn. Has no effect if the opponent withdraws before that.
Zap Cannon	Electric	Special	100	50	5	Normal		Inflicts Paralyze condition on an opponent.
Zen Headbutt	Psychic	Physical	80	90	15	Normal	○	Makes your opponent Flinch with a 20% probability. (Disables the opponent's move during that turn.)

FIELD MOVES

MOVES	EFFECTIVENESS
Cut	Cuts small trees so you can proceed.
Defog	Clears the "Deep Fog" and gives you better vision.
Dig	Lets you escape from a cave, cavern, etc., brings you back to the last entrance.
Flash	Lights up dark caves.
Fly	Transport in a flash to places you've been to before.
Rock Climb	Lets you climb up and down on craggy mountain walls.
Rock Smash	Crushes cracked rocks so you can proceed.

MOVES	EFFECTIVENESS
Softboiled	Your Pokémon shares its HP with others in the party.
Strength	Removes huge rocks so you can proceed.
Surf	Travel on water.
Sweet Scent	Used in the wild, it lures wild Pokémon to appear on the spot.
Teleport	Transport to the last visited Pokémon Center. (Not effective in towns or caves.)
Waterfall	Lets you climb up on a waterfall.

ADDITIONAL EFFECTS OF BATTLE MOVES (P.258-262)

*1 Recovers 2/3 of HPs under sunny conditions. Usually recovers 1/2 of HPs. Under Rain, Sandstorm, Hail, and Deep Fog, recover 1/4 of HPs.

*2 Effect decreases in Double Battles.

*3 If the weather is Sunny, Rain, Hail or Sandstorm, then it doubles the strength of Fire-type moves, Water-type moves, Ice-type moves and Rock-type moves respectively.

*4 Causes 2x damage when used on the opponent who is using Dive.

*5 Melts the ice, even if you're frozen yourself. In that case, it melts your ice.

*6 Cause 2x damage when used on the opponent who is using Fly or Bounce.

*7 Attack is always a hit when used under rainy weather. Under intense sun Accuracy is 50%. Can attack opponent that's using Fly or Bounce.

*8 Disables your opponents moves like Light Screen, Reflect, Safeguard, Mist, Spikes, Toxic Spikes, and nullifies the effect of Deep Fog.

*9 Makes it easier to produce a critical hit.

*10 Causes 2x damage if used after the move Defense Curl.

*11 Causes 2x damage when used on the opponent who is using Dig. Effect decreases in Double Battles.

*12 Causes a decrease of half of the opponent's Defense. Effect decreases in Double Battles.

*13 Makes your Ground-type moves hit on Flying-type Pokémon and the ones that have the Ability Levitate. Prevents your opponent from using moves Fly, Splash, Bounce and Magnet Rise. (If they are already in use, they will be disabled).

*14 Won't hit if the opponent's level is higher than yours. The lower your opponent's level, the higher the Accuracy.

*15 Under sunny conditions, you can skip the build-up and attack on the first turn. Strength will be reduced by half under Rain, Sandstorm, Hail, and Deep Fog.

*16 Cause 2x damage when used on opponent using Fly or Bounce. Effect decreases in Double Battles.

*17 Use move Poison Spikes twice and it causes your opponent to be Badly Poisoned. Not effective on Poison-type Pokémon, Flying-type Pokémon and Pokémon with the Levitate Ability.

*18 First attack moves will come first regardless of the effect of this move. If used again during the turn that the move is still effective, it kills the effect.

*19 Causes 2x damage when used on the opponent who is using Dive. Effect decreases in Double Battles.

*20 If opponent uses Flying-type Pokémon or the ones with the Ability Levitate, allows your Ground-type moves to hit them.

*21 Can't use this move unless you've used Stockpile previously. Your Defense and Special Defense raised by Stockpile will go back down to normal.

*22 If used by Ghost-type Pokémon, decreases your HP by half of your max HPs but also decreases the opponent's HP by 1/4 of its max HPs per turn.

*23 Effect will last for the duration of the turn after you switch Pokémon. Effect decreases in Double Battles.

*24 The following effects will be added with a 30% probability. Causes Sleep when used in tall grass and water puddle. Lowers Accuracy by 1 when used on sandy ground. Makes opponent Flinch when used on craggy surface or in caves. Lowers Speed in marsh. Lower Attack by 1 on water. Causes Freeze on snow fields and ice. Causes Paralyze on building floors.

*25 Cause 2x damage if used when the opponent is using Minimize.

*26 When in grass and water puddle, you'll become Grass-type. Sandy land and marsh will make you Ground-type. Rocky surfaces and caves, Rock-type. On water, Water-type. Snowy field and ice, Ice-type. And on building floor, Normal-type.

*27 Causes damage regardless of your opponent's types.

TMS

NO.	MOVES	HOW TO OBTAIN	PRICE
1	Focus Punch	Oreburgh Gate, B1F. (After winning Canalave City Gym battle) / Also, you can use the Ability Pickup.	
2	Dragon Claw	Mt. Coronet (2nd) 1 FL (After visiting Spear Pillar).	
3	Water Pulse	Ravaged Path. (After winning Hearthome City Gym battle.)	
4	Calm Mind	After obtaining the National Pokédex.	48bp
5	Roar	Route 213. (After winning Snowpoint City Gym battle.)	
6	Toxic	Route 212.	
7	Hail	Route 217 / Trade with 10 Green Shards in a home on Route 212.	
8	Bulk Up	After obtaining the National Pokédex. (Battle Park)	48bp
9	Bullet Seed	Route 204.	
10	Hidden Power	At Trainers' School in Jubilife City / As a prize at Veilstone Game Corner.	6000gc
11	Sunny Day	Route 212 / Trade with 10 Red Shards in a home on Route 212.	
12	Taunt	Route 211.	
13	Ice Beam	Route 216 (After winning Snowpoint City Gym battle.) / As a prize at Veilstone Game Corner.	10000gc
14	Blizzard	Lake Acuity / Veilstone Dept. Store 3 FL in Veilstone City.	5500
15	Hyper Beam	Veilstone Dept. Store 3 FL in Veilstone City.	7500
16	Light Screen	Veilstone Dept. Store 3 FL in Veilstone City.	2000
17	Protect	Veilstone Dept. Store 3 FL in Veilstone City.	2000
18	Rain Dance	Route 223 / Trade with 10 Blue Shards in a home on Route 212.	
19	Giga Drain	Route 209. (After winning Hearthome City Gym battle.)	
20	Safeguard	Veilstone Dept. Store 3 FL in Veilstone City.	2000
21	Frustration	Galactic Veilstone Building 3 FL / As a prize at Veilstone Game Corner.	1000gc
22	Solar beam	Veilstone Dept. Store 3 FL in Veilstone City.	3000
23	Iron Tail	Iron Island B2F.	
24	Thunderbolt	Valley Windworks (After winning Hearthome City Gym / As a prize at Veilstone Game Corner.)	1000gc
25	Thunder	Lake Valor (After visiting Spear Pillar) / Veilstone Dept. Store 3 FL in Veilstone City.	5500
26	Earthquake	Wayward Cave (After winning Canalave City Gym battle.) / Also, you can use the Ability Pickup.	
27	Return	Lost Tower 4 FL / As a prize at Veilstone Game Corner.	8000gc
28	Dig	Ruin Maniac Cave.	
29	Psychic	Route 211 (After winning Snowpoint City Gym battle.) / As a prize at Veilstone Game Corner.	10000gc
30	Shadow Ball	Route 210 (After obtaining SecretPotion.)	
31	Brick Break	Oreburgh Gate, B1F. (After obtaining Bicycle.)	
32	Double Team	Wayward Cave / As a prize at Veilstone Game Corner.	4000gc
33	Reflect	Veilstone Dept. Store 3rd FL in Veilstone City.	2000
34	Shock Wave	Route 215.	
35	Flamethrower	Fuego Ironworks / As a prize at Veilstone Game Corner.	10000gc
36	Sludge Bomb	Galactic HQ B2F. (On a passageway between their warehouse and HQs.)	
37	Sandstorm	Trade with 10 Yellow Shards in a home on Route 212.	
38	Fire Blast	Lake Verity (After visiting Spear Pillar) / Veilstone Dept. Store 3 FL in Veilstone City.	5500
39	Rock Tomb	Ravaged Path.	
40	Aerial Ace	Route 213.	
41	Torment	Victory Road 1 FL.	
42	Façade	After obtaining the National Pokédex. (Survival Area)	
43	Secret Power	Amity Square in Hearthome City.	
44	Rest	As a prize at Veilstone Game Corner / Also, you can use the Ability Pickup.	10000gc
45	Attract	Amity Square in Hearthome City.	
46	Thief	Eterna City. (After winning Eterna City Gym battle.)	
47	Steel Wing	Route 209.	
48	Skill Swap	A girl in a house in Canalave City.	
49	Snatch	Galactic HQ 1 FL.	
50	Overheat	After obtaining the National Pokédex.	
51	Roost	Route 210.	
52	Focus Blast	Veilstone Dept. Store 3 FL in Veilstone City.	
53	Energy Ball	After obtaining the National Pokédex.	
54	False Swipe	Veilstone Dept. Store 3 FL in Veilstone City.	
55	Brine	Pastoria City Gym battle.	
56	Fling	A man in a house on Route 222.	
57	Charge Beam	Sunyshore City Gym battle.	
58	Endure	As a prize at Veilstone Game Corner.	2000gc
59	Dragon Pulse	Victory Road 1 FL.	
60	Drain Punch	Veilstone City Gym battle.	
61	Will-O-Wisp	After obtaining the National Pokédex.	32bp
62	Silver Wind	Route 212.	
63	Embargo	A man in Veilstone City.	
64	Explosion	As a reward for your 10 consecutive slot wins at the Game Corner.	
65	Shadow Claw	Hearthome City Gym battle.	
66	Payback	Route 215.	
67	Recycle	An old Lady in Eterna Condominium 2 FL in Eterna City.	
68	Giga Impact	As a prize at Veilstone Game Corner.	20000gc
69	Rock Polish	Mt. Coronet (1st) 1 FL. (After visiting Lake Verity. (2nd))	
70	Flash	Oreburgh Gate B1F. (after winning Oreburgh City Gym battle.) / Veilstone Dept. Store 3 FL in Veilstone City.	
71	Stone Edge	Victory Road 2 FL.	
72	Avalanche	Snowpoint City Gym battle.	
73	Thunder Wave	After obtaining the National Pokédex.	32bp
74	Gyro Ball	As a prize at Veilstone Game Corner.	15000gc
75	Sword Dance	As a prize at Veilstone Game Corner.	4000gc
76	Stealth Rock	Oreburgh City Gym battle.	
77	Psych Up	A boy on Route 211. (After visiting Lake Verity. (2nd))	

bp......battle points
gc......game coins

TMS, CONT.

NO.	MOVES	HOW TO OBTAIN	PRICE
78	Captivate	Route 204. (After winning Eterna City Gym battle.)	
79	Dark Pulse	Victory Road 2 FL.	
80	Rock Slide	Mt. Coronet 2 FL. (2nd).	
81	X-Scissor	Route 221.	
82	Sleep Talk	Eterna Forest. (After winning Eterna City Gym battle.)	
83	Natural Gift	Veilstone Dept. Store 3 FL in Veilstone City.	2000
84	Poison Jab	Route 212. (After winning Hearthome City Gym battle.)	
85	Dream Eater	Valor Lakefront. (After winning Snowpoint City Gym battle.)	
86	Grass Knot	Eterna City Gym battle.	
87	Swagger	Pokémon Mansion.	
88	Pluck	A girl in a house in Floaroma Town.	
89	U-Turn	As a prize at Veilstone Game Corner / Canalave City.	6000gc
90	Substitute	A small room on 2 FL of Forest Mansion. / As a prize at Veilstone Game Corner.	2000gc
91	Flash Cannon	Canalave City Gym battle.	
92	Trick Room	A clown at a cottage on Route 213.	

HMS

NO.	MOVES	HOW TO OBTAIN	PRICE
01	Cut	From Cynthia when she comes to Eterna City.	
02	Fly	At Galactic Warehouse in Veilstone City.	
03	Surf	From the elder of Celestic Town. (After examining a fresco.)	
04	Strength	From an old lady on 5 FL of Lost Tower.	
05	Defog	From a man in Pastoria Great Marsh.	
06	Rock Smash	From a mountain man at Oreburgh Gate.	
07	Waterfall	From Jasmine on the beach front in Sunyshore City. (After visiting Sunyshore City.)	
08	Rock Climb	Route 217.	

CONTEST MOVES

MOVE	CONTEST	POWER	APPEAL
Absorb	Smart	❤	If Voltage goes up two in a row, you earn +3.
Acid	Smart	❤❤❤	A basic performance.
Acid Armor	Tough	-	Doubles your score in the next turn.
Acupressure	Cool	-	Doubles your score in the next turn.
Aerial Ace	Cool	❤❤	If the Pokémon performs first, earn +2.
Agility	Cool	❤❤	Causes your Pokémon to move first in next round.
Air Cutter	Cool	❤❤❤	A basic performance.
Air Slash	Cool	❤❤	If the Pokémon performs first, earn +2.
Amnesia	Cute	-	Doubles your score in the next turn.
Ancientpower	Tough	❤❤	If the Pokémon performs last, earn +2.
Aqua Jet	Beauty	❤❤	Causes your Pokémon to move first in next round.
Aqua Ring	Beauty	-	Appeal Point matches Voltage of judge.
Aqua Tail	Cute	❤❤❤	A basic performance.
Aromatherapy	Smart	-	Appeal Point matches Voltage of judge.
Assist	Cute	❤❤	All Pokémon in next round go in random order.
Assurance	Beauty	❤❤	Earn double the score if your performance is last.
Astonish	Smart	❤❤❤	A basic performance.
Attack Order	Smart	❤❤	If the judges' Voltage goes up, you earn +2.
Attract	Cute	❤❤	No Voltage decrease during same turn.
Aura Sphere	Beauty	❤❤	If the Pokémon performs first, earn +2.
Aurora Beam	Beauty	❤❤	If the Pokémon performs first, earn +2.
Avalanche	Cool	❤❤	Earn double the score if your performance is last.
Barrier	Cool	❤❤	No Voltage increase during same turn.
Baton Pass	Cute	-	High score for low Voltage.
Beat Up	Smart	❤❤	Perform same move twice in a row.
Belly Drum	Cute	-	Doubles your score in the next turn.
Bide	Tough	❤❤	Earn double the score if your performance is last.
Bind	Tough	-	Appeal Point equals round you perform in (1st=1, 2nd=2, etc).
Bite	Tough	❤❤❤	A basic performance.
Blizzard	Beauty	❤❤	If the Pokémon performs first, earn +2.
Block	Cute	❤❤	No Voltage increase during same turn.
Body Slam	Tough	❤❤❤	A basic performance.
Bone Club	Tough	❤❤❤	A basic performance.
Bone Rush	Tough	❤❤	Perform same move twice in a row.
Bounce	Cute	❤	If the same judge has not already been picked, earn +3.
Brave Bird	Cute	❤❤	If the Pokémon performs last, earn +2.
Brick Break	Cool	❤❤❤	A basic performance.
Brine	Smart	❤❤	If the judge's Voltage goes up, earn +2.
Bubble	Cute	❤❤	Causes your Pokémon to move last in next round.
BubbleBeam	Beauty	❤❤	Causes your Pokémon to move last in next round.
Bug Buzz	Cute	❤❤	If the judge's Voltage goes up, earn +2.
Bulk Up	Beauty	-	Doubles your score in the next turn.
Bullet Seed	Cool	❤❤	Perform same move twice in a row.
Calm Mind	Smart	-	Doubles your score in the next turn.
Camouflage	Smart	❤❤	No Voltage increase during same turn.
Captivate	Beauty	❤❤	No Voltage decrease during same turn.
Charge	Smart	-	Doubles your score in the next turn.
Charge Beam	Beauty	❤❤	If the Pokémon performs first, earn +2.
Charm	Cute	❤❤	No Voltage decrease during same turn.
Chatter	Smart	❤	If Pokémon gets the lowest score, you earn +3.
Close Combat	Smart	❤❤	If the previous Pokémon hit max Voltage, earn +3.
Confuse Ray	Smart	❤❤	Lowers Voltage of judges by 1.
Confusion	Smart	❤❤❤	A basic performance.
Constrict	Tough	-	Appeal Point equals round you perform in (1st=1, 2nd=2, etc).
Copycat	Cool	-	If previous performer hits max Voltage, then you earn points equal to its Voltage rating.
Cosmic Power	Cool	-	Doubles your score in the next turn.
Cotton Spore	Beauty	❤❤	Causes your Pokémon to move first in next round.
Counter	Tough	❤❤	Earn double the score if your performance is last.
Cross Chop	Cool	❤❤	If the Pokémon performs last, earn +2.
Cross Poison	Cool	❤❤❤	A basic performance.
Crunch	Tough	❤❤	If the Pokémon performs last, earn +2.
Curse	Tough	-	Appeal Point equals round you perform in (1st=1, 2nd=2, etc).
Cut	Cool	❤❤❤	A basic performance.
Dark Pulse	Cool	❤❤	If the Pokémon performs first, earn +2.
Defend Order	Smart	-	Doubles your score in the next turn.
Defense Curl	Cute	❤❤	No Voltage increase during same turn.
Defog	Beauty	❤❤	No Voltage increase during same turn.
Destiny Bond	Smart	-	If all Pokémon choose the same Judge, earn +15.
Detect	Cool	-	High score for low Voltage.
Dig	Smart	❤	If the same judge has not already been picked, earn +3.
Disable	Smart	❤❤	No Voltage decrease during same turn.
Discharge	Cool	❤❤	If the Pokémon performs first, earn +2.
Dive	Beauty	❤	If the same judge has not already been picked, earn +3.
Dizzy Punch	Cool	-	High score for low Voltage.
Double Hit	Smart	❤❤	Perform same move twice in a row.
Double Team	Cool	❤❤	Causes your Pokémon to move first in next round.
Doubleslap	Tough	❤❤	Perform same move twice in a row.

CONTEST MOVES, CONT.

MOVE	CONTEST	POWER	APPEAL
Dragon Claw	Cool	❤❤	If the Pokémon performs first, earn +2.
Dragon Dance	Cool	-	Doubles your score in the next turn.
Dragon Pulse	Smart	❤❤	If the judge's Voltage goes up, earn +2.
Dragon Rage	Cool	❤❤❤	A basic performance.
Dragon Rush	Cool	❤❤	If the Pokémon performs last, earn +2.
Dragonbreath	Cool	❤❤	If the Pokémon performs first, earn +2.
Drain Punch	Beauty	❤	If Voltage is raised by two Pokémon in a row, earn +3.
Dream Eater	Smart	❤	If Voltage is raised by two Pokémon in a row, earn +3.
Drill Peck	Cool	❤❤❤	A basic performance.
DynamicPunch	Cool	❤❤	If the Pokémon performs last, earn +2.
Earth Power	Smart	❤❤	If the Pokémon performs last, earn +2.
Earthquake	Tough	❤❤	If the Pokémon performs last, earn +2.
Egg Bomb	Tough	❤❤❤	A basic performance.
Embargo	Cute	❤❤	Prevents Voltage from going up in the same turn.
Ember	Beauty	❤❤❤	A basic performance.
Encore	Cute	❤	If Voltage is raised by two Pokémon in a row, earn +3.
Endeavor	Tough	❤❤	Earn double the score if your performance is last.
Endure	Tough	❤❤	No Voltage increase during same turn.
Energy Ball	Beauty	❤❤	If the Pokémon performs first, earn +2.
Explosion	Beauty	-	If all Pokémon choose the same Judge, earn +15.
Extrasensory	Cool	❤❤	If the Pokémon performs first, earn +2.
Extremespeed	Cool	❤❤	Causes your Pokémon to move first in next round.
Facade	Cute	❤❤	Earn double the score if your performance is last.
Faint Attack	Smart	❤❤	If the Pokémon performs last, earn +2.
Fake Out	Cute	❤❤	If the Pokémon performs first, earn +2.
Fake Tears	Smart	❤❤	No Voltage decrease during same turn.
False Swipe	Cool	-	High score for low Voltage.
Featherdance	Beauty	❤❤	No Voltage decrease during same turn.
Feint	Beauty	-	High score for low Voltage.
Fire Blast	Beauty	❤❤	If the Pokémon performs first, earn +2.
Fire Fang	Beauty	❤❤❤	A basic performance.
Fire Punch	Beauty	❤❤	If the Pokémon performs first, earn +2.
Fire Spin	Beauty	-	Appeal Point equals round you perform in (1st=1, 2nd=2, etc).
Fissure	Tough	-	If all Pokémon choose the same Judge, earn +15.
Flail	Cute	❤❤	Earn double the score if your performance is last.
Flame Wheel	Beauty	❤❤	Perform same move twice in a row.
Flamethrower	Beauty	❤❤	If the Pokémon performs first, earn +2.
Flare Blitz	Smart	❤❤	If the previous Pokémon hit max Voltage, earn +3.
Flash	Beauty	❤❤	Lowers Voltage of judges by 1.
Flash Cannon	Smart	❤❤	If the Pokémon performs first, earn +2.
Flatter	Smart	❤❤	No Voltage decrease during same turn.
Fling	Tough	❤	If Pokémon gets the lowest score, you earn +3.
Fly	Smart	❤	If the same judge has not already been picked, earn +3.
Focus Blast	Cool	❤❤	If the Pokémon performs first, earn +2.
Focus Energy	Cool	-	Doubles your score in the next turn.
Focus Punch	Tough	❤	If the same judge has not already been picked, earn +3.
Follow Me	Cute	❤❤	All Pokémon in next round go in random order.
Force Palm	Cool	❤❤	If the Pokémon performs last, earn +2.
Foresight	Smart	❤	If Voltage is raised by two Pokémon in a row, earn +3.
Frustration	Cute	❤❤	If the Pokémon performs last, earn +2.
Fury Attack	Cool	❤❤	Perform same move twice in a row.
Fury Cutter	Cool	❤❤	Perform same move twice in a row.
Fury Swipes	Tough	❤❤	Perform same move twice in a row.
Future Sight	Smart	❤❤	If the Pokémon performs first, earn +2.
Giga Drain	Smart	❤	If Voltage is raised by two Pokémon in a row, earn +3.
Giga Impact	Beauty	❤❤	If the previous Pokémon hit max Voltage, earn +3.
Grass Knot	Smart	❤❤	If the judge's Voltage goes up, earn +2.
Grasswhistle	Smart	❤❤	No Voltage decrease during same turn.
Gravity	Beauty	❤❤	No Voltage increase during same turn.
Growl	Cute	❤❤	No Voltage decrease during same turn.
Growth	Beauty	-	Doubles your score in the next turn.
Grudge	Tough	❤❤	Lowers Voltage of judges by 1.
Guard Swap	Cute	-	High score for low Voltage.
Gunk Shot	Cool	❤❤❤	A basic performance.
Gust	Smart	❤❤❤	A basic performance.
Gyro Ball	Beauty	❤❤	Earn double the score if your performance is last.
Hail	Beauty	❤❤	No Voltage increase during same turn.
Hammer Arm	Cool	❤❤	Causes your Pokémon to move last in next round.
Harden	Tough	❤❤	No Voltage increase during same turn.
Haze	Beauty	❤❤	No Voltage increase during same turn.
Head Smash	Tough	❤❤	If the previous Pokémon hit max Voltage, earn +3.
Heal Bell	Beauty	-	Appeal Point matches Voltage of judge.
Heal Block	Cute	❤❤	No Voltage increase during same turn.
Heal Order	Smart	-	Appeal Point matches Voltage of judge.
Healing Wish	Cute	-	Appeal Point matches Voltage of judge.
Heart Swap	Cool	-	High score for low Voltage.
Helping Hand	Smart	❤	If Voltage is raised by two Pokémon in a row, earn +3.

CONTEST MOVES, CONT.

MOVE	CONTEST	POWER	APPEAL
Hi Jump Kick	Cool	♥♥♥	A basic performance.
Hidden Power	Smart	♥	If Pokémon gets the lowest score, you earn +3.
Horn Attack	Cool	♥♥♥	A basic performance.
Horn Drill	Cool	-	If all Pokémon choose the same Judge, earn +15.
Hydro Pump	Beauty	♥♥	If the Pokémon performs first, earn +2.
Hyper Beam	Cool	♥♥	If the previous Pokémon hit max Voltage, earn +3.
Hyper Fang	Cool	♥♥	If the Pokémon performs last, earn +2.
Hyper Voice	Cool	♥♥♥	A basic performance.
Hypnosis	Smart	♥♥	No Voltage decrease during same turn.
Ice Beam	Beauty	♥♥	If the Pokémon performs first, earn +2.
Ice Fang	Cool	♥♥♥	A basic performance.
Ice Punch	Beauty	♥♥	If the Pokémon performs first, earn +2.
Ice Shard	Beauty	♥♥	Causes your Pokémon to move first in next round.
Icy Wind	Beauty	♥♥	Causes your Pokémon to move last in next round.
Imprison	Smart	♥	If Voltage is raised by two Pokémon in a row, earn +3.
Ingrain	Smart	-	Appeal Point equals round you perform in (1st=1, 2nd=2, etc).
Iron Defense	Tough	♥♥	No Voltage increase during same turn.
Iron Head	Tough	♥♥	If the Pokémon performs last, earn +2.
Iron Tail	Cool	♥♥	If the Pokémon performs last, earn +2.
Jump Kick	Cool	♥♥♥	A basic performance.
Karate Chop	Tough	♥♥♥	A basic performance.
Kinesis	Smart	-	Doubles your score in the next turn.
Knock Off	Smart	♥♥♥	A basic performance.
Last Resort	Cute	-	Appeal Point equals round you perform in (1st=1, 2nd=2, etc).
Leaf Storm	Cute	♥♥	If the previous Pokémon hit max Voltage, earn +3.
Leech Life	Smart	♥	If Voltage is raised by two Pokémon in a row, earn +3.
Leech Seed	Smart	-	Appeal Point equals round you perform in (1st=1, 2nd=2, etc).
Leer	Cool	♥♥	No Voltage decrease during same turn.
Lick	Tough	-	High score for low Voltage.
Light Screen	Beauty	♥♥	No Voltage increase during same turn.
Lock-On	Smart	♥	If Voltage is raised by two Pokémon in a row, earn +3.
Low Kick	Tough	♥♥♥	A basic performance.
Lucky Chant	Cute	♥♥	No Voltage increase during same turn.
Mach Punch	Cool	♥♥	Causes your Pokémon to move first in next round.
Magic Coat	Beauty	♥♥	Earn double the score if your performance is last.
Magical Leaf	Beauty	♥♥	If the Pokémon performs first, earn +2.
Magnitude	Tough	♥♥	If the Pokémon performs last, earn +2.
Me First	Cute	♥♥	Causes your Pokémon to move first in next round.
Mean Look	Beauty	♥♥	Lowers Voltage of judges by 1.
Meditate	Beauty	-	Doubles your score in the next turn.
Mega Drain	Smart	♥	If Voltage is raised by two Pokémon in a row, earn +3.
Megahorn	Cool	♥♥	If the Pokémon performs last, earn +2.
Memento	Tough	-	If all Pokémon choose the same Judge, earn +15.
Metal Burst	Beauty	♥♥	Earn double the score if your performance is last.
Metal Claw	Cool	♥♥	If the Pokémon performs last, earn +2.
Metal Sound	Smart	♥♥	Lowers Voltage of judges by 1.
Meteor Mash	Cool	♥♥	If the Pokémon performs last, earn +2.
Metronome	Cute	♥♥	All Pokémon in next round go in random order.
Mimic	Cute	-	If previous performer hits max Voltage, then you earn points equal to its Voltage rating.
Mind Reader	Smart	♥	If Voltage is raised by two Pokémon in a row, earn +3.
Minimize	Cute	♥♥	No Voltage increase during same turn.
Miracle Eye	Cute	♥	If Voltage is raised by two Pokémon in a row, earn +3.
Mirror Coat	Beauty	♥♥	Earn double the score if your performance is last.
Mirror Move	Smart	♥♥	Earn double the score if your performance is last.
Mirror Shot	Cute	♥♥	If the Pokémon performs first, earn +2.
Mist	Beauty	♥♥	No Voltage increase during same turn.
Moonlight	Beauty	-	Appeal Point matches Voltage of judge.
Morning Sun	Beauty	-	Appeal Point matches Voltage of judge.
Mud Bomb	Smart	♥♥	If the Pokémon performs last, earn +2.
Mud Shot	Tough	♥♥	Causes your Pokémon to move last in next round.
Muddy Water	Tough	♥♥	If the Pokémon performs last, earn +2.
Mud-Slap	Cute	♥♥♥	A basic performance.
Nasty Plot	Cute	-	Doubles your score in the next turn.
Natural Gift	Cool	♥♥	If the Pokémon performs last, earn +2.
Night Shade	Smart	♥♥♥	A basic performance.
Night Slash	Beauty	♥♥♥	A basic performance.
Nightmare	Smart	♥♥	No Voltage decrease during same turn.
Octazooka	Tough	♥♥	If the judge's Voltage goes up, earn +2.
Odor Sleuth	Smart	♥	If Voltage is raised by two Pokémon in a row, earn +3.
Ominous Wind	Smart	-	Doubles your score in the next turn.
Overheat	Beauty	♥♥	If the previous Pokémon hit max Voltage, earn +3.
Pain Split	Smart	♥♥	Lowers Voltage of judges by 1.
Payback	Cool	♥	If the same judge has not already been picked, earn +3.
Peck	Cool	♥♥♥	A basic performance.
Perish Song	Beauty	♥♥	Lowers Voltage of judges by 1.
Petal Dance	Beauty	-	Appeal Point equals round you perform in (1st=1, 2nd=2, etc).
Pin Missile	Cool	♥♥	Perform same move twice in a row.

CONTEST MOVES, CONT.

MOVE	CONTEST	POWER	APPEAL
Pluck	Cute	-	If previous performer hits max Voltage, then you earn points equal to its Voltage rating.
Poison Fang	Smart	❤❤	If the judge's Voltage goes up, earn +2.
Poison Gas	Smart	❤❤❤	A basic performance.
Poison Jab	Smart	❤❤	If the judge's Voltage goes up, earn +2.
Poison Sting	Smart	❤❤	No Voltage decrease during same turn.
Poisonpowder	Smart	❤❤	No Voltage decrease during same turn.
Pound	Tough	❤❤❤	A basic performance.
Powder Snow	Beauty	❤❤❤	A basic performance.
Power Gem	Beauty	❤❤❤	A basic performance.
Power Swap	Beauty	-	High score for low Voltage.
Power Trick	Cool	-	High score for low Voltage.
Power Whip	Beauty	❤❤❤	A basic performance.
Protect	Cute	-	High score for low Voltage.
Psybeam	Beauty	❤❤	If the Pokémon performs first, earn +2.
Psych Up	Smart	-	Doubles your score in the next turn.
Psychic	Smart	❤❤	If the Pokémon performs first, earn +2.
Psycho Shift	Cool	-	High score for low Voltage.
Psy-Cutter	Cool	❤❤	If the Pokémon performs first, earn +2.
Psywave	Smart	❤❤❤	A basic performance.
Punishment	Smart	❤	If Pokémon gets the lowest score, you earn +3.
Pursuit	Smart	❤	If Voltage is raised by two Pokémon in a row, earn +3.
Quick Attack	Cool	❤❤	Causes your Pokémon to move first in next round.
Rage	Cool	-	Doubles your score in the next turn.
Rain Dance	Tough	❤❤	No Voltage increase during same turn.
Razor Leaf	Cool	❤❤❤	A basic performance.
Razor Wind	Cool	❤	If the same judge has not already been picked, earn +3.
Recover	Smart	-	Appeal Point matches Voltage of judge.
Recycle	Smart	-	If previous performer hits max Voltage, then you earn points equal to its Voltage rating.
Reflect	Smart	❤❤	No Voltage increase during same turn.
Refresh	Cute	-	Appeal Point matches Voltage of judge.
Resort	Smart	❤❤	If the previous Pokémon hit max Voltage, earn +3.
Rest	Cute	-	Appeal Point matches Voltage of judge.
Return	Cute	❤❤	If the Pokémon performs first, earn +2.
Revenge	Tough	❤❤	Earn double the score if your performance is last.
Reversal	Cool	❤❤	Earn double the score if your performance is last.
Roar	Cool	❤❤	No Voltage decrease during same turn.
Roar of Time	Cool	❤❤	If the previous Pokémon hit max Voltage, earn +3.
Rock Blast	Tough	❤❤	Perform same move twice in a row.
Rock Climb	Cool	❤❤	If the Pokémon performs last, earn +2.
Rock Polish	Tough	❤❤	Causes your Pokémon to move first in next round.
Rock Slide	Tough	❤❤❤	A basic performance.
Rock Smash	Tough	❤❤	If the Pokémon performs last, earn +2.
Rock Throw	Tough	❤❤❤	A basic performance.
Rock Tomb	Smart	❤❤	Causes your Pokémon to move last in next round.
Role Play	Cute	❤	If Pokémon gets the lowest score, you earn +3.
Rollout	Tough	❤❤	Perform same move twice in a row.
Roost	Cool	-	Appeal Point matches Voltage of judge.
Safeguard	Beauty	❤❤	No Voltage increase during same turn.
Sand Tomb	Smart	-	Appeal Point equals round you perform in (1st=1, 2nd=2, etc).
Sand-Attack	Cute	❤❤	No Voltage decrease during same turn.
Sandstorm	Tough	❤❤	No Voltage increase during same turn.
Scary Face	Tough	❤❤	Causes your Pokémon to move last in next round.
Scratch	Tough	❤❤❤	A basic performance.
Screech	Smart	❤❤	Lowers Voltage of judges by 1.
Secret Power	Smart	❤❤	All Pokémon in next round go in random order.
Seismic Toss	Tough	❤❤❤	A basic performance.
Selfdestruct	Beauty	-	If all Pokémon choose the same Judge, earn +15.
Shadow Ball	Smart	❤❤	If the Pokémon performs first, earn +2.
Shadow Claw	Cute	❤❤	If the Pokémon performs first, earn +2.
Shadow Punch	Smart	❤❤	If the Pokémon performs first, earn +2.
Shadow Sneak	Smart	❤❤	Causes your Pokémon to move first in next round.
Sheer Cold	Beauty	-	If all Pokémon choose the same Judge, earn +15.
Shock Wave	Cool	❤❤	If the Pokémon performs first, earn +2
Signal Beam	Beauty	❤❤	If the judge's Voltage goes up, earn +2.
Silver Wind	Beauty	❤❤	If the judge's Voltage goes up, earn +2.
Sing	Cute	❤❤	No Voltage decrease during same turn.
Skill Swap	Smart	-	If previous performer hits max Voltage, then you earn points equal to its Voltage rating.
Sky Attack	Cool	❤	If the same judge has not already been picked, earn +3.
Slack Off	Cute	-	Appeal Point matches Voltage of judge.
Slam	Tough	❤❤❤	A basic performance.
Slash	Cool	❤❤❤	A basic performance.
Sleep Talk	Cute	❤❤❤	A basic performance.
Sludge Bomb	Tough	❤❤	If the Pokémon performs last, earn +2.
Smokescreen	Smart	❤❤	Lowers Voltage of judges by 1.
Snatch	Smart	-	If previous performer hits max Voltage, then you earn points equal to its Voltage rating.
Snore	Cute	❤❤❤	A basic performance.
Softboiled	Beauty	-	Appeal Point matches Voltage of judge.

CONTEST MOVES, CONT.

MOVE	CONTEST	POWER	APPEAL
Solarbeam	Cool	♥	If the same judge has not already been picked, earn +3.
Sonicboom	Cool	♥♥♥	A basic performance.
Spacial Rend	Tough	♥♥	If the judge's Voltage goes up, earn +2.
Spark	Cool	♥♥♥	A basic performance.
Spit Up	Tough	♥♥	If the Pokémon performs last, earn +2.
Spite	Tough	♥♥	No Voltage decrease during same turn.
Splash	Cute	-	High score for low Voltage.
Stealth Rock	Cool	♥♥	No Voltage increase during same turn.
Steel Wing	Cool	♥♥♥	A basic performance.
Stockpile	Tough	-	Doubles your score in the next turn.
Stomp	Tough	♥♥♥	A basic performance.
Stone Edge	Tough	♥♥	If the judge's Voltage goes up, earn +2.
Strength	Tough	♥♥♥	A basic performance.
String Shot	Smart	♥♥	No Voltage decrease during same turn.
Stun Spore	Smart	♥♥	No Voltage decrease during same turn.
Submission	Cool	♥♥♥	A basic performance.
Substitute	Smart	♥	If Pokémon gets the lowest score, you earn +3.
Sucker Punch	Smart	♥♥	Causes your Pokémon to move first in next round.
Sunny Day	Beauty	♥♥	No Voltage increase during same turn.
Super Fang	Tough	♥♥♥	A basic performance.
Superpower	Tough	♥♥	If the Pokémon performs last, earn +2.
Supersonic	Smart	♥♥	No Voltage decrease during same turn.
Surf	Beauty	♥♥	If the Pokémon performs first, earn +2.
Swagger	Cute	♥♥	No Voltage decrease during same turn.
Swallow	Tough	-	Appeal Point matches Voltage of judge.
Sweet Kiss	Cute	♥♥	No Voltage decrease during same turn.
Sweet Scent	Cute	♥♥	No Voltage decrease during same turn.
Swift	Cool	♥♥	If the Pokémon performs first, earn +2.
Swords Dance	Beauty	-	Doubles your score in the next turn.
Synthesis	Smart	-	Appeal Point matches Voltage of judge.
Tackle	Tough	♥♥♥	A basic performance.
Tail Glow	Beauty	-	Doubles your score in the next turn.
Tail Whip	Cute	♥♥	No Voltage decrease during same turn.
Tailwind	Smart	♥♥	Causes your Pokémon to move first in next round.
Take Down	Tough	♥♥♥	A basic performance.
Taunt	Smart	-	High score for low Voltage.
Teleport	Cool	♥♥	Causes your Pokémon to move first in next round.
Thief	Tough	-	If previous performer hits max Voltage, then you earn points equal to its Voltage rating.
Thrash	Tough	♥♥	Perform same move twice in a row.
Thunder	Cool	♥♥	If the Pokémon performs first, earn +2.
Thunder Fang	Smart	♥♥♥	A basic performance.
Thunder Wave	Cool	♥♥	No Voltage decrease during same turn.
Thunderbolt	Cool	♥♥	If the Pokémon performs first, earn +2.
Thunderpunch	Cool	♥♥	If the Pokémon performs first, earn +2.
Thundershock	Cool	♥♥♥	A basic performance.
Tickle	Cute	♥♥	No Voltage decrease during same turn.
Torment	Tough	-	High score for low Voltage.
Toxic	Smart	♥♥	No Voltage decrease during same turn.
Toxic Spikes	Smart	♥♥	No Voltage increase during same turn.
Trick	Smart	-	If previous performer hits max Voltage, then you earn points equal to its Voltage rating.
Trick Room	Cute	♥♥	All Pokémon in next round go in random order.
Twister	Cool	♥♥♥	A basic performance.
Uproar	Cute	♥♥	Lowers Voltage of judges by 1.
U-turn	Cute	-	High score for low Voltage.
Vine Whip	Cool	♥♥♥	A basic performance.
Vital Throw	Cool	♥♥	Causes your Pokémon to move last in next round.
Volt Tackle	Cool	♥♥	If the previous Pokémon hit max Voltage, earn +3.
Wakeup Slap	Smart	-	High score for low Voltage.
Water Gun	Cute	♥♥♥	A basic performance.
Water Pulse	Beauty	♥♥	If the Pokémon performs first, earn +2.
Water Sport	Cute	♥♥	No Voltage increase during same turn.
Waterfall	Tough	♥♥♥	A basic performance.
Weather Ball	Smart	♥♥	If the judge's Voltage goes up, earn +2.
Whirlpool	Beauty	-	Appeal Point equals round you perform in (1st=1, 2nd=2, etc).
Whirlwind	Smart	-	If all Pokémon choose the same Judge, earn +15.
Will-O-Wisp	Beauty	♥♥	If the Pokémon performs first, earn +2.
Wing Attack	Cool	♥♥♥	A basic performance.
Withdraw	Cute	♥♥	No Voltage increase during same turn.
Wood Hammer	Tough	♥♥	If the Pokémon performs last, earn +2.
Worry Seed	Beauty	♥♥	No Voltage decrease during same turn.
Wrap	Tough	-	Appeal Point equals round you perform in (1st=1, 2nd=2, etc).
Wring Out	Smart	♥♥	If the previous Pokémon hit max Voltage, earn +3.
X-Scissor	Beauty	♥♥	If the Pokémon performs first, earn +2.
Yawn	Cute	♥♥	No Voltage decrease during same turn.
Zen Headbutt	Beauty	♥♥	If the Pokémon performs last, earn +2.

POKÉMON NATURES AND CHARACTERISTICS

POKÉMON NATURES

EACH POKÉMON has its own nature which makes a difference in how their stats grow upon leveling up. They have preferences in Poffin flavors, too. Feed them the Poffin they like and it raises their conditions better.

POKÉMON'S NATURE — STATS	ATTACK	DEFENSE	SPEED	SPECIAL ATTACK	SPECIAL DEFENSE
POFFIN FLAVOR	SPICY	SOUR	SWEET	DRY	BITTER
Hardy					
Lonely	○	▲			
Brave	○		▲		
Adamant	○			▲	
Naughty	○				▲
Bold	▲	○			
Docile					
Relaxed		○	▲		
Impish		○		▲	
Lax		○			▲
Timid	▲		○		
Hasty		▲	○		
Serious					
Jolly			○	▲	
Naive			○		▲
Modest	▲			○	
Mild		▲		○	
Quiet			▲	○	
Bashful					
Rash				○	▲
Calm	▲				○
Gentle		▲			○
Sassy			▲		○
Careful				▲	○
Quirky					

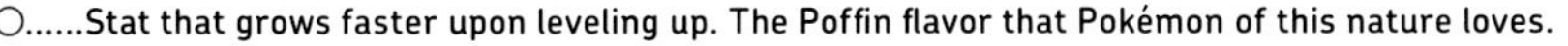

○......Stat that grows faster upon leveling up. The Poffin flavor that Pokémon of this nature loves.

▲......Stat that won't grow much upon leveling up. The Poffin flavor that Pokémon of this nature hates.

POKÉMON'S CHARACTERISTICS

BESIDES NATURE, each Pokémon has characteristics, too. What stat grows faster varies based on these characteristics. For instances, the Pokémon that has a characteristic that makes HP grow faster levels up to have its HP grow faster than other stats.

STAT THAT GROWS FASTER	CHARACTERISTICS
HP	Loves eating Takes naps a lot Daydreams a lot Untidy Loves to relax

STAT THAT GROWS FASTER	CHARACTERISTICS
Attack	Proud of its strength Loves to thrash around Short tempered Loves to fight Hot blooded

STAT THAT GROWS FASTER	CHARACTERISTICS
Defense	Strong Tolerant Tenacious Patient Enduring

STAT THAT GROWS FASTER	CHARACTERISTICS
Speed	Loves to race Sensitive to sound Spaz Clown Runs away fast

STAT THAT GROWS FASTER	CHARACTERISTICS
Special Attack	Curious Mischievous Shrewd Pondering Very organized

STAT THAT GROWS FASTER	CHARACTERISTICS
Special Defense	Obstinate Vanity Competitive Hates to lose Stubborn

POKÉMON ABILITIES

ABILITY	EFFECTS FOR BATTLING POKÉMON	EFFECTS FOR STANDING-BY ALLY POKÉMON
Aftermath	When fainting because of a Direct Attack, causes damage equal to 1/4 of his max HPs to the inflicting opponent.	
Anticipation	Detects if the opponent has super effective moves or one-hit KO moves.	
battle Armor	Prevents your opponent from gaining a critical hit on you.	
Blaze	Increases the strength of your Fire-type moves by 1.5x when your HP falls below 1/3 of its max HPs.	
Chlorophyll	Double your Speed when it's sunny.	
Clear Body	Defends against moves that lower your stats.	
Cloud Nine	Prevents all Pokémon in battle from being affected by weather conditions.	
Cute Charm	When attacked with a Direct Attack, cast Cute Charm over your opponent with a 30% probability.	
Damp	Stops moves like Selfdestruct and Explosion. The Ability Aftermath doesn't work, either.	
Dry Skin	Restores your HP without receiving damage when attacked by Water-type moves. Recovers your HP every turn when it is Raining. (*3)	
Early Bird	Recovers from Sleep.	
Filter	Decreases the damage you receive from super effective moves.	
Flash Fire	Protects you from receiving Fire-type moves and increases the strength of your Fire-type moves by 1.5x.	
Flower Gift	Increases your and your allies' Attack and Special Defense by 1.5x when it's Sunny.	
Guts	Raises your Attack by 1.5x when suffering from status conditions.	
Heatproof	Halves the damages inflicted on you by your opponent's Fire-type moves and by having the Burn condition.	
Honey Gather	Sometimes gathers Honey during battles. (In regular, non-battle situations, too.) (*8)	
Huge Power	Raises your Attack. When you lose your Ability (i.e. Skill Swap), it will only be 1/2.	
Hustle	Raises your Attack by 1.5x but lowers your Physical Attack Accuracy to 80%.	Makes it less probable to encounter high-leveled wild Pokémon.
Hydration	Recovers from status conditions at the end of the turn when it is Raining.	
Immunity	Protects you from the Poison condition.	Makes it more probable for male Pokémon to meet female Pokémon and vice versa.
Inner Focus	Prevents Flinch condition.	
Insomnia	Prevents you from being inflicted with the Sleep condition.	
Intimidate	Upon entering the battle the user of this move lowers the opponent's Attack by 1.	Makes it less probable to come across low-leveled wild Pokémon.
Keen Eye	Prevents your opponent from lowering your Accuracy.	Makes it less probable to encounter low-leveled wild Pokémon.
Klutz	Prevents your effective items from being effective in battles.	
Levitate	Protects you from Ground-type moves.	
Limber	Prevents you from being inflicted with the Paralyze condition.	
Liquid Ooze	Inflicts damage on your opponent when they use a healing move that absorbs your HP.	
Magic Guard	Prevents all moves (except Direct Attacks) from decreasing your HP. (*7)	
Marvel Scale	Increases your Defense by 1.5x when affected by status conditions.	
Mold Breaker	Lets you use your moves without being affected by your opponent's Abilities. (*1)	
Natural Cure	Heals your status conditions when you withdraws from the battle.	
No Guard	Makes each others' moves always land without fail.	Makes it more probable to come across wild Pokémon.
Oblivious	Prevents you from Attract.	
Overgrow	Increases the strength of your Grass-type moves by 1.5x when your HP falls below 1/3 of its max HPs.	
Own Tempo	Protects you from the Confuse condition.	
Pick Up	Occasionally picks up items during battles. (In regular, non-battle situations, too.) (*9)	
Poison Point	When attacked with a Direct Attack, causes your opponent to be Poisoned with a 30% probability.	
Pressure	When attacked, it decreases PP of your opponent's move by 2.	Makes it less probable to encounter high-leveled wild Pokémon.
Pure Power	Raises your Attack. When you lose your Ability (i.e. Skill Swap), it will only be 1/2.	
Rivalry	Raises your Attack towards the same-gender opponents. Lowers it towards opposite gender opponents. (*5)	
Rock Head	Prevents you from suffering the effects of moves like Take Down and Double-Edge.	
Run Away	Lets all Pokémon flee except for Trainer battles.	
Sand Stream	Upon entering the battle the user of this move creates a Sandstorm.	
Sand Veil	Raises your Accuracy when a Sandstorm occurs.	Makes it less probable that you will encounter wild Pokémon when a Sandstorm occurs.
Serene Grace	Doubles the probability of producing the move's additional effects.	
Shed Skin	Heals your status conditions in each turn with a 1/3 probability.	
Shield Dust	Defends against additional effects of moves.	
Simple	Doubles your stat changes.	
Sniper	Increases the damage of the move when it is a critical hit.	
Snow Warning	Makes it Hail upon entering the battle.	
Sound Proof	Defends against sound moves (*6) like Uproar and Sing.	
Static	When attacked with a Direct Attack, causes your opponent to be Paralyzed with a 30% probability.	Makes it more probable that you will encounter Electric-type Pokémon.
Steadfast	Raises your Speed by 1 every time your opponent flinches.	
Stench	(No effect.)	Makes it less probable to come across wild Pokémon.
Sticky Hold	Prevents theft of your items.	Makes it more probable you will catch Pokémon when you fish.
Storm Drain	Draws all Water-type moves to you in 2-on-2 battles.	
Sturdy	Defends against one-hit-knock-out moves like Horn Drill and Sheer Cold.	
Suction Cups	Defends against moves that makes you switch in and out such as Whirlwind and Roar.	Makes it more probable you will catch Pokémon when you fish.
Super Luck	Makes it more probable that you produce a critical hit.	
Swarm	Increases the strength of your Bug-type moves by 1.5x when your HP falls below 1/3 of its max HPs.	
Swift Swim	Doubles your Speed when it is raining.	
Synchronize	Makes your opponent suffer from the same status conditions when you are inflicted with the Poison, Paralyze or Burn condition.	Makes it more probable that you will encounter Pokémon with the same nature as you.
Tangled Feet	Raises your Accuracy when you're Confused.	
Technician	Increases the power of moves that are less than 60 in Power by 1.5x. (*4)	
Thick Fat	Halves the damage inflicted on you by your opponent's Fire and Ice-type moves.	
Torrent	Increases the strength of your Water-type moves by 1.5x when your HP falls below 1/3 of its max HPs.	
Unaware	You are unaffected by your opponent's stats changes.	
Unburden	Doubles your Speed when you run out of items. Your Speed will be back to normal when you have items again. (*2)	
Water Absorb	Restores your HP without receiving damage when attacked by Water-type moves.	
Water Veil	Protects you from the Burn condition.	

ADDITIONAL EFFECTS OF ABILITIES

*1 Except for Abilities that have post-attack effects. For instance, you can deliver a critical hit on an opponent with battle Armor, but still suffer damage by Rough Skin.
*2 Not effective if you don't have any items in the beginning.
*3 Increases the damage by Fire-type moves. Receive damage every turn when it's sunny.
*4 Includes the moves that change the strength, and cases the effects of moves change the strength.
*5 Has no effect on Pokémon that have no gender.
*6 The moves, Snore, Heal Bell, Screech, Sing, Chatter, Metal Sound, Grasswhistle, Uproar, Super Sonic, Growl, Hyper Voice, Roar, Perish Song, Bug Buzz.
*7 Liquid Ooze and Aftermath, Sandstorm and Hail Conditions, Poison, Badly Poisoned, Burn, Nightmare, Curse, Bind, Sand Tomb, Fire Spin, Wrap. Effects from moves Poison Spikes, Stealth Rock. Effects of items Black Sludge, Sticky Barb. Backlash of your own move. Backlash of your unsuccessful moves.
*8 Probability of Gathering (Pickup) increases as Pokémon's level goes up.
*9 Items change based on Pokémon's level.

ITEMS

ITEM	DESCRIPTION	HOW TO OBTAIN	PRICE
Adamant Orb	Exclusively for Dialga. Raises the strength of Dragon- and Steel-type moves.	Spear Pillar. (Diamond only)	
Air Mail	A colorfully printed letter.	Jubilife City / Eterna City.	50
Amulet Coin	Let your Pokémon battle at least once and the prize will be doubled.	Amity Square in Hearthome City.	
Antidote	Cures special condition Poisoned.	Pokémart. (From the beginning.)	100
Armor Fossil	A Pokémon fossil. Will be restored into Shieldon.	Dig out in Underground. (Pearl only)	
Awakening	Cures special condition Sleep.	Pokémart. (After winning Oreburgh City Gym battle.)	250
Big Mushroom	Can be sold for 2500 Poké Dollars.	Mt. Coronet.	
Big Pearl	Can be sold for 3750 Poké Dollars.	Route 213.	
Big Root	Allows you to heal more with HP absorbing moves.	Route 214.	
Black Belt	Raises the strength of Fighting-type moves.	An old man in a house on Route 221.	
Black Glasses	Raises the strength of Dark-type moves.	Talk to an old man in a house in Celestic Town in the daytime.	
Black Sludge	Restores your HPs during battles. (*3)	Wild Croagunk sometimes have it.	
Bloom Mail	A letter that has pretty flower patterns printed on it.	Floaroma Town.	50
Blue Scarf	Pokémon will score high in a Beauty Contest.	A Scarf man in Pastoria City.	
Blue Shard	Collect 10 of them and you can trade them for TM18 Rain Dance.	Dig out in Underground.	
Bubble Mail	A letter that has a picture of a world of blue water printed on it.	Veilstone Dept. Store 1 FL.	50
Burn Heal	Cures Burn.	Pokémart. (After winning Oreburgh City Gym battle.)	250
Calcium	Raises the basic points of Special Attack.	Veilstone Dept. Store 2 FL / Route 209.	9800
Carbos	Raises the basic points of Speed.	Veilstone Dept. Store 2 FL / Route 220.	9800
Choice Specs	Lets you use only one same move but raises your Special Attack by 1.5x.	Talk to a man in a house in Celestic Town.	
Cleanse Tag	Less likely to encounter wild Pokémon if held by the first Pokémon in the party.	An old lady on the Lost Tower 5 FL.	
Clefairy Doll	Makes sure that you will be able to elude wild Pokémon.	Veilstone Dept. Store 1 FL.	1000
Damp Mulch	Keeps the soil moist which slows down the berry's growing process.	Old Man in Berry House on Route 208.	200
Damp Rock	Makes the effect of the move Rain Dance last longer.	Dig out in Underground.	
Dawn Stone	Makes a specific Pokémon evolve.	Mt. Coronet (2nd) 1 FL.	
Dire Hit	Makes it easier that your Pokémon's move will be a critical hit.	Veilstone Dept. Store 2 FL / Route 207.	650
Draco Plate	Raises the strength of Dragon-type moves.	Dig out in Underground.	
Dread Plate	Raises the strength of Dark-type moves.	Old Chateau / Dig out in Underground.	
Dusk Stone	Makes a specific Pokémon evolve.	Galactic Warehouse.	
Earth Plate	Raises the strength of Ground-type moves.	Oreburgh Gate B1F / Dig out in Underground.	
Elixir	Restores PP of all the moves by 10 points.	Route 212 / Galactic Veilstone Building 2 FL.	
Energy Root	Restores Pokémon's HP by 200 points. Very bitter.	Herb Shop in Eterna City.	800
EnergyPowder	Restores Pokémon's HP by 50 points. Very bitter.	Herb Shop in Eterna City.	500
Escape Rope	When deep inside of caves and caverns, it enables you to come back to the entrance.	Pokémart. (After winning Oreburgh City Gym battle.)	550
Ether	Restores PP of one move by 10 points.	Eterna Forest / Route 215.	
Everstone	Prevents Pokémon from evolving.	Dig out in Underground.	
Exp. Share	Gains experience points without fighting in battles.	From Prof. Rowan's assistant in Eterna City.	
Expert Belt	Raises the strength of a move when it is super effective.	An old man in a house on Route 221.	
Fire Stone	Makes a specific Pokémon evolve.	Fuego Ironworks / Dig out in Underground.	
Fist Plate	Raises the strength of Fighting-type moves.	Route 215 / Dig out in Underground.	
Flame Mail	A letter that has a picture of a world of red blazing fire printed on it.	Veilstone Dept. Store 1 FL.	50
Flame Plate	Raises the strength of Fire-type moves.	Dig out in Underground.	
Focus Band	When HP is full, always leaves 1 HP even after receiving a move that makes you faint.	An old man in a house on Route 221.	
Fresh Water	Restores Pokémon's HP by 50 points.	Veilstone Dept. Store 5 FL.	200
Full Heal	Cures all the special conditions.	Pokémart. (After winning Hearthome City Gym battle.)	600
Full Incense	Makes you attack second.	Veilstone City.	
Full Restore	Restores all your HP and cures all the special conditions.	Pokémart. (After winning Sunyshore City Gym battle.)	3000
Gooey Mulch	Makes your berry ripe and fall quicker and germinate more frequently.	Old Man in Berry House on Route 208.	200
Grass Mail	A letter that has a picture of refreshing green grass field printed on it.	Veilstone Dept. Store 1 FL.	50
Green Scarf	Pokémon will score high in a Smartness division.	A Scarf Man in Pastoria City.	
Green Shard	Collect 10 of them and you can trade them for TM07 Hail.	Dig out in Underground.	
Grip Claw	Makes the effect of the moves Bind and Wrap last longer.	Wayward Cave B1F.	
Growth Mulch	Keeps the soil relatively dry which makes the berry grow faster.	Old Man in Berry House on Route 208.	200

ITEMS, CONT.

ITEM	DESCRIPTION	HOW TO OBTAIN	PRICE
Guard Spec.	Prevents your ally's stats from decreasing (being lowered) for 5 turns.	Veilstone Dept. Store 2 FL / Route 215.	700
Hard Stone	Raises the strength of Rock-type moves.	Dig out in Underground.	
Heal Powder	Cures all the special conditions. Very bitter.	Herb Shop in Eterna City.	450
Heart Mail	A letter that has a picture of a big heart printed on it.	Hearthome City.	50
Heart Scale	Lets you learn a move from Move Tutor in Pastoria City.	Dig out in Underground.	
Heat Rock	Makes the effect of the move Sunny Day last longer.	Dig out in Underground.	
Honey	Lures wild Pokémon. You can use it on trees.	Floaroma Town / Wild Combee always have it.	100
HP Up	Permanently raises a Pokémon's HP.	Veilstone Dept. Store 2 FL / Iron Island B2F.	9800
Hyper Potion	Restores Pokémon's HP by 200 points.	Pokémart (After winning Hearthome City Gym battle).	1200
Ice Heal	Recovers from being Frozen.	Pokémart (After winning Oreburgh City Gym battle).	250
Icicle Plate	Raises the strength of Ice-type moves.	A house on Route 217 / Dig out in Underground.	
Icy Rock	Makes the effect of the move Hail last longer.	Dig out in Underground.	
Insect Plate	Raises the strength of Bug-type moves.	Dig out in Underground.	
Iron	Raises the basic points of Defense.	Veilstone Dept. Store 2 FL / Route 217.	9800
Iron Ball	Lowers your Speed. (*2)	Iron Island B1F / Dig out in Underground.	
Iron Plate	Raises the strength of Steel-type moves.	Dig out in Underground.	
King's Rock	Sometimes makes the opponent flinch when your Pokémon uses attack moves.	Pokémon with Ability Pickup sometimes pick them up.	
Lava Cookie	A Lavaridge specialty. Cures all the special conditions.	Return a Suite Key to a woman at Valor Lakefront.	
Leaf Stone	Makes specific Pokémon evolve.	Floaroma Meadow / Dig out in Underground.	
Leftovers	Gradually restores your HPs every turn.	Wild Munchlax always have it.	
Lemonade	Restores your HPs by 80.	Veilstone Dept. Store 5 FL.	350
Light Ball	Equipped on Pikachu, doubles Attack and Special Attack.	Wild Pikachu sometimes have it.	
Light Clay	Makes the effect of the moves Reflect and Light Screen last longer.	Mt. Coronet B1F / Dig out in Underground.	
Luck Incense	Let the Pokémon holding it battle at least once and the prize will be doubled.	Ravaged Path.	
Lucky Egg	Lets you gain a little extra bonus experience points.	Wild Chansey sometimes have it.	
Lustrous Orb	Exclusively for Palkia. Raises the strength of Dragon- and Water-type moves.	Spear Pillar (Pearl only)	
Macho Brace	Lowers your Speed by half but raises your stats basic points.	Show 3 kinds of Burmy to the boy in a house in Pastoria City.	
Magnet	Raises the strength of Electric-type moves.	Iron Island B2F.	
Max Elixir	Restores all the PP of all moves.	Mt. Coronet (1st) B1F.	
Max Ether	Restores all the PP of one move.	Iron Island B2F / Wayward Cave.	
Max Potion	Restores all HP.	Pokémart (After winning Snowpoint City Gym battle).	2500
Max Repel	Prevents you from encountering wild Pokémon during the time you walk for 250 steps.	Pokémart (After winning Hearthome City Gym battle).	700
Max Revive	Restores all of the HPs of a fainted Pokémon.	Route 214 / Galactic Veilstone Building 2 FL / Dig out in Underground.	
Meadow Plate	Raises the strength of Grass-type moves.	Dig out in Underground.	
Mental Herb	Cures Cute Charm. Good for one use.	Route 216.	
Metal Coat	Raises the strength of Steel-type moves.	Wild Steelix and Bronzor sometimes have it.	
Metronome	Raises the strength of a certain move if used consecutively.	As a prize item at Veilstone Game Corner (for 1000 coins).	
Mind Plate	Raises the strength of Psychic-type moves.	Solaceon Ruins B4F / Dig out in Underground.	
Miracle Seed	Raises the strength of Grass-type moves.	Floaroma Town / Floaroma Meadow.	
Moomoo Milk	Restores your HP by 100.	At Café Cabin on Route 210.	500
Moon Stone	Makes a specific Pokémon evolve.	Wild Clefairy sometimes have it / Dig out in Underground.	
Mystic Water	Raises the strength of Water-type moves.	Pastoria City.	
NeverMeltIce	Raises the strength of Ice-type moves.	Wild Snover have it sometimes.	
Nugget	Can be sold for 5000 Poké Dollars.	Solaceon Ruins B4F.	
Odd Incense	Equipped on Pokémon, it raises the strength of Psychic-type moves.	Solaceon Ruins B4F.	
Odd Keystone	A stone to be framed in on the broken stone tower on Route 209.	A man on Route 208.	
Old Gateau	A secret specialty of Eterna City. Cures all the special conditions.	Old Chateau 2 FL.	
Oval Stone	Makes specific Pokémon evolve.	Lost Tower 2 FL.	
Parlyz Heal	Cures Paralysis.	Pokémart (from the beginning).	200
Pearl	Can be sold for 700 Poké Dollars.	Route 223.	
Pink Scarf	Pokémon will score high in the Cuteness Contest.	A Scarf Man in Pastoria City.	
Poison Barb	Raises the strength of Poison-type moves.	Route 206 / Wild Budew and Roselia sometimes have it.	
Potion	Restores Pokémon's HP by 20 points.	Pokémart (from the beginning).	300
PP Up	Raises the max PP of a move by 1.	Veilstone City / Route 213.	
Protein	Raises the basic points of your Attack.	Veilstone Dept. Store 2 FL / Route 221.	9800
Pure Incense	Less likely to encounter wild Pokémon if held by the first Pokémon in the party.	Route 221.	
Quick Claw	Makes you able to attack first sometimes.	A woman on 1 FL in condominiums in Jubilife City.	
Rare Bone	Can be sold for 5000 Poké Dollars.	Dig out in Underground.	
Rare Candy	Raise your Pokémon's level by 1.	Wayward Cave / Solaceon Ruins B4F.	
Razor Claw	Makes it easier that your Pokémon's move will be a critical hit.	Victory Road 1 FL.	
Red Scarf	Pokémon will score high in a Coolness contest.	A Scarf man in Pastoria City.	
Red Shard	Collect 10 of them and you can trade them for TM11 Sunny Day.	Dig out in Underground.	
Repel	Prevents you from encountering wild Pokémon during the time you walk for 100 steps.	Pokémart (After winning Oreburgh City Gym battle).	350
Revival Herb	Fully recovers from fainting.	Herb Shop in Eterna City.	2800
Revive	Restores half of the HPs of a fainting Pokémon.	Pokémart (After winning Veilstone City Gym battle) / Dig out in Underground.	1500
Rock Incense	Raises the strength of Rock-type moves.	Fuego Ironworks.	
Rose Incense	Raises the strength of Grass-type moves.	Route 212.	
Sea Incense	Raises the strength of Water-type moves.	Route 204.	
Shed Shell	Makes it certain that your Pokémon's able to switch with its ally.	Wild Beautifly and Dustox sometimes have it.	
Shell Bell	Restores HP by 1/8 of the damage done to your opponent.	A woman on 2 FL of a condominium in Hearthome City.	
Shiny Stone	Makes specific Pokémon evolve.	Iron Island B3F.	
Silk Scarf	Raises the strength of Normal-type moves.	As a prize item at Veilstone Game Corner (for 1000 coins).	
Silverpowder	Raises the strength of Bug-type moves.	Eterna Forest.	
Skull Fossil	A Pokémon fossil. Will be restored into Cranidos.	Dig out in Underground (Diamond only).	
Sky Plate	Raises the strength of Flying-type moves.	Dig out in Underground.	
Smoke Ball	Makes sure that you will be able to escape from wild Pokémon.	Route 210.	
Smooth Rock	Makes the effect of the move Sandstorm last longer.	Dig out in Underground.	

ITEMS, CONT.

ITEM	DESCRIPTION	HOW TO OBTAIN	PRICE
Snow Mail	A letter that has a picture of a world of cold snow printed on it.	Snowpoint City.	50
Soda Pop	Restores Pokémon's HP by 60 points.	Veilstone Dept. Store 5 FL / Route 212.	300
Soft Sand	Raises the strength of Ground-type moves.	Mt. Coronet (1st) B1F.	
Soothe Bell	Makes your Pokémon bond better.	Pokémon Mansion.	
Space Mail	A letter that has a picture of outer space printed on it.	Veilstone Dept. Store 1 FL.	50
Spell Tag	Raises the strength of Ghost-type moves.	A woman in a house on Route 217.	
Splash Plate	Raises the strength of Water-type moves.	Route 220 / Dig out in Underground.	
Spooky Plate	Raises the strength of Ghost-type moves.	At Amity Square in Hearthome City / Dig out in Underground.	
Stable Mulch	Makes your berry take longer to ripen and fall.	Old Man in Berry House on Route 208.	200
Star Piece	Can be sold for 4900 Poké Dollars.	Dig out in Underground.	
Stardust	Can be sold for 1000 Poké Dollars.	Oreburgh Gate B1F / Mt. Coronet (1st) B1F.	
Steel Mail	A letter that has a picture of cool machinery printed on it.	Sunyshore City.	50
Sticky Barb	Receives damage in each turn (*1).	A man on Veilstone Dept. Store 5 FL.	
Stone Plate	Raises the strength of Rock-type moves.	Dig out in Underground.	
Sun Stone	Makes specific Pokémon evolve.	Dig out in Underground.	
Super Potion	Restores Pokémon's HP by 50 points.	Pokémart (After winning Oreburgh City Gym battle).	700
Super Repel	Prevents you from encountering wild Pokémon during the time you walk for 200 steps.	Pokémart (After winning Veilstone City Gym battle).	500
Thunderstone	Makes a specific Pokémon evolve.	Sunyshore City / Dig out in Underground.	
TinyMushroom	Can be sold for 250 Poké Dollars.	Mt. Coronet.	
Toxic Plate	Raises the strength of Poison-type moves.	Dig out in Underground.	
Tunnel Mail	A letter that has a picture of a coal mine printed on it.	Oreburgh City.	50
TwistedSpoon	Raises the strength of Psychic-type moves.	Wild Abra and Kadabra sometimes have it.	
Water Stone	Makes a specific Pokémon evolve.	Route 214 / Dig out in Underground.	
Wave Incense	Raises the strength of Water-type moves.	Route 210.	
White Herb	Restores the lowered stats. Good for only one use.	Pokémon with Ability Pickup sometimes pick them up.	
Wide Lens	Raises your accuracy.	As a prize item at Veilstone Game Corner (for 1000 coins).	
Wise Glasses	Raises the strength of Special Attacks.	Talk to a man in a house in Celestic Town at night.	
X Accuracy	Raises the user Pokémon's Accuracy.	Veilstone Dept. Store 2 FL / Route 209.	950
X Attack	Raises the user Pokémon's Attack by 1.	Veilstone Dept. Store 2 FL / Route 205.	500
X Defend	Raises the user Pokémon's Defense by 1.	Veilstone Dept. Store 2 FL / Oreburgh Mine.	550
X Sp. Def	Raises the user Pokémon's Special Defense by 1.	Veilstone Dept. Store 2 FL / Route 214.	350
X Special	Raises the user Pokémon's Special Attack by 1.	Veilstone Dept. Store 2 FL / Route 212.	350
X Speed	Raises the user Pokémon's Speed by 1.	Veilstone Dept. Store 2 FL / Route 208.	350
Yellow Scarf	Pokémon will score high in a Tough division.	A Scarf man in Pastoria City.	
Yellow Shard	Collect 10 of them and you can trade them for TM37 Sandstorm.	Dig out in Underground.	
Zap Plate	Raises the strength of Electric-type moves.	Dig out in Underground.	
Zinc	Raises the basic points of Special Defense.	Veilstone Dept. Store 2 FL / Route 212.	9800
Zoom Lense	Makes it probable that your move will land when you attack after your opponent.	As a prize item at Veilstone Game Corner (for 1000 coins).	

KEY ITEMS

KEY ITEMS	DESCRIPTION	HOW TO OBTAIN	PRICE
Bicycle	A fast running Bicycle. Can shift gears.	From a store manager of a Bike Shop.	
Coin Case	A case that can contain 50000 coins.	From a clown in a house in Veilstone City.	
Coupon 1	A ticket to be exchanged for a Pokétch application.	Correctly answer the clown's quiz in Jubilife City.	
Coupon 2	A ticket to be exchanged for a Pokétch application.	Correctly answer the clown's quiz in Jubilife City.	
Coupon 3	A ticket to be exchanged for a Pokétch application.	Correctly answer the clown's quiz in Jubilife City.	
Explorer Kit	A set of tools that are useful for explorations. You can go to the Underground.	From Underground Man in Eterna City.	
Fashion Case	A case that neatly contains your stickers.	From an employee of Jubilife TV in Jubilife City.	
Galactic Key	A card key that decipher the security code to Team Galactic HQs.	B2F in Galactic Warehouse to Galactic Veilstone Building.	
Good Rod	A new good fishing rod. Catches Pokémon when used on waterfront.	From a fisher on Route 209.	
Journal	A notebook that records the details of your journey.	From your mom in Twinleaf Town.	
Old Charm	A charm Cynthia entrusted you with to be handed over to the elder of Celestic Town.	From Cynthia that appears after you use Secret Potion on Route 210.	
Old Rod	An old ragged fishing rod. Catches Pokémon when used at waterfront.	From a fisher in Jubilife City.	
Pal Pad	A pad that registers your friends, records the details of your plays.	From Teala at Pokémon Wi-Fi Club in Oreburgh City.	
Parcel	You are keeping for your rival's mom to later deliver to your rival.	From your rival's mom in Twinleaf Town.	
Poffin Case	A case that keeps Poffin you've made.	From the president of Pokémon Fan Club in Hearthome City.	
Seal Case	A case that contains stickers to put on your Ball Capsule.	From a woman in a house in Solaceon Town.	
Secret Potion	A medicine to cure headaches of a group of Psyduck on Route 201.	From Cynthia on Valor Lakefront.	
Sprayduck	A watering tool. Used to grow your berries.	From a sales person at a flower shop in Floaroma Town.	
Storage Key	A key to Galactic warehouse in Veilstone City.	From a Team Galactic grunt at Galactic Veilstone Building in Veilstone City.	
Suite Key	A key from the Hotel Grand Lake.	Route 213.	
Town Map	A map that's ready and usable at anytime. Check your current whereabouts as well.	Deliver the package to your rival in Jubilife City.	
Vs. Seeker	Detects other Pokémon Trainers who want to battle. Gets charged by your walking.	From Professor's assistant on Route 207.	
Works Key	A key to enter the Valley Windworks in the valley.	From a Team Galactic Grunt in Floaroma Town.	

ADDITIONAL DESCRIPTIONS

1 Sometimes it sticks to something it touches and cause damage.
2 It makes Flying-type Pokémon or the ones with Ability Levitate susceptible to Ground-type moves.
3 It works only for Poison-type Pokémon. Decreases HPs of all other Pokémon that are not Poison-type.

ITEMS – POKÉ BALLS

ITEM	DESCRIPTION	HOW TO OBTAIN	PRICE
Poké Ball	For catching wild Pokémon	Pokémart (From the beginning).	200
Great Ball	Easier to catch Pokémon with than Poké Ball.	Pokémart (After winning Veilstone City Gym battle).	600
Ultra Ball	Easier to catch Pokémon with than Great Ball.	Pokémart (After winning Hearthome City Gym battle).	1200
Master Ball	Always catches any wild Pokémon.	From Cyrus on Galactic Veilstone Building 4 FL.	
Net Ball	Works well on Bug- and Water-type Pokémon.	Oreburgh City / Floaroma City.	1000
Nest Ball	The weaker the Pokémon is, the easier the capture.	Eterna City / Hearthome City.	1000
Repeat Ball	Works well on Pokémon you've caught before.	Canalave City / Pokémon League.	1000
Timer Ball	The more turns, the easier the capture.	Celestic Town / Snowpoint City.	1000
Luxury Ball	Makes your captured Pokémon bond with you.	Sunyshore City / Pokémon League.	1000
Dusk Ball	Makes it easier to catch Pokémon at night or in dark places.	Solaceon Town / Pastoria City.	1000
Heal Ball	Heals HP and special conditions of the Pokémon you've caught.	Jubilife City / Oreburgh City.	300
Quick Ball	Use this ball right in the beginning of a battle.	Pastoria City / Celestic Town.	1000
Dive Ball	Makes it easier to catch Pokémon living in water.	Pokémon News Press in Solaceon Town.	
Premier Ball	A rare Poké Ball that commemorates something.	Purchase 10 Poké Balls at a time.	
Safari Ball	A special ball you can use only in Pastoria Great Marsh.	Pastoria Great Marsh (you get 30 balls for 500 Poké Dollars admission).	

WILD POKÉMON ITEMS

NO.	POKÉMON	ALWAYS	OFTEN	SOMETIMES
10	Starly			Yache Berry
11	Staravia			Yache Berry
14	Bibarel		Oran Berry	Sitrus Berry
15	Kricketot			Metronome
16	Kricketune			Metronome
20	Abra			Twisted Spoon
21	Kadabra			Twisted Spoon
25	Budew			Poison Barb
26	Roselia			Poison Barb
31	Geodude			Everstone
32	Graveler			Everstone
35	Steelix			Metal Coat
50	Beautifly (Diamond only)			Shed Shell
52	Dustox (Pearl only)			Shed Shell
53	Combee	Honey		
56	Buizel			Wacan Berry
57	Floatzel			Wacan Berry
58	Cherubi			Miracle Seed
67	Buneary			Chople Berry
76	Glameow (Pearl only)			Cheri Berry
77	Purugly (Pearl only)			Cheri Berry
82	Chingling			Colbur Berry
83	Chimecho			Colbur Berry
84	Stunky (Diamond only)			Pecha Berry
85	Skuntank (Diamond only)			Pecha Berry
88	Bronzor			Metal Coat
89	Bronzong			Metal Coat
90	Ponyta			Shuca Berry
94	Mime Jr. (Diamond only)			Leppa Berry
95	Mr. Mime (Diamond only)			Leppa Berry
97	Chansey		Oval Stone	Lucky Egg
99	Cleffa		Leppa Berry	Moon Stone
100	Clefairy		Leppa Berry	Moon Stone
102	Chatot			Metronome
103	Pichu			Oran Berry
104	Pikachu		Oran Berry	Light Ball
109	Gible			Haban Berry
112	Munchlax	Leftovers		
121	Girafarig			Persim Berry
127	Skorupi			Poison Barb
129	Croagunk			Black Sludge
134	Finneon			Rindo Berry
136	Tentacool			Poison Barb
137	Tentacruel			Poison Barb
142	Snover			NeverMeltIce
143	Abomasnow			NeverMeltIce
144	Sneasel		Grip Claw	Quick Claw

ITEMS POKÉMON PICK UP WITH THE ABILITY PICK UP

ITEMS	LEVEL OF POKÉMON THAT HAS PICKUP									
	LOW LEVEL								HIGH LEVEL	LEVEL 100
Potion	◎									
Antidote	○	◎								
Super Potion	○	○	◎							
Great Ball	○	○	○	◎						
Repel	○	○	○	○	◎					
Escape Rope	○	○	○	○	○	◎				
Full Heal	○	○	○	○	○	○	◎			
Hyper Potion	△	○	○	○	○	○	○	◎		
Ultra Ball	△	△	○	○	○	○	○	○	◎	
Revive		△	△	○	○	○	○	○	○	◎
Rare Candy			△	△	○	○	○	○	○	○
Dusk Sone				△	△	○	○	○	○	○
Shiny Stone					△	△	○	○	○	○
Dawn Stone						△	△	○	○	○
Full Restore							△	△	○	○
Max Revive								△	△	○
PP Up									△	△
Max Elixir										△
Hyper Potion	▲									
Nugget	▲	▲								
King's Rock		▲	▲							
Full Restore			▲	▲						
Ether				▲	▲					
White Herb					▲	▲				
TM44 Rest						▲	▲			
Elixir							▲	▲		
TM01 Focus Punch								▲	▲	
Leftovers									▲	▲
TM26 Earthquake										▲

◎........Often ○........Sometimes △........Occasionally ▲........Rarely

ACCESSORIES POKÉMON PICK UP AT AMITY SQUARE

PROBABILITY	POKÉMON				
	CLEFAIRY	DRIFLOON	PACHIRISU / PSYDUCK	PIKACHU	BUNEARY / HAPPINY
Sometimes	White Fluff	Pink Fluff	Jagged Boulder	Orange Fluff	Pink Scale
Sometimes	Orange Fluff	Red Feather	Snaggy Pebble	Brown Fluff	Shed Horn
Sometimes	White Feather	Yellow Feather	Brown Fluff	Small Leaf	Pink Fluff
Sometimes	Mini Pebble	Black Beard	Mini Pebble	Red Feather	Yellow Feather
Sometimes	Small Leaf	Narrow Scale	Black Moustache	Yellow Feather	Shed Claw
Sometimes	Blue Scale	White Fluff	Shed Horn	Yellow Fluff	Black Fluff
Sometimes	Magost Berry	Magost Berry	Magost Berry	Magost Berry	Magost Berry
Sometimes	Cornn Berry	Cornn Berry	Cornn Berry	Cornn Berry	Cornn Berry
Sometimes	Rabuta Berry	Rabuta Berry	Rabuta Berry	Rabuta Berry	Rabuta Berry
Sometimes	Nomel Berry	Nomel Berry	Nomel Berry	Nomel Berry	Nomel Berry
Occasionally	White Beard	White Moustache	Narrow Scale	Glitter Boulder	Mini Pebble
Occasionally	Thin Mushroom	Shed Claw	Mini Pebble	Big Scale	Big Leaf
Occasionally	Big Scale	Narrow Leaf	Green Scale	Black Moustache	Green Scale
Occasionally	Spelon Berry	Spelon Berry	Spelon Berry	Spelon Berry	Spelon Berry
Occasionally	Pamtre Berry	Pamtre Berry	Pamtre Berry	Pamtre Berry	Pamtre Berry
Occasionally	Watmel Berry	Watmel Berry	Watmel Berry	Watmel Berry	Watmel Berry
Occasionally	Durin Berry	Durin Berry	Durin Berry	Durin Berry	Durin Berry
Occasionally	Belue Berry	Belue Berry	Belue Berry	Belue Berry	Belue Berry
Rarely	Stump	Purple Scale	Thick Mushroom	Purple Scale	Black Pebble

TYPE COMPATIBILITY CHART

THERE ARE TWO "TYPES" - The type of the moves Pokémon use in attacking and the types of Pokémon that receive the attacks. The amount of damage varies based on the compatibility of these two types. Master this chart and use it to your advantage!!!

ATTACK MOVE TYPES \ TYPES OF POKéMON (THAT RECEIVE THE ATTACKS)	NORMAL	FIRE	WATER	GRASS	ELECTRIC	ICE	FIGHTING	POISON	GROUND	FLYING	PSYCHIC	BUG	ROCK	GHOST	DRAGON	DARK	STEEL
NORMAL													▲	✕			▲
FIRE		▲	▲	◎		◎						◎	▲		▲		◎
WATER		◎	▲	▲					◎				◎		▲		
GRASS		▲	◎	▲				▲	◎	▲		▲	◎		▲		▲
ELECTRIC			◎	▲	▲				✕	◎					▲		
ICE		▲	▲	◎		▲			◎	◎					◎		▲
FIGHTING	◎					◎		▲		▲	▲	▲	◎	✕		◎	◎
POISON				◎				▲	▲				▲	▲			✕
GROUND		◎		▲	◎			◎		✕		▲	◎				◎
FLYING				◎	▲		◎					◎	▲				▲
PSYCHIC							◎	◎			▲					✕	▲
BUG		▲		◎			▲	▲		▲	◎			▲		◎	▲
ROCK		◎				◎	▲		▲	◎		◎					▲
GHOST	✕										◎			◎		▲	▲
DRAGON															◎		▲
DARK							▲				◎			◎		▲	▲
STEEL		▲	▲		▲	◎							◎				▲

SYMBOLS

◎ = VERY EFFECTIVE X 2	▲ = NOT VERY EFFCTIVE X 0.5
NO SYMBOL = EFFECTIVE X 1	✕ = NO EFFECT AT ALL X 0

* Fire-type Pokémon don't get burnt. Ice-type Pokémon don't get frozen. Poison-type Pokémon don't get poisoned.

STICKERS

CUSTOMIZE YOUR Poké Ball by putting Stickers on it. You can buy Stickers at the Sunyshore Market in Sunyshore City, where the selection changes daily. To collect alphabet Stickers, show your Unown to a boy in Solaceon Town.

STICKERS FOR MONDAY SALE

ITEMS	DESCRIPTION	LOCATION	PRICE
Heart Sticker A	Small pink heart.	Sunyshore Market in Sunyshore City.	50
Star Sticker B	Yellow stars with a big sparkle.	Sunyshore Market in Sunyshore City.	50
Line Sticker C	Black line.	Sunyshore Market in Sunyshore City.	100
Electric Sticker B	Green light shooting upward.	Sunyshore Market in Sunyshore City.	100
Fire Sticker A	Small orange flame.	Sunyshore Market in Sunyshore City.	50
Party Sticker D	White confetti.	Sunyshore Market in Sunyshore City.	100
Song Sticker A	Green treble clef shape.	Sunyshore Market in Sunyshore City.	50

STICKERS FOR TUESDAY SALE

ITEMS	DESCRIPTION	LOCATION	PRICE
Heart Sticker B	Big pink heart.	Sunyshore Market in Sunyshore City.	50
Star Sticker C	Blue stars with a small sparkle.	Sunyshore Market in Sunyshore City.	50
Line Sticker D	Blue line .	Sunyshore Market in Sunyshore City.	100
Electric Sticker C	Yellow light shooting downward.	Sunyshore Market in Sunyshore City.	100
Fire Sticker B	Big orange flame.	Sunyshore Market in Sunyshore City.	50
Flower Sticker A	Falling pink petals.	Sunyshore Market in Sunyshore City.	50
Song Sticker B	Red note.	Sunyshore Market in Sunyshore City.	50

STICKERS FOR WEDNESDAY SALE

ITEMS	DESCRIPTION	LOCATION	PRICE
Heart Sticker C	Small black heart.	Sunyshore Market in Sunyshore City.	50
Star Sticker D	Blue stars with a big sparkle.	Sunyshore Market in Sunyshore City.	50
Smoke Sticker A	White smoke puffs.	Sunyshore Market in Sunyshore City.	100
Electric Sticker D	Green light shooting downward.	Sunyshore Market in Sunyshore City.	100
Fire Sticker C	Small blue flame	Sunyshore Market in Sunyshore City.	50
Flower Sticker B	Pink flower petals.	Sunyshore Market in Sunyshore City.	50
Song Sticker C	Orange note.	Sunyshore Market in Sunyshore City.	50

STICKERS FOR THURSDAY SALE

ITEMS	DESCRIPTION	LOCATION	PRICE
Heart Sticker D	Big black heart.	Sunyshore Market in Sunyshore City.	50
Star Sticker E	Color changing stars with a small sparkle.	Sunyshore Market in Sunyshore City.	100
Smoke Sticker B	Black smoke puffs.	Sunyshore Market in Sunyshore City.	100
Bubble Sticker A	A little bit of blue bubbles.	Sunyshore Market in Sunyshore City.	50
Fire Sticker D	Big blue flame.	Sunyshore Market in Sunyshore City.	50
Flower Sticker C	Falling purple petals.	Sunyshore Market in Sunyshore City.	50
Song Sticker D	Yellow note.	Sunyshore Market in Sunyshore City.	50

STICKERS FOR FRIDAY SALE

ITEMS	DESCRIPTION	LOCATION	PRICE
Heart Sticker E	Floating pink heart.	Sunyshore Market in Sunyshore City.	100
Star Sticker F	Color changing stars with a big sparkle.	Sunyshore Market in Sunyshore City.	100
Smoke Sticker C	White smoke puffs going downward.	Sunyshore Market in Sunyshore City.	100
Bubble Sticker B	A lot of blue bubbles.	Sunyshore Market in Sunyshore City.	50
Party Sticker A	Red confetti.	Sunyshore Market in Sunyshore City.	50
Flower Sticker D	Purple petals.	Sunyshore Market in Sunyshore City.	50
Song Sticker E	Blue note.	Sunyshore Market in Sunyshore City.	50

STICKERS FOR SATURAY SALE

ITEMS	DESCRIPTION	LOCATION	PRICE
Heart Sticker F	Floating pink heart.	Sunyshore Market in Sunyshore City.	100
Line Sticker A	White line.	Sunyshore Market in Sunyshore City.	100
Smoke Sticker D	Black smoke puffs going downward.	Sunyshore Market in Sunyshore City.	100
Bubble Sticker C	A little bit of pink bubbles.	Sunyshore Market in Sunyshore City.	50
Party Sticker B	Blue confetti.	Sunyshore Market in Sunyshore City.	50
Flower Sticker E	Falling yellow petals.	Sunyshore Market in Sunyshore City.	50
Song Sticker F	Yellow note.	Sunyshore Market in Sunyshore City.	50

STICKERS FOR SUNDAY SALE

ITEMS	DESCRIPTION	LOCATION	PRICE
Star Sticker A	Yellow stars with a small sparkle.	Sunyshore Market in Sunyshore City.	50
Line Sticker B	Yellow line.	Sunyshore Market in Sunyshore City.	100
Electric Sticker A	Yellow light shooting upward.	Sunyshore Market in Sunyshore City.	100
Bubble Sticker D	A lot of pink bubbles.	Sunyshore Market in Sunyshore City.	50
Party Sticker C	Green confetti.	Sunyshore Market in Sunyshore City.	100
Flower Sticker F	Yellow petals.	Sunyshore Market in Sunyshore City.	50
Song Sticker G	Navy blue note.	Sunyshore Market in Sunyshore City.	50

THE ALPHABET STICKERS

DESCRIPTION	LOCATION	PRICE
A Sticker shaped like the letter A	Show Unown A to a boy in a house in Solaceon Town.	—
A Sticker shaped like the letter B	Show Unown B to a boy in a house in Solaceon Town.	—
A Sticker shaped like the letter C	Show Unown C to a boy in a house in Solaceon Town.	—
A Sticker shaped like the letter D	Show Unown D to a boy in a house in Solaceon Town.	—
A Sticker shaped like the letter E	Show Unown E to a boy in a house in Solaceon Town.	—
A Sticker shaped like the letter F	Show Unown F to a boy in a house in Solaceon Town.	—
A Sticker shaped like the letter G	Show Unown G to a boy in a house in Solaceon Town.	—
A Sticker shaped like the letter H	Show Unown H to a boy in a house in Solaceon Town.	—
A Sticker shaped like the letter I	Show Unown I to a boy in a house in Solaceon Town.	—
A Sticker shaped like the letter J	Show Unown J to a boy in a house in Solaceon Town.	—
A Sticker shaped like the letter K	Show Unown K to a boy in a house in Solaceon Town.	—
A Sticker shaped like the letter L	Show Unown L to a boy in a house in Solaceon Town.	—
A Sticker shaped like the letter M	Show Unown M to a boy in a house in Solaceon Town.	—
A Sticker shaped like the letter N	Show Unown N to a boy in a house in Solaceon Town.	—
A Sticker shaped like the letter O	Show Unown O to a boy in a house in Solaceon Town.	—
A Sticker shaped like the letter P	Show Unown P to a boy in a house in Solaceon Town.	—
A Sticker shaped like the letter Q	Show Unown Q to a boy in a house in Solaceon Town.	—
A Sticker shaped like the letter R	Show Unown R to a boy in a house in Solaceon Town.	—
A Sticker shaped like the letter S	Show Unown S to a boy in a house in Solaceon Town.	—
A Sticker shaped like the letter T	Show Unown T to a boy in a house in Solaceon Town.	—
A Sticker shaped like the letter U	Show Unown U to a boy in a house in Solaceon Town.	—
A Sticker shaped like the letter V	Show Unown V to a boy in a house in Solaceon Town.	—
A Sticker shaped like the letter W	Show Unown W to a boy in a house in Solaceon Town.	—
A Sticker shaped like the letter X	Show Unown X to a boy in a house in Solaceon Town.	—
A Sticker shaped like the letter Y	Show Unown Y to a boy in a house in Solaceon Town.	—
A Sticker shaped like the letter Z	Show Unown Z to a boy in a house in Solaceon Town.	—
A Sticker shaped like the letter !	Show Unown ! to a boy in a house in Solaceon Town.	—
A Sticker shaped like the letter ?	Show Unown ? to a boy in a house in Solaceon Town.	—

ACCESSORIES

ACCESSORIES	HOW TO OBTAIN	MAX (PIECES)
Award Podium	Win 1st place in Tough Contest / Master Rank.	1
Big Leaf	Take a stroll in Amity Square with Buneary and Happiny.	9
Big Scale	Take a stroll in Amity Square with Pikachu and Clefairy.	9
Big Tree	From a woman outside of Eterna Forest.	1
Black Beard	Take a stroll in Amity Square with Drifloon.	9
Black Fluff	Take a stroll in Amity Square with Buneary and Happiny.	9
Black Moustache	Take a stroll in Amity Square with Pikachu, Pachirisu and Psyduck.	9
Black Specs	Trade 20 Wepear Berries at the Pick a Peck of Colors Flower Shop.	9
Black Stone	Take a stroll in Amity Square with Buneary and Happiny.	9
Blue Balloon	Win 1st place in Beauty Contest / Great Rank.	1
Blue Barrette	Win 1st place in Beauty Contest / Normal Rank.	1
Blue Feather	Take a stroll in Amity Square with Shroomish and Jigglypuff (after receiving the National Pokedex).	9
Blue Flower	Trade 30 Cornn Berries at the Pick a Peck of Colors Flower Shop.	9
Blue Scale	Take a stroll in Amity Square with Clefairy.	9
Brown Fluff	Take a stroll in Amity Square with Pikachu, Pachirisu and Psyduck.	9
Cape	Trade 250 Cornn Berries at the Pick a Peck of Colors Flower Shop.	1
Carpet	Trade 100 Spelon Berries at the Pick a Peck of Colors Flower Shop.	1
Chimchar Mask	From a man at the Jubilife TV station (2 FL) in Jubilife City. (*1)	1
Colorful Parasol	Trade 30 Magost Berries at the Pick a Peck of Colors Flower Shop.	1
Confetti	Trade 30 Razz Berries at the Pick a Peck of Colors Flower Shop.	9
Crown	Insert FireRed game, then goto the right-corner of the 2nd floor of Pal Park after obtaining the National Pokédex.	1
Cube Stage	Win 1st place in Smart Contest / Master Rank.	1
Eerie Thing	Massage House in Veilstone City once a day.	9
Flag	From a woman near a gate of Cycling Road.	1
Flower Stage	Win 1st place in Cute Contest / Master Rank	1
Fluffy Bed	Trade 150 Watmel Berries at the Pick a Peck of Colors Flower Shop.	1
Glass Stage	Win 1st place in Beauty Contest/Master Rank.	1
Glitter Powder	Massage House in Veilstone City once a day.	9
Glitter Stone	Take a stroll in Amity Square with Pikachu.	9
Gold Pedestal	Win 1st place in Cool Contest / Master Rank.	1
Googly Spec	Trade 20 Nomal Berries at the Pick a Peck of Colors Flower Shop.	9
Gorgeous Specs	Trade 40 Pinap Berries at the Pick a Peck of Colors Flower Shop.	9
Green Balloon	Win 1st place in Smart Contest / Great Rank.	1
Green Barrette	Win 1st place in Smart Contest / Normal Rank.	1
Green Scale	Take a stroll in Amity Square with Pachirisu, Psyduck, Buneary and Happiny.	9
Gutsy Determination	Massage House in Veilstone City once a day.	9
Headdress	Win 1st place in Cute Contest / Ultra Rank.	1
Heroic Headband	Win 1st place in Tough Contest / Ultra Rank.	1
Humming Note	Massage House in Veilstone City once a day.	9
Jagged Stone	Take a stroll in Amity Square with Pachirisu or Psyduck.	9
Mini Stone	Take a stroll in Amity Square with Pachirisu and Psyduck.	9
Mirror Ball	Trade 250 Durin Berries at the Pick a Peck of Colors Flower Shop.	1
Mystic Fire	Massage House in Veilstone City once a day.	9
Narrow Leaf	Take a stroll in Amity Square with Drifloon.	9
Narrow Scale	Take a stroll in Amity Square with Pachirisu, Psyduck and Drifloon.	9

ACCESSORIES, CONT.

ACCESSORIES	HOW TO OBTAIN	MAX (PIECES)
Nostalgic Pipe	Trade 120 Pamtre Berries at the Pick a Peck of Colors Flower Shop.	1
Old Umbrella	Trade 50 Pamtre Berries at the Pick a Peck of Colors Flower Shop.	1
Orange Flower	Trade 15 Magost Berries at the Pick a Peck of Colors Flower Shop.	9
Orange Fluff	Take a stroll in Amity Square with Pikachu and Clefairy.	9
Peculiar Spoon	Massage House in Veilstone City once a day.	9
Photo Board	Trade 200 Belue Berries at the Pick a Peck of Colors Flower Shop.	1
Pink Balloon	Win 1st place in Cute Contest / Great Rank.	1
Pink Barrette	Win 1st place in Cute Contest / Normal Rank.	1
Pink Flower	Trade 10 Bluk Berries at the Pick a Peck of Colors Flower Shop.	9
Pink Fluff	Take a stroll in Amity Square with Buneary, Happiny and Drifloon.	9
Pink Scale	Take a stroll in Amity Square with Buneary and Happiny.	9
Piplup Mask	From a man at the Jubilife TV station (2 FL) in Jubilife City. (*1)	1
Poison Extract	Massage House in Veilstone City once a day.	9
Pretty Dewdrop	Massage House in Veilstone City once a day.	9
Professor Hat	Win 1st place in Smart Contest/Ultra Rank.	1
Puffy Smoke	Massage House in Veilstone City once a day.	9
Purple Scale	Take a stroll in Amity Square with Pikachu and Drifloon.	9
Red Balloon	Win 1st place in Cool Contest / Great Rank.	1
Red Feather	Take a stroll in Amity Square Pikachu and Drifloon.	9
Red Flower	Trade 10 Razz Berries at the Pick a Peck of Colors Flower Shop.	9
Round Stone	Take a stroll in Amity Square with Clefairy, Pachirisu and Psyduck.	9
Scarlet Barrette	Win 1st place in Cool Contest/Normal Rank.	1
Seashell Shard	Massage House in Veilstone City once a day.	9
Shed Claw	Take a stroll in Amity Square with Buneary, Happiny and Drifloon.	9
Shed Horn	Take a stroll in Amity Square with Pachirisu, Psyduck, Buneary and Happiny.	9
Shimmering Fire	Massage House in Veilstone City once a day.	9
Shiny Powder	Massage House in Veilstone City once a day.	9
Silk Veil	Win 1st place in Beauty Contest / Ultra Rank.	1
Small Leaf	Take a stroll in Amity Square with Pikachu and Clefairy.	9
Snaggy Stone	Take a stroll in Amity Square with Pachirisu and Psyduck.	9
Snow Crystal	Massage House in Veilstone City once a day.	9
Sparks	Massage House in Veilstone City once a day.	9
Spotlight	Trade 80 Nomel Berries at the Pick a Peck of Colors Flower Shop.	1
Spring	Massage House in Veilstone City once a day.	9
Standing Mike	Trade 80 Bluk Berries at the Pick a Peck of Colors Flower Shop.	1
Stump	Take a stroll in Amity Square with Clefairy.	9
Surfboard	Trade 180 Wepear Berries at the Pick a Peck of Colors Flower Shop.	1
Sweet Candy	Trade 30 Nanab Berries at the Pick a Peck of Colors Flower Shop.	9
Thick Mushroom	Take a stroll in Amity Square with Pachirisu and Psyduck.	9
Thin Mushroom	Take a stroll in Amity Square with Clefairy.	9
Tiara	Insert LeafGreen game, then go to the right-corner of the 2 FL of Pal Park. After obtaining the National Pokédex.	1
Top Hat	Win 1st place in Cool Contest / Ultra Rank.	1
Turtwig Mask	From a man at the Jubilife TV station (2 FL) in Jubilife City. (*1)	1
Wealthy Coin	Massage House in Veilstone City once a day.	9
White Beard	Take a stroll in Amity Square with Clefairy.	9
White Feather	Take a stroll in Amity Square with Clefairy.	9
White Flower	Trade 10 Nanab Berries at the Pick a Peck of Colors Flower Shop.	9
White Fluff	Take a stroll in Amity Square with Clefairy and Drifloon.	9
White Moustache	Take a stroll in Amity Square with Drifloon.	9
Yellow Balloon	Win 1st place in Tough Contest / Great Rank.	1
Yellow Barrette	Win 1st place in Tough Contes t/ Normal Rank.	1
Yellow Feather	Take a stroll in Amity Square with Pikachu, Buneary, Happiny and Drifloon.	9
Yellow Flower	Trade 15 Rabuta Berries at the Pick a Peck of Colors Flower Shop.	9
Yellow Fluff	Take a stroll in Amity Square with Pikachu.	9

*1: If you go to the man at Jubilife TV, you'll receive the player's initial Pokémon mask. A mask of the first Pokémon you chose in the beginning of your jouney. If you talk to a woman on 1 FL in Veilstone Dept. Building, you'll receive a mask of your rival's initial Pokémon. If you go to the woman beneath the observatory in Pastoria City, you will receive a mask of your support character's initial Pokémon.

BACKGROUND

DRESS UP (*1)	YOU HAVE IT FROM THE BEGINNING
Candy Room	4th place prize at Pokémon Lotto in the Jubilife TV station.
City at Night	You have it from the beginning (*2) /4th place prize at Pokémon Lotto in the Jubilife TV station.
Cumulus Cloud	You have it from the beginning (*2) /4th place prize at Pokémon Lotto in the Jubilife TV station.
Desert	You have it from the beginning (*2) /4th place prize at Pokémon Lotto in the Jubilife TV station.
Fiery Stage	You have it from the beginning (*2) /4th place prize at Pokémon Lotto in the Jubilife TV station.
Flower Patch	You have it from the beginning (*2) /4th place prize at Pokémon Lotto in the Jubilife TV station.
Future Room	4th place prize at Pokémon Lotto in the Jubilife TV station.
Open Sea	4th place prize at Pokémon Lotto in the Jubilife TV station.
Ranch	You have it from the beginning (*2) /4th place prize at Pokémon Lotto in the Jubilife TV station.
Seafloor	Insert Pokémon Sapphire game. Speak to a woman in the right-corner of the 2 FL of Pal Park.
Serene Room	4th place prize at Pokémon Lotto in the Jubilife TV station.
Sky	Insert Pokemn Emerald game. Speak to a woman in the right-corner of the 3 FL of Pal Park.
Snowy Town	You have it from the beginning (*2) /4th place prize at Pokémon Lotto in the Jubilife TV station.
Space Stage	You have it from the beginning (*2) /4th place prize at Pokémon Lotto in the Jubilife TV station.
Total Darkness	4th place prize at Pokémon Lotto in the Jubilife TV station.
Underground	Insert Pokémon Ruby game. Speak to a woman in the right-corner of the 2 FL of Pal Park.

*2: You have 2 of the following items from the beginning: Ranch, City at Night, Snowy Town, Fiery Stage, Space Stage, Cumulus Cloud, Desert, Flower Patch.

ACCESSORIES

YOU'LL BE ASKED to accessorize your Pokémon in the first round of the Super Contest. To earn a high score, be sure to choose accessories that fit the theme you're given.

NAME	SHAPELY	SHARPNESS	THE CREATED	NATURE	THE COLORED	THE SOLID
Award Podium	High	Normal	High	Low	Normal	High
Big Leaf	High	Normal	Low	High	Normal	Normal
Big Scale	Normal	High	Low	High	Normal	High
Big Tree	High	Normal	Low	High	Normal	High
Black Beard	Normal	High	High	Low	High	Normal
Black Fluff	Normal	Low	Low	High	High	Normal
Black Moustache	Normal	Normal	High	Low	High	Normal
Black Pebble	High	Low	Normal	Normal	High	High
Black Specs	High	Normal	High	Low	High	High
Blue Balloon	Normal	Low	High	Low	High	Low
Blue Barrette	Normal	Normal	High	Low	High	Normal
Blue Feather	Normal	High	Low	High	High	Normal
Blue Flower	High	Normal	Low	High	High	Normal
Blue Scale	Normal	High	Low	High	High	High
Brown Fluff	Normal	Low	Low	High	High	Normal
Cape	High	High	High	Low	High	Normal
Carpet	High	Low	High	Low	High	High
Chimchar Mask	High	Low	High	Low	Normal	Normal
Colored Parasol	High	High	High	Low	High	High
Confetti	Normal	Normal	High	Low	High	Normal
Cube Stage	High	Normal	High	Low	Normal	High
Determination	Low	Normal	Normal	Normal	Normal	Low
Eerie Thing	Normal	Low	Normal	High	High	Low
Flag	High	High	High	Low	High	High
Flower Stage	High	Normal	High	Low	Normal	High
Fluffy Bed	High	Low	High	Low	Normal	Normal
Glass Stage	High	Normal	High	Low	Normal	High
Glitter Boulder	High	Low	Normal	Normal	Normal	High
Glitter Powder	Normal	Low	High	Normal	Normal	Normal
Gold Pedestal	High	Normal	High	Low	High	High
Googly Specs	High	Normal	High	Low	Normal	High
Gorgeous Specs	High	Normal	High	Low	High	High
Green Balloon	Normal	Low	High	Low	High	Low
Green Barrette	Normal	Normal	High	Low	High	Normal
Green Scale	Normal	Low	Low	High	High	High
Heroic Headband	High	Normal	High	Low	Normal	Normal
Humming Note	Low	Normal	High	Normal	Normal	Normal
Jagged Boulder	High	Low	Low	High	Low	High
Lace Headdress	High	High	High	Low	Low	Normal
Mini Pebble	High	Low	Normal	Normal	Normal	High
Mirror Ball	High	Low	High	Low	Normal	High
Mystic Fire	Low	Low	Normal	High	Normal	Low
Name	Shapes	Pointy	Artificial	Natural	Colorful	Sturdy
Narrow Leaf	Normal	High	Low	High	Normal	Normal
Narrow Scale	Normal	High	Low	High	Normal	High
Old Umbrella	High	High	High	Low	Normal	High

BRIGHTNESS	THE GAUDY	FLEXIBILITY	THE FESTIVE	THE INTANGIBLE	RELAXATION	NAMES
High	High	Low	Normal	Low	Normal	Award Podium
Normal	Normal	High	Low	Normal	Normal	Big Leaf
High	High	Normal	Normal	Normal	Low	Big Scale
Normal	Normal	Normal	Normal	Low	Normal	Big Tree
Low	High	High	Low	Normal	High	Black Beard
Low	Normal	High	Normal	Normal	High	Black Fluff
Low	High	High	Low	Normal	High	Black Moustache
Low	High	Low	Normal	Low	High	Black Pebble
Low	High	Low	Low	Normal	High	Black Specs
Normal	High	High	Normal	High	Normal	Blue Balloon
Normal	High	Normal	Normal	Normal	Normal	Blue Barrette
Normal	High	Normal	Normal	Normal	Normal	Blue Feather
Normal	Normal	Normal	Normal	Normal	Normal	Blue Flower
Normal	High	Normal	Normal	Normal	High	Blue Scale
Normal	Normal	High	Normal	Normal	High	Brown Fluff
Low	High	High	Normal	Normal	High	Cape
Normal	High	High	High	High	Normal	Carpet
Normal	High	Normal	Normal	Normal	Normal	Chimchar Mask
High	High	Normal	High	Normal	Normal	Colored Parasol
Normal	High	High	Normal	High	Normal	Confetti
Normal	High	Low	Normal	Low	Normal	Cube Stage
High	High	High	Normal	High	Normal	Determination
Low	Low	High	Low	High	High	Eerie Thing
Normal	High	High	Normal	High	Normal	Flag
Normal	High	Low	High	Low	Normal	Flower Stage
Normal	High	High	Normal	Normal	Normal	Fluffy Bed
High	High	Low	High	Low	Normal	Glass Stage
High	High	Low	High	Low	Low	Glitter Boulder
High	High	High	High	High	Low	Glitter Powder
High	High	Low	High	Low	Low	Gold Pedestal
Normal	Normal	Low	Low	Normal	High	Googly Specs
Low	High	Low	High	Normal	Normal	Gorgeous Specs
Normal	High	High	Normal	High	Normal	Green Balloon
Normal	High	Normal	Normal	Normal	Normal	Green Barrette
Normal	High	Normal	Normal	Normal	Normal	Green Scale
Normal	High	High	Normal	High	Normal	Heroic Headband
Normal	High	High	High	High	Normal	Humming Note
Normal	Normal	Low	Low	Low	High	Jagged Boulder
High	High	Normal	High	Normal	Normal	Lace Headdress
Normal	High	Low	Normal	Low	Normal	Mini Pebble
High	High	Low	High	Normal	Low	Mirror Ball
High	Normal	High	High	High	Normal	Mystic Fire
Bright	Flashy	Elegant	Glamorous	Shapeless	Simple	Names
Normal	Normal	High	Low	Normal	Normal	Narrow Leaf
Low	High	Normal	Normal	Normal	High	Narrow Scale
Normal	Normal	Normal	Low	Normal	High	Old Umbrella

CHARTS & INFO

ACCESSORIES, CONT.

NAME	SHAPELY	SHARPNESS	THE CREATED	NATURE	THE COLORFUL	THE SOLID
Orange Flower	High	Normal	Low	High	High	Normal
Orange Fluff	Normal	Low	Low	High	High	Normal
Peculiar Spoon	High	Normal	High	Low	Low	High
Photo Board	High	Normal	High	Low	Normal	High
Pink Balloon	Normal	Low	High	Low	High	Low
Pink Barrette	Normal	Normal	High	Low	High	Normal
Pink Flower	High	Normal	Low	High	High	Normal
Pink Fluff	Normal	Low	Low	High	High	Normal
Pink Scale	Normal	Normal	Low	High	High	High
Piplup Mask	High	Low	High	Low	Normal	Normal
Poison Extract	Low	Low	Normal	High	High	Low
Pretty Dewdrop	Normal	Low	Low	High	Normal	Low
Professor Hat	High	High	High	Low	High	High
Puffy Smoke	Low	Low	Low	High	Normal	Low
Purple Scale	Normal	High	Low	High	High	High
Red Balloon	Normal	Low	High	Low	High	Low
Red Barrette	Normal	Normal	High	Low	High	Normal
Red Feather	Normal	High	Low	High	High	Normal
Red Flower	High	Normal	Low	High	High	Normal
Retro Pipe	High	Normal	High	Low	Normal	High
Round Pebble	High	Low	Normal	Normal	Normal	High
Seashell	High	Normal	Low	High	Low	High
Shed Claw	High	High	Normal	High	Low	High
Shed Horn	High	High	Normal	High	Low	High
Shimmering Fire	Low	Low	Normal	High	Normal	Low
Shiny Powder	Normal	Low	High	Normal	Normal	Normal
Silk Veil	High	Normal	High	Low	Normal	Normal
Small Leaf	Normal	Normal	Low	High	Normal	Normal
Snaggy Pebble	High	Low	Low	High	Low	High
Snow Crystal	Normal	Normal	Low	High	Normal	Low
Sparks	Low	Low	Normal	High	Normal	Low
Spotlight	High	Normal	High	Low	Low	High
Spring	High	High	High	Low	Normal	High
Standing Mike	High	High	High	Low	Normal	High
Stump	High	Normal	Normal	High	Low	High
Surfboard	High	High	High	Low	Normal	High
Sweet Candy	High	Normal	High	Low	Normal	High
Thick Mushroom	High	Normal	Normal	High	Normal	Normal
Thin Mushroom	Normal	High	Normal	High	Normal	Normal
Top Hat	High	Normal	High	Low	High	Normal
Turtwig Mask	High	Low	High	Low	Normal	Normal
Wealthy Coin	High	Low	High	Low	Normal	High
White Beard	Normal	High	High	Low	Normal	Normal
White Feather	Normal	High	Low	High	High	Normal
White Flower	High	Normal	Low	High	Normal	Normal
White Fluff	Normal	Low	Low	High	Normal	Normal
White Moustache	Normal	Normal	High	Low	Normal	Normal
Yellow Balloon	Normal	Low	High	Low	High	Low
Yellow Barrette	Normal	Normal	High	Low	High	Normal
Yellow Feather	Normal	High	Low	High	High	Normal
Yellow Flower	High	Normal	Low	High	High	Normal

BRIGHTNESS	THE GAUDY	FLEXIBILITY	THE FESTIVE	THE INTANGIBLE	RELAXATION	NAMES
Normal	Normal	Normal	Normal	Normal	Normal	Orange Flower
Normal	Normal	High	Normal	Normal	Normal	Orange Fluff
Normal	Normal	Normal	Normal	Low	Normal	Peculiar Spoon
Normal	High	Normal	Normal	High	Normal	Photo Board
Normal	High	High	Normal	High	Normal	Pink Balloon
Normal	High	Normal	Normal	Normal	Normal	Pink Barrette
Normal	Normal	Normal	Normal	Normal	Normal	Pink Flower
Normal	Normal	High	Normal	Normal	Normal	Pink Fluff
Normal	High	Normal	Normal	Normal	Normal	Pink Scale
Normal	High	Normal	Normal	Normal	Normal	Piplup Mask
Low	Low	High	Low	High	High	Poison Extract
Normal	Normal	High	High	High	Low	Pretty Dewdrop
Normal	High	Normal	Normal	Normal	Normal	Professor Hat
Normal	Normal	High	Low	High	Normal	Puffy Smoke
Normal	High	Normal	Normal	Normal	Normal	Purple Scale
Normal	High	High	Normal	High	Normal	Red Balloon
Normal	High	Normal	Normal	Normal	Normal	Red Barrette
Normal	High	Normal	Normal	Normal	Normal	Red Feather
Normal	Normal	Normal	Normal	Normal	Normal	Red Flower
Normal	Normal	Low	Low	Low	Normal	Retro Pipe
Normal	High	Low	Normal	Low	Normal	Round Pebble
High	Normal	Low	Normal	Normal	Normal	Seashell
High	Normal	Low	Normal	Normal	Low	Shed Claw
High	Normal	Low	Normal	Normal	Low	Shed Horn
High	High	High	High	High	Normal	Shimmering Fire
High	High	High	High	High	Low	Shiny Powder
High	High	High	High	High	Low	Silk Veil
Normal	Normal	High	Low	Normal	Normal	Small Leaf
Normal	Normal	Low	Low	Low	Normal	Snaggy Pebble
High	Normal	High	High	High	Low	Snow Crystal
High	Normal	High	High	High	Normal	Sparks
High	High	Normal	High	High	Low	Spotlight
Normal	High	High	Normal	Normal	Normal	Spring
Normal	High	Normal	Normal	Normal	Normal	Standing Mike
Normal	Normal	Low	Low	Normal	Normal	Stump
Normal	High	Low	Normal	Normal	Normal	Surfboard
Normal	High	Normal	Normal	Normal	Normal	Sweet Candy
Normal	Normal	Normal	Normal	Normal	Low	Thick Mushroom
High	Normal	Normal	Normal	Normal	Low	Thin Mushroom
Low	High	Normal	High	Normal	High	Top Hat
Normal	High	Normal	Normal	Normal	Normal	Turtwig Mask
Normal	High	Low	High	Low	Low	Wealthy Coin
High	High	High	Low	Normal	Low	White Beard
High	High	Normal	Normal	Normal	Low	White Feather
High	Normal	Normal	Normal	Normal	Low	White Flower
High	Normal	High	Normal	Normal	Low	White Fluff
High	High	High	Low	Normal	Low	White Moustache
High	High	High	Normal	High	Normal	Yellow Balloon
High	High	Normal	Normal	Normal	Normal	Yellow Barrette
High	High	Normal	Normal	Normal	Normal	Yellow Feather
High	Normal	Normal	Normal	Normal	Normal	Yellow Flower

DECORATIVE GOODS

THESE ARE ITEMS you can use to decorate your secret base. You can obtain them by trading spheres or visiting Mr. Goods.

GOODS	LOCATIONS AND CONDITIONS	PRICE
Beauty Cup	Mr. Goods in Hearthome City (After winning the Master Rank in Beauty Contest).	
Big Bookshelf	Trade with 20-25 Jade Spheres in the Underground.	
Big Oil Drum	Trade with 10-40 Pale Spheres in the Underground.	
Big Table	Trade with 12-15 Blue Spheres in the Underground.	
Bike Rack	Trade with 35-49 Jade Spheres in the Underground.	
Binoculars	Trade with 10-40 Pale Spheres in the Underground.	
Blue Crystal	Mr. Goods in Hearthome City (After greeting 100 people in Underground).	
Blue Cushion	Trade with 8-10 Red Spheres In the Underground.	
Blue Tent	Trade with 20-70 Pale Spheres in the Underground.	
Bonsai	Trade with 8-10 Jade Spheres in the Underground.	
Bonsly Doll	Veilstone Dept. Store 4 FL in Veilstone City.	2000
Buizel Doll	Veilstone Dept. Store 4 FL in Veilstone City.	3000
Buneary Doll	Trade with 15-30 Pale Spheres in the Underground / Underground Man in Eterna City.	
Chatot Doll	Veilstone Dept. Store 4 FL in Veilstone City.	3000
Chimchar Doll	Trade with 25-40 Red Spheres in the Underground / Underground Man in Eterna City.	
Clear Tent	Trade with 40-99 Pale Spheres in the Underground.	
Clefairy Doll	Trade with 40-70 Pale Spheres in the Underground.	
Container	Trade with 10-40 Pale Spheres in the Underground.	
Cool Cup	Mr. Goods in Hearthome City (After winning the Master Rank in Cool Contest).	
Crate	Trade with 33-40 Red Spheres in the Underground.	
Cupboard	Trade with 20-25 Jade Spheres in the Underground / Veilstone Dept. Store 4 FL in Veilstone City.	1000
Cupboard Box	Trade with 20-25 Red Spheres in the Underground / Veilstone Dept. Store 4 FL in Veilstone City.	
Cute Cup	Mr. Goods in Hearthome City (After winning the Master Rank in Cute Contest).	
Dainty Flowers	Trade with 8-10 Jade Spheres in the Underground.	
Display Shelf	Trade with 12-15 Jade Spheres in the Underground	
Drifloon Doll	Trade with 33-40 Blue Spheres in the Underground.	
Feathery Bed	Trade with 33-40 Blue Spheres in the Underground.	
Game System	Trade with 48-50 Hard Spheres in the Underground.	
Glameow Doll	Trade with 15-20 Blue Spheres in the Underground.	
Glitter Gem	Underground Man in Eterna City (Take 50 flags).	
Globe	Mr. Goods in Hearthome City (After GTS opens, use Nintendo Wi-Fi Connection).	
Green Bike	Trade with 33-40 Jade Spheres in the Underground.	
Gym Statue	Mr. Goods in Hearthome City (After obtaining 8 Gym badges).	
Happiny Doll	Trade with 40-70 Pale Spheres in the Underground.	
Healing Machine	Trade with 90-99 Hard Spheres in the Underground.	
Iron Beam	Trade with 9-10 Hard Spheres in the Underground.	
Lab Machine	Trade with 28-30 Hard Spheres in the Underground.	
Lavish Flowers	Trade with 8-10 Jade Spheres in the Underground.	
Long Table	Trade with 12-15 Blue Spheres in the Underground.	
Lovely Flowers	Trade with 8-10 Jade Spheres in the Underground.	
Mantyke Doll	Veilstone Dept. Store 4 FL in Veilstone City.	3000
Maze Block 1	Trade with 48-50 Hard Spheres in the Underground.	
Maze Block 2	Trade with 48-50 Hard Spheres in the Underground.	
Maze Block 3	Trade with 48-50 Hard Spheres in the Underground.	
Maze Block 4	Trade with 48-50 Hard Spheres in the Underground.	
Maze Block 5	Trade with 48-50 Hard Spheres in the Underground.	
Mime Jr. Doll	Veilstone Dept. Store 4 FL in Veilstone City.	2000
Munchlax Doll	Veilstone Dept. Store 4 FL in Veilstone City.	2000
Mystic Gem	Underground Man in Eterna City (Take 10 flags).	
Oil Drum	Trade with 10-40 Pale Spheres in the Underground.	
Pachirisu Doll	Trade with 70-99 Pale Spheres in the Underground.	
Pikachu Doll	Trade with 70-99 Pale Spheres in the Underground.	
Pink Crystal	Mr. Goods in Hearthome City (After giving decorative goods to 100 people in Underground).	
Pink Dresser	Trade with 50-60 Jade Spheres in the Underground.	
Piplup Doll	Trade with 35-40 Blue Spheres in the Underground / Underground Man in Eterna City.	
Plain Table	Trade with 8-10 Blue Spheres in the Underground / Underground Man in Eterna City.	
Poké Center Flower	Trade with 10-40 Pale Spheres in the Underground.	
Poké Center Table	Trade with 20-25 Blue Spheres in the Underground.	
Potted Plant	Trade with 20-25 Red Spheres in the Underground.	
Pretty Flowers	Trade with 8-10 Jade Spheres in the Underground.	
Pretty Gem	Underground Man in Eterna City (Take 1 flag).	
Pretty Sink	Trade with 9-10 Hard Spheres in the Underground / Veilstone Dept. Store 4 FL in Veilstone City.	3000
Red Bike	Trade with 33-40 Red Spheres in the Underground.	
Red Crystal	Mr. Goods in Hearthome City (after digging 100 fossils in the Underground).	
Red Tent	Trade with 20-70 Pale Spheres in the Underground.	
Refrigerator	Trade with 12-15 Jade Spheres in the Underground / Veilstone Dept. Store 4 FL in Veilstone City.	1000
Research Shelf	Trade with 12-15 Jade Spheres in the Underground.	
Shiny Gem	Underground Man in Eterna City (take 3 flags).	
Shop Shelf	Trade with 35-49 Jade Spheres in the Underground.	
Small Bookshelf	Trade with 8-10 Jade Spheres in the Underground / Underground Man in Eterna City.	
Small Table	Trade with 8-10 Blue Spheres in the Underground.	
Smart Cup	Mr. Goods in Hearthome City (after winning the Master Rank in Smart Contest).	
Snorlax Doll	Trade with 80-99 Red Spheres in the Underground.	
Test Machine	Trade with 28-30 Hard Spheres in the Underground.	
Tough Cup	Mr. Goods in Hearthome City (after winning the Master Rank in Tough Contest).	
Trash Can	Trade with 8-10 Red Spheres in the Underground.	

DECORATIVE GOODS, CONT.

GOODS	LOCATIONS AND CONDITIONS	PRICE
Turtwig Doll	Trade with 35-40 Jade Spheres in the Underground / Underground Man in Eterna City.	
TV	Trade with 9-10 Hard Spheres in the Underground / Veilstone Dept. Store 4 FL in Veilstone City.	4500
Vending Machine	Trade with 8-10 Jade Spheres in the Underground.	
Weavile Doll	Trade with 28-30 Hard Spheres in the Underground.	
Wide Sofa	Trade with 20-25 Blue Spheres in the Underground.	
Wide Table	Trade with 12-15 Blue Spheres in the Underground.	
Wood Dresser	Trade with 20-25 Jade Spheres in the Underground.	
Wooden Chair	Trade with 8-10 Red Spheres in the Underground / Underground Man in Eterna City.	
Yellow Crystal	Mr. Goods in Hearthome City (after using 100 times in the Underground).	
Yellow Cushion	Trade with 8-10 Red Spheres in the Underground / Veilstone Dept. Store 4 FL in Veilstone City.	500

UNDERGROUND TREASURES

MANY ITEMS ARE BURIED in the walls of the Underground. They vary between Diamond and Pearl, with some items being easier to find in one game than the other.

TREASURES FOR A TRADE	CHANCES OF DISCOVERY		NUMBER OF SPHERES FOR A TRADE
	DIAMOND	PEARL	
Armor Fossil	E	B	Blue Sphere (30-50)
Blue Shard	B	C	Blue Sphere (20-25)
Blue Sphere	A	A	
Damp Stone	D	D	Blue Sphere (40-50)
Draco Plate	D	D	Red Sphere (70-80)
Dread Plate	D	D	Red Sphere (70-80)
Earth Plate	D	D	Jade Sphere (70-80)
Everstone	D	D	Pale Sphere (25-35)
Fire Stone	D	D	Red Sphere (25-35)
Fist Plate	D	D	Hard Sphere (70-80)
Flame Plate	D	D	Red Sphere (70-80)
Green Shard	C	B	Jade Sphere (25-35)
Hard Sphere	B	B	
Hard Stone	D	D	Red Sphere (25-35)
Heart Scale	B	B	Red Sphere (5-10)
Heat Stone	D	D	Red Sphere (40-50)
Icicle Plate	D	D	Blue Sphere (70-80)
Icy Stone	D	D	Pale Sphere (35-40)
Insect Plate	D	D	Jade Sphere (70-80)
Iron Plate	D	D	Hard Sphere (70-80)
Iron Sphere	D	D	Hard Sphere (40-50)
Jade Sphere	A	A	
Leaf Stone	D	D	Jade Sphere (25-35)
Light Clay	D	D	Pale Sphere (40-50)
Max Revive	D	D	Pale Sphere (40-50)
Meadow Plate	D	D	Jade Sphere (70-80)
Mind Plate	D	D	Pale Sphere (70-80)
Moon Stone	D	D	Pale Sphere (25-35)
Pale Sphere	B	B	
Rare Bone	D	D	Pale Sphere (25-35)
Red Shard	C	B	Red Sphere (20-25)
Red Sphere	A	A	
Revive	C	C	Pale Sphere (5-10)
Skull Fossil	B	E	Jade Sphere (30-50)
Sky Plate	D	D	Blue Sphere (70-80)
Smooth Rock	D	D	Hard Sphere (35-40)
Splash Plate	D	D	Blue Sphere (70-80)
Spooky Plate	D	D	Pale Sphere (70-80)
Star Piece	D	D	Pale Sphere (35-45)
Stone Plate	D	D	Hard Sphere (70-80)
Sun Stone	D	D	Red Sphere (25-35)
Thunderstone	D	D	Hard Sphere(25-35)
Toxic Plate	D	D	Pale Sphere (70-80)
Water Stone	D	D	Blue Sphere (25-35)
Yellow Shard	B	C	Hard Sphere (20-25)
Zap Plate	D	D	Hard Sphere (70-80)

A......High B......Not very high C......Relatively low D......Low E......Zero

UNDERGROUND TRAPS

THESE CAN BE buried in the floor of the Underground. Gather them by trading with spheres, or release traps buried by other players.

TRAPS	DESCRIPTION	HOW TO RELEASE	LOCATION
Alert Trap 1	"Hello! Nice to meet you!" is displayed on the top screen.		Trade with 5-9 Pale Spheres in the Underground.
Alert Trap 2	"Good-bye! I'm going back up!" is displayed on the top screen.		Trade with 5-9 Pale Spheres in the Underground.
Alert Trap 3	"Let's go to Union Room!" is displayed on the top screen.		Trade with 5-9 Pale Spheres in the Underground.
Alert Trap 4	"Please come here!" is displayed on the top screen.		Trade with 5-9 Pale Spheres in the Underground.
Bubble Trap	Creates large bubbles that trap you.	Touch the bubble.	Trade with 12-16 Blue Spheres in the Underground.
Confuse Trap	Makes you move in random directions.	Take 50 steps.	Trade with 10-12 Pale Spheres in the Underground.
Crater Trap	Gets you stuck in a hole where you can't move for a long time.	Press the button 20 times.	Trade with 12-15 Hard Spheres in the Underground.
Digger Drill	Allows you to build a secret base in a wall in front of you.		Trade for 15-30 random sphere in the Underground.
Ember Trap	A small fire appears to immobilize you.	Blow on your mic.	Trade with 5-9 Red Spheres in the Underground.
Fire Trap	A huge fire appears to immobilize you.	Blow on your mic.	Trade with 20-30 Red Spheres in the Underground.
Flower Trap	Petals whirl up all over the screen so you can't move.	Blow on your mic.	Trade with 30-40 Jade Spheres in the Underground.
Foam Trap	Creates small bubbles that trap you.	Touch the foam.	Trade with 5-7 Blue Spheres in the Underground.
Fog Trap	Smoke completely clouds the screen.	Touch the smoke.	Trade with 12-16 Red Spheres in the Underground.
Hurl Trap →	Throws you far to the right.		Trade with 12-15 Red Spheres in the Underground.
Hurl Trap ←	Throws you far to the left.		Trade with 12-15 Red Spheres in the Underground.
Hurl Trap ↑	Throws you far upward.		Trade with 12-15 Blue Spheres in the Underground.
Hurl Trap ↓	Throws you far downward.		Trade with 12-15 Blue Spheres in the Underground.
Leaf Trap	Leaves whirl up all over the screen so you can't move .	Blow on your mic.	Trade with 15-19 Jade Spheres in the Underground.
Move Trap ↑	Throws you upward.		Trade with 3-6 Blue Spheres in the Underground.
Move Trap →	Throws you to the right.		Trade with 3-6 Red Spheres in the Underground.
Move Trap ←	Throws you to the left.		Trade with 3-6 Red Spheres in the Underground.
Move Trap ↓	Throws you downward.		Trade with 3-6 Blue Spheres in the Underground.
Pit Trap	Gets you stuck in a hole where you can't move.	Press the button 10 times.	Trade with 3-6 Hard Spheres in the Underground.
Reverse Trap	Makes you move in the opposite direction of the side of the d-pad you press.	Take 20 steps.	Trade with 10-12 Pale Spheres in the Underground.
Rock Trap	A rock falls on you so you can't move.	Touch the rock.	Trade with 3-6 Blue Spheres in the Underground.
Rockfall Trap	A big rock falls on you so you can't move.	Touch the big rock.	Trade with 8-15 Blue Spheres in the Underground.
Smoke Trap	Smoke clouds the screen.	Touch the smoke.	Trade with 5-7 Red Spheres in the Underground.

BERRIES–SINNOH VERSION

No.	Name	No. of Berries: Min.	No. of Berries: Max.	Time to Grow to the Next Stage	Time the Berry Takes to Ripe	Spicy	Dry	Sweet	Bitter	Sour	Smoothness
1	Cheri	2	5	3 hours	12 hours	Normal					☆☆☆☆
2	Chesto	2	5	3	12		Normal				☆☆☆☆
3	Pecha	2	5	3	12			Normal			☆☆☆☆
4	Rawst	2	5	3	12				Normal		☆☆☆☆
5	Aspear	2	5	3	12					Normal	☆☆☆☆
6	Leppa	2	5	4	16	Normal		Normal	Normal	Normal	☆☆☆☆☆
7	Oran	2	5	4	16	Normal	Normal		Normal	Normal	☆☆☆☆☆
8	Persim	2	5	4	16	Normal	Normal	Normal		Normal	☆☆☆☆☆
9	Lum	2	5	12	48	Normal	Normal	Normal	Normal		☆☆☆☆☆
10	Sitrus	2	5	8	32		Normal	Normal	Normal	Normal	☆☆☆☆☆
11	Figy	2	5	5	20	Normal					☆☆☆☆
12	Wiki	2	5	5	20		Normal				☆☆☆☆
13	Mago	2	5	5	20			Normal			☆☆☆☆
14	Aguav	2	5	5	20				Normal		☆☆☆☆
15	Iapapa	2	5	5	20					Normal	☆☆☆☆
16	Razz	2	10	2	8	Normal	Normal				☆☆☆☆☆
17	Bluk	2	10	2	8		Normal	Normal			☆☆☆☆☆
18	Nanab	2	10	2	8			Normal	Normal		☆☆☆☆☆
19	Wepear	2	10	2	8				Normal	Normal	☆☆☆☆☆
20	Pinap	2	10	2	8	Normal				Normal	☆☆☆☆☆
21	Pomeg	2	5	8	32	Normal		Normal	Normal		☆☆☆☆☆
22	Kelpsy	2	5	8	32		Normal		Normal	Normal	☆☆☆☆☆
23	Qualot	2	5	8	32	Normal		Normal		Normal	☆☆☆☆☆
24	Hondew	2	5	8	32	Normal	Normal		Normal		☆☆☆☆☆
25	Grepa	2	5	8	32		Normal	Normal		Normal	☆☆☆☆☆
26	Tamato	2	5	8	32	Relatively rich	Normal				☆☆☆☆

☆......Not smooth ☆☆......Not very smooth ☆☆☆......Relatively smooth ☆☆☆☆......Smooth ☆☆☆☆☆......Very smooth

SUCTION FORCE	AVAILABLE ON THE FIELD	EFFECT	LOCATIONS	NAME	NO.
Relatively strong	○	Pokémon heals itself when Paralyzed.	Floaroma Town / Route 205 / A flower shop in Floaroma Town.	Cheri	1
Relatively strong	○	Pokémon heals itself when put to sleep.	Route 205 / Route 209 / A flower shop in Floaroma Town.	Chesto	2
Relatively strong	○	Pokémon heals itself when Poisoned.	Route 205 / Route 215 / A flower shop in Floaroma Town.	Pecha	3
Relatively strong	○	Pokémon heals itself when Burned.	Route 206 / Route 213 / A flower shop in Floaroma Town.	Rawst	4
Relatively strong	○	Pokémon heals itself when Frozen.	Route 210 / Route 211 / A flower shop in Floaroma Town.	Aspear	5
Relatively strong	○	Pokémon restores its PP by 10 when it's down to 0.	Route 209 / Route 221 / Berry Master on Route 208.	Leppa	6
Relatively strong	○	Pokémon restores its HP by 10 when it's down to less than a half.	Floaroma Town / Route 205 / Berry Master on Route 208.	Oran	7
Relatively strong	○	Pokémon heals itself when Confused.	Solaceon Town / Pastoria City / Berry Master on Route 208.	Persim	8
Relatively weak	○	Pokémon cures special conditions by itself.	Route 212 / Berry Master on Route 208.	Lum	9
Relatively weak	○	Pokémon restores its HP by 1/4 of its max HP when it's down to less than a half.	Fuego Ironworks / Route 210 / Berry Master on Route 208.	Sitrus	10
Normal	○	Pokémon restores its HP when it's less than a half but can be Confused if it dislikes spicy flavor.	Solaceon Town / Route 218 / Berry Master on Route 208.	Figy	11
Normal	○	Pokémon restores its HP when it's less than a half but can be Confused if it dislikes dry flavor.	Route 215 / Route 210 / Berry Master on Route 208.	Wiki	12
Normal	○	Pokémon restores its HP when it's less than a half but can be Confused if it dislikes sweet flavor.	Route 215 / Route 221 / Berry Master on Route 208.	Mago	13
Normal	○	Pokémon restores its HP when it's less than a half but can be Confused if it dislikes bitter flavor.	Route 213 / Route 210 / Berry Master on Route 208.	Aguav	14
Normal	○	Pokémon restores its HP when it's less than a half but can be Confused if it dislikes sour flavor.	Route 213 / Route 211 / Berry Master on Route 208.	Iapapa	15
Strong	○	An ingredient of Poffin.	Route 206 / Route 208 / Berry Master on Route 208.	Razz	16
Strong	○	An ingredient of Poffin.	Eterna Forest / Route 207 / Berry Master on Route 208.	Bluk	17
Strong	○	An ingredient of Poffin.	Solaceon Town / Route 208 / Berry Master on Route 208.	Nanab	18
Strong	○	An ingredient of Poffin.	Fuego Ironworks / Berry Master on Route 208.	Wepear	19
Strong	○	An ingredient of Poffin.	Route 208 / Route 210 / Berry Master on Route 208.	Pinap	20
Relatively weak	○	Makes your Pokémon bond but lowers the basic points of HP.	Route 214 / Berry Master on Route 208.	Pomeg	21
Relatively weak	○	Makes your Pokémon bond but lowers the basic points of Attack.	Fuego Ironworks / Berry Master on Route 208.	Kelpsy	22
Relatively weak	○	Makes your Pokémon bond but lowers the basic points of Defense.	Route 222 / Berry Master on Route 208.	Qualot	23
Relatively weak	○	Makes your Pokémon bond but lowers the basic points of Special Attack.	Route 221 / Berry Master on Route 208.	Hondew	24
Relatively weak	○	Makes your Pokémon bond but lowers the basic points of Special Defense.	Route 211 / Berry Master on Route 208.	Grepa	25
Relatively weak	○	Makes your Pokémon bond but lowers the basic points of Speed.	Route 212 / Berry Master on Route 208.	Tamato	26

BERRIES, CONT.

	NO.	NAME	NO. OF BERRIES		TIME TO GROW TO THE NEXT STAGE	TIME THE BERRY TAKES TO RIPE	FLAVORS AND RICHNESS					SMOOTHNESS
			MIN	MAX			SPICY	DRY	SWEET	BITTER	SOUR	
	27	Cornn	2	10	6	24		Relatively rich	Normal			☆☆☆☆
	28	Magot	2	10	6	24			Relatively rich	Normal		☆☆☆☆
	29	Rabuta	2	10	6	24				Relatively rich	Normal	☆☆☆☆
	30	Nomel	2	10	6	24	Normal				Relatively rich	☆☆☆☆
	31	Spelon	2	15	15	60	Rich	Normal				☆☆☆
	32	Pamtre	2	15	15	60		Rich	Normal			☆☆☆
	33	Watmel	2	15	15	60			Rich	Normal		☆☆☆
	34	Durin	2	15	15	60				Rich	Normal	☆☆☆
	35	Belue	2	15	15	60	Normal				Rich	☆☆☆
	36	Occa	2	5	18	72	Normal		Normal			☆☆☆☆
	37	Passho	2	5	18	72		Normal		Normal		☆☆☆☆
	38	Wacan	2	5	18	72			Normal		Normal	☆☆☆☆
	39	Rindo	2	5	18	72	Normal			Normal		☆☆☆☆
	40	Yache	2	5	18	72		Normal			Normal	☆☆☆☆
	41	Chople	2	5	18	72	Normal			Normal		☆☆☆☆
	42	Kebia	2	5	18	72		Normal			Normal	☆☆☆☆
	43	Shuca	2	5	18	72	Normal		Normal			☆☆☆☆
	44	Coba	2	5	18	72		Normal		Normal		☆☆☆☆
	45	Payapa	2	5	18	72			Normal		Normal	☆☆☆☆
	46	Tanga	2	5	18	72	Relatively rich				Normal	☆☆☆
	47	Charti	2	5	18	72	Normal	Relatively rich				☆☆☆
	48	Kasib	2	5	18	72		Normal	Relatively rich			☆☆☆
	49	Haban	2	5	18	72			Normal	Relatively rich		☆☆☆
	50	Colbur	2	5	18	72				Normal	Relatively rich	☆☆☆
	51	Babiri	2	5	18	72	Relatively rich	Normal				☆☆☆
	52	Chilan	2	5	18	72		Relatively rich	Normal			☆☆☆

☆......Not smooth ☆☆......Not very smooth ☆☆☆......Relatively smooth ☆☆☆☆......Smooth ☆☆☆☆☆......Very smooth

SUCTION FORCE	AVAILABLE ON FIELD	EFFECT	LOCATIONS	NAME	NO.
Normal		An ingredient of Poffin.	Amity Square in Hearthome City.	Cornn	27
Normal		An ingredient of Poffin.	Amity Square in Hearthome City.	Magot	28
Normal		An ingredient of Poffin.	Amity Square in Hearthome City.	Rabuta	29
Normal		An ingredient of Poffin.	Amity Square in Hearthome City.	Nomel	30
Relatively weak		An ingredient of Poffin.	Amity Square in Hearthome City.	Spelon	31
Relatively weak		An ingredient of Poffin.	Amity Square in Hearthome City.	Pamtre	32
Relatively weak		An ingredient of Poffin.	Amity Square in Hearthome City	Watmel	33
Relatively weak		An ingredient of Poffin.	Amity Square in Hearthome City.	Durin	34
Relatively weak		An ingredient of Poffin.	Amity Square in Hearthome City.	Belue	35
Relatively weak		Halves the damage of super effective Fire-type moves.	A berry lady in Pastoria City.	Occa	36
Relatively weak		Halves the damage of super effective Water-type moves.	A berry lady in Pastoria City.	Passho	37
Relatively weak		Halves the damage of super effective Electric-type moves.	A berry lady in Pastoria City / Wild Buizel and Floatzel sometimes have it.	Wacan	38
Relatively weak		Halves the damage of super effective Grass-type moves.	A berry lady in Pastoria City / Wild Finneon sometimes have it.	Rindo	39
Relatively weak		Halves the damage of super effective Ice-type moves.	A berry lady in Pastoria City / Wild Starly and Staravia sometimes have it.	Yache	40
Relatively weak		Halves the damage of super effective Fighting-type moves.	A berry lady in Pastoria City / Wild Buneary sometimes have it.	Chople	41
Relatively weak		Halves the damage of super effective Poison-type moves.	A berry lady in Pastoria City.	Kebia	42
Relatively weak		Halves the damage of super effective Ground-type moves.	A berry lady in Pastoria City / Wild Ponyta sometimes have it.	Shuca	43
Relatively weak		Halves the damage of super effective Flying-type moves.	A berry lady in Pastoria City.	Coba	44
Relatively weak		Halves the damage of super effective Psychic-type moves.	A berry lady in Pastoria City.	Payapa	45
Relatively weak		Halves the damage of super effective Bug-type moves.	A berry lady in Pastoria City.	Tanga	46
Relatively weak		Halves the damage of super effective Rock-type moves.	A berry lady in Pastoria City.	Charti	47
Relatively weak		Halves the damage of super effective Ghost-type moves.	A berry lady in Pastoria City.	Kasib	48
Relatively weak		Halves the damage of super effective Dragon-type moves.	A berry lady in Pastoria City / Wild Gible sometimes have it	Haban	49
Relatively weak		Halves the damage of super effective Dark-type moves.	A berry lady in Pastoria City / Wild Chingling and Chimecho sometimes have it.	Colbur	50
Relatively weak		Halves the damage of super effective Steel-type moves.	A berry lady in Pastoria City.	Babiri	51
Relatively weak		Halves the damage of super effective Normal-type moves.	A berry lady in Pastoria City.	Chilan	52

POFFIN

POFFIN	COLOR	FLAVORS	EFFECTIVE FOR (CONTEST)
Spicy Poffin	Red	Spicy.	Cool contest
Dry Poffin	Blue	Dry.	Beauty contest
Sweet Poffin	Pink	Sweet.	Cute contest
Bitter Poffin	Green	Bitter.	Smart contest
Sour Poffin	Yellow	Sour.	Tough contest
Spicy-Dry Poffin	Red / Blue	Spicy and Dry (More Spicy than Dry).	Cool contest
Spicy-Sweet Poffin	Red / Pink	Spicy and Sweet (More Spicy than Sweet).	Cool contest
Spicy-Bitter Poffin	Red / Green	Spicy and Bitter (More Spicy than Bitter).	Cool contest
Spicy-Sour Poffin	Red / Yellow	Spicy and Sour (More Spicy than Sour).	Cool contest
Dry-Spicy Poffin	Blue / Red	Dry and Spicy (More Dry than Spicy).	Beauty contest
Dry-Sweet Poffin	Blue / Pink	Dry and Sweet (More Dry than Sweet).	Beauty contest
Dry-Bitter Poffin	Blue / Green	Dry and Bitter (More Dry than Bitter).	Beauty contest
Dry-Sour Poffin	Blue / Yellow	Dry and Sour (More Dry than Sour).	Beauty contest
Sweet-Spicy Poffin	Pink / Red	Sweet and Spicy (More Sweet than Spicy).	Cute contest
Sweet-Dry Poffin	Pink / Blue	Sweet and Dry (More Sweet than Dry).	Cute contest
Sweet-Bitter Poffin	Pink / Green	Sweet and Bitter (More Sweet than Bitter).	Cute contest
Sweet-Sour Poffin	Pink / Yellow	Sweet and Sour (More Sweet than Sour).	Cute contest
Bitter-Spicy Poffin	Green / Red	Bitter and Spicy (More Bitter than Spicy).	Smart contest
Bitter-Dry Poffin	Green / Blue	Bitter and Dry (More Bitter than Dry).	Smart contest
Bitter-Sweet Poffin	Green / Pink	Bitter and Sweet (More Bitter than Sweet).	Smart contest
Bitter-Sour Poffin	Green / Yellow	Bitter and Sour (More Bitter than Sour).	Smart contest
Sour-Spicy Poffin	Yellow / Red	Sour and Spicy (More Sour than Spicy).	Tough contest
Sour-Dry Poffin	Yellow / Blue	Sour and Dry (More Sour than Dry).	Tough contest
Sour-Sweet Poffin	Yellow / Pink	Sour and Sweet (More Sour than Sweet).	Tough contest
Sour-Bitter Poffin	Yellow / Green	Sour and Bitter (More Sour than Bitter).	Tough contest
Heavy Poffin	Gray	3 or more flavors are mixed.	Depends on flavors
Too-heavy Poffin	White	4 or more flavors are mixed.	Depends on flavors
Poor-flavored Poffin	Black	3 or more flavors are mixed but each flavor is weak.	Not effective
Mild Poffin	Gold	One of 5 flavors is much richer than others.	Depends on flavors

REMATCH TRAINERS – SINNOH REGION VERSION

LOCATION	TRAINER'S NAME
Route 202	Tristan,Youngster
Route 202	Logan, Youngster
Route 202	Natalie, Lass
Route 203	Michael, Youngster
Route 203	Dallas, Youngster
Route 203	Sebastian, Youngster
Route 203	Madeline, Lass
Route 203	Kaitlin, Lass
Route 204 (Jubilife City side)	Tyler, Youngster
Route 204 (Jubilife City side)	Samantha, Lass
Route 204 (Jubilife City side)	Sarah, Lass
Route 204 (Floaroma Town side)	Taylor, Aroma Lady
Route 204 (Floaroma Town side)	Liv and Liz, Twins
Route 204 (Floaroma Town side)	Brandon, Bug Catcher
Route 205 (Floaroma Town side)	Elizabeth, Aroma Lady
Route 205 (Floaroma Town side)	Jacob, Camper
Route 205 (Floaroma Town side)	Zackary, Camper
Route 205 (Floaroma Town side)	Kelsey, Battle Girl
Route 205 (Floaroma Town side)	Siena, Picnicker
Route 205 (Floaroma Town side)	Karina, Picnicker
Route 205 (Floaroma Town side)	Daniel, Hiker
Route 205 (Floaroma Town side)	Nicholas, Hiker
Route 205 (Eterna City side)	Andrew, Fisherman
Route 205 (Eterna City side)	Joseph, Fisherman
Route 205 (Eterna City side)	Zachary, Fisherman
Route 206	Axel, Cyclist
Route 206	James, Cyclist
Route 206	John, Cyclist
Route 206	Ryan, Cyclist
Route 206	Megan, Cyclist
Route 206	Nicole, Cyclist
Route 206	Kayla, Cyclist
Route 206	Racheal, Cyclist
Route 206	Theodore, Hiker
Route 207	Anthony, Camper
Route 207	Austin, Youngster
Route 207	Helen, Battle Girl
Route 207	Lauren, Picnicker
Route 207	Kevin, Hiker
Route 207	Justin, Hiker
Route 208	Hannah, Aroma Lady
Route 208	Kyle, Black Belt
Route 208	William, Artist
Route 208	Cody, Fisherman

LOCATION	TRAINER'S NAME
Route 208	Robert, Hiker
Route 208	Alexander, Hiker
Route 208	Jonathan, Hiker
Route 209	Shelley, Cow Girl
Route 209	Richard, Jogger
Route 209	Raul, Jogger
Route 209	Emma and Lil, Twins
Route 209	Danielle, Poké Kid
Route 209	Albert, Pokémon Breeder
Route 209	Jennifer, Pokémon Breeder
Route 209	Ty and Sue, Young Couple
Route 210 (Solaceon Town side)	Wyatt, Jogger
Route 210(Solaceon Town side)	Fabian, Ninja Boy
Route 210 (Solaceon Town side)	Brennan, Ninja Boy
Route 210 (Solaceon Town side)	Bruce, Ninja Boy
Route 210 (Solaceon Town side)	Teri and Tia, Twins
Route 210 (Solaceon Town side)	Marco, Rancher
Route 210 (Solaceon Town side)	Ava and Matt, Belle and Pa
Route 210 (Solaceon Town side)	Kahlil, Pokémon Breeder
Route 210 (Solaceon Town side)	Amber, Pokémon Breeder
Route 210 (Celestic Town side)	Alyssa, Ace Trainer
Route 210 (Celestic Town side)	Adam, Black Belt
Route 210 (Celestic Town side)	Zac and Jen, Double Team
Route 210 (Celestic Town side)	Patrick, Dragon Tamer
Route 210 (Celestic Town side)	Brianna, Bird keeper
Route 210 (Celestic Town side)	Joel, Ninja Boy
Route 210 (Celestic Town side)	Nathan, Ninja Boy
Route 210 (Celestic Town side)	Davido, Ninja Boy
Route 210 (Celestic Town side)	Brian, Veteran
Route 211 (Eterna City side)	Alexandra, Bird keeper
Route 211 (Eterna City side)	Zach, Ninja Boy
Route 211 (Eterna City side)	Louis, Hiker
Route 211 (Celestic Town side)	Harry, Ruin Maniac
Route 211 (Celestic Town side)	Sean, Black belt
Route 211 (Celestic Town side)	Katherine, Bird Keeper
Route 211 (Celestic Town side)	Nick, Ninja Boy
Route 212 (Pastoria City side)	Danny, Policeman
Route 212 (Pastoria City side)	Stefano, Scientist
Route 212 (Pastoria City side)	Shaun, Scientist
Route 212 (Pastoria City side)	Juan, Fisherman
Route 212 (Pastoria City side)	Cameron, Fisherman
Route 212 (Pastoria City side)	Travis, Fisherman
Route 212 (Pastoria City side)	Alexa, Parasol Lady
Route 212 (Pastoria City side)	Sabrina, Parasol Lady

REMATCH TRAINERS – SINNOH REGION VERSION, CONT.

LOCATION	TRAINER'S NAME
Route 212 (Pastoria City side)	Dominique, Collector
Route 212 (Pastoria City side)	Taylor, Pokémon Ranger
Route 212 (Pastoria City side)	Jeffrey, Pokémon Ranger
Route 212 (Pastoria City side)	Allison, Pokémon Ranger
Route 212 (Hearthome City side)	Melissa, Lady
Route 212 (Hearthome City side)	Jason, Rich Boy
Route 212 (Hearthome City side)	Bobby, Policeman
Route 212 (Hearthome City side)	Alex, Policeman
Route 212 (Hearthome City side)	Dylan, Policeman
Route 212 (Hearthome City side)	Caleb, Policeman
Route 212 (Hearthome City side)	Jeremy, Gentleman
Route 212 (Hearthome City side)	Reina, Socialite
Route 213	Chelsea, Tuber
Route 213	Jared, Tuber
Route 213	Cyndy, Beauty
Route 213	Sheltin, Swimmer (m)
Route 213	Evan, Swimmer (m)
Route 213	Kenneth, Fisherman
Route 213	Haley, Swimmer (f)
Route 213	Mary, Swimmer (f)
Route 213	Paul, Sailor
Route 214	Bryan, Ruin Maniac
Route 214	Hunter, Ruin Maniac
Route 214	Devon, Beauty
Route 214	Carlos, P.I.
Route 214	Mitchell, Psychic
Route 214	Abagail, Psychic
Route 214	Douglas, Collector
Route 214	Brady, Collector
Route 214	Jamal, Collector
Route 215	Calvin, Ruin Maniac
Route 215	Dennis, Ace Trainer
Route 215	Maya, Ace Trainer
Route 215	Gregory, Black Belt
Route 215	Derek, Black Belt
Route 215	Nathaniel, Black Belt
Route 215	Scott, Jogger
Route 215	Craig, Jogger
Route 216	Blake, Ace Trainer
Route 216	Garrett, Ace Trainer
Route 216	Laura, Ace Trainer
Route 216	Maria, Ace Trainer
Route 216	Philip, Black Belt
Route 216	Bradley, Skier
Route 216	Edward, Skier
Route 216	Kaitlyn, Skier
Route 216	Andrea, Skier
Route 217	Dalton, Ace Trainer
Route 217	Olivia, Ace Trainer

LOCATION	TRAINER'S NAME
Route 217	Luke, Black Belt
Route 217	Shawn, Skier
Route 217	Bjorn, Skier
Route 217	Madison, Skier
Route 217	Antonio, Ninja Boy
Route 217	Ethan, Ninja Boy
Route 218	Tony, Guitarist
Route 218	Miguel, Fisherman
Route 218	Luc, Fisherman
Route 218	Skyler, Sailor
Route 219	Mariel, Tuber
Route 219	Trenton, Tuber
Route 220	Adrian, Swimmer (m)
Route 220	Erik, Swimmer (m)
Route 220	Vincent, Swimmer (m)
Route 220	Jessica, Swimmer (f)
Route 220	Erica, Swimmer (f)
Route 220	Katelyn, Swimmer (f)
Route 220	Claire, Swimmer (f)
Route 221	Jake, Ace Trainer
Route 221	Shannon, Ace Trainer
Route 221	Dillon, Swimmer (m)
Route 221	Cory, Fisherman
Route 221	Vanessa, Swimmer (f)
Route 221	Ivan, Collector
Route 222	Holly, Tuber
Route 222	Conner, Tuber
Route 222	Nicola, Beauty
Route 222	Trey, Rich Boy
Route 222	Thomas, Policeman
Route 222	Brett, Fisherman
Route 222	Alec, Fisherman
Route 222	George, Fisherman
Route 222	Cole, Fisherman
Route 222	Luther, Sailor
Route 222	Marc, Sailor
Route 223	Wesley, Swimmer (m)
Route 223	Ricardo, Swimmer (m)
Route 223	Fransisco, Swimmer (m)
Route 223	Colton, Swimmer (m)
Route 223	Troy, Swimmer (m)
Route 223	Oscar, Swimmer (m)
Route 223	Aubree, Swimmer (f)
Route 223	Paige, Swimmer (f)
Route 223	Crystal, Swimmer (f)
Route 223	Cassandra, Swimmer (f)
Route 223	Gabrielle, Swimmer (f)
Route 223	Zachariah, Sailor

WEAKNESS LOOKUP: SINNOH REGION VERSION

NORMAL

TYPES		MOVE TYPES THAT CAUSE 2x OR MORE DAMAGE								MOVE TYPES THAT ARE INCAPABLE OF DAMAGE		
		4x DAMAGE		2x DAMAGE								
Normal				Fighting						Ghost		
Normal	Flying			Electric	Ice	Rock				Ground	Ghost	
Normal	Water			Grass	Electric	Fighting				Ghost		
Normal	Psychic			Bug	Dark					Ghost		

FIRE

TYPES		MOVE TYPES THAT CAUSE 2x OR MORE DAMAGE								MOVE TYPES THAT ARE INCAPABLE OF DAMAGE		
		4x DAMAGE		2x DAMAGE								
Fire				Water	Ground	Rock						
Fire	Fighting			Water	Ground	Flying	Psychic					

WATER

TYPES		MOVE TYPES THAT CAUSE 2x OR MORE DAMAGE								MOVE TYPES THAT ARE INCAPABLE OF DAMAGE		
		4x DAMAGE		2x DAMAGE								
Water				Grass	Electric							
Water	Steel			Electric	Fighting	Ground				Poison		
Water	Flying	Electric		Rock						Ground		
Water	Ground	Grass								Electric		
Water	Poison			Electric	Ground	Psychic						
Water	Dragon			Dragon								

GRASS

TYPES		MOVE TYPES THAT CAUSE 2x OR MORE DAMAGE								MOVE TYPES THAT ARE INCAPABLE OF DAMAGE		
		4x DAMAGE		2x DAMAGE								
Grass				Fire	Ice	Poison	Flying	Bug				
Grass	Ground	Ice		Fire	Flying	Bug				Electric		
Grass	Poison			Fire	Ice	Flying	Psychic					
Grass	Ice	Fire		Fighting	Poison	Flying	Bug	Rock	Steel			

ELECTRIC

TYPES		MOVE TYPES THAT CAUSE 2x OR MORE DAMAGE								MOVE TYPES THAT ARE INCAPABLE OF DAMAGE		
		4x DAMAGE		2x DAMAGE								
Electric				Ground								

FIGHTING

TYPES		MOVE TYPES THAT CAUSE 2x OR MORE DAMAGE								MOVE TYPES THAT ARE INCAPABLE OF DAMAGE		
		4x DAMAGE		2x DAMAGE								
Fighting				Flying	Psychic							
Fighting	Psychic			Flying	Ghost							
Fighting	Steel			Fire	Fighting	Ground				Poison		

POISON

TYPES		MOVE TYPES THAT CAUSE 2x OR MORE DAMAGE								MOVE TYPES THAT ARE INCAPABLE OF DAMAGE		
		4x DAMAGE		2x DAMAGE								
Poison	Flying			Electric	Ice	Psychic	Rock			Ground		
Poison	Dark			Ground						Psychic		
Poison	Bug			Fire	Flying	Psychic	Rock					
Poison	Fighting	Psychic		Ground	Flying							

GROUND

TYPES		MOVE TYPES THAT CAUSE 2x OR MORE DAMAGE								MOVE TYPES THAT ARE INCAPABLE OF DAMAGE		
		4x DAMAGE		2x DAMAGE								
Ground				Grass	Water	Ice				Electric		

PSYCHIC

TYPES		MOVE TYPES THAT CAUSE 2X OR MORE DAMAGE								MOVE TYPES THAT ARE INCAPABLE OF DAMAGE		
		4x DAMAGE		2x DAMAGE								
Psychic				Bug	Ghost	Dark						

BUG

TYPES		MOVE TYPES THAT CAUSE 2x OR MORE DAMAGE								MOVE TYPES THAT ARE INCAPABLE OF DAMAGE		
		4x DAMAGE		2x DAMAGE								
Bug				Fire	Flying	Rock						
Bug	Grass	Fire	Flying	Ice	Poison	Bug	Rock					
Bug	Ground			Fire	Water	Ice	Flying			Electric		
Bug	Steel	Fire								Poison		
Bug	Flying	Rock		Fire	Electric	Ice	Flying			Ground		
Bug	Poison			Fire	Flying	Psychic	Rock					
Bug	Fighting	Flying		Fire	Psychic							

ROCK

TYPES		MOVE TYPES THAT CAUSE 2x OR MORE DAMAGE								MOVE TYPES THAT ARE INCAPABLE OF DAMAGE		
		4x DAMAGE		2x DAMAGE								
Rock				Grass	Water	Fighting	Ground	Steel				
Rock	Ground	Grass	Water	Ice	Fighting	Ground	Steel			Electric		
Rock	Steel	Fighting	Ground	Water						Poison		

GHOST

TYPES		MOVE TYPES THAT CAUSE 2x OR MORE DAMAGE								MOVE TYPES THAT ARE INCAPABLE OF DAMAGE		
		4x DAMAGE		2x DAMAGE								
Ghost				Ghost	Dark					Normal	Fighting	
Ghost	Flying			Electric	Ice	Rock	Ghost	Dark		Normal	Fighting	Ground
Ghost	Poison			Ground	Psychic	Ghost	Dark			Normal	Fighting	
Ghost	Dark									Normal	Fighting	Psychic

DRAGON

TYPES		MOVE TYPES THAT CAUSE 2x OR MORE DAMAGE								MOVE TYPES THAT ARE INCAPABLE OF DAMAGE		
		4x DAMAGE		2x DAMAGE								
Dragon	Ground	Ice		Dragon						Electric		

DARK

TYPES		MOVE TYPES THAT CAUSE 2x OR MORE DAMAGE								MOVE TYPES THAT ARE INCAPABLE OF DAMAGE		
		4x DAMAGE		2x DAMAGE								
Dark	Flying			Electric	Ice	Rock				Ground	Psychic	
Dark	Ice	Fighting		Fire	Bug	Rock	Steel			Psychic		

STEEL

TYPES		MOVE TYPES THAT CAUSE 2x OR MORE DAMAGE								MOVE TYPES THAT ARE INCAPABLE OF DAMAGE		
		4x DAMAGE		2x DAMAGE								
Steel	Ground			Fire	Water	Fighting	Ground			Electric	Poison	
Steel	Psychic			Fire	Ground					Poison		
Steel	Dragon			Fighting	Ground					Poison		

SINNOH POKÉDEX COMPLETE RECORD GUIDE